Resistance and Representation

Rethinking Childhood

Joe L. Kincheloe and Jan Jipson
General Editors

Vol. 12

PETER LANG
New York • Washington, D.C./Baltimore • Boston • Bern
Frankfurt am Main • Berlin • Brussels • Vienna • Oxford

Resistance and Representation

Rethinking Childhood Education

Edited by
Janice A. Jipson
and Richard T. Johnson

PETER LANG
New York • Washington, D.C./Baltimore • Boston • Bern
Frankfurt am Main • Berlin • Brussels • Vienna • Oxford

Library of Congress Cataloging-in-Publication Data

Resistance and representation: rethinking childhood education /
edited by Janice A. Jipson and Richard T. Johnson.
p. cm. — (Rethinking childhood; vol. 12)
Includes bibliographical references and index.
1. Early childhood education—Cross-cultural studies. 2. Educational anthropology—
United States. 3. Educational anthropology—Canada. 4. Educational anthropology—
Pacific Area. I. Jipson, Janice. II. Johnson, Richard T. III. Series.
LB1139.23.R47   372.21—dc21   99-49955
ISBN 0-8204-4250-X
ISSN 1086-7155

Die Deutsche Bibliothek-CIP-Einheitsaufnahme

Resistance and representation: rethinking childhood education /
ed. by: Janice A. Jipson and Richard T. Johnson.
–New York; Washington, D.C./Baltimore; Boston; Bern;
Frankfurt am Main; Berlin; Brussels; Vienna; Oxford: Lang.
(Rethinking childhood; Vol. 12)
ISBN 0-8204-4250-X

Cover art by Erik Van Deventer
Cover design by Lisa Dillon

© 2001 Peter Lang Publishing, Inc., New York

All rights reserved.
Reprint or reproduction, even partially, in all forms such as microfilm,
xerography, microfiche, microcard, and offset strictly prohibited.

Contents

List of Figures and Tables	ix
Acknowledgements	xi

Introduction

Resistance and Representation: Rethinking Childhood Education Janice A. Jipson	1

Part I: Resistance and Representation: The Child

1	Natural Born Curriculum: Popular Culture and the Representation of Childhood Gaile S. Cannella	15
2	Interrupting Dominant Images: Critical and Ethical Issues Christine Woodrow and Marie Brennan	23
3	Resisting Institutionalized Ageism Mark D. Bailey and Nancy Meltzoff	45

Part II: Resistance and Representation: The Teacher

4	Good Teacher or Feminist Teacher?: Investigating the Ethics of Early Childhood Curriculum Glenda Mac Naughton	59

5	The Early Childhood Teacher as Professional: An Archaeology of University Reform Katharina Heyning	77
6	Resisting the Norms of Elementary Education: One Primary Teacher's Stories Lisa Goldstein	107
7	Eh, No Act!: The Power of Being on the Margin Kerri-Ann Hewett	117

Part III: Resistance and Representation: The Curriculum

8	Critical Perspectives on Social Studies in Early Childhood Education Shirley A. Kessler	127
9	Pointed Noses and Yellow Hair: Deconstructing Children's Writing on Race and Ethnicity in Hawai'i Julie Lokelani Kaomea	151
10	What Does a Child Deserve in a Book? Harlan Quist and the Politics of Childhood Knowledge Nicholas Paley	181
11	If You Think You're Naked, You Are! Mary Jane Fox	193

Part IV: Resistance and Representation: Society

12	"The Proof of the Home Is the Nursery": An American Proverb Revisted Larry Prochner	205

13	Beating Mom: How to Win the Power Game Susan Grieshaber	223
14	Who's Making These Policies Anyway?: How Head Start Staff Interpret Official Policies Deborah Ceglowski	239
15	Restructuring Governing in Eastern Europe: Constructing New Needs for Families, Children, and Childcare Marianne N. Bloch	253
16	Resisting Normative Representation in the Pacific Islands: Domestic Enemies Meet over Coffee Richard T. Johnson and Maria Gaiyabu	279
17	To Speak: Problematizing of the Use of Personal Stories in Early Childhood Research Chelsea Bailey	291

Epilogue

Reconceptualization as Interruption, Interrogative Punctuation, and Opening — 305
Richard T. Johnson

References — 311

Contributors — 345

Figures and Tables

Figure 3.1: Effective Forms of Resistance for each Arena	55
Figure 9.1: Student response 1	152
Figure 9.2: Student response 2	153
Figure 9.3: Student response 3	154
Figure 9.4: Student response 4	155
Figure 9.5: Student response 5	156
Figure 9.6: Student response 6	157
Figure 9.7: Facts and Figures chart from an encyclopedic entry on Japan	160
Figure 9.8: A page from a children's field guide to endangered birds	162
Figure 9.9: Close-up comparison of Kau'i's description of blacks and the children's field guide description of Bali Mynahs	163
Figure 12.1: La Pouponnière.—Promenade, et Becquée ou repas simultané	214
Figure 12.2: Crèche D'Youville, Montreal, 1920s	214
Figure 12.3: Die Kinderkrippe. Albert Anker, 1890	215
Figure 12.4: Dining Room, East End Day Nursery, Toronto, 1902–1903	216
Figure 12.5: The Meal Hour in the Franciscan Nunnery on the Via Giusti	218
Figure 12.6: Dinner Time, Handsworth Day Nursery, Birmingham	219

Table 15.1: Annual Percentage Change in GDP, 263
  1990–1995
Table 15.2: Unemployment Rates, 1990–1994 265
Table 15.3: Nursery and Kindergarten Coverage (%) 268
  1980, 1985, 1990–1994

Acknowledgments

We would like to thank the many individuals who have contributed to the creation of this book. First, we would like to acknowledge the very significant support and encouragement we have received from the Reconceptualizing Early Childhood Education community. Opportunities to present early versions of many of these chapters at the annual "reconceptualizing" conferences have allowed us to benefit from your valuable feedback and suggestions.

We would also like to thank our chapter contributors: Chelsea Bailey, Mark Bailey, Mimi Bloch, Marie Brennan, Gaile Cannella, Deborah Ceglowski, Mary Jane Fox, Maria Gaiyabu, Lisa Goldstein, Susan Grieshaber, Kerri-Ann Hewett, Katharina Heyning, Shirley Kessler, Glenda Mac Naughton, Nancy Meltzoff, Nicholas Paley, Larry Prochner, Julie Kaomea, and Christine Woodrow. Your careful work in examining issues of resistance and representation in early childhood education and your responsiveness in preparing and editing their chapters have made the timely publication of this book possible.

Additional thanks go to members of the Critical Perspectives on Childhood Education Special Interest Group of the American Educational Research Association (AERA), for their sponsorship of our interactive symposium on issues of resistance and representation in early childhood research and for providing a supportive place for us to test, question, and validate our thinking.

The institutional support of National Louis University and the University of Hawaii has been essential to the completion of this book. We would like to offer special thanks to our colleagues and students who enthusiastically encouraged our work on this project by reading, listening, reacting, and critiquing our efforts and by sharing our joy and struggles in creating this book.

Thanks, too, to Joe Kincheloe and the Rethinking Childhood Education series of Peter Lang Publishing Company for providing us with the opportunity to publish this collection of essays. Chris Myers and Shirley Steinberg of Peter Lang provided editorial and technical support in the actual production of the book and also, through their encouragement and interest, allowed us to proceed through this project with confidence and enthusiasm.

***

In addition to these shared acknowledgments, we each would like to offer our individual appreciation and thanks to those who supported us in this work.

Jan would like to express appreciation to friends, mentors, and colleagues who have contributed in important ways to her own rethinking of early childhood education and to her continued interest in examining issues of resistance and representation within the field. Petra Munro, Tina Lozano, Shirley Kessler, Nicholas Paley, Jeffrey Lewis, Rubena Azhar, and Beth Swadener have long shared my interests in rethinking early childhood curriculum and policy, as well as child development and diversity. Through our many discussions and readings, you have helped me focus my commitment to critical practice within our field and have supported me in addressing issues of privilege and resistance throughout my scholarly work.

I would also like to express my gratitude to my coauthor, Rich Johnson, for his enthusiasm and efforts in putting this book together. Despite geographical and technical barriers, Rich's insights and commitment to this book were truly essential to its completion. If all coauthors were like you, Rich, publishing would be a continual pleasure.

Thanks also to Michael Apple, Mimi Bloch, and Gary Price, who, as friends and mentors in my early studies of childhood education at the University of Wisconsin, encouraged me to look thoughtfully and critically at the seemingly hidden and taken-for-granted practices in the field of education. My work has been greatly enriched by your guidance and interest.

Finally, I would like to express my appreciation to my family for supporting me through a very long and difficult writing process—Bob for his love and affection, as well as for taking care of me on a day-to-day basis; Jenny for being the best daughter-scholar-friend that any academic mom could ever want; Emmie for being the lovely, independent companion of my wanderings and for teaching me, through her own life, about courage and art and love; and Erik for being funny, and creative, and smart, but most of all for interjecting the reality of childhood into my work.

***

Acknowledgments

Just as Jan mentioned I too would like to express appreciation to colleagues and friends who have contributed in important ways to my own revisioning early childhood education. With the support of these people I have found my way through many hard choices about how to intellectualize tough issues in my writing, in my thinking. I would first like to express my gratitude to my coauthor, Jan Jipson, for her assistance in making this book come to fruition. The miles apart made things difficult at times, but with her persistence and wealth of authorial experience, in the end it seemed easy. I look forward to continued collaborative ventures Jan! My very dear friend and chapter coauthor, Maria Gaiyabu, is the model of resistance. Her desire to question, inquire, question again, all in the name of what is right for the collective is truly inspirational. If I could only collaborate with Maria the rest of my life, my way of perceiving the world, my way of representing those perceptions on paper, would be more than fulfilled. To my students and colleagues here at the University of Hawai'i and my colleagues in the Pacific, we have much work to be done.

I too would like to honor my family here. Tina supports my work in the Pacific and pushes me to discover stories never told. Her support and patience helps these stories come to life, come to realization. My children, Nicholas, Nathan, and Haleigh keep me honest by keeping me focused on the cares and concerns of children and childhood. Without this loving support system, my work would have little personal meaning.

Introduction

Resistance and Representation: Rethinking Childhood Education
Janice A. Jipson

History

"We have to do something about this DAP thing[1] you know," Shirley Kessler remarked as we shared a cup of coffee in a sidewalk French Quarter cafe. We were attending an American Educational Research Association (AERA) meeting and had slipped out of a session to "debrief" and to complain of how difficult it was to gain access to the "early childhood establishment." We did not even imagine that the seeds of our resistance were planted in the Louisiana sun that day.

It actually had begun much earlier, of course. Having recently finished our dissertations at the University of Wisconsin-Madison and having worked with Michael Apple and Herbert Kliebard, as well as the early childhood faculty, we shared a concern about the increasing dominance of our field by a child development perspective and were in the habit of plotting ways to upset that dominance, perhaps replacing it with a critical curriculum perspective. Our earlier, separate involvements with the anti-war movement, the TAA (Teaching Assistants Association) strikes, and the Civil Rights movement had made us accustomed to looking at things from the perspective of resistance. The growing hegemony of psychologically based curricular models in early childhood, be they behavioral or developmental, had made each of us increasingly uncomfortable across the tenure of our graduate school years. By 1987, we were wondering what to do.

It was Shirley who organized the first efforts. Calling together a group of like-minded early childhood educators from the Midwest during the summer of 1988, she initiated plans for a public discussion of the developmentally appropriate practice issue at AERA and for a special conference aimed at "reconceptualizing early childhood education." We took as our first course of resistance the presentation of a panel discussion critically examining developmentally appropriate practice to a largely sympathetic audience at the Bergamo Conference on Curriculum Theorizing. Bergamo had long been, and still is for many of us, a primary site for sharing and developing our work. It also had a strong influence on how the Reconceptualizing Early Childhood Education conference was originally conceptualized. The following spring, 1989, a revised symposium was presented to a somewhat less receptive audience of early childhood educators at the AERA annual meeting in Boston.

In 1991, Shirley and Beth Swadener edited a special issue of *Early Education and Development*, which brought together the papers from the AERA symposium, along with other, similarly focused, essays critically examining developmentally based early childhood curriculum. And, the first annual Reconceptualizing Early Childhood Education conference was convened in Madison, Wisconsin, in October, 1991, providing an annual site for the critical consideration of research and practice in early childhood education. The conference has continued to serve as a site of resistance and for alternative representations of research knowledge throughout the 1990s, expanding to include a large, international membership.

Following the special issue of *Early Education and Development*, in 1992, Shirley and Beth published an edited volume of essays and research studies entitled *Reconceptualizing Early Childhood Education*. And in 1995, the *Rethinking Childhood* academic book series was launched by editors Janice Jipson and Joe Kincheloe (Peter Lang Publishing Company) to provide an on-going publication site for the reconceptualization of childhood education.

In retrospect, it appears that the reconceptualist movement represented by this group of early childhood educators emerged for several reasons. Perhaps initially one of the most compelling was the practical desire of this group of scholars to find a site for the active discussion and dissemination of their work and for the sharing of research which seemed to fall outside the psychologically driven parameters of the Society for Research in Child Development or the Early Childhood Special Interest Group (SIG) of AERA.

Also significant to the founding of the reconceptualist group was the belief that research grounded in a critical perspective on curriculum and schooling was, perhaps, too theoretically estranged from the conventions of the early childhood education community and its professional associations. Recognizing their shared commitment to a reanalysis of the conditions through which many children and their families are positioned outside the dominant discourse of development and education, the reconceptualist researchers sought opportunities for dialogue and collaboration in applying feminist, critical, multicultural, postcolonial and postmodern theories and methodologies to questions of early childhood curriculum, research, and theorizing. In the end, what connected them was their shared commitment to creating social change and improving the lives of children.

Thus, we had begun to create a space for ourselves, a "homeplace" (hooks, 1990), where we could engage each other in serious debate and discussion around the issues that were important to us. I do not recall any desires to proselytize or recruit, to offer salvation or redemption; to the contrary, it seemed in the beginning as if we were seeking a communal refuge from the seemingly un-accepting and sometimes battering reactions of the early childhood field to our ideological perspectives. The conference continued to grow in membership, providing a shelter, of sorts, an opportunity to address issues of early childhood education differently. Encouraged by the interest in our perspective, and utilizing theories and methods of feminism, postmodernism, and critical theory, we persisted in our examination of curricular questions of what knowledge and experiences were of most worth for young children (including but not constrained to issues of development), and of questions concerning the meaning of knowledge to the individual knower and the concomitant cultural and social interests that constitute the experienced curriculum. We reconsidered our own positions as early childhood educators committed to social change. And out of this reconsideration came other acts of resistance.

It is from within the historical context of the reconceptualist movement in early childhood education that this book, *Resistance and Representation: Rethinking Childhood Education,* takes its form. The aim of the collection is multiple: the critical, crosscultural consideration of issues of identity and theory-making in early childhood education, the examination of current resistances and reconceptualizations of traditional practices, the consideration of issues of research practice and research representation, and the discussion of the role of crosscultural, feminist, critical and postmodern theories as lenses for early childhood curriculum and research. Written by researchers from Australia, Canada, and the United States, the intent of these essays is to present a broad array of perspectives on curricular, social, and pedagogical issues within the early childhood field.

The past decade of "reconceptualizing early childhood education" has involved an intensive, scholarly rethinking of childhood education, with multicultural, critical, feminist, neocolonial, and postmodern early childhood researchers calling to question dominant ideologies, knowledges, and educational practices. This recent work in early childhood education has opened up dialogue in the field by focusing on such issues as power relations within the adult/child dichotomy, the manifestation of societal fears and obsessions about curriculum content, and the control of women and children through the construction of educational standards. Crossing disciplinary boundaries, this reconceptualized inquiry has also focused scholarly research in early childhood education on a broad variety of critical, feminist, postcolonial, and postmodern research methods and representations.

Re: Conceptualization

The ongoing reconceptualization of early childhood education is, at its very center, a process of reflection and realignment across multiple, intersecting terrains—those of identity, both of the child and of the early childhood professional; those of curriculum, both in its development and in its enactment; and those of social context and of social responsibility. Central to each of these, and to much of contemporary early childhood theorizing, has been the assumption that knowledge of the world takes the form of firm and steady truths that can be directly accessed through one's senses—by observation and experimentation (Beyer & Bloch, 1996) but often without reference to social, historical, or cultural contexts.

Thus we have "knowledge" of the developing child and of the designated and acceptable roles of the teacher, mother, childcare worker, etc.; we have understandings of what constitutes an 'appropriate' teaching practice or a standard and often standardized curriculum; we have routinized methodologies for the conducting of early childhood research (Jipson, 1999); and we have prescriptions and programs for child advocacy and educational reform, all of which assume certain universal regularities in the child's personal and educational worlds. It is this set of knowledges that has provided the seemingly consistent base for early childhood research and the understanding of child development and curriculum throughout the last half century. These assumptions and the political implications of generalizing Euro-American expectations and knowledge of child development and curriculum to the rest of the world provide the base for much of the reconceptualizing work that has taken place over the past ten years. And it is within the active resistance to these assumptions that new representations of childhood, curriculum, etc., have been created.

Researchers such as Jeffrey Lewis (1995), in analyzing current research in developmental psychology and early education, challenge the notion of developmental regularities, pointing out that the existence of 'universal' and 'immutable' stages of child development (Bredekamp, 1987; New, 1994) is contradicted by contemporary crosscultural research in psychology and anthropology. Lewis critiques the current focus on individual development, independence, and cognitive learning, critiquing characterizations of theories of child development as 'cultural scripts' and 'folk theories.' Valerie Walkerdine (1984) has also critiqued the notion of the universality of research-based developmental psychology, arguing that "developmental psychology is premised on a set of claims to truth which are historically specific and which are not the only or necessary way to understand children" (p. 154).

Early childhood educators working within the frame of critical theory have offered the strongest resistance to traditional perspectives in early childhood education, noting that because of inherent assumptions about knowledge and truth, many early childhood educators have failed to recognize the social and cultural values inherent in curricular decision making and thus have failed to consider whose interests are served by the curricula they employ (Jipson, 1991; Kessler & Swadener, 1992). From the perspective of critical theory, curriculum reflects the particular, usually Western and middle class, social, historical and cultural traditions upon which it is based. The imposition of any particular curriculum thus reproduces classed, raced, and gendered distortions in its representation of the world.

In the case of early childhood research, multiple interferences are evident. In addition to the notions about childhood that early childhood educators bring from their own experiences as children, they are influenced by their individual beliefs about what is important for children to know, about what children are able to do, and about what meanings children's activities have for them. These personal beliefs are grounded in the specificities of each educator's own historical, social, and cultural traditions. Furthermore, understandings of early childhood education are influenced by competing social constructions of the young child (Cannella, 1997; James, Jenks, & Prout, 1998) as an object of adult attention and care, as a developmentally maturing organism, and as unequally able to participate in rational problem solving or adult discourse may constrain.

The resultant constructions of childhood and of early childhood programs, which emanate primarily from Euro-American cultural experience, serve to impose both limitations and expectations on children and their teachers, actively reproducing dominant Euro-American patterns, relationships, and behaviors. In the end, both the representations of childhood constructed by educators in their minds and in their expectations and the representations of the world constructed by educators through their curricula determine what the experience of early childhood education is. Thus, while seemingly based on "objective," psychological research, contemporary perspectives on early childhood curriculum and on the institution of early childhood education carry multiple alternate and impressionistic representations of childhood which serve to inscribe power and privilege in specific ways, thus creating particular social texts and engendering particular educational possibilities.

Resistances

Early childhood educators working from a critical perspective are actively engaged in resistance to the dynamics described above. Often those who work directly with young children face the dilemma of balancing their roles as educators with their personal commitments to social change, their concerns with the cultural appropriateness of children's educational experiences, and their commitment to facilitating the social construction of meaning.

The inherent conflict in being committed to a liberatory, critical perspective, while not imposing personal values and agenda on others, also raises serious issues for early childhood educators striving to employ egalitarian and nonexploitative research methodologies with children. Research is the process of constructing representations of evolving understandings, representations called knowledge. Critically informed early childhood researchers assert that such knowledge is socially constructed and mediated. They believe that knowledge is invariably culturally and historically embedded in the concrete specifics of the situation. Thus, for critically informed researchers, knowledge must always be [re]viewed in the context of its constitution. By resisting and interrogating readily apparent forms of knowledge, critically informed researchers assert that what appears to be "objective reality" is actually what one's mind constructs based on its prior experience. Forms of knowledge, once constructed, must be examined from a cultural and historical perspective in terms of their role or potential within social evolution. For example, the concept of "child-centeredness" or "developmentally appropriate practice" or "optimal birthrate" can be understood as emerging within privileged Eurocentric cultural systems and societies which can afford to put their children at the center of their lives—as objects of their devotion, upward mobility, and material consumption, rather than as contributors to the family economy (Azhar, 1998).

From a critical perspective, knowledge is also valued in terms of its potential to contribute to progressive social change and social justice and is thereby a representation of resistance to dominant perspectives. Critically informed educators assert that the knowing individual can shape and re-shape the world through her/his instrumental action, through symbolic and communicative activity, and through the dialectical interplay between the two. In the case of research with young children this would involve both children's actions, in work and play, and their understandings of their activity, within the historical, cultural, and social context in which they live. Believing that knowledge and values are fundamentally interrelated, critically informed educators focus their concern on the emancipatory or repressive potential of knowledge. They assert that knowledge can never be neutral or disinterested, and that notions of "truth" are always tied to values. Furthermore, critically informed educators recognize that knowledge is unequally distributed and that knowledge-makers inevitably use their knowledge to enhance their own status and to support their own interests.

And this is where resistance and representation come in. Since critically informed educators believe that the world is socially constructed and shaped by human action, they believe it can also be re-shaped and transformed through human action. In resisting dominant forms of knowledge production and knowledge which privileges particular ways of knowing and being, the critically informed educator begins with a commitment to intersubjective understanding and the continual examination of boundaries which may enable or constrain relations of power related to discourse, culture, location, and subjectivity. In working with young children, this involves identifying how children's understanding and subjectivity are shaped through their interactions with each other and with adults. It also involves considering the historical and social situatedness of the discourses that frame and colonize their experiences and serve to position and represent them in particular ways. Thus, critically informed early childhood educators must repeatedly consider the local, partial, and contingent nature of their discourse with and about children—and the representations they create. By grounding early childhood education in the experiences of children and by recognizing that subjective understandings are partially determined by context, early childhood educators can develop an awareness of how their own understandings may also have been distorted or repressed through the process of their own resistance and reflection.

Representations

Resisting ensconced understandings of childhood and of early childhood practice, many reconceptualist early childhood educators have continued to explore questions of knowledge, knowledge production, and representation. Variously immersed in feminist, poststructuralist, and postcolonial theorizing, these researchers began to consider research questions outside the norms of early childhood practice,[2] and more actively experiment with different ways of representing "data," employing unconventional and unexpected genres, textual designs, and representations.[3] Working within interchanging theoretical frameworks and responsive to the intellectual strategies of deconstruction and semiotics, these researchers experimented with nontraditional forms of aural and textual representation and the application of strategies of rhyzomatic construction, discontinuous cadence, polyphonous voice, and bricolage to their research representations (Paley, 1995).

Recognizing that diverse, hidden understandings—contradictions, ambiguities, disconnections, disagreements, and displacements—were often overlooked in official research narratives, these researchers are also beginning to look at the 'hidden curriculum' of research representation and the representation of the painful, the prohibited, and the confused, while simultaneously identifying the same secret, messy, and contradictory processes in their own work. Explorations into the non-unitary identity of the child, the teacher or the mother (Bailey, 1998a; Jipson, 1992; Jipson & Munro, 1993), consideration of curricular topics such as AIDS (Silin, 1987), and deconstruction of discourses of risk (Swadener, 1995) or of no-touch policies (Johnson, 1997) exemplify the turn of some reconceptualist early childhood researchers toward heretofore unexamined and forbidden territory. And in doing this research, they encountered boundaries which both enabled and constrained their examination of relations of power, positionality, discourse, culture, and subjectivity. For these early childhood educators, research came to be a process for resisting dominant identities, arrangements, and perspectives within their field and also a process for constructing new representations of their understandings—even while realizing that knowledge and its representations is under continual construction/[re]construction, is always a partial, shifting amalgamation of fleeting and indistinct realities.

Resistance & Representation

In exploring the ongoing resistance within early childhood to dominant models of curriculum and inquiry and in examining current issues in constructing and representing knowledge about young children, this book presents alternatives which have emerged within contemporary early childhood research and practice and which challenge historically and ideologically fixed notions of the representation of children, teachers, families, and curriculum. Individual chapters focus on what the authors see as the sometimes insidious culture of early childhood education, addressing the nature of the contemporary culture of early childhood, the historic and philosophical foundations of early childhood curriculum, and the question of how a more authentic and culturally responsive early childhood practice can be created.

In our focus on issues of resistance and representation and as editors of this volume, we have repeatedly confronted our own conflicting desires to stay practically grounded while still exploring theoretical questions at the margins of early childhood and beyond. In seeking to adequately represent issues of polyvocality and inter-subjectivity as they relate to early childhood research, we recognize and yet cannot quite escape the dualistic trap seemingly inherent in talking about the role of the expert, the researcher, or the early childhood professional in working with children and families. In struggling with dilemmas of elasticity/plasticity—the circling around and positioning we assume relative to one another, to theory, and to our research, we acknowledge the difficulties inherent in this work, in working with one another. And in engaging the issues of power, control, affirmation, and connection as they are engaged through our positions and impositions to/from/of each other, we hope that we, too, continue to resist and represent ourselves in ever new and promising ways.

The individual chapters in this book have been arranged into 4 sections, focusing on issues of resistance and representation as they relate to the child, the teacher, the curriculum, and the social context. In the first section, essayists Gail Cannella in "Natural Born Curriculum: Popular Culture and the Representation of Childhood," Christine Woodrow and Marie Brennan in "Interrupting Dominant Images: Critical and Ethical Issues," and Mark Bailey and Nancy Meltzoff in "Resisting Institutionalized Ageism" examine widespread assumptions about the nature of childhood. Taken as a whole in their efforts to call into question dominant representations of the child, these chapters serve as an effective resistance to socioculturally determined beliefs about childhood and the education of young children.

In the second section of the book, Glenda MacNaughton in "Good Teacher or Feminist Teacher?: Investigating the Ethics of Early Childhood Curriculum," Katharina Heyning in "The Early Childhood Teacher as Professional: An Archaeology of University Reform," Lisa Goldstein in "Resisting the Norms of Elementary Education: One Primary Teacher's Stories," and Kerri-Ann Hewett "Eh, No Act!: The Power of Being on the Margin," problematize the collective identity and common representations of "early childhood teacher." In analyzing the complex and multidimensional nature of early childhood work, these essayists explore the construction of teacher identity, thereby both resisting and disrupting the notion of a singular early childhood educator role.

The third section of the book examines the core of early childhood education in its focus on issues of resistance and representation in regard to curricular practices in early childhood education. In "Critical Perspectives on Social Studies in Early Childhood Education," Shirley Kessler calls to question the function of social studies as citizenship education for young children and the process by which this socialization curriculum was developed, implemented, and maintained. She suggests we look to our history for visions of the way we want to live together in the future as a guide for curriculum planning, implementation, and evaluation and as a way to develop alternative perspectives on citizenship education and social studies education for young children. Julie Kaomea, in "Pointed Noses and Yellow Hair: Deconstructing Children's Writing on Race and Ethnicity in Hawaii," turns the focus of the curriculum discussion to language arts education, and, in particular, to issues of culture, race, and ethnicity as they find representation in the educational experiences of children. Nicholas Paley, in "What Does a Child Deserve in a Book? Harlan Quist and the Politics of Childhood Knowledge," continues the discussion of the language arts from another perspective. In analyzing the relationship between the nature of children's picture books and common beliefs about what children should know and experience, he calls into question many prevailing assumptions about the curricular appropriateness of educational materials for young children. Lastly, through considerations of cultural and identity politics, Mary Jane Fox reflects on other critical issues which should be part and parcel of any curricular deliberations.

The last section of the book focuses on broader historical, social, and philosophical issues of resistance and representation in early childhood education. Larry Prochner, in "The Proof of the Home Is the Nursery: An American Proverb Revisited," looks closely at assumptions about early childhood from a historical perspective, tracing the development of Euro-American notions of child care across several centuries. Susan Grieshaber, in "Beating Mom: How to Win the Power Game," Deb Ceglowski, in "Who's Making These Policies Anyway?: How Head Start Staff Interpret Official Policies," and Marianne Bloch in "Restructuring Governing in Eastern Europe: Constructing New Needs for Families, Children, and Childcare" examine social and political issues of power as they relate to programs for young children across an international context. The final chapters in this section, "Resisting Normative Representation in the Pacific Islands: Domestic Enemies Meet Over Coffee" by Richard Johnson and Maria Gaiyabu and "To Speak: Problematizing the Use of Personal Stories in Early Childhood Research," by Chelsea Bailey, bring the book's focus back around to issues of identity and representation in early childhood education, but from an intensely personal perspective and through the genre of story, thus challenging the very assumptions of early childhood research as objective and distanced.

The contributors to this book are themselves the reconceptualizers of early childhood education. The lives and work of these authors have connected and reconnected in many ways across their commitment to early childhood education, their rethinking of educational practice in its many forms, and their relationships with each other. In selecting the essays for this book, we chose to include a broad range of topics, ideas, methodologies, and representational styles, reflecting the diversity among the early childhood educators who have participated in the reconceptualist work of the past decade. *Resistance and Representation* is, thus, also about connection and collaboration, and about the complex and tightly woven interrelationships between a group of scholars and their efforts to re-form their field. We offer this book, both as resistance and affirmation.

NOTES

[1] Developmentally Appropriate Practice' (DAP), as described in the document published by the National Association of Young Children (Bredekamp, 1987), delineates both age-appropriate and inappropriate practices in the education of young children. Based on research in child development, the DAP document became the focus of much criticism of both the inappropriate and sometimes inaccurate use of psychological research in educational contexts (Canella, 1997) and the application of such research across cultural contexts (Jipson, 1991).

[2] For example, the exploration of issues such as passion, sex, love, and death by early childhood researchers including reconceptualists Chelsea Bailey, Lisa Goldstein, Richard Johnson, Jonathan Silin, and Joe Tobin.

[3] Recent work by Karen Anijar, Jan Jipson, Elijah Mirochnik, and Nicholas Paley exemplifies some of these experimentations.

Part I: Resistance and Representation:

THE CHILD

Chapter 1

Natural Born Curriculum: Popular Culture and the Representation of Childhood
Gaile S. Cannella

Education is dominated by the conviction that the child is a universal, naturally progressing being who is innocent, needs protection, and is distinctly different from adults. This deterministic perspective has been fostered through enlightenment/modernist discourses (Foucault, 1978) that focused on reason, universal man, natural truth, and the evolutionary search for the origins of knowledge in the human infant. Perpetuated by medicine and psychology, a popular culture has emerged in which adults believe that they have uncovered the Natural Truth of childhood and can universally prescribe curriculum content and methods for use with all children. The beliefs are so pervasive that only a given set of behaviors are expected and accepted for children or parents. Evidenced in media appeals to "Read to your children" or "Save the children of the world," and in school-based attempts to offer appropriate experiences for young children, these beliefs have become so embedded within everyday life that they are taken-for-granted as truth. We have come to believe that we as adults have scientifically discovered the nature of the child, the natural being. This "natural born" universal child discourse so dominates that counter perspectives are virtually silenced. Through movies, television, newspapers, music, parent education materials, political and religious rhetoric, and of course the capitalist artifacts that are constructed with consumers in mind, the "expert" construction of "child" permeates both the dominant and subordinate ideologies of our everyday lives.

The purposes of this chapter are to (1) examine the various discourses of childhood that have become popularized as part of everyday culture, (2) expose adult/child power relations that are generated through these discourses, and (3) explore how these constructions limit and devalue the multiple ways in which younger human beings are part of the diverse contexts of the world in which they find themselves (Merleau-Ponty, 1964; Silin, 1987; Silin, 1995). The childhood discourses that have been legitimized as truth in both dominant and counter ideologies include the existence of the natural, universal human "child"; the representation of the child as innocent and needy, with a specific focus on the need for protection; and, finally, the representation of the child as Other than the adult.

Childhood as Natural and Universal

From television commercials that represent younger human beings as those who are "most concerned about the type of diaper that they wear" to parent advice books explaining the "best toys for children of different ages" to political rhetoric that would position "all 8-year-olds as reading independently," childhood is constructed as the human condition that is natural and scientifically definable. After all, everyone was once a child. We have accepted the concept of the universal child with only limited analysis of the historical and political context or assumptions from which it has emerged. The construction of the child represents the enlightenment focus on the existence of natural laws that could be universally applied. Combined with the modernist focus on scientific thought and empirically based science (Weiner, 1966), the notion of "child" emerged as the ultimate object of the belief that human beings are natural, constant, understandable, and controllable. Psychology arose as the vehicle for the nineteenth- and twentieth-century application of these positivist assumptions to human beings. Further, within the context of "childhood," younger human beings were not only psychologized, but biologized. We now function as if we "know" the natural, universal truth of the child. Experts in development, medicine, and psychology teach courses and write books on child growth, explaining what to expect from children of different ages and how to interpret the child's thoughts. Educators, whether claiming to be developmentalists or academics, declare sets of child learning needs that are viewed as applicable to all younger human beings. Toys can be found everywhere, in stores of all types and even through toy clubs, designed specifically to further that predetermined learning. In commercials, television programs, and movies, childhood is presented as a universal way of being in the world, from the children who are "accent free" speakers of English in commercials to the middle-class dress and behavior of Barney children.

How are adult/child power relations generated through natural child discourse?

First, universalization of any group of people reifies them into simple predetermined entities. The constructions generated by psychology are excellent examples, essentializing the child as comprised of social, emotional, language, cognitive, physical, and moral domains. Complex, ambiguous human beings are reduced to listings of functions at particular ages, descriptions of behaviors, and categorization as "cute" or "sweet," "normal" or "smart." Second, the discourse of the natural, universal child perpetuates the dominant belief in truth and the privileging of scientific thought in the revelation of that truth. Third, a form of cultural elitism emerges for the group of people who have constructed the universal child. Those who would identify that child are given power over everyone else. This claim to the truth of childhood legitimizes experts like psychologists, social workers, physicians, and some educators as they define childhood and maintain control over children, parents, and other educators. A judgmental surveillance of these populations is even justified (Burman, 1994; Walkerdine, 1984). A language of normality and pathology is generated within the larger universalist discourse. Younger human beings are labeled as normal or abnormal, as gifted or slow, as competent or inept. The power is created that supports intervention into the lives of others that legitimizes social regulation for universalization. Finally, power is generated for those children who "fit" the truth while power is denied to those who for cultural, individual, or other reasons do not accept or fit the dominant construction. Those who embody the "truth" are viewed as the real children, allowed to have a real childhood.

These power issues lead to the recognition that natural child discourse actually limits and devalues all children. Predetermined constructions of younger human beings immediately limit our abilities to see the diversity of humankind (Kessen, 1993). For example, as a society, we have constructed the desire and the expectation to see self-concept revealed by other human beings. We have learned to be concerned about the notion of self through the language of experts like psychologists and educators and through the media as we observe commercials that focus on how we look and feel about ourselves. If a child revealed the belief that the earth, nature, and human beings are one, we might accept that the child was following a particular cultural belief, but we would still make judgments concerning the child's individual self-concept development. We would not hear the child at all (Delpit, 1995). The discourse of universalized truth further denies the political, historical, and social contexts from which we have emerged. We accept the existence of such "truths" as personality, cognition, self-concept, and individualism and represent them in the media, in literature, in toys that are provided for children, and in our everyday conversations. Positioning children within predetermined discourses and expectations immediately devalues them by placing limits on how they see themselves, on how we see them, and on how we hear what they want to say.

Children as Innocent and Needy

Popular dialogue with and about children is dominated by the construction of younger human beings as both "innocent" and "needy." Dialogue includes such statements as "Kids can't see fear, pain, or uncertainty" (from a television program), "crying babies are trying to communicate needs" (parent advise column in newspaper), "first we determine the child's needs" (an early childhood educator), "children need to stay home with their mothers" (a minister). Both the discourse of innocence and the construction of the child as needy signifies a being who is weak, lacking, and dependent, a human who is deficient and without agency. The fifteenth-century Christian church had constructed the child as the "holy innocent" (Kennedy, 1988). This belief combined with the dualistic perspectives of enlightenment Cartesian ideology constructed a group of human beings that were viewed as needing protection from a corrupt society and separation from a contaminated world (Block, 1995). The child has been constructed as innocent and needy; the child needs not only food and care, but nurturance, protection, and the knowledge possessed by others.

Woodhead (1990) discussed the questionable positivist discourse of child needs that clearly implies that adults should predetermine the life of those who are younger. Universalist needs have been generated as if value-free and appropriate for all. For example, dominant psychological and medical perspectives have posed that children need one consistent care giver. Yet, studies in diverse cultures have demonstrated that children can have happy, healthy lives with as many as ten care givers (Smith, 1980). Beyond those needs that we all have such as food and possibly shelter (although Victor contradicted some of our notions about shelter), we cannot name universal needs for all younger human beings. However, experts, authors, publishers, parents, and film makers continue to popularize child needs through child-rearing manuals, literature, bedtime stories, and the mass media.

Besides implying some form of angelic goodness (as represented on jewelry, pictures, and television programs), the discourse of innocence has been clearly defined as the opposite of intelligence. Children are still learning, do not yet understand, have not had experience. Silin (1995) has demonstrated the problem with this construction of the child as innocent in his discussion of human beings as faced with illness and death. No longer does any "group" appear more or less innocent or knowledgeable. AIDS and death call to question any of our certainties.

How are adult/child power relations generated through the discourses of child needs and innocence?

Those who are older are immediately privileged over those who are younger. First, the notion that child needs can be decided on by someone who is not the child creates authority for those constructing the need. One group makes the determination and imposes that certainty on the other. Referred to by some as imperialism, older human beings (and perhaps a particular group of experts) are deciding exactly what life will be like for those who are younger (Cahan, Mechling, Sutton-Smith, & White, 1993). Human society is oversimplified through the discourse of child needs, implying that we can actually understand the complexity of each other's lives. Our uncertainties, our doubts, our ambiguities are concealed and denied as judgments made for others. Further, the discourse of child innocence fosters dualistic thinking in which children are created as innocent, naive, ignorant, unknowing, and helpless. Those who know about the world and have experience in it are legitimized as the teachers and instructors of those who are unknowing. As Walkerdine (1984) has demonstrated, innocence requires that access to knowledge be withheld; only "safe" knowledge is allowed and only when the authority deems appropriate. Finally, surveillance (continued observation), a condition that would be objectionable to most adults, is justified in the name of protection.

These power issues lead to the recognition that younger human beings are harmed through our constructions of them as "needy" and "innocent." Within both constructions, child knowledge is not only disqualified, but its existence denied. Imperialist adult expectations and practices silence children with the messages that they do not know enough, that they are not yet competent to make decisions for themselves, and that it is appropriate for others to intervene in their lives. Clearly, younger human beings are smaller than most of us who are older, and all of us need protection at various points in our lives, dependent on the context and social circumstance. However, we must address the possibility that through our discourses that construct children as needy and innocent, perhaps a target group is created, a group that is accepted as victims for others. After all, they have no knowledge; they are stripped of all power; they have been told that they must depend on us for all their needs. Children are constructed as the ideal victim.

Children as the Ultimate Other (Child vs. Adult)

Remaining consistent with (previously discussed) Cartesian dualisms, the concept of "child" is perpetuated as the opposite from the "adult," defined by the older members of society as the "not me." Represented in children's programming through puppets, cartoons, and make-believe, through toys such as Water Babies, Baby Wiggles, Mr. Potato Head, Puffalump Pets, and Bert & Ernie, through businesses like McDonald's, Tyco, or Chuck E. Cheese ("where a kid can be a kid"), and in school through play, bulletin boards, and the assumed need for concrete and colorful materials, children are signified as the ultimate "Other" than the adult. Distinctly separate worlds have been popularized for adults and children. Adults are those who are intelligent, strong, competent, mature, and civilized; adults are those who work and are in control. Children are those who are ignorant, fearful, incompetent, immature, and savage; children are those who play and need control. The construction of "child" is consistent with the Western patriarchal notion that more "superior" groups must govern and regulate others (Lerner, 1993; 1986), the assumption that led to enlightenment subjugation of the poor, women, the mentally ill, and children (Foucault, 1965). Even the counter-discourse of the romantic period fostered oppositional dualisms; irrational as opposed to rational, feelings as opposed to thoughts. Further, the characteristics that are imposed on children are applied to adults who are viewed as deficient by labeling them as "childish," "immature," or "dependent." The child is constructed in opposition and clearly inferior to the adult.

How are power relations generated through the construction of the adult/child dichotomy?

The creation of the "child" by those who identify themselves as "adults" gives those adults total power, legitimizing both explicit and implicit subjugation. First, younger human beings are constructed as object, illustrated well in the popular comment "Children are our greatest natural resource." Children are placed in the same object category as trees, water, and food, positioned as nationally owned and for use by others. Children are "used" in everything from political rhetoric to commercials in which they are represented as the reason for the "safest tire on the road." Children are "used" to legitimize colonialist discourse and actions. The "First World" (Nsamenang, 1992) is constructed as the savior in the name of children of the "Third World." Whether through hunger, child labor, education, or living conditions, the discourse that would "Save the Children" or "Guarantee Childhood" perpetuates a colonialist power perspective, masking the imperialism that has led to poverty and fostering notions that people who live in poverty are responsible for the condition (Burman, 1994). The strength and agency of groups of children and their families are denied as "childhood" is used to conceal our role in the imperialist subjugation of others.

Second, the adult/child dichotomy results in the construction of a life period as separate from others, an isolated, insulated period of human existence. Even though we were all younger human beings, this disconnection with childhood legitimizes our own autobiographical constructions of the adult self as superior to the child self. We, as adults, privilege notions of sophistication and refinement and apply them to what we think and do as distinct from the time in our lives when we had not "come of age."

The adult/child dichotomy, and all the power associated with it, has resulted in a group of human beings who are only heard when being "spoken for" by those who are older. Whether younger human beings are affluent and living in the United States or labeled as destitute and living in a so-called underdeveloped country, they are only allowed to speak through the voices of adults. We hear them through the biological, psychological, sociological, cognitive, or linguistic sciences that we have created. We hear them through the discourses of need and ignorance that we have fostered. We hear and see through our constructions of them as consumers or learners. We have constructed a world in which we only hear another group of human beings from our position as the "more experienced," "sophisticated," "competent" adult. We hear them from a position in which we have appropriated all the power.

Challenging Thoughts

Our constructions of the "natural born child" have so dominated all forms of culture and discourse that younger human beings have been given little opportunity to either construct their own worlds or speak for themselves. They have been denied any power that did not fit our constructions of them. They have no counter-discourse, no popular culture other than what we have imposed on them or tolerated in our adult benevolence. Their resistance has gone unnoticed or has been silenced. The complexity of their worlds as human beings, the multiple ways in which they may know the world, and the expressiveness and wonder of their voices have been denied.

Chapter 2

Interrupting Dominant Images:
Critical and Ethical Issues
Christine Woodrow and Marie Brennan

Imagery associated with childhood surrounds us. As Patricia Holland comments, "Childhood lends itself to spectacular presentation" (Holland, 1992, p. 3). From images of emaciated waifs in aid agency brochures to babies in flowerpots on calendars and cards, these images clamor for attention as they silently contribute to public and collective notions of childhood. These versions of childhood are both influential on and reflected in the diversity of visual, aural, and textual representations of childhood that surround all of us in the carrying out of our daily lives, our rituals and ceremonies. Taken on their own, pictures of children may seem innocuous, the imagery ambiguous. However, the proliferation of these pictures, and their domination of public space, provides the opportunity to discern certain emerging themes and underpinning conceptual messages. Holland argues that pictures of children form part of 'interweaving narratives of childhood' (1992, p. 10), narratives that are both public and private, personal and social. In the wide eyes of the appealing child, the crouched body of the abused child, the structured placing of child in the arms of the mother or the family constellation, are guides for behavior and relationship and the telling of familiar "stories."

These images are powerful and diverse in the way they offer positions to women and men, teachers and children, people of color and whites, establishing various power relationships through the exercise of how the images are connected to central social practices. It can be argued that these (and other) representations of children and childhood are also reflections of, and resources for, practice in the early childhood profession and contribute to conceptions of childhood on which early childhood educators draw. We might argue too that images of children significantly influence how children see themselves. They construct a set of resources for identity-building from which children as well as adults draw. Understanding how these images might operate for children and shape understandings about their place in the world is as much a project of relevance to the early childhood educator as understanding how the images work in relation to producing practice in the field.

Whilst the argument sustaining the potential of these images in defining, resourcing, and reflecting conceptions of childhood is powerful, it is important to consider how definitive their effect is. These images and their meanings interrupt one another and are contestable. Competing versions of childhood images struggle for dominance in the public domains of community discussion, political rhetoric, and policy formation and enactment. Pictures are constructions: they offer both reality and illusion, including representations and fantasy. It is partly in this tension that we can find the opportunity to resist, find new stories, create different narratives, develop new practices, whether they are practices of identity formation or practices of teaching in early childhood. Interruption, we thus propose, is a strategic intervention into the field, offering critical possibilities for early childhood educators, practitioners, and children.

In this chapter, we explore the significance of three main sets or themes of dominant images of childhood: the child as innocent, the child as monster/threat, and the child as embryo adult. Each of the sets of images we show is quite widespread in Australia and offers a number of resources which are drawn upon in the field of early childhood education, as well as in the broader society, perhaps even more widely than in Australia. All three themes, we argue, are problematic and offer limited space for conceptualizing childhood or change. We thus explore the potential of agency for the child and for the early childhood educator by using the lens of ethics. Ethics, we suggest, provide a way to understand both how particular values are embedded in existing practices and how in the reflexive moments of redesigning practices it is possible to explore new value orientations which allow for—indeed demand—a place for change. Adequate ethical resources to help us explore the significance of possible strategic directions for the field of early childhood educators and for the children with whom we work are required for this task. In provoking critique and encouraging contestation, we consider how dominant images work, including how they fail to work uniformly to determine the field. In this discussion, it is necessary to explore the capacity to weave new images, to resist and act on in forming identity and the practices that support it. We also question how our own arguments and images position the child—and ourselves—within the field of early childhood power relations.

In the first section of the chapter, we outline the range of different themes underlying the dominant images of the child. We show the implications that these have for the child and for the early childhood educator, both as teachers and as academics and advocates for the field. In the second section, we outline some early work on ethical principles which allows for a more active construction of the child and a space for early childhood educators to work toward a new set of practices around images of childhood. In the third section, we then put forward some suggestions for strategic activities for interrupting these dominant images through teaching, advocacy, and research.

Section 1: Dominant Images and How They Work

It is not yet widely understood that childhood is a socially constructed concept, emanating from a net of social relationships that have developed over time and in specific places (see James, Jenks, & Prout, 1998). In the early childhood field, we need to understand how the images which we use have been shaped by culturally specific sets of ideas, philosophies, attitudes, and practices which define the nature of childhood for that setting and situation. In each of those pictures of children on cereal packets, chocolate wrappers, and greeting cards are represented aspects of childhood which, Holland (1992) suggests, contribute to our collective notion of childhood. Representing as they do an amalgam of perspectives, the power of these images is mostly unresisted, their themes uncritiqued. The images that we work with have become so naturalized, so taken-for-granted, that questioning them often makes us uncomfortable, and is likely to raise accusations of political bias, as was recently experienced when one of the authors presented related ideas to a public forum.

The continued emphasis on images of children places children in the public gaze and in so doing allows adults to reassert their control of children and childhood. Unexamined images carry a potential to blind us to the realities of children's own experience, reinforce stereotypes and power relationships and lead to the marginalization of minority groups and indifference to issues of social justice and difference. Unchallenged, the images have the potential to create false hopes and influence the proliferation of copies of "celebrated" images, many of which leave unresolved serious ethical issues about the treatment of children. Unless challenged these images also have the potential to reinscribe the traditional ideology, practices, and ethical understandings of practice associated with early childhood. Holding up these images and their underpinning assumptions to closer scrutiny gives potential benefits to the early childhood field by reexamining values and allowing examination of ethical concerns.

Early childhood has built itself around certain key ideas and images of children, teaching, and families. In the day to day practices of early childhood settings, particular dominant views of childhood, underpinned by a range of assumptions, have become naturalized. Our contention is that these views are contained by images in the profession, drawn on by early childhood educators in developing their philosophy, pedagogy, and curriculum. We also understand that a dynamic exists between the images and the responses that they generate, which helps create a construction of childhood that embraces certain political, cultural, and social positions. The images that are embedded in the profession are linked to public images, and the images associated with early childhood thus work both outside and inside the profession.

In our analysis of the images that predominate in Australian coverage of childhood, we have identified three main themes or sets of images which seem to dominate. In exploring these three dominant sets of images, we are providing a framework within which to explore and analyze the construction and implementation of curriculum for young children, the roles of adults who work in early childhood settings, and the dimensions of ethical issues embedded in them. Our analysis in this chapter does not go into detail, but aims to provide an overview of the range of images and some assumptions and implications that are embedded in them (see Woodrow, 1996, for a fuller discussion of these images). For each major image, we examine in brief the educational assumptions that fit with the image, the embedded ethical assumptions associated with that image, and provide some examples from the Australian setting.

Child as Innocent

The image of the child as innocent is a pervasive and resilient one. It is a cherished image, and one that is perpetuated and promoted incessantly in the drama of international and local news items, and the sentimental world of greeting cards. Yet it is an image that has been significantly influential on the field of early childhood. The image of an innocent child is represented in a variety of ways and includes pictures of children as helpless and vulnerable, and can be seen in pictures of premature babies in the hands of adults, or the angel-winged child accompanying the December page of the calendar. The image of the child as innocent is deeply embedded in the aid for third world countries promotional material (with the wide-eyed supplicating child) and can work to reinforce the dominance of developed countries. It also warns of the price of resistance. The image of innocence also embraces the notion of cuteness—a notion that is strongly perpetuated in popular representations of children. Holland describes how cuteness itself is "an acceptable play on the co-existence of innocence and knowledge" (1992, p. 14).

Emanating from the nineteenth-century progressive movement and embedded in the retelling of Bible stories, the tabula rasa of John Locke, and the walled garden of childhood idealized by John Holt, the image is the antithesis to the notion of child with original sin. Early childhood pedagogy underpinned by such an image places teachers in powerful positions of protection; the teacher role is dominated by the demonstration of competence, understood as the manipulation of a carefully structured, planned, safe, and sanitized environment. The teacher nurtures potential, facilitates the learning, and protects the child. How does such a perspective position the child? In a recent critique of contemporary early childhood curriculum, Jonathan Silin claimed the pervading belief in innocence is only a short step from believing in childhood ignorance. Silin (1995) argued that when childhood innocence is the dominant framework, children are frequently denied the opportunity to explore the realities of their life or to develop responses to it. Perhaps we attempt to protect children from the knowledge they already have. James (1996) talks about what could be seen as the Western mythologizing surrounding the idealization of a safe, protected, and innocent childhood—far removed from her experiences as a researcher in the north of England exploring children's peer relationships, where she saw children attempting to actively construct and renegotiate their place in the world. Constructing the child as innocent requires adults to maintain positions of power, to be all-knowing, to consider and make the "right" decisions on behalf of children. Yet many have a claim on acting on the child's behalf. Deciding whose claim is legitimate, what is "right" and issues about who decides are questions of significant ethical importance. What ethically are the responsibilities of the early childhood educator when conflict occurs, as it must, between perceptions of a community, a parent, and a child of what is in a child's best interests?

The innocence frame places children as weak and non-agentic, denying the capability of children to act and determine action for themselves. It inhibits the potential of children to explore the injustices and social realities of their existence and develop skills to deal with the moral inconsistencies and challenges that they encounter. This frame can work to reinforce power differentials between adults and children. Maintaining the image of the child as innocent usually works to reassert the power and control of the adult.

Much of the rights discourse, including the UN Convention on the Rights of the Child, is grounded in the child as innocent framework. Emanating from a focus on rights is the rhetoric of needs. Conceptualizing the adults' role as one of establishing children's needs is highly problematic in terms of agency. Such a move tends to hide the specific cultural and social choices that are made on children's behalf and works against the idea of rights in its own terms: that children may have a 'right' to claim for themselves the definition of their own needs.

The early childhood profession, as a highly feminized workforce, has its own associated issues and challenges to do with power, operating as it does within an established patriarchy. Confronting and considering the ethical issues emanating from the power differentials between adults and children that are so deeply embedded in the image of childhood innocence offers multiple new questions to the consideration of the profession and its practices.

Child as Threat/Monster

In addition to the prevalence of the child as innocent image, there is also a widely used set of images about the child as monster or threat. One of the best-selling child-rearing books for parents in Australia, written by a pediatrician, is entitled *Toddler Taming*. Other examples of representations of the child as threat or monster include the strident call for the return of corporal punishment, the imposition of night curfews on children under certain ages. Imaging the child as a threat helps society justify inhumane and humiliating practices to children. This set of images works as the obverse of the innocent child: the child who is not protected, or the inherently evil tendencies of the *little animal* is to be tamed and organized into higher order activities through education. However, the danger is always present that the inner monstrous qualities of the child might escape the civilized constraints provided.

Whilst the use of image of the child as threat or monster might shock those working in early childhood, close examination of a range of schooling practices demonstrates that this image is deeply embedded in them. It has, for example, given rise to practices such as streaming children, school uniforms, and classifying children into groups such as gazelles and snails, snakes and kangaroos. The image underpins many discipline policies and the discourse associated with attention deficit disorder (ADD), and helps support a medical treatment model for "dysfunctional" behavior. Further, the image allows and even encourages the promotion of reward systems and competition.

When this image dominates, schooling practices tend to be framed by rules and expectations of socially acceptable behaviors. Some rules lead to more rules as children explore the boundaries of that acceptability. Teachers become the expert lion tamer. Fear of a mob of unruly 'animals' justifies the protection role of the professional—though whether this is protecting themselves or other children is open to question. Education thus is seen as a bastion of civilization, building on nineteenth-century models of savage or 'primitive' exotic others, to be tamed through literacy and socialization.

When the image of child as threat or monster dominates, adult power and control are valorized and conformity is given priority. Teachers' roles are constructed around maintaining the social order as they protect themselves and other children from the monster children. In these circumstances the conditions that allow children to undertake the social negotiation of power and autonomy in a social context are not present and as a consequence children are denied the opportunity to grow in their own understanding and construction of ethical responsibility. An ethic that promotes domination, conformity, and autonomy precludes the development of relationships and trust that underpin an ethic of caring and connection and the promotion of justice.

Child as Embryo Adult
Images of the child as embryo adult represents a third powerful theme in early childhood. In many ways, this image is the reversal of the first. Children are seen as the raw material from which will be shaped the socially acceptable adult, and childhood as a time of preparation for "life." This statement "preparation for life" seems to suggest that childhood is not life. The image is indeed a dominant one in education and from it emanates many early childhood philosophies, policies, and practices that have become hallmarks of early childhood practice. Most significantly for education and training, the image is informed by and relies on stage theories of child development. The image positions the

teacher as the magic facilitator, preparing the right environment through which development will unfold. Themes that underpin development and natural growth are notions of rationality, naturalness, and universality. And so we see the child as moving from irrationality to the rationality of adulthood along a preestablished sequence of development.

Piaget's work, in which child development is seen to have a particular structure, and to consist of predetermined stages leading to the eventual achievement of logical competence and adult rationality, has been hugely influential on the discourses associated with early childhood education. It has inspired the entrenchment of the scientific construction of irrationality, naturalness, and universality of childhood and led to theories of socialization which are still strongly embedded in early childhood philosophy and practice. Socialization theories construct the child as passive, immature, incompetent, and irrational in contrast to the adult as mature, rational, competent, social, and autonomous. Socialization theory provides the framework for childhood to be seen as a rehearsal for life and strongly endorses social conformity. Within a stage development framework, children are positioned as marginalized beings, awaiting some temporal passage into the social world. Among the many outcomes of the dominance of this framework is the focus on the family and school as socializing agents, allowing the possibly negative impact of these institutions on children's lives to be largely ignored. The dominance of a notion of universal development works to blind teachers and children to consideration of difference and the effects of varying social experience and conditions.

The citizenship and civics education movement which is gaining ground in the Australian education context reflects this image of childhood as preparation for life, as do the graduation ceremonies from the childcare setting, complete with academic dress. The popular slogan "Children are the nation's richest resource," and the seemingly endless collection of pictures of children dressed as adults posed to reenact one version or another of the classic seduction or love scene that adorn the cards, wrapping paper, and shelves of our gift shops, all rely on the notion that the child is an adult in embryonic form.

The consequent focusing on the individual and masking of the role of social institutions in shaping the child and childhood embedded in this image reinforces notion of autonomy, differentiation, and abstract ideals of justice, keystones of traditional ethical frameworks. The consequent promotion of individualism has a tendency to disconnect children from their lives, promotes conformity above difference, and privileges certain clear-cut definitions of knowledge above others. Most importantly when early childhood curriculum draws strongly on this image the outcome is invariably an orientation to reproduction rather than transformation.

It is also clear that the economic and cultural moves associated with globalization are central to the spread and dominance of certain sets of images such as these discussed here. Here the issues associated with globalization are significant. Mass communication technologies, mass marketing, and other processes of globalization have contributed to the development of movements that attempt to universalize conceptions of childhood. This is most evident in the advocacy movement surrounding the advancement of the rights of the child. New words, images, products, and expectations mediated through merchandising, Internet, television, and the experiences of "other" children unseat and reconstruct the identity children develop of themselves and that created for them: identities which transcend regions, cultures, and countries. The process of globalization of childhood provides both risks and opportunities. Risks lie in homogenizing the experience of childhood and ignoring the vast range of cultural conditions, across time and place, and risks exist in the exploitation of the exotic aspects of certain cultures without exploration of the processes that surround and produce these representations. Opportunities for change and improvement lay in opening up possibilities for identity formation outside the dominant paradigms. As well as this move toward universalization, part of the process of globalization is to ensure that the images are anchored locally. Thus we see images of "Aussie" kids, "Vegemite" kids—eating brand names that are locally familiar—as well as being consumers of multinational toys and fast food.

Section 2: Agency and Ethics: Toward a Conceptual Framework

In section one we have presented an argument that the three dominant sets of images remain largely uncontested and contain serious questions and inadequacies in relation to ethical and educational relations. This has led to our questioning their appropriateness for use in early childhood practices. In particular we noted that there are problems with the lack of agency able to be ascribed to those in the field, including children themselves, and implied that we need to work toward an alternate conceptual framework for discerning shared understandings and making judgments within the field of early childhood. If early childhood practitioners are to engage critically with the assumptions of their work and the construction of their own work—and if they are to help children to engage critically in the construction of themselves and their world—then the explanation of how this world works needs to include a concept of agency. In this chapter we cannot hope to achieve a full outline of such a conceptual framework, but we argue for the importance of addressing ethics as part of this project. Clarifying the understanding of the moral voice(s) with which the early childhood field can speak is a task of considerable timeliness, if we accept Hekman's argument that moral voices are constitutive and thus morality and subjectivity are inseparably linked (1995, p. 129).

For our purposes here, a concern with ethics denotes an orientation to critical interrogation of the values and consequences of practices—in this case the practices drawing on and producing images of children. This is a practice-based version of ethics: ethics-in-use. This approach avoids defining ethics tightly, as we have found the tendency to define ethics only in terms of one particular ethical approach (see Denise & Peterfreund, 1992)—when there are many in disarray—actually detracts from our capacity to raise ethical debate within the field. In this section of the chapter we briefly outline our concern with the limited resources provided by traditional approaches to addressing ethics in ways which are useful for early childhood practitioners. We then outline a concept of situated ethics which is not only concerned with the local but is also interested in the connections with the field of practice—including the institutions in which practices occur.

Traditions of ethics have tended to remain highly abstract, the province of philosophy rather than treated as part of any practice. The "grand ethical theories" known to students of philosophy seem to be identified by attempts to develop principles with the following characteristics (Tong, 1993, p. 13):

- prescriptive
- universalizable
- over-riding
- public
- practicable

The effect of hundreds of years of ethical debate within such a dominant framework has been to reinforce social inequality, since the universalist ethic tends to support the interests of dominant groups. It is presumed to cover everyone, and by refusing to recognize that some groups are systematically obscured or ignored in the development and application of such principles, this framework for ethics has further removed ethical issues from the purview of ordinary practitioners. Notions of impartiality characterize traditional ethical frameworks, thereby setting up oppositions such as public-private, reason-passion, universal-particular, the consequences of which are to reinforce dominance of hegemonic groups (Young, 1990). We have seen these concepts at work in our brief analysis of the three sets of images.

The practices which have emerged in a range of fields such as early childhood have masked the interests at stake by the semblance of neutrality and the call for universal prescriptions for practice. Concerned largely with questions of social control and freewill, the traditional ethical approaches have either failed to address or dismissed issues about connection, interdependence, and relationship, features which tend to characterize early childhood as it is practiced.

Recent advances in feminist, postmodern, and postcolonial ethical debates have suggested the importance of challenging this way of approaching ethics. For such critics, the "grand theories" have failed to provide an ethical theory relevant to the realities of people's lives, especially to those of women and other groups less powerful. Feminist approaches to ethics have highlighted how ethical issues are traditionally conceived as arising from competing rights, requiring formal and abstract approaches to resolution. Consequently, resources have not developed to assist people's ability to analyze and reflect on their ethical responsibilities, and to act in ways that interrupt the dominant power relations to introduce new norms in their practices. Attempts to redefine ethics and to find new possibilities for ethical relations characterize much of this work.

In providing critique of the traditional ethical frameworks, theorists from feminist perspectives, in particular, have drawn attention to how these theories ignore and dismiss the importance of connection and a "care" perspective. Embedded in the images that we have considered are a range of ethical issues and positions that we have questioned. Protection from harsh realities of the world is embedded in a discourse of care in particular. Consider how the image of the child as threat or monster denies agency to the child and reinforces traditional understandings of power and authority. In protecting ourselves from this threatful child, an ethic that inscribes justice and autonomy for the adult is privileged and one that values care and connection is alienated. Yet the adult role, in protecting one child from another, or concern for specific individuals, calls on an ethic of care as well. Similarly the image of the child as innocent, constrained most obviously by notions of the unitary rational subject of the adult and the entrenchment of unequal power relationships between adult and child, must also contain an element of care and connection when adults are concerned to ensure the safety and well-being of the child. In the final image of the child as embryo adult, might not too much be expected of the child in developing the rational, autonomous perspective inscribed in the image? Questions must arise about the dominance of an ethic which values autonomy, rationality, and abstracted notions of justice over interdependence, relationship, and connection.

There has been a tendency in contemporary debates to dichotomize care and justice, resulting in some theories that valorize care as a distinctly feminine value. Whilst these perspectives may speak easily and convincingly to people working in professions such as early childhood, who characteristically espouse a strong care orientation, a note of caution needs to be sounded. Could this "care voice," claiming distinctiveness of the woman's perspective, both reflect and reinforce the inferiority of women (Tronto, 1987)? The essentialist and universalist approach which sees all women as a homogenous group, in agreement by virtue of their sex, precludes the capacity for men to be caring—or even for some women not to be caring, or not caring all of the time. This makes it difficult to reconstruct both care and justice as dimensions to an ethics of lived daily life. If men are to be concerned with justice and women with care, there is no prospect of reconstructing gender relations in early childhood settings or anywhere else. By dichotomizing care and justice, abstract rights-based notions of justice are also allowed to remain unproblematized. The opposite strategy of embracing an ethic of care and the exclusion of an ethic of justice is just as problematic as a basis of ethical work among early childhood educators and for the children with whom they work. Moral relativism and a noncritical stance on relationship are potential traps. For example, in early childhood should some relationships, such as the parent-child, be considered as universal caring relationships? How the moral worth and dignity of human beings might be considered within a theory of care is still to be answered. Tronto (1987) suggests that social institutions might be arranged in ways to expand understandings of the boundaries of care. This would have implications for how we understand care and how it operates in families, schools and teaching.

A concern with justice and the centrality of the features of rules and rights that characterize traditional ethical frameworks pose many problems for developing a more critical orientation to the understanding of ethical relations in early childhood practice. In the context of working toward alternative ethical frameworks that privilege connection and relationship and see ethical issues arising from conflicting responsibilities rather than from conflict about rights and rules, the perspective of justice built mainly around rights seems limited and limiting. A more adequate version could be developed by consideration of the embodiment of people engaged in questions of injustice, with a particular emphasis on examining how they are situated in institutional practices and relations which have developed in ways beyond their own understanding or choosing.

However, the language of rights does remind us that the interests of the oppressed and marginalized ought to be raised and discussed. If this is applied to the problem of who is "in" the relationship—in particular whether children themselves are part of the active agency constituting the relationship—important questions can be raised, about child-adult relations as well as about which children are advantaged/disadvantaged through the practices of early childhood. A more hopeful position is to move, as Iris Marion Young (1990) advocates, to a reconstituted understanding of justice which moves away from a universal, autonomous understanding of justice situated outside social institutions and instead considers social groupings, difference, and notions of oppression and dominance as central. In this way, Young argues, issues about decision making, division of labor, and culture allow an examination of the practices and institutions that produce injustice. If we were able to rework care and justice as necessarily related, there would be possibilities for reworking the nature of relations between privileged and oppressed, between powerful and the not so powerful, between adults and children.

Ethical debates in the early childhood sector need to address questions of how we are to live and work in the field, and specifically how we are to work with children in ways which allow for critical reflection and constructive building of ethical subjects. We refer to ethics rather than values, since we are emphasizing here the shared understandings (and disagreements) within the field, rather than the individual beliefs and opinions of practitioners. Clearly we need to include the social values of integrity, justice, and caring within our explanation. We conceive of ethics as being socially and historically produced, and see them as embedded in the practices that occur within the social institutions of families, early childhood centers, and schools. We thus take a "situated"

approach to ethics rather than one which emphasizes abstraction of universal principles. Issues which need to be considered as part of this reworking of ethics include attention to:
- the social context of the production of ethics as part of practices;
- the kinds of professional and personal issues in which ethics is involved;
- the kinds of issues and events that raise ethics away from their embedded aspects; and
- the constitution of ethics as an aspect of practice.

A central related question for any adequate conception of ethics is how we are to conceive of the ethical subject. If we take this back to the issue of images as discussed in section one, we are asking whether the child and the early childhood educator are determined by these images—i.e., constituted by them—or whether there is also space for a subject or group of subjects to constitute themselves in ways which draw upon but are not limited to the existing framing provided through those dominant images. We wish to argue for the second view: that active subjects are both constituted and constitute themselves, and that, as a consequence, new forms of identity and subjectivity are possible, though not fully open to redefinition. In order to make this point, we need to consider the question of how to explain agency in a way which avoids privileging the unitary, rational, individualistic subject on the one hand and on the other avoid seeing the subject as totally determined by the discourses, images, and practices already existing, with no capacity for reason at all.

In particular we point to a notion of autonomy which focuses on relations as well as separation. Thus, agency is not merely about having an individual capacity to contribute to the ongoing production of practice but also emphasizes the community within which the individual works and practices. Ethics are the basis on which interaction among humans and between humans and their world is organized. The problem is that most versions of ethics emerge from an enlightenment notion of the independent/autonomous rational subject, individualistic and free to choose. From such a view of the subject we are likely to fall into the trap of voluntarism—the belief in the freedom to choose that fails to acknowledge the historical and institutional constraints that help to constitute the options from which we are to choose, that shape our identities though not in predetermined ways. The other trap is to assume that humans are determined by their circumstances and without the capacity to affect their own lives and institutions.

In this section we have explored some dimensions for rethinking ethics. These frameworks contest notions of the universal rational subject and the separation of self and others which is inherent in traditional approaches to ethics. These newer resources for renegotiating and understanding ethical relations hold potential for the development of new sets of relationships in the early childhood field that enable:

- children to be seen as active
- recognition of the social nature of practice and the ethics embedded in it
- changes to practice to occur and thus to the ethical relations embedded in these new practices.

In resisting the ethical positions embedded in the dominant images of childhood, it may become possible to develop other ethical positions and possibilities for both children and early childhood teachers. When issues about positioning of the child, the assignation and claiming of voice and agency, and the nature of relationship between child and adult, teacher and student are considered. The reconceptualization of an ethic of justice, and the possibilities for an ethical framework which privileges embodied relationships, linking care and justice, offers exciting and important possibilities for early childhood.

Section 3: Strategies to Interrupt the Dominant Images of Childhood

In the previous sections of this chapter we have suggested the problematic nature of a range of images of childhood that reflect and resource early childhood practice. Early childhood philosophy and practices have their roots in a historical tradition in which certain practices have developed within specific institutional forms. They draw on a range of cultural practices and multiple images of schooling, mothering, teaching, and childhood. These images work both within and outside the profession and are embedded in a range of practices. Whilst we argue that these images, public and professional, contain and illustrate certain ethical positions and issues, we need to understand that in conceiving the images as both constituted and constitutive, the early childhood profession is not always constrained or contained within them. Although the sets of images might be claimed to be dominant, no single image has automatic priority. As we move between the images, including ones from other fields, drawing on the lessons and practices inscribed by one or the other, new possibilities for action are created in the spaces between them and between the images and the realities of the situation. That is, the field of images itself is significant in opening up opportunities for alternative positions. Even the uniqueness of each child interrupts these images.

We have identified some ethical questions embedded in these images. The problematic nature of the images, their power in reproducing dominant power positions, and the inadequacy of the traditional models and resources with which to consider alternative ethical positions all imply that resistance to these images is an important task in the early childhood field. It is timely to consider what strategies can be adopted to allow people in early childhood to interrupt these dominant images, and in so doing create possibilities for the development of new ethical relations. Possibilities for interrogation, resistance, and interruption of the dominant images is possible through at least three projects: teaching, advocacy work, and research.

Teaching

In early childhood teacher education, there are a number of opportunities which can be used to develop questions about and possible substitutes for the dominant images of childhood, even though many students who come into the field do so because of their interest in children conceived in traditional terms. We provide an example drawn from "Images of Childhood," a university course at Central Queensland University. In the development and teaching of this subject, and through workshops with practicing early childhood educators, the authors have had the opportunity to engage people in examination and critique of childhood images. Insights into the problematic nature of these images and their role in representation, production, and reproduction of early childhood ideology and practices have been achieved by encouraging the identification of themes and conceptual messages in a range of public and professional images. Examining just what is at stake in these visual representations and images and who has an interest in maintaining the status quo facilitates analysis and reflection on values and power relations inherent in the images in the practices inscribed and naturalized in the profession. Projects such as these provide the opportunity to illuminate and investigate the values that underpin certain childhood images and allow the exploration on the inherent ethical constraints, as well as considering the range of practices they produce. Examining the relationships between different images and analysis of the resonance and dissonance of certain themes within and between them has also allowed the interrogation of the power relationships and provided resources for the interruption of the dominant images.

Working with the language that surrounds childhood in everyday discourse has also been instructive in explorations of images and meanings about childhood. When combined with the personal creation of new representations and images, this can provide meaningful insights into how early childhood work is constructed, how the images position children and teachers, and what possibilities might exist or be created that restructure and reposition these relationships.

Consistent with the concern with child agency, a further project to advance the interruption of these dominant images is to involve children in critique and analysis of these images as part of the teaching in early childhood settings. Children have a significant stake in how they are represented, and what are the dominant images and discourses that are central to their experiences of life. Engaging children in reflection and critique within the early childhood classroom offers potential for renegotiating the meanings we make of the images and for children to contribute to their own construction of childhood. Allowing opportunities in the early childhood classroom for the children's voice in the curriculum offers the possibility for a more emancipatory curriculum.

Advocacy

Early childhood educators can undertake a range of advocacy work in questioning images of childhood, calling attention to important questions such as who produces these images, the claims they make, and whose interests they serve. Our knowledge of the field suggests that most early childhood professionals have been reticent to act politically, yet our reading of the dominant images suggest we/they themselves are politically very powerful in maintaining the status quo in images of children. Critiquing these images and encouraging debate through political activism, lobbying and the use of the media, as well as developing new images, seem important projects for the field to undertake.

The advocacy role is also important in work with other educational and caring professionals such as health and welfare workers, since images of childhood are also central to their professional self-definition and to their daily work with children and families. Professional associations might also undertake in-service training courses, perhaps by including a range of professionals with a stake in working with children, to explore the results of these images in their own work. Parent groups, particularly those of disadvantaged groups, might be able to provide alternative readings to the dominant images, ones which question innocence, monstrous children, and embryonic adults as central representations of their children's experience of life.

Policy domains, too, need to be the focus for increased advocacy on behalf of children and the images which constrain them and ourselves. Policy, especially at a time when there is high contestation about funding for human services and education, is particularly influential in extending and structuring particular images of children. In particular, children become the object of the surveillance gaze, the target of policy. To alter those images can be part of consultation processes with government and nongovernment agencies and employment bodies for the field.

In Australia, recent efforts to eradicate corruption, particularly in the public sector, have resulted in a number of attempts to formalize ethical attention, through the development of codes of conduct and codes of ethical practice among professionals. Codes of ethics are often seen as tools in which power and control can be exercised for some common good, rather than as frameworks for considering alternative ways of being and acting ethically. Typically they are highly abstracted, disconnected from practice and give rise to a search for universal principles to guide ethical action. In Australia, the development of a Code of Ethics for early childhood has been helpful in signaling some discussion about ethical responsibilities and providing some resources for this discussion.

In relation to dealing with images of childhood as they operate within the field of early childhood, while approaches such as a code of ethics may be one part of a strategy to raise ethical debates within the professional field, there is little that can be done through such strategies to interrupt the continued operation and reinscription of images. Nor do they address such questions as the alternative possibilities in relation to a position of agency and the ethical frameworks in which justification and consequences of agency can be considered. How different groups in different places might understand "justice" or "democracy," for example, needs local attention and local readings. While ethics remains an abstract and highly individual tradition, those engaged in fields such as early childhood will not be supported to engage in interrogation of their practices and their embedded ethical stances. Codes of ethics may raise levels of debate but these are not enough to address local lived practice.

Research

The field of early childhood is not well researched; it often suffers from a need to gain credibility by the use of outmoded methodologies or empirical work. Consequently its theoretical work can be derivative or trivial, failing to address significant questions and issues for practitioners or for substantive theoretical areas. Our work here suggests some important foci for research which might support greater practitioner interest in research findings and in participation in research projects since there are some obvious connections to practice. Our work in the field suggests that many of the dominant images of children are actively used in early childhood settings and often lie unchallenged. Collaborative research that allows the exploration of these images has potential to contribute to the development of new images, practices, and relations among children and between children and adults.

We are also interested in exploring further questions of children's agency. Important opportunities for research, teaching, and theory building can be found in opening up issues of agency in relation to the construction of images and their connection to identity formation and to changing the teacher-child relationship. As well, we have suggested that there are important research areas to explore in the links between the images of children in the public domain, the work of professionals in early childhood, and how ethics is embedded and produced in those images and practice. Research that explores and analyzes the experiences of ethics in early childhood practice might include focus on the social context of the production of ethics, conditions under which practices are produced in early childhood and their ethical dimensions, and identification of the kind of event that raises ethical issues into explicit concern. All of this research might contribute to more ethical relations in early childhood.

In this chapter we have advocated a move toward a reconstruction of the relationships between adult and children, and among educators in early childhood. We have urged the interruption and resistance of the dominant images of childhood as an important part of this move, since it shows up the current workings of those images—which operate even among those most interested in being critical in their theoretical and teaching practice. We have suggested that for this reconstruction to occur and possibilities for greater agency and action to be realized, an alternative framework for understanding and developing ethical relationships is required. We have argued that significant ethical issues arise from the consideration of these images and that traditional resources for understanding ethics in practice can be shown to be inadequate in a field in which care and connection are dominant priorities. In a tentative discussion of a possible framework with this potential, the directions indicate the need to avoid privileging an ethic of care and connection over autonomy and impartiality in favor of a new understanding of the relationship between care and justice.

Interrogating and interrupting some of the dominant images currently working in early childhood opens the way to taking a more critical look at ethical relations in practice and working toward a vision of possibilities for agency, changing practice and new sets of ethical relationships embedded in that practice. The project of interrogation and interruption can be undertaken at multiple levels, including through partnerships with children within early childhood programs; through action and advocacy in the field; and through collaborative research projects. In each case the social nature of professional practice and the ethical relations that are produced and embedded in them need to be explored. Such projects carry the promise of enhancing understanding, changing practice in the field and leading to a reconceptualized and more powerful field of early childhood.

In this brief space, we cannot hope to address the full complexity of changing the images and uses of images of children. However, we are suggesting that a fuller exploration of the ethical dimensions of our work has the potential to be strategically useful at a time when, in Australia at least, the "profession" is emerging just as the crisis of the state, the downsizing of the human services in the public sector, and the re-gendering of educational workplaces are being put into place. In a context where resources are tight, where efficiency, economy, and productivity are the dominant frameworks for responses to social concerns and the rhetoric of old fashioned family values is pervasive, there is a temptation to work only within the system, and thus within the current definitions of the paradigms for childhood already enshrined in the media and our practices. In a period of such change it is easier and more obvious to attribute tensions and difficulties to professional and industrial issues than explore the deeper and complex issues related to ethical dimensions of restructuring the field. Allowing such tensions to masquerade as industrial or professional issues can inhibit significant and meaningful critical reflection when what we need to do is to confront the shortcomings of the dominant images of childhood already incorporated in the early childhood field. To raise questions about the images is confronting. However, we have to dare to be critical if we are to interrupt these images, and for many of us the process can be quite discomforting. To be critical, then, involves us in evoking normative judgments. As Iris Marion Young (1990) suggests, "social description and explanation must be critical, that is aim to evaluate the given in normative terms" (p. 5). She continues, "normative reflection must begin from historically specific circumstances because there is nothing but what is, the given, the situated interest in justice from which to start. Reflecting from within a particular social context, good normative theorizing cannot avoid social and political description and explanation" (p. 5).

Chapter 3

Resisting Institutionalized Ageism
Mark D. Bailey and Nancy Meltzoff

"Rug rats," "ankle biters," "snot jockeys," and "carpet critters" are all deprecating terms used to refer to young children. Although they are intended to cause a chortle by those who use them, these phrases carry negative connotations as did endearments directed at women such as "bimbo" or "babe." Slang of this nature is always denigrating and it is indicative of feelings of resentment and/or the need to feel superior. It also tends to be emblematic of a lack of sensitivity on the part of the user.

In our society, ageism has long been institutionalized. It is manifest as a condescending attitude not only toward young children, but toward those professionals who work with them as well. While it is tempting to provide an extensive deconstruction of the origins of this ageism and the power differential that it represents and sustains, that is not the purpose of the present chapter; this analysis can be found elsewhere (e.g., Cannella, 1997). Our purpose will instead be to focus on the ways in which we can recognize and respond to this ageism, educating its purveyors along the way.

Throughout the history of humanity, conceptions of children and of childhood have been rooted in social convenience and evolving philosophical perspective (Aries, 1962; de Mause, 1974). The retelling of this history varies depending on whose account you read. Aries (1962) depicts the history of childhood as rooted equally in religious and cultural necessity and consisting of the gradual movement from "coddling" to control. In contrast, de Mause (1974) paints a radically different picture. Filled with mistreatment, abuse, and neglect, deMause's depiction is of horrific violation that improved gradually in the last century as parents developed the "capacity to identify and satisfy the needs of their children" (p. 51). Despite their differences, the thread that appears to connect both of these depictions of childhood is the philosophical acceptance of the child as fundamentally distinct from and unequal to adults.

Contemporary philosophical perspectives recognize that the concept of child should not be considered axiomatic, but is instead a categorical construction that may serve to limit and control individuals of this age group (Cannella, 1997). From the constructivist perspective, childhood is recognized as a social construction and not an independent reality (Cannella, 1997). This recognition is also found in the writing of critical theorists (e.g., Morrow & Brown, 1994) who suggest that one result of this categorical construction is the justification of ongoing domination.

The nature of this culture of domination has been carefully illuminated by resistance theorists such as Giroux (1983) and Willis (1977). Resistance theory itself is an integral part of critical theory, which is founded on "the premise that men and women are essentially unfree and inhabit a world rife with contradictions and asymmetries of power and privilege" (McLaren, 1989, p. 166). Critical educators seek to make changes in this unequal world, to participate in the construction of a just and non-exploitative society for children of all ages, and to take part in "creating history" (McLaren, 1989, p. 154).

An exploration of ageism is a concern of critical educators, who are committed to transforming social inequalities and confirming the "voices of subordinate groups in the student population" (McLaren, 1989, p. 165). Young children are a subordinate group that is particularly susceptible to ageist practices. In this chapter we will refer to the ageist practices directed at this population of young children as well as those who work with them as "juvenile ageism."

Resistance theorists have explored the role of conflict and contradiction within the process of social reproduction in schools, examining such issues as the means by which inequities are transmitted, how schools sustain the status quo, and the manner in which dominant practices are sustained in a gendered, classed, and aged society. Much of this work on resistance has focused upon student resistance (Giroux, 1983; McLaren, 1989). As McLaren notes, resistance by students "is a rejection of their reformulation as docile objects where spontaneity is replaced by efficiency and productivity, in compliance with the needs of the corporate marketplace" (1989, p. 188). In the case of adolescents, students find ways to speak up for themselves, through overt and covert acts of resistance. Indeed, it is this emerging voice and ability to resist that are one of the hallmarks of adolescence. Although variously analyzed and categorized as a period of storm and stress (Hall, 1904) or argumentativeness (Elkind, 1984), adolescence is period in an individual's life when the ability to comprehend the ageist treatment to which one is subjected, and the voice with which to speak out against that treatment, come together. This can be particularly empowering for adolescents.

In the case of juvenile ageism, much of the resistance must emanate from the allies of young children. This includes enlightened parents, teachers, and other socially conscious adults who recognize the inequities of power inherent in a system where representation is power and where children have limited representation. Yet it is critical that as allies in resistance, we not see ourselves as members of a superior culture. The resistance ally is akin to "the image of Giroux's resisting intellectual, someone who questions prevailing norms and established regimes of truth" (McLaren, 1989, p. 189). As allies we ask questions about dominant modes of behavior. How is political power structured to achieve social control of children? To what extent does the public arena dictate the manner in which children can interact socially with members of the larger community? What fosters the conditions that lead to ageist professional hierarchies? What sociocultural conditions nourish juvenile ageism? We support the necessity for challenging assumptions and engaging in resistance against dominating logic and restrictions that are inherent in the system as it stands.

Resistance to juvenile ageism has been steadily growing in the early childhood educational community as we endeavor to seek an appropriate level of respect and legitimacy. Yet many of us still struggle to find ways we can resist these ageist attitudes and skillfully focus our efforts to raise the consciousness of others. In this chapter, we discuss the arenas wherein resistance to juvenile ageism is necessary, and provide effective forms of resistance for each arena.

We propose that juvenile ageism is evident and must be confronted in four major arenas in our society: the political, the professional, the personal, and the public. In each of these arenas, we will examine the manifestations of condescension and control that support negative attitudes and actions, and we will suggest the types of resistance that can be generated in response.

The Manifestations of Ageism
The Political Arena
In the political arena, juvenile ageism is evident on the national, state, and local levels. In America, political power is both directly and indirectly responsible for status and the allocation of resources. Young children don't vote, and because of this, they have a minimal amount of

power to affect public policy. The occasional child, such as Ryan White, Samantha Smith, or Zlata Filipovic, does capture the public's eye, but more often than not the attention is focused on a single issue and the public's attention is short lived. Therefore, at the political level we see ageism manifest in issues that concern children. The education of children tends to receive less support than do issues involving those groups who, because of their vote, wield more power. Even in government-funded programs for children such as public schooling, early childhood education programs are continually underfunded in relation to the programs of older students.

Although developmental research indicates that a very significant amount of learning goes on before the age of seven, we see that politicians have continued to make kindergarten optional in some states, and full-day kindergarten is offered in only a limited number of states. Early childhood education research indicates that every dollar invested in high-quality early childhood programs for young children living in poverty can save three to seven dollars in reduced social program allocations during the adolescent and adult years. However, this information has not significantly changed the emphasis the government places on early intervention programs.

Head Start is a classic example of a successful program truly making a difference in the lives of young children, only to be cut back by a shortsighted conservative Congress. Even with the many efforts directed at improving the educational system, there is still a lack of respect for the importance of providing resources for these efforts at the beginning of a student's educational experience. This results in a lack of resources for early childhood programs.

We see this political ageism at the state and local levels as well. Whenever there is a budgetary crisis, money for the early programs tends to be cut first. In 1997 in Portland, Oregon, there was a $15 million shortfall in the public school budget. The first cuts that were made involved early childhood education. The entire full-day kindergarten program was cut throughout the school district. Furthermore, of the teachers in the district who were cut, more than half of them taught kindergarten–third grade. How is this justified? Districts prioritized programs and cut those on the bottom until the monetary goal was reached. Kindergarten teachers were cut with the understanding that remaining teachers could teach larger classes and both a morning and an afternoon class. One kindergarten teacher might have more than 60 students a day in two 2.5-hour classes. Even though there was an outcry at the loss of funds and the cutting of teachers that resounded from the citizens of Portland, the emphasis on cutting early childhood programs was not a topic of public comment or question.

The Professional Arena
Early childhood educators are all too familiar with the condescension attendant a profession that involves working with young children; stratification and ageism exists at all professional levels. At the university level, it can be found in relationships between faculty members, even between teacher educators, where an academic hierarchy frequently exists that is inversely related to student age. When early childhood educators communicate and work with their university peers, there tends to be a certain respect for their abilities as an educator. However, there are times when it is possible to see that respect undermined and the tone and tenor of conversation change to a more simplistic level when the topic turns to early childhood education. It is a form of intellectual patronization. This condescension even extends to relationships between teacher educators, who by their actions and words at times imply that there is less academic rigor associated with working with the future teachers of younger students than with future secondary teachers: "...after all, they are only kindergartners."

Within the public schools there appears to be a pecking order between teacher/practitioners where an age-related hierarchy exists. This is intertwined with gender issues as well, in that traditionally women have taught at the lower grades and men have dominated secondary schools. However, male kindergarten teachers are regularly treated as intellectual lightweights by members of both genders. The attitude appears to be "What exactly can these young children learn and therefore how difficult can your job be?" In a recent conversation one of the authors had with a district superintendent, the superintendent commented on his desire to assess students' abilities as they enter the public school system to determine whether or not they were "ready to learn." The belief that real learning doesn't actually begin until children start in public schools is so institutionalized that it can be found in the first statement of Goals 2000: "All children in the United States will begin school ready to learn," implying that what they do prior to public schooling is not actual learning but some lesser cognitive activity.

In graduate education programs, ageism is repeatedly exhibited between students. This is manifest in a detachment between the teachers of older grade levels and those of younger grades, and there is even an interesting reflection of professional self-concept that may be affected by student age. This tends to be especially true of men studying to be early childhood educators. When asked what level he would be doing his student teaching at, one particularly large male in our program responded self-consciously "kindygarten," as if to say "kindergarten" would seem like he was putting on airs. Similarly, many students refer to children's literature as "Kiddy Lit," because they consider it intellectually inferior.

Finally, it is illuminating to examine the pecuniary inequity that exists between educational professionals who work with preschool students, and those who work with high school students. Our society does not support paying a preschool teacher the same amount regardless of whether the teachers at each age level are equally qualified, a case of juvenile ageism as ingrained economic policy.

Personal Arena

The personal arena includes those interactions that each of us experience with friends, or family. The most effective means of examining the personal arena will be for one of us to relate our personal experiences as an early childhood educator. We have already discussed the low educational status traditionally accorded early childhood educators, where the perceptions of the challenge of the job and the legitimacy of the teaching that takes place appear to be related to student age. This was made painfully evident when I was an early childhood educator at the preschool and then kindergarten level. The kinds of value-laden comments directed at teachers ranged from "oh, that must be fun getting to play with kids all day," to a sarcastic remark I once received from an acquaintance, "tough job, it must be hard to choose what to have at snack time every day." Even now, with a doctoral degree and as a faculty member in a respected university, when people learn that I teach early childhood educators, there is a tendency for many of them to respond in ways that belie their conception of this job as a lightweight intellectual challenge.

The families of early childhood educators exhibit these tendencies as well. It seems that there is something legitimately educational about teaching only at a grade level that has a number next to it; the larger the number, the more legitimate. The graduate students with whom I work regularly receive these sorts of comments. The parents of a current student mentioned to me that an early childhood education endorsement was good because, "This will always give my daughter something she can fall back on later if she needs to." Once, when discussing a colleague's current job as a preschool teacher, the parents of this colleague wondered when he might get a "real job" and start doing the "real teaching" that he was trained for and that his teaching license would allow. How does one respond to such innuendoes, overtones, or direct questions? Sometimes they are based in ignorance, yet at other times they are intentionally employed as a means of social stratification. How can we resist these attitudes and behaviors, and enlighten their purveyors?

The Public Arena
Until very recently the public arena was the major source of conflict between ageist structures and practices, and the needs of young children. While the public arena includes places ranging from adult-only to child-oriented facilities, we refer only to those public facilities that should, by their nature, provide equal accessibility for children as well as adults. This includes public travel, certain stores and restaurants, museums and any place that adults should legitimately take young children. In these public places, meeting the safety and comfort needs of children has often been made difficult by a lack of consideration for these younger, and therefore second-class, citizens. Implicit in this is the valuing of adult activities, while children are treated as a distraction at best.

Of all the arenas, the public arena is the most progressive for being non-ageist. However, the reason for this change was not a reconceptualizing of children and their role in society, but the power of money. Owners of restaurants, airlines, and other public facilities realized that parents of young children were making decisions about spending their time and money based on the accommodations available for young children. "Do you have a changing table?" "Are there facilities that are accessible and safe for young children?" Proprietors began to recognize that meeting the legitimate needs of children might entice the whole family. We now see movie theaters that have soundproof rooms to which parents can bring their children for child-centered movie viewing. Many stores have added facilities for children that recognize and accommodate their play needs.

Whereas economic considerations have changed some practices in the public arena, ageism is still a strong undercurrent that is only addressed when it is in the immediate best interest of adults. Although there has been some improvement, there is still work to be done. Resisting ageist practices continues to be in the best interests of children and families. Let us now examine some forms that this resistance can take.

Forms of Resistance

The word resistance comes from: *re* meaning back and *sistere*, which is traced to the Latin *stare*, meaning stand (the same root that developed into the word statue). Therefore "to resist" means to take a stand in opposition, to push back. We propose that there are five major types of resistance that individuals can use to take an oppositional stand.

A. The first type of resistance is to proactively fight, argue, or work for change: when we are aggressive or assertive for the purpose of achieving a goal. This is an offensive movement that may be preemptive. In physical and practical terms, this is a moving forward, a purposeful, planned action.

B. The second type of resistance is to actively counter: when we speak up and push back against the actions of others that keep us from achieving a goal. This is more of a defensive movement. We can imagine this concretely in the following manner: when pushed, push back.

C. The third type of resistance is to withstand or fend off: when we do not allow ourselves to be pushed where we don't want to go. Resistance, in this sense, is to stand firm and hold fast to our own ground.

D. The fourth type of resistance is to passively resist, which is to refuse to cooperate with or submit to another's actions. This alternative to direct resistance takes its impetus from the martial art of Aikido, which redirects the energy of the initiator.

E. The fifth type of resistance is to boycott. Not a capitulation, this form of resistance works by intentionally not engaging. We choose to turn our backs or stay away in order to deliver a strong message.

While it is the case that each of these forms of resistance can be skillfully used in each of the arenas, there are some forms of resistance that are more effective for each specific arena. The key to maximizing the effectiveness of any resistance lies in the skillful selection of the form most appropriate for each specific situation. Figure 3.1 provides a graphic representation of the relation between the forms and arenas. In the political arena, simply withstanding or refusing is less effective in bringing about change. In this arena, it is necessary to be more proactive, to fight, argue, or work for what we believe in. Figure 3.1 depicts this connection between the arena and the most effective form of resistance. For instance, in the political arena, this might mean such actions as proposing new legislation that will reform ageist conventions. It might involve serious lobbying for the formation of new legislative committees, or actively running and supporting candidates sensitive to issues and supportive of change. One example is the worthy wage campaign where early childhood educators seek to increase the pay and respect that they receive. It should be noted that proactive fighting is not the only form of resistance that can be effective in the political arena. To actively counter (B) can also be skillful. An example would be to actively counter the efforts of school officials who propose ageist changes or policies such as those tendered in the Portland School District example above.

In the professional arena, we can resist by withstanding the actions of colleagues and clients (C). For instance, we can speak up against the ageist attitudes of others, and not allow condescending comments to pass without a response. When ageist assumptions are made, we can question them, refuse to except them, ask for clarification, and work to deconstruct them: confronting by not accepting. Also helpful in the professional arena is (B). An example of resisting by pushing back would be to actively counter school officials who propose ageist changes or policies.

In the personal arena, perhaps the most useful form is passive resistance (D). When friends or family make ageist comments, it is possible to rephrase to eliminate the ageist references. For instance, in the example given above, where a student's father said, "This will always give my daughter something she can fall back on later if she needs to," it is possible and useful to respond "Yes, your daughter is a gifted teacher and this degree will provide her with multiple possibilities for carrying out this important job." This is a sincere attempt to educate and change language, behaviors, and attitudes without direct confrontation. But there may also be times in the personal arena when it can be useful to more forcefully counter comments like this by pushing back (B) and directly challenging deprecating statements. The use of one form over another will depend on the individuals involved and the outcome that is desired.

In the public arena, one of the effective means of resisting has been to boycott, another passive form of a resistance that involves voting with one's presence. For instance, boycotting the local family restaurant because there are no highchairs or changing facilities, or refusing to be a patron at a store that will not allow children to use their bathroom, can be effective means of fostering changes. Once these practices begin to evolve, the actions of these institutions will be reinforced with increased public support. Often, however, a more forceful approach is needed such as (B). In the public arena, we can actively counter these practices either through organized and publicized campaigns, or by face-to-face discussions with those who are making the ageist decisions.

As depicted in Figure 3.1, all forms of resistance can be applicable to some degree in each of the four arenas. However, (B), active countering, is particularly appropriate in all four arenas. The implication is that it is important to be skilled at engaging in multiple forms of resistance, and that as we resist it is critical to know which form to use in a given situation in order to maximize effectiveness. The five forms of resistance are very different experiences and many result in different reactions by the persons involved.

In conclusion, where do we go from here? Often in the quest to deconstruct and reconceptualize, we are left knowing there is inequality, yet feel uncertain about how to begin to affect change. If we agree that resistance can be a positive act necessary for fostering change, we must be willing to engage in dialogue about when and how to resist both individually and collectively. The purpose of this chapter has been to provide a starting point for those seeking to resist the practice of juvenile ageism. As has been suggested above, there are many arenas within which to engage in this effort. We agree with Cannella that a vital element in the work of early childhood education should be "...the resistance to dominant forces that inhibit social justice and the caring tasks of hearing the voices of others. This work can be found in classrooms, communities, and even in scholarly research publications" (1997, p. 172).

This work will not always be easy, yet the endeavor is necessary if the reconceptualization of early childhood education is to become a nexus for resistance to traditional juvenile ageist practices. The hope is that this paper will provide some guidance as we consider how best to resist the manifestations of condescension and control which reinforce negative attitudes and actions.

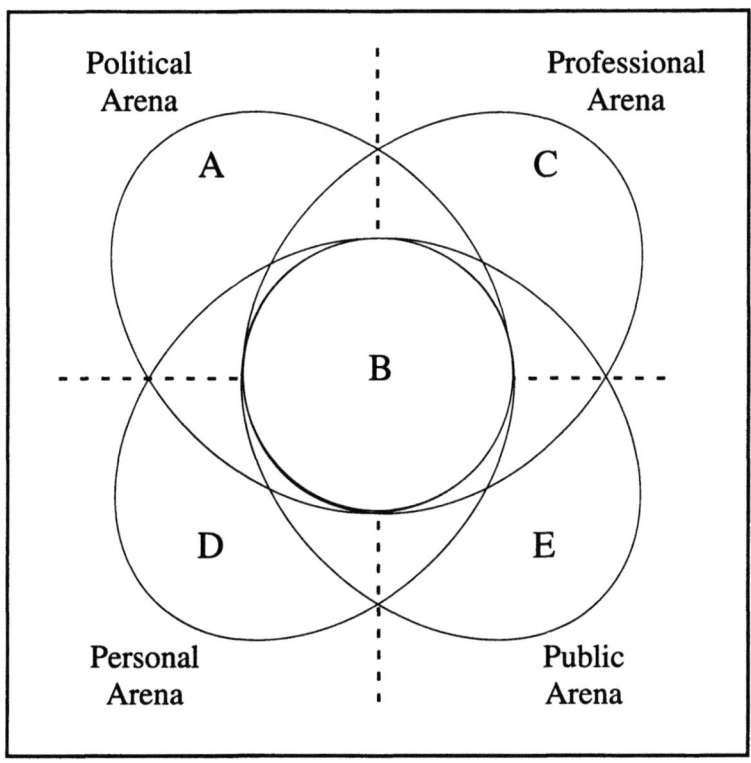

Forms of Resistance:
A. Fight proactively
B. Actively counter
C. Withstand
D. Passively Resist
E. Boycott

Figure 3.1. Effective Forms of Resistance for each Arena

Part II: Resistance and Representation:

THE TEACHER

Chapter 4

Good Teacher or Feminist Teacher?: Investigating the Ethics of Early Childhood Curriculum

Glenda Mac Naughton

Dewey argued, we must be clear what social vision will underpin our curriculum work with young children because it is and should be the foundation of all we do: "Fostering growth makes little sense without a vision of where the children should be headed" (Dewey, 1938, cited in Goldstein, 1994, p. 14).

In this chapter I argue that the everyday pragmatics of early childhood curriculum work, such as how we organize our rooms, can lead to unwitting collusion with conservative social visions. I will show how this happens and outline strategies through which early childhood educators can reconceptualize their work together for an alternative, progressive social vision.

A very simple story I've called *The Block Play Story* begins my argument. It is about two educators, one who decided to reorganize the inside area of her kindergarten and one who didn't. For reasons of confidentiality the people in the story have been given pseudonyms.

Block Play: The Story

The two educators were part of a larger group of twelve early childhood educators who decided to explore the practical dilemmas and issues involved in challenging traditional sex-role stereotypes in their centers. They met monthly to talk about the gender issues surfacing in their work and how to plan for them. For several months, they monitored children's play choices and interests and found that there were very traditionally gendered play patterns between the children in ten of the centers. For instance, boys were dominating in a learning area of the center called block play and in other construction material areas and girls were dominating in the home corner and in less physically active play areas. Not surprisingly, given the research project's aims, the teachers tried to alter these patterns.

Nette was one such teacher. She wanted to change how she organized the children's inside play area. Nette decided to bring the outside blocks inside and combine these with home corner equipment in order to disrupt the idea that blocks were for boys and home corner was for girls. As she explained to the group:

> My current aim is to present kindergarten equipment to children in a manner which discourages gender bias. Blocks, dolls and dramatic play equipment are all stored in the same area to present opportunities for combined play with this equipment by both girls and boys, thus challenging some of the stereotypical use of these items. (Baird, Jones, Sharpe, Payne, & MacNaughton, 1992, p. 2)

Nette was very excited by her work. She worked part-time in two kindergartens sharing each with another teacher, so she had to negotiate her decision to alter equipment positionings with these teachers. She explained her work and tried to gain their support for her experiment. One teacher told her she was "crazy." The other teacher "just couldn't accept it" and found it impossible to work with outdoor blocks inside. Consequently, for seven weeks Nette repositioned *all* indoor and outdoor blocks twice a week to ensure that the room organization was back to 'normal' for this teacher.

A little later in the year Nette did gain agreement from one teacher to reorganize block play and home corner for a special project. It went extremely well with boys and girls each playing in the redesigned area in constructive and collaborative ways for much of the time. Nette decided she wanted the change to remain once the project was completed. Her colleague was "surprised by the fact that I wasn't going to put it all back at the end of the term." This was despite a discussion in which her colleague admitted she found the "set-up easier to use with the group of children she'd got." Summarizing the reactions of several of her colleagues to the changes she had made, Nette said:

> Discussions with colleagues about my concerns over the different ways boys and girls are treated in many kindergartens has resulted in me being labeled a radical feminist by some or as worrying about something that doesn't exist.

Back in the monthly meetings of the research group there was considerable uncertainty about whether Nette's reorganization was appropriate. For instance, Edna argued that the kindergarten room should be set up with separate spaces for home corner and blocks because each offered specific and distinctive learning opportunities for the children. As she explained to the group:

> It gives a sense of order and categories for the children.... These are expectations of us from our training and because we are preparing the children for the next step. It's why we are doing it. But whether it's the right thing to do...we would have to look very closely to justify ourselves if we were doing it differently. If we had everything down one end of the room and the children just went and got what they wanted to use where ever and however they wanted...(fades). I know of a lot of teachers who would get very upset if children moved the equipment together.

Another member of the group felt concerned about how the local government Children's Services Advisor in her area would react if she did such a thing whilst a third member just felt it "was wrong." She couldn't explain why. She just knew it was. Another wondered at "what College would say" and yet another felt the parents in her center would be "dead against it because it wouldn't look like a normal kindergarten."

A simple change in room organization based on a desire for greater gender equity in children's play choices had led to Nette being seen by several of her colleagues as a 'crazy radical feminist.' In particular, she was seen as acting in ways that went against what had been learned "at college" and went against normal practice as defined by several colleagues and parents.

Carlie, another teacher in the group, was interested in the changes Nette was making and supported them. However, she decided that she just couldn't experiment in her own center. The reasons for this related to Carlie's history of working for gender equity.

When I met Carlie she had been working in what she described as "non-sexist" ways with children for over fifteen years and described herself as being "committed to non-sexist education for a long time." Carlie saw herself as: "feminist. Yes although not a fiercely radical one, but I believe in equal rights, opportunities, etc." I'll use some of Carlie's words to give you a flavor of what this meant:

> We have two children of our own. A girl who is nine and a boy four and a half. Always both have been given equal opportunity and equal access to experiences. Laura's second birthday gift was a train-set. I've always worked full-time outside of the home apart from two lots of maternity leave—so we have always shared the shopping, housework, lawn-mowing etc.

For Carlie, gender equity was a deeply personal, as well as professional, issue. She had acted and thought in nonsexist ways over many years in both her personal and professional lives. Some parents and colleagues had reacted positively:

> I did have a lot of parents that commented on my program in that they appreciated what I was doing for their girls, more so than parents of boys... and some of those families have actually followed me from one kindergarten to another.

That some parents supported her work was completely countered by the larger number of parents for whom gender equity was a non-issue, or who actively discouraged it. If parents didn't want to talk about gender, Carlie felt uncertain about how to broach it with them. This was understandable, given parents' power within kindergarten services. Formally, they were her employer. In addition, parents could move their child/children to another center if they were unhappy with the approach/views of the teacher. Carlie knew this occurred as some parents had recently moved to her kindergarten due to unhappiness with other kindergarten teachers' work. She suspected this could also work in reverse, affecting attendance numbers. The funding basis of Victorian kindergartens meant child attendance quotas had to be met to qualify for government operational subsidies. Parents leaving could jeopardize numbers, and thus funding, for the next calendar year.

Alongside this economic issue, Carlie's feelings of difference and uncertainty were intensified by other teachers' negative reactions to her interest in gender equity:

> I was on a lot of committees for organizing conferences and we would brainstorm.... I would always bring up gender stuff and I would always get howled down and they say "What do you want that for?"

When she tried to discuss her gender equity philosophy with colleagues in her center, responses ranged from them "getting upset" and being "fairly negative," to "being ignored" and "indifference."

May (Carlie's untrained assistant) exemplified what happened when they "got upset." Carlie had been concerned about May's sexist language and decided to raise this with her. The conversation centered on the merits of using the term "children," rather than "boys" and "girls." Carlie saw 'children' as an inclusive, gender-neutral term. May said Carlie was making "a fuss about nothing" and tried to avoid speaking to Carlie for the next couple of days.

Around the same time Carlie talked with two of her co-teachers about a decision she had made to purchase materials to support her attempts to interest boys in the home corner area. She explained how their "indifference" to one such purchase made her feel.

> Carlie: "... the other day at the Op Shop I bought a little boy's, supposedly, a boy's jacket with an emblem on, like a school uniform thing, and I think they thought I was a bit off the deep end because I was putting that out as another dress up. It's just little things that I do, I am sure they think 'She's really mad,' 'cos they don't react at all. I just said 'Oh I think that it's a bit female oriented in here. I saw this at the Op Shop for $1, so I bought it.'"
> Glenda: "They don't give you any reaction?"
> Carlie: "No, I just think they think I'm really radical."

Carlie's colleagues reactions and non-reactions to her gender concerns were clearly unsettling. It was hard for her to judge what they felt or why, but she felt that purchasing equipment to support her nonsexist curriculum was a problem. Because she worked where few adults visibly talked and acted in nonsexist ways she was constantly made to feel "different," "odd" or "weird." This was unsettling, uncomfortable, frustrating and, in many instances, was undermining. She did feel that her beliefs were "right" but she also experienced them as a problem because of other people's views.

Carlie's sense of being different was intensified by her difficulty in obtaining resources and information such as research reports on gender in early childhood and books and posters, to use in her teaching.

Carlie talked often of the impact on her nonsexist curriculum of having little active support for her work and it was clear that she found this personally wearing. Hence, Carlie was reluctant to get involved in projects which required her colleagues' collaboration. For instance, whilst she wished she could reorganize block play and home corner, she didn't because she didn't want to risk being made to feel 'weird' yet again.

Theorizing the Stories

To explain how daily, pragmatic curriculum decisions such as room organization and equipment purchase often unwittingly support conservative social visions I will draw from Foucault's work on regimes of truth (Gore, 1993). He believed that all social institutions in the modern world survive and thrive through creating and maintaining 'regimes of truth' about how we should think, act, and feel toward ourselves and others (Foucault, 1977a, 1977b, 1978, 1982; Gore, 1993; 1991). For instance, educational institutions, such as early childhood centers or the academy, survive and thrive through creating and maintaining a set of "truths" about how we should think, act, and feel toward ourselves as early childhood professionals and toward children, parents, and colleagues. These 'truths' are woven together into a regime (or system of management) that governs what is seen to be normal and desirable ways of thinking, acting, and feeling in all early childhood institutions. In doing so, they create and maintain a system of morality that says this is a "good," "true" way to be an early childhood professional and this is not.

I will use *The Block Play Story* to illustrate how current 'regimes of truth' in early childhood operate in practice to marginalize progressive social goals and practices in our field and show how they can provide a platform from which to rethink the ethics of early childhood curriculum. There are three propositions about the relationship between knowledge and modern organizations that intertwine to form Foucault's concept of "regimes of truth" and they help illustrate my point. (See, for example, Davies, 1991, 1990a, 1989a, 1989b; Dreyfus & Rabinow, 1982; Gore, 1993; Weedon, 1987).

Proposition One: *Different interpretations of our social world compete for the status of "truth."*

Foucault shares with other postmodernist theorists, such as Derrida and Lyotard, the belief that nothing is inherently "true." Foucault believed that within any field of knowledge (e.g., child development, early childhood education) there are many different interpretations of our social world that compete for the status of truth. Some gain that status, reaching a point where they appear to be right, correct, and immutable—true—but are not. They are just one of the many possible versions of truth about any social phenomena. They are seen as truth because they have successfully competed to achieve this status.

To illustrate: Foucault would argue that there is no one right or "true" way to offer blocks and home corner as some of Nette's colleagues believed. There are many ways. Nette had one "truth" about how to offer blocks and home corner, her colleagues had a different "truth." Nette interpreted what was the right and correct (or true) way differently to her other colleagues. However, that there are different ways of interpreting the world is *not* Foucault's key point. His point is that some are seen to be more 'true' than others.

So, from his point of view, Nette faced such opposition to her changes and Carlie would not introduce changes in room organization because particular ways of organizing space and materials in the early childhood curriculum had competed successfully with others to gain the status of "truths." By this Foucault means that particular approaches to room organization had become normal, accepted, taken-for-granted, not in need of questioning. In the block play story the idea of having separate spaces for blocks and homecorner had achieved this status of a "truth" for many of Nette's colleagues. It was right and it should not, indeed, be questioned. They believed their way to be normal, correct, and, therefore, the 'true' way.

Proposition Two: *Ideas about how to act and be in our social world stand out as truths not because of any inherent "truth" within them but because they have institutional and personal support.*

The institutional support Foucault called the political substance of a regime of truth. The personal support he called the ethical substance of a regime of truth. Individuals support particular regimes of truth about how we should think and behave toward ourselves and others because all "regimes of truth" about our social world and social relationships institutionalize particular systems of morality (Davies, 1993) and constitute particular ways of being as normal, right, and, therefore, desirable.

These systems of morality tell us how we should act, feel, and think if we want to be seen as normal. To be normal we have to learn to tame, create, or style ourselves in ways that ensure we look and sound normal to others and feel and sound normal to ourselves. Most of us try to be "normal" because only individuals who act "normally" gain institutional backing and support. In doing so, the ethical, personal substance becomes integrated with the political, institutional substance of the regime.

To illustrate: In the block play story, the political substance of the regime was evident in the institutional power of the academy to construct notions of "good" teaching in preservice training. For instance, Nette's colleagues beliefs about room organization had the status of "truth" for them because they had been articulated and circulated by "college"—the very institution that certifies who is competent to practice as an early childhood educator. Colleagues such as Edna regarded Nette's work as odd and different because of what they had learned at "college." "College" was used to provide a powerful institutional justification for their 'truth' that blocks and home corner should be separately provided. Nette had no comparable institutional knowledge base with which to defend her decisions and so they became questionable and, therefore, problematic. Whilst this did not stop Nette's work, it required her to be prepared to regard herself as "radical," to accept what she did as odd and different to the norm and to be totally committed to her project.

The same was true for Carlie: she was unable to find institutional backing for her nonsexist work. It was lacking in her local teachers' network and in the journals and researchbase of the academy. There was also no institutional backing from the providers of educational materials as she searched for suitable nonsexist materials. This lack of institutional support for her nonsexist work made her feel different to the norm and highly marginalized.

The personal substance of the regime was evident in how colleagues wove together their personal power to sanction changes at the local level and to tame difference. Nette's local colleagues used their personal power of sanction to marginalize her approach to organizing space and materials and to maintain their way of organizing them as preeminent. One colleague directly blocked her work and the other colleague tolerated it, rather than supported it.

Carlie's colleagues used their personal power to teach Carlie to tame herself as a feminist teacher, and to style herself as an early childhood teacher who was silent on gender. It was only if she did this that she felt she would be seen as normal by her colleagues. Speaking of gender, purchasing equipment to support gender equity, and questioning others' language needed to be tamed to maintain a sense of being OK or normal among colleagues and parents. The moment Carlie did things that were associated with her feminism she felt she had transgressed some boundary in her teaching that she shouldn't. She learned that to be a feminist early childhood teacher who acted on her feminist beliefs was to be not normal. There was no 'truth' that said "it's OK to be a feminist early childhood teacher." Carlie had internalized the "truth" that this was not normal to such an extent that she constantly self-disciplined her desires and actions as a feminist educator to protect herself from constantly being on the margins of normality.

Proposition Three: *We can learn what ideas have the status of "truths" by looking at who and what is seen as "other" to the normal.*

To illustrate: In the block play story, Nette was clearly seen as "other" to the norm for her views on block play organization, Carlie was seen as another "other" for her belief in gender equity. Carlie's work for gender equity meant she was seen as weird, odd, and radical and was, at times, ignored by colleagues. Hence, working for gender equity and experimenting with the organization of space and materials were, in this instance, regarded by the majority as not normal. In this instance, the norms, the "truths" about early childhood curriculum worked against experimentation and against working for gender equity. In other words, it is not normal to experiment and it is not normal to work for gender equity. Neither is necessary to dominant understandings of good practice....and that's the truth! Hence, the current regime of truth implicitly condones a conservative social vision of gender inequality. It does this through silencing and marginalizing those who work for greater gender equity in our field.

In summary, Foucault argued that we live in a world in which there is no inherent truth, but many truths. Of the many truths that circulate in a given field of knowledge, for example, in early childhood education, some gain that status of truths and create a regime of truth that governs our ideas and practices. This regime is held in place by complex webs of power between the ethical (personal) and political (institutional) substance of a regime.

Beyond the Block Play Story

Current research (Alloway, 1995a, 1995b; Davies, 1989a; MacNaughton, 1995; Walkerdine, 1989, 1990, 1992a) suggests that room organization is not the only area of curriculum practice that has acquired the status of a "truth" that cannot and should not be questioned. Alloway (1995a) has argued that:

> ...all early childhood educators...observe a common language, a common set of beliefs that are elevated to the status of 'truths' about child development...(and are) articulated in a shared language, in immediately identifiable terms such as: child development, developmental stages, development of the 'whole child', developmentally appropriate practice, integrated curriculum, children's interest driven programs, individual needs, individual readiness, individual planning, close observation of the individual child's development.

These beliefs regulate the practice of early childhood staff on a daily basis. I believe that the elevation of particular early childhood discourses to the status of "truths" has an essentially conservative influence on early childhood education and makes it hard to innovate in many areas of curriculum work. In particular, it has silenced and marginalized a progressive social agenda within this work by defining it as different and "other" to the mainstream. In the *Block Play Story* a set of truths about how and why to organize space and materials in particular ways marginalized those wanting to rethink these 'truths' by defining them and their practices as different and 'other' to the mainstream.

In a social world in which inequalities and injustices flourish the mainstream visions and practices in early childhood education have yet not seriously grappled with what this means for how we work and in whose interests we educate and care for children. What does it mean for our selection of resources, our teaching practices, our understandings of child development, and our assessment of children's learning to construct a curriculum that is anti-classist or anti-heterosexist? Should we do so, in whose interests are we educating and caring for young children if we do not and thus implicitly support homophobia and classism? To say that our current practices are in the interests of all children is to homogenize children and deny the social diversity that constructs and, at times, constricts them and their families.

In my view, any work for progressive social change within the early childhood curriculum must start by understanding how particular discourses gain and maintain ascendancy and reach the status of truths. Foucault argued that there is a political and ethical substance to the construction of a regime of truth (Gore, 1993) and I want to ask what can be learned from analyzing the ethical substance of how the particular discourses which gain the status of truths in early childhood education. Such analysis takes us to the heart of how we can collaborate to produce progressive change.

The Ethics of Regimes of Truth in Early Childhood Education

Foucault saw ethics as the personal relationship to the self: how we should discipline and style ourselves to create and maintain certain ways of being as normal and true and to establish that we are normal and correct in how we are acting and feeling (Gore, 1993). In other words, from our ethics flow the questions, how should we be acting and feeling to ensure that we are being "true" to ourselves as educators and to prove to ourselves and others that this is the case? Our ethics are governed by a "regime of truth" about what is a "true" way to act as an early childhood professional.

The Foucauldian sense of ethics in early childhood education has been powerfully documented by Walkerdine (1990, 1992a). She argued that the child-centred pedagogies which are at the heart of early childhood education and constitute its current "regime of truth" are based on an ethics of individualism and on the "dream of democratic harmony" (Walkerdine, 1992a, p. 22). Child-centred education assumes that the child's growth and development is a natural, individually determined process which should be allowed full expression. It is the moral imperative of the educator to accomplish the fully expressed individual with judicious but minimal intervention (see, for example, Arthur, Beecher, Dockett, Farmer, & Richards, 1993; Beaty, 1992; Bredekamp, 1987; Mallory & New, 1994).

In curriculum work with the child, this requires each of us to develop curriculum processes within ourselves to "know the child" and to "facilitate the child's development" and each of us has to learn to tame, style and discipline ourselves in ways that achieve this (MacNaughton, 1995).

As the majority of current early childhood texts emphasize, curriculum planning for young children should be based on developmental observations of individual children taken by the individual educator (MacNaughton, 1995). This is the foundation of all that follows and it requires the individual educator to have a confident autonomy in curriculum planning. This creates the ethics of individualism in our curriculum work talked of by Walkerdine: only the individual educator can know the individual children within her or his center, so only the individual educator can plan for each child's learning.

This individualism and its associated planning approaches are highly problematic for anyone committed to curriculum change and particularly for those committed to progressive social change. As I have just suggested, this ethic sustains reflection on the child and curriculum decisions for the child at the site of the individual educator. In *The Block Play Story* this was problematic for anyone working for gender equity in three ways.

First, traditions about how to offer materials and equipment were able to remain unquestioned by individual staff and were reinforced by colleagues. Going against tradition to achieve gender equity goals was not seen as "innovation" but as "abnormal." Whether things should/could be done differently is a key question in any process of change but it did not arise until educators began debating their decisions *in a group* with other educators. The catalyst for change was not just any group of educators. It was a group that had as its raison d'être a progressive social agenda to change gender relations. Without this catalyst, traditions that were inadvertently contributing to sexism between children would have remained unchallenged.

Second, working for progressive social goals, in this case, gender equity goals, was problematic because knowledge learned in preservice training was constructed and reconstructed as 'truth.' "College" was seen as the holder of "truths" about what constitutes good and normal practice. Going against "college," irrespective of what was taught at "college," was seen by individuals, as problematic. In this instance, working for gender equity clashed with what "college" taught. If preservice training has ignored issues of social justice, equity, and education for the "practice of freedom" (Friere, 1990), then how can the individuals begin to reconstruct their knowledge and practices to support progressive social visions and practices? Who gives permission to construct new "truths" about good practice? The occasional one-off inservice session that constitutes most professional development in the field is unlikely to challenge fundamental "truths" from "college." So, whilst individuals remain the key reflectors on their own practices the hegemony of white, Western, middle-class truths about "good practice" that have dominated key elements of early childhood theory and practice will remain unchallenged.

Third, to publicly own and advocate a clear progressive social change vision was to be odd, abnormal, and wrong. Colleagues and parents silenced and/or marginalized Carlie's antisexist/feminist understandings and practices. Carlie was a highly committed and motivated educator who had struggled in isolation to feel proud of her work. It was only in collaboration with others that she began to redefine her work as valid. Whilst individual early childhood staff articulate their social vision in isolation from others, such marginalization is likely to confront other committed and motivated staff working for progressive social change. Research (e.g., Kenway, Willis, Blackmore, & Rennie, 1994; MacNaughton, 1995) and anecdotal material certainly suggests that this is the case.

In summary: the ethics of individualism that underpins curriculum decisions in child-centred education makes working for progressive social goals difficult. This is because traditions about how to offer materials and equipment can remain unquestioned by individual staff and can be reinforced by colleagues, because knowledge learned in pre-service training can be constructed and reconstructed as "truth" and because to publicly own and advocate a clear social change vision can be seen as odd, abnormal, and wrong. If these traditions and this knowledge unintentionally support conservative social goals and practices, as much research suggests that they do, then I believe we need to reconstruct the ethical substance of our curriculum work.

Ways Forward

If we want progressive social change in and via early childhood education, and I believe there are good reasons why we should, we need to move beyond the ethics of individualism that has permeated curriculum work to date to an ethics of what I have begun to call critical collectivism. Before I explain what is involved in such an ethical shift I want to briefly explore why I believe that a progressive social vision should underpin our curriculum work in early childhood. Such a discussion is essential, because in order to construct the ethics that will underpin our "truth" decisions, we have to have clear goals and aspirations for ourselves (Gore, 1993). Foucault labels these goals and aspirations the telos of the regime (Gore, 1993). I believe that in the early childhood field we have debated this telos insufficiently in recent years, although the need for such work has never been more pressing given the shared conservative vision that is driving our federal and state governments.

The basis for arguing that our goals and aspirations should be based on a progressive social vision and should embrace the need for greater equity, social justice, and human rights comes from within our own claims for early childhood curriculum. We have repeatedly claimed to care about and work for the interests of all children and to work so that each child can develop to their full potential. However, research (see Byrnes & Kiger, 1992; Dau & Creaser, 1995; Dermon-Sparks, 1989; Siraj-Blatchford & Siraj-Blatchford, 1995) has consistently shown that children cannot develop if they are living in a society where they and their families face oppression, inequality, and injustice. It touches and constrains the children as deeply as it touches and constrains their families and the rest of us. In most Western countries now, and in the immediate future, such groups include indigenous peoples, women of different racial and ethnic backgrounds, working-class people, the out-of-work and under-employed, gays and lesbians, people defined as disabled by themselves and or others, travelers and gypsies, recently arrived refugees, and rural and isolated people.

Yet, to what extent can we claim to work in the interests and from the concerns and perspectives of these groups? We, and in this I include the academy, the government, resource agencies, and individual centers cannot claim to work in the interests of all children if we marginalize and silence the concerns, experiences, interests, and demands of these groups within early childhood education and ignore them in our curriculum work. With hand held over our heart can we claim genuine progress in including the combined concerns of gender equity and the multicultural perspectives in their curriculum? To what extent do we address class inequality in and through our curriculum? Where are the perspectives of children and parents from families headed by gays or lesbians in our curriculum?

Individuals are making changes in how they do curriculum based on a desire for greater equity and social justice. But we are far from a collective shared vision about the processes, form, and content of early childhood curriculum for progressive social change. I believe we cannot imagine and reconstruct our practices and theories in ways that support the goals and aspirations of the oppressed and marginalized until we learn to collaborate with them around the content and processes of our curriculum and move to what I am calling an ethics of critical collectivism.

Another glimpse at the gender research project from which the *Block Play Story* came provides some insights into how such collaboration might begin and what an ethics of critical collectivism might look like. During the eighteen months of this research project individuals changed many of their beliefs and practices about early childhood. Key to each of these changes was a shift in their relationship with the knowledge they used for curriculum planning. This shift occurred along several dimensions which were implicated in restyling themselves as early childhood educators. One of the key shifts was from individual responsibility for curriculum knowledge to collective responsibility for critiquing and developing this knowledge. This required learning to look and think on others' work and have others look and think on your work. This occurred because the research group required that each person discuss their individual teaching decisions across a range of curriculum issues with others in the group on a monthly basis. It also required that the gendering implications of these decisions be explored with others.

This process of group sharing and exploration challenged the view that early childhood teaching is an individual responsibility and an individual negotiation with the self. Therefore, it challenged the view that knowledge of the individual child is and should be the sole knowledge for curriculum planning. You now had to include what others in the group felt was appropriate or not from a gender equity perspective. Through this there was an addition to what Foucault calls the disciplinary gaze to which group participants were prepared to subject themselves to. Orner (1992, p. 83) described the disciplinary gaze as one in which the "...regulation of the self (occurs) through the internalization of the regulation of others." All project members, including myself, had always given a privileged position to the disciplinary gaze of "college." Project members had unquestioningly remembered and acted upon the pedagogic "truths" of their preservice training, over many years. Membership of the research group offered the opportunity for an additional disciplinary 'gaze' into the equation of the self as an educator. It required that the participants expose and negotiate pedagogic "truths" with others, including me, someone from "college." These others had a clear social vision about the need for gender equity perspectives in the curriculum so project members had to take account of gender equity concerns and negotiation with the group, as well as "college" when they took their curriculum decisions. This often led to conflicts between different "truths" about what can and should be done.

These conflicts went beyond the reorganization of space and materials to questions of if, how, and when to intervene in children's play; how to observe and evaluate children's learning; what can and should be the goals of gender equity in early childhood curriculum work? To style ourselves as early childhood educators for gender equity we had to learn to open ourselves to collective critique of our curriculum visions and practices and to see such critique as necessary, and positive. We also had to take this back into our daily practice. In Foucault's language we needed to "style" ourselves as people willing, and able, to do this, and as people prepared to think of how we might collectively determine our relationships with our pedagogic knowledge. We had to be prepared to subject ourselves to the gaze of others. We had to be prepared to be more reflexive in relation to our knowledges of the child and how to 'be' with the child as early childhood educators. We had to reconstruct our ethical relationships with our self and take on the progressive gaze of others.

Through this, each of us began to pay attention to the relationship between our daily curriculum decisions and our broader social visions. In many of the research group meetings, we talked informally about what we liked and disliked about how the world was currently organized. How did we feel about violence toward women? How did we feel about the position of women in various occupations? How did we feel about a racist incident we had read about? How did we feel about the latest policy changes to community services? These "wider issues" coiled through each meeting and nearly always emerged as in discussion about a particular child or parent. The social and political context of our curriculum work was inseparable from what was said and done in the name of the children.

Hence, I believe that to reconstruct our ethics of the self and to move to an ethics of critical collectivism we need to be prepared to do two things. First, we (once again I am using we to include the academy, the government, the resource agencies, and individual centers), must come together with others who embody the visions and aspirations of the oppressed, marginalized, and silenced. For instance, if we are committed to including indigenous peoples' perspectives in our curriculum, we must form groups/networks in which the needs, goals, and understandings of indigenous peoples are paramount and in which we explore what these mean for our curriculum theories and practices. Second, in this coming together we need to open our curriculum decisions and the knowledge of the child upon which they are based to radical critique from the group (or collective). In this way we can collectively critique and negotiate our theories and practices in ways that are consistent with and relevant to a progressive social vision.

The reasons for doing this build from the postmodernist proposition, referred to earlier, that there is no such thing as "truth." This proposition raises several questions about our curriculum decisions in early childhood: How do we decide between competing "truth" claims about what is in the best interests of children? How do we decide what knowledge should underpin our curriculum decisions? Whose version of the "truth" about what is appropriate for young children do we privilege? Foucault argued that we must judge the validity of knowledge through reference to other than "truth claims" (see Weedon, 1987). In his view we need to judge such claims politically and ethically, and we do this through asking: "Who benefits from this truth?' "In whose interest is this truth?" "Who gains power through this truth?" "In whose interest should I be investing?" These questions require us to recognize the different and competing power effects of these "truths" and to decide whose interests we want to support. Not all truths serve all interests equally. For those committed to greater equity and social justice then the "truths" that benefit the interests of the oppressed, silenced and marginalized must be privileged. For example, feminists must privilege those "truths" that support greater equity for women and girls and work against patriarchy.

To illustrate: In the *Block Play Story* we must judge what the teachers did through recognizing who benefited from each way of organizing blocks and home corner? My own research has shown that traditional ways of organizing space and materials very often benefit boys and reinforce patriarchal ways of being masculine and feminine. Nette's special project work also showed this. Hence, as a feminist early childhood educator I must, as Nette did, choose to privilege the "truth" that traditional ways of organizing space and materials are problematic for gender equity and reject the truth that separation is best.

However, Carlie found this is difficult to do without institutional backing. This lack of institutionalization silenced her, despite her beliefs. Her experiences indicate how difficult it can be to go against the norm in isolation from others. As I said at the outset, she was a mature, committed and experienced teacher, yet years of feeling on the margins had taken their toll.

Until we have in our field a process of deciding between competing curriculum "truths" that is collective and that shares this responsibility more widely, we will continue to extract a high personal and professional price from those in our field working for progressive social goals and practices. Individuals *beavering* away in individual centers cannot readily create the scale of change needed to enable us to genuinely claim that we are working in the interests of all children.

An individual working in a field alone has little chance of:
- convincing others to break with early childhood traditions.
- effectively challenging colleagues about their social visions and educational practices.
- going against, or reassembling, knowledge learned in preservice training.
- discussing and negotiating their educational visions and practices

with others committed to progressive social change.

Yet, each of these processes is at the heart of an ethics of the self, based on critical collectivism. I would ask the reader to consider the extent to which an ethics of critical collectivism is desirable and possible and whether the inevitable challenges to tradition it would generate are worth the risks.

In conclusion, I would argue that we need to search for a telos (goal) in early childhood curriculum which is based on the desire for a world in which all those groups that have faced inequality, oppression, and discrimination can enjoy greater freedom and choice about ways of being and ways of living. But we must collaborate with all groups in our society working for progressive social change and justice to collectively negotiate and critique the details of this vision. If we remain cocooned in the currently dominant ethics of individualism which insulates us from critiques of our traditions, our practice, and our goals, this cannot happen. But it must happen if we are to continue to claim to work in the interests of all children.

Note: An earlier version of this paper was presented to the Weaving Webs Conference, July 12, 1996, Melbourne.

Chapter 5

The Early Childhood Teacher as Professional: An Archaeology of University Reform
Katharina Heyning

Introduction

In the spring of 1991 approximately thirty students at the University of Wisconsin-Madison enrolled in a newly created program leading to teacher certification in preschool through grade three (PK3). The new PK3 concentration was unusual for several reasons. First it reflected a national discourse about the "professionalism" of early childhood educators. Second, it emerged as a direct result of the Wisconsin Department of Public Instruction's (DPI) efforts to mandate teacher education reform through altered teacher licensure requirements. Third, it allowed students to pursue early childhood certification through either the School of Family Resources and Consumer Sciences (FRCS) or the School of Education (SOE).

The purpose of this chapter is to explore the multiple effects of "professionalization" discourse during a ten-year span of time leading up to the construction of the PK3 program. Using archival texts, a Foucauldian archaeological investigation is utilized to examine discursive formations without temporal relationships. In so doing, distinctions that are made about teacher education and the historical contexts through which they emerge become more visible. Two questions are asked of the text. First, how is professional ideology and expertise distinguished in the text during the construction of the PK3 program? Second, what examples of professional early childhood identities are represented in the text?

My interest in the professionalization of early childhood education revolves around how a program or course of study is defined and classified. Specifically, I am interested in the distinctions that are made about teacher education and the internal relations through which they emerge. I am also interested in how the creation of a PK3 program relates to the larger political, economic, and social culture of a university.

To enable such an examination, I will use a social epistemology of education reform as a method of social inquiry. This methodology views elements of institutional practice as historically formed patterns of power relations. Knowledge, as linked with power, is intertwined with social practices and becomes accessible to social inquiry (Popkewitz, 1991). This technique will allow a more in-depth analysis of how knowledge about the program is constructed within the social and political arena of the university.

The primary significance of this study lies in its use of interpretive social inquiry to examine teacher education reform. A new range of questions are asked that differ from "traditional" educational inquiry. Archival text is analyzed as a form of discourse to help expose the power dynamics and complexities of teacher education reform in a large research-oriented university. The archival texts chosen for this study consist of faculty meeting minutes, memos, and informational handouts periodically catalogued in notebooks and filed in a department office.[1] Throughout this chapter I will use the broader term "texts" to refer to these records.

The first section of this chapter will present a framework for analyzing history and historical texts as a form of discourse. The second section will discuss specific points related to "professionalization" and early childhood education as historic and contemporary issues. This will foreshadow the textual analysis and guiding questions, which completes the third section. The final section will review the findings and summarize the results.

History as Textual Archaeology

One of the fundamental aspects of this project was determining how to study the history of a program that was influenced by the ideology of professionalization. Indeed, the very idea of writing or reading "history" is not without debate. In the past half century, there has been an increased focus on history's relationship with sociology, psychology, and semiotics—particularly within the study of history and the philosophy of science (Hunt, 1986, 1989). The historian, in interpreting the past, necessarily takes an active role in re-creating the reality he or she sees there. Interpretive historical neutrality, while tempting, is impossible.

History is often thought of as a study remote from the present. In *Debates with Historians*, Pieter Geyl writes "history is an active force in the struggles of every generation and the historian by his interpretation of the past, consciously or half-consciously or even unconsciously, takes his part in them, for good or for evil" (Geyl, 1958, p. 264). History is not inevitably useful and the historian cannot choose to remain neutral.

Howard Zinn compares history to a jungle and states "The only thing I am really sure of is that we who plunge into the jungle need to think about what we are doing, because there is somewhere we want to go" (Zinn, 1985). The study of any historical episode, therefore, involves more than the chronologicalization of "facts." It involves the perceptions of the researcher through their interpretation of the subject matter. The idea that historical study is more than the documentation of individual political acts has been taken up by various theorists. Nowhere has this idea been more thoroughly explored than in France, where the disciplines of epistemology, history, and the philosophy of science have been areas of continual philosophic debate for the past fifty years (Lemert, 1981).[2]

The archival data chosen for this examination consisted of faculty meeting minutes and memos. It is important to recognize that these texts were not seen as a complete representation of the events that happened in the department. In using them I was not trying to re-create or piece together a specific chronology of events that happened, but rather I used them as a "window" on the action. The choice of texts may, at first glance, appear limited in scope. Other records of events are available and could have been used in this study. However, my decision to limit the data to faculty meeting minutes, departmental memos, and informational handouts does not equate a limitation in analysis. It was the intent of this study to demonstrate how the historically formed rules and patterns of regulation apparent in the text helped to form an apparatus of power which embodied principles for action within the university. The texts under examination represent the "everyday spaces" of teacher education practice, and the rules and regulations that become apparent in the analysis are not limited to the use of these texts alone. The rituals of documentation become a construction that is visible in other texts and the daily lives of individuals. Therefore, the analysis of any university text can yield important information about the historical constructions of teacher education reform and practice.

One long-standing methodology used in the examination of historical documents is to view them as keys to unlocking the thoughts and actions of those who produced them. Using the "objective" linguistic data of the text, historians attempt to reconstruct the inner thoughts and life of the author. The aim of the researcher is to locate meaning within some underlying framework, metaphorical system, or secret decoding process. Text is seen as a purely symbolic artifact of human symbolic activity. It is a written representation of "reality" or statement of experience where "truth" is in the eye of the beholder (Bazerman, 1992). The trouble with this type of examination is that it can result in discursive abstractions where texts mean nothing beyond those of the writer. There is the ever-present chance of developing postmodern rhetoric or textual narcissism (Baker, 1991; Cocks, 1989).

In contrast, this study draws upon the work of Michel Foucault to employ an archaeological investigation where the texts are examined as *artifacts* in the study. Foucault views the statements made in documents as monuments and objects of study in their own right, subject to specific rules of discursive formation (Gutting, 1989). This form of investigation describes discursive formations without temporal relationships (Foucault, 1972). Similar to structuralist methodologies such as linguistics and ethnology, an archaeology of knowledge displaces "man" from his privileged position at the center of thought. Foucault's archaeology of knowledge differs from structuralism, however, in its concern for actual occurrences and their effects instead of their structural possibilities. Instead of looking for long-term continuities and gradual changes, the move away from "man" as the fundamental subjects places a greater emphasis on the sharp ruptures in a procession of ideas. Instead of looking for a succession of thought, an archaeological investigation uncovers discontinuities and breaks in the chronology. This allows for a more careful examination of how a series of events may become an object of discourse that can be recognized, described, clarified, and elaborated. For this study, the creation of the PK3 program is examined through the meeting minutes and memos kept during a ten-year span of time.

In my use of Foucault, I have examined the text as a form of socially constructed discourse. By discourse, I mean that the interpretation of the text is viewed as a negotiated endeavor concerned with the nature of interpretation and the subject matter being interpreted (White, 1978). All discourse takes into account differences of opinion as to its own authority. When applied to textual analysis, these differences of opinion are found between the reader's analysis and the (unknown) meaning set forth by the writer. Not only does the language used indicate various forms of meaning by the way it shifts, recedes, fractures, and disperses and defers dialogue, but it also represents a singular interpretation of a social event recorded in a particular way (Cherryholmes, 1990). There has been a growing recognition that any statement of experience, oral or written, can be "read" as discursive practice (Klein, 1992). This widened view has linked power and authority to text and placed it in a social space that can be examined and interpreted.

Examining the faculty meeting minutes as discourse presents unique problems as they are constrained by form, objectivity, and an emphasis on parliamentary procedure. They are events recorded by one person and represent the viewpoint of one person. When circulated as a fair representation of a historical event, they become more of a rhetorical enterprise centered on persuasion (Brown, 1987, 1992a, 1992b). In order to examine these texts as social discourse, I also rely on Pierre Bourdieu's concept of authorized language.

Bourdieu suggests that the power of authorized language lies in the delegated power of the spokesperson (Bourdieu, 1991). In other words, the authority of the university is delegated to the departmental texts because the are a *product* of the institution. The substance of discourse is a guarantee of delegation by the way it represents the authority of the establishment. Its power is limited only to the extent of delegation and the social positioning of the spokesperson. The stylistic features which characterize authorized language—such as routinization, stereotyping and neutralization—all stem from the position the spokesperson occupies in the competitive field of the institution. The structure of the field governs the form of expression and access to the text. Bourdieu uses the term "structural censorship" to signify how the authorized spokesperson is subjected to the norms of official protocol when reporting events. Text is actually the product of a dialectical compromise between the expressive interest of the spokesperson and the structural censorship of the field.

The faculty meeting minutes are generally kept by a department secretary and are reviewed by the chair prior to being sent out to the faculty. Following standard "note taking" techniques, certain events are recorded and others left out. Unless the event can be recorded in "acceptable" form, it will go unstated in the minutes. This represents the authority of the institution and the power of the faculty to regulate the "official" minutes. The minutes are a physical manifestation of the compromise between what was actually said during the meeting and what was recorded by the note-taker. The structural censorship of the institution is visible in what the note-taker writes and what is published and circulated after the meeting. Using Bourdieu's notion of authorized language the texts can be examined to study how professional ideology influenced the construction of the PK3 program. This differs from textual narcissism because an emphasis is put on the relationships of the text within the context of the university instead of trying to find "truth" or "reality" in the *correct* reading of the text.

The purpose of this study was to explore the effect of professional ideology on the creation of the PK3 program. The next section will explore two aspects of professionalization related to early childhood teacher education reform. First, specific points concerning the history of early childhood education as an emerging profession will be examined as historic and contemporary issues. Second, the various ways professional ideology can be conceptualized will be outlined to provide a framework for understanding the textual analysis.

Early Childhood Education as a Unique Juncture

There are several specific issues related to the professionalization of the early childhood education field that require attention as an aid to understanding the text. In suggesting this, I am not attempting to "write" the history of professional early childhood education nor present an exhaustive review of the literature. Rather, I am including the following sketch as a way to add depth to the textual analysis. This includes the rather unique history of early childhood professionalism and its relationship to science, gender, and psychology during the first half of this century.

Early childhood programs have always been a part of the educational fabric in the U.S. Early programs included infant, dame, primary, or petty schools from colonial rule through the establishment of the first English-language kindergartens in the 1860s (Bloch, 1987; Cremin, 1988; Spodek, Saracho, & Peters, 1988). Often described as a history of movements (the kindergarten movement, the nursery school movement, the day care movement, etc.), the way in which the early childhood education profession emerged continues to impact how teachers approach professionalism in their field today. During the early part of the twentieth century, early childhood education in urban areas was frequently associated with working-class immigrant children. Nursery schools were often sponsored by settlement houses and philanthropic agencies in the belief that middle-class children were lacking specific socio-emotional experiences (Bloch, 1987; Cremin, 1988). As teachers organized their efforts to "help" children in the cities, national organizations were formed to debate methodologies and promote professional agendas (Hewes, 1976).

Science, Welfare, and Psychology. One professional *"identity"* that developed during this time was scientism. Heavily influenced by the emerging field of psychology, early childhood certification courses began training teachers in new "scientific" methodologies. Although the teachers began to think of themselves as professionals, they often had difficulty convincing others of their elevated status. Bloch suggests the following scenario:

> Kindergarten teaching was more and more frequently provided by certified and trained teachers, and innovations in kindergarten curriculum development began to be discussed by 'experts'. Those working in programs concerned with the care of young children, and particularly the leaders in the field, wanted to be and, in many cases, were beginning to be considered 'professionals.' Yet, while the burgeoning group of people identifying themselves with the kindergarten and 'early education' were convinced of the importance of education for the young, they were still trying to convince others that this was a critical and professional field of endeavor. (Bloch, 1987, pp. 41–42)

To further their efforts toward professionalization, early childhood teachers began increasing their affiliation with scientific ideas about children, child study research techniques, and university-based research programs. Child development "professionals" aligned themselves heavily with scientific methodologies in an effort to appear to be more deserving of professional status. This affiliation continues to color notions of professionalization within the field of early childhood education today (Bloch, 1992).

A second professional identity that emerged in early childhood education during the first half of this century was *welfarism* based upon gender. Unlike elementary and secondary teachers, early childhood teachers have historically identified with the need to protect children by elevating motherhood, housekeeping, child rearing, and child nurture to a specialized moral status (Finkelstein, 1988). In America, women were seen as agents of moral and cultural nurture, as child advocates, and custodians of the young. These notions were backed by popular early childhood theorists of the time such as F. W. Fröbel, who expressed the special gift women had to teach young children as an "educational calling." Early childhood educators popularized the ideas of educators like Hall and Thorndike, to provide scientific authorization for women as natural guardians of the young (Bloch, 1987; Finkelstein, 1988; Tallberg Broman, 1993). As with their elementary education counterparts, the professionalization of kindergarten teaching marked the emergence of a "women's profession." It was by teaching and advocating for early childhood programs and welfare that women first began to be seen as "professional" workers. Although it appears sexist by today's standards to underscore the "educational calling" of women, the continued emphasis on nurture, care, and child advocacy—long associated with women's work—still dominates debates about the professionalization of early childhood education.

These "twin" professional identities, welfarism and scientism, are often expressed through the language of psychology in early childhood education. On one hand early childhood professionals identify with the science of early childhood education and the application of psychologically derived child development practices. On the other, their historical commitment to child welfare often indicates a profession based on maternal nurturing (Finkelstein, 1988; Seifert, 1988).

Both of these identities are visible through the use of psychological language in teacher education program texts as well. For instance, the science of teaching early childhood education is visible when psychological terms are used to justify educational practices. An example of this was the increasing dependence on testing in early childhood programs after psychologists popularized intelligence testing in America. It was through psychometrics that psychology first began to establish its claim as the appropriate authority to judge children and administer them in a way that would increase their utility to society (Rose, 1989). Intelligence testing, combined with observations of large numbers of young children deemed both "normal" and "defective" by society's standards, enabled the establishment of norms of behavior. For the first time the child was beginning to be described in psychological terms. Developmental stages, defined by psychologists, became a popular measuring stick against which all young children were measured.

Nurturing and child welfare issues are also often described in psychological terms. As children were measured against statistical norms of behavior, deviance from these norms were often linked to family culture. The family was now judged for its ability to produce "normal" and well-adjusted, psychologically sound children. Psychologists believed that parents needed help in producing well-adjusted children and advocated familiarizing them with the principles of child development (Napoli, 1981). Accordingly, early childhood educators, acting in a maternal advocacy role, turned their attention to the family and its influence in the young child's life. The values, ideas, and norms of psychology were asserted into the family through routines like infant testing and medical checkups. Books, pamphlets, and magazine articles published by early childhood professionals were directed at parents in hopes of educating the family to produce children that were psychologically and developmentally sound (Rose & Miller, 1992). Evidence of this can be seen in early childhood programs that often place specific emphasis on the child's family and community in the curriculum.

Professional Ideology and Expert Authority

Although the reliance on behavioral scientific and gendered traditions of early childhood education provide insights to the profession, links to national reform rhetoric during the construction of the PK3 program are also important. During the time period when the PK3 certification was being discussed by both DPI and the UW-Madison faculty, there was a marked increase in the number of published reports and books critical of teacher education in the United States.[3] Two key aspects of these reports were an ideological belief in professionalism and a reliance on expert authority. By examining how these notions became integral parts of the reform reports generated during this period, the influence of professionalism during the construction of the PK3 program can be investigated further in the archival text.

Most of the reform reports published between 1980 and 1991 stated a need to increase the professionalism of teaching. A profession is generally thought to have certain benchmarks that delineate it from other occupations. These include a specialized body of knowledge, juried entry, and a sense of social service.[4] Conventional wisdom in education typically views teachers as professionals or semi-professionals and the idea of what a "professional" is influences how teachers act (Densmore, 1987). This conception of professionalism is often used to justify teachers' relatively high social status and job-related privileges. The "cultural appeal" of professionalism is often grounded in notions of upward mobility and it is believed that teachers will receive higher professionals status if they become more like doctors and lawyers, who are assumed to be efficiently serving society (Ginsburg & Newman, 1985; Popkewitz, 1994). Along with inferences of dependability, quality, and effectiveness, professionalism is sometimes described as a "state of mind" that must be earned through integrity, commitment, trust, and honest hard work (Clamp, 1990). Accordingly, many of the reform reports of the 1980s and early 1990s emphasized a need to provide teachers with more autonomy, privilege, and professional status so that teaching could be viewed as a "full-fledged" profession.[5]

Another translation of professional ideology in the reports and articles of this period was the suggested adoption of certification testing and professional board regulated standards for beginning teachers.[6] This form of juried entry to the field was designed to assure "professional" competence through testing. Like medical and legal bar exams, those who could not pass the test would not become teachers. This view of professionalization derives authority from its scientific claims and the assumption that only a few self-governing professionals can exercise trained judgment in their field of expertise (Popkewitz, 1994). The emphasis to "professionalize" teaching through competency testing continues to be especially popular within the publications of early childhood professional organizations such as NAEYC (e.g., Bredekamp, 1992; Bredekamp & Willer, 1993; Willer & Bredekamp, 1993).

In addition to professional ideology, the reports relied heavily on notions of "expert" knowledge or authority. Such a reliance was not unique to this point in time. Throughout history people have claimed that various experts have used their authority to order human life (Rose, 1994). The university's involvement in this reliance can be traced to medieval centers of learning and their social function of extending knowledge, instruction, and service to the community through the professional preparation and exportation of professorial expertise (Duryea, 1981). This reliance upon technical expertise can be viewed as a form of trust in technical knowledge. Society places trust in professions whose claim to specialized knowledge is taken-for-granted. Professionals are believed to hold specialized knowledges that have validity independent of the practitioners and clients that make use of them (validity determined because of the general aura of respect toward knowledge deemed scientific). Giddens suggests this type of trust is typical of society's faith in abstract systems that disembed social relations from local contexts (Giddens, 1990, 1991). In other words, society places trust in professionals because they are known to hold specialized or technical knowledge of some sort. This trust is determined by the relative ignorance of technical knowledges held by the majority of people and a general pragmatic attitude toward abstract systems.

In an attempt to professionalize teaching, the reform reports of the 1980s and early 1990s frequently called for increased recognition of the specialized knowledges held by the teaching profession. One popular "solution" was the use of a pedagogical knowledge base for guiding coursework and teacher competency testing.[7] The knowledge base would consist of pedagogy broken into "chunks" of knowledge taught to beginning teachers. Many of the purveyors of these reports held strong ties with the universities long recognized for their reliance on scientific and technical knowledge (Labaree, 1992a). The idea that all "good" teaching is basically similar and can be broken down into chunks of defined knowledge to be taught concretely exemplifies a social trust in expert knowledge and abstract systems such as those found in research institutions.

Textual Analysis

The question to be decided, then, is how to examine the professional influence during the construction of the PK3 program while keeping in mind the various ways it can be expressed and translated (such as through professional ideology and expert authority) and the unique history of early childhood education as a profession. One way to do this would be to look at the proliferation of the professional expertise and its relationship to power in the text. This could include: (1) the history of problemizations or the way in which groups become manageable by expertise, (2) the generosity of expertise or how explanatory vocabularies, procedures, and techniques are lent to the public, (3) the transformations of the political to non-political or how something that was once politically volatile becomes technically understood and apolitical, and (4) the relationship between subjects that are dominated by and subjected to professional expertise in terms of professional norms and knowledges.[8]

To apply this to the text during the construction of the PK3 program one would look at the ways in which the new early childhood certification program was described as an emergent field of expertise, how the program was described through unique or technical vocabularies, the a priori acceptance of such language as non-political, and the way the new program was described in relationship to existing faculty standards. Using Rose's guiding principles, the questions to be asked of the text are: (1) How is professional ideology and expertise distinguished in the text during the construction of the PK3 program? and (2) What examples of early childhood professional identities are represented in the text? How are they expressed through the discourses of science and child welfare? These questions will be explored in the next two sections.

I. How is professional ideology and expertise distinguished in the text during the construction of the PK3 program?

University Prestige. As discussed above, the influence of professional ideology upon the construction of the PK3 program can be investigated by looking at the various ways in which the program was linked to emergent expertise, depicted through unique or technical vocabularies, and the way the new program was described in relationship to existing standards. For example, in December of 1988 the early childhood area faculty circulated a memo to the rest of the elementary education area faculty describing why they supported the development of a FRCS and SOE joint major at the PK3 level.[9]

> UW-Madison, as the largest and most prestigious higher educational institution in the state, should be supportive of this pedagogically reasonable (for a change) shift by DPI, despite the fact that the timing is not our own, and develop a cohesive, integrated program to correspond to the new certification level. (Early Childhood Education Area Faculty memo circulated in December 1988)

What is interesting about this passage is the way the need for a new program is framed in terms of the university's reputation as the "most prestigious higher educational institution in the state." There are several possible interpretations of linking the new PK3 concentration with the prestige of UW-Madison as visible in the text.

One reading of this statement is that the PK3 program should be a part of the elementary education curriculum at UW-Madison *because* it is the most prestigious institution in Wisconsin. If DPI was earlier certification ranges offered by UW-Madison (the nursery and nursery/kindergarten certification) and replacing them with the PK3 certification, then UW-Madison, as the state's flagship educational institution, should be offering it. UW-Madison's role as Wisconsin's educational leader has a long history. When the Wisconsin State Legislature outlined plans for the university in 1848 a primary purpose of the institution was to become a "central point of union and harmony to the educational interests of the Commonwealth" (Curti & Carstensen, 1949). Nine of the eleven cluster campuses that make up the University of Wisconsin System are former teacher preparation institutions or normal schools. UW-Madison, however, was designed as a university that contained a teacher-training program for high-school teachers. Unlike other institutions, it was not a normal school that "grew into" university status. The faculty at UW-

Madison has historically viewed their program as "different" from other teacher education programs around the state (Prestine, 1992).

This situation is not unique to Wisconsin. Schools of education within large, research-driven campuses often think of themselves as providing scholarly leadership in education—especially when compared to smaller campuses in the area that also offer teacher-training programs (Clifford & Guthrie, 1988). Wanting to continue in the "leadership" role in Wisconsin education could have influenced the early childhood faculty to press for inclusion of a PK3 program in the department.

Another interpretation of this statement is that early childhood education was becoming professionally legitimized through certification and recognition by DPI—therefore UW-Madison should recognize this shift in DPI's thinking by offering the new certification program. Stating that DPI's decision was "pedagogically reasonable (for a change)" suggests that DPI was sanctioning a new certification grouping and UW-Madison should recognize and support this "legitimate shift" in thinking by DPI by offering the new certification. The early childhood faculty could have viewed UW-Madison's support of DPI's certification changes as a way to call statewide attention to the importance of early childhood education and show their approval of DPI's decision.

A third interpretation of this statement refers to the historical relationship between the early childhood area and elementary area faculty. By eliminating the nursery/kindergarten and the kindergarten "add-on" certification, the faculty who worked in early childhood education would be effectively eliminated from teacher education programs at UW-Madison. Approximately 5 to 8 faculty members would have to be moved to other positions within other faculties. By asking the elementary area faculty to be supportive of the PK3 certification program, the early childhood faculty were also calling upon their *own* professional expertise within UW-Madison. As faculty in the most prestigious university in Wisconsin, they were taking a "stand" for something they believed was immensely important for the future of their own professional field.

A common denominator for each of these interpretations is the way the prestige accorded the university is linked with the emerging recognition of early childhood education as a "certifiable" program. The reasons for offering a PK3 program were coupled with UW-Madison's prominence in teacher education. As discussed earlier, there is a documented link between professional ideology and prestige. Professional ideology often assumes that with professional status comes recognition and prestige. It is believed that the "true" professions have an aura of distinction. The early childhood teacher, long considered to have low professional standing when compared to teachers of older children, would benefit by an association with the prestige of a large research-driven institution like UW-Madison.

Expert Knowledge

DPI also implied specific notions of professional ideology in its construction of the administrative code that delineated the PK3 certification requirements by the way it linked professional status with social commitments and expertise. The faculty was given various drafts of the rules as they were being created by DPI and were discussed in the monthly faculty meetings. The following section on the professional sequence required for early childhood certification changed very little from its earliest draft to the present-day format.[10] It is part of the meeting minutes on several occasions as an attached document:

> PI 4.12 (7) this program shall require the study of professionalism, program and staff development, supervision and evaluation of support staff, advisory groups, community agencies and resources and public services personnel as related to early childhood programs. (Wisconsin Department of Public Instruction, 1989, Subchapter V-Professional Education Sequences, 4.12 (7), draft given to faculty December 5, 1988)

In this section, DPI states that early childhood teachers must be enrolled in a course of study that meets specific "professional education sequence standards." What is intriguing about this particular rule is how "professionalism" is defined through association—a commitment to society and public need and job accountability through supervision and evaluation. The distinctions that are made about professionalism here are key. Students studying early childhood education are to be made aware of the hierarchy in agency work, such as the responsibilities of supervision and evaluation of support staff. A "professional" early childhood teacher should also know how to work with advocacy groups and community agencies to best meet the needs of society.

The ideological construction of professionalism in the PI4 rules text correlates well with two of the three "benchmarks" of professionalism discussed earlier: specialized knowledge and a sense of social service. Recognizing the supervision and evaluation of support staff calls attention to the specialized body of knowledge early childhood "professionals" have. A commitment to social service is alluded to when early childhood professionals are asked to work with advocacy groups and community agencies.

Both of these sections suggest the proliferation of *expertise* in the development of the program (Rose, 1994). In the first example the university is seen as the legitimator and grantor of expertise. The early childhood program, if it were to become part of UW-Madison's education curriculum, would be given status and access to the expert knowledge of the institution. By being part of the university's well-known, established, and nationally recognized teacher education program, early childhood education would be given more attention and funding for research projects and broader access to university knowledge and expertise. This also correlates with the role of a school of education within a research university, where the overriding emphasis is on the production of scholarly publications and procurement of funding, which in turn increases institutional expertise.

In the second example, DPI has outlined what a "professional" early childhood program must consist of if graduates are to be certified. The language used to describe the professional duties of an early childhood educator draws attention to DPI's "expert" knowledge to determine what the program should look like. In this example, DPI provides the expertise determining early childhood professionalism: a commitment to society and public need and job accountability through supervision and evaluation. Instead of the university's expertise, it is DPI's which determines the "professional" early childhood teacher education program.[11]

The proliferation of expertise is linked with both the legitmation of professional knowledge and the production of professionals. The PK3 program as "part of" the university's expertise and knowledge relates the structure of the program to the "expert-advisor" role of the university. In this light, the university is seen as serving society as a whole through the production of "rational" knowledge that is "useful" for the professional teacher. Through categorization and structuring, certain knowledge is legitimized and taught to prospective teachers. Graduates of the program are seen as "holding" this knowledge and are deemed professional. The rational knowledge transmitted by the university is part of a style of scientific discourse associated with empiricism and positivism seen through the interpretive lens of "practicality" (Popkewitz, 1987b). It is not neutral. The university privileges a form of instrumental reasoning that assumes a common framework of experience defined through scientific study. The theories and practices of the university form a method of social management through the professionalization of knowledge.[12]

Professional expertise arises out of a claim to knowledge, neutrality, and efficacy and provides various "solutions" to the problem of governing society (Hunter, 1990; Rose, 1996). Instead of setting direct government rule, professional expertise acts with authority to set the norms of individual conduct in society. Governmental analysis and decision becomes a product of professional expertise. Professionals are vested with a certain responsibility and power on the basis of their close association with "true" discourses. The production of professional experts plays a role in translating society into an object of government. In the first example, the PK3 program is linked with the university's expertise through association with a prestigious research institution. In the second example, early childhood professional expertise is determined by DPI in the form of knowing how to meet the needs of society through a sense of social service. In this example society is made accessible to government through the state-defined PK3 certification rules.

Besides its association with expertise, professionalism is also defined through *adequate preparation* in a third textual example. In April of 1984 the text documents the faculty as discussing a recently completed departmental review report by DPI. A major recommendation of the report cited the need to maintain a "professional" early childhood teacher education program to adequately prepare students for their future role as early childhood teachers:[13]

> The basic professional program for teachers should be shaped by a single overriding purpose; specifically, to prepare teachers for work success in the classroom, school and community. Every course should be scrutinized with respect to its contribution to this end. (April 9, 1984, meeting minutes attachment)

The report went on to suggest that the early childhood program be broadened to include methods courses in teaching art, music, and physical education to preschool/kindergarten-age children. The report equates professionalism with *adequate preparation*. Although the DPI report complimented the department for having a program that emphasized the arts and physical education, it also criticized it because it did not have specific methods courses for early childhood teachers in the teaching of these subjects.

The distinctions that are made in this statement show the relationship between "becoming professional" and "adequate preparation" where *adequate* is defined by the expert knowledge of DPI and the university. This knowledge was to be conveyed in the form of specific methods courses. In other words, to be adequately prepared as an early childhood teacher, students needed to take methods courses specifically tailored to early childhood education. The idea that there could be an overarching theme to early childhood professional education is also suggested in the text. The choice of the words "single overriding purpose" adds emphasis to the idea that the program should be centered on learning specific techniques and methods for teaching in the early childhood arena.

Both UW-Madison and DPI are positioned in the text as having expertise related to the professionalization of early childhood education. One way to think of this is to view DPI and UW-Madison as part of an expert "system" that enables one to remove social relationships from the immediacies of context (Giddens, 1990). DPI is positioned as providing "expert knowledge" of the early childhood program through the construction of the PI4 rules document. In so doing they acted as a protector for the consumer (the consumer being both the teacher-to-be and those in the community depending upon the expert knowledge of the certified teacher) by regulating the profession of early childhood teachers. The university is positioned as part of the expert system by using its access to scientific knowledge to interpret and augment the rules set by DPI and by creating a professional program for students to pass through. This expert system of knowledge "splits" time and space because the teacher is disembedded from the local contexts of teaching through codification, rules, and descriptions of expert knowledge. Let me explore this further.

The expert system created by the university and DPI that certifies graduates of the early childhood program as "professional" brackets time and space by deploying modes of technical knowledge which have validity *independent* of the practitioners and clients who make use of them. For instance, the expert or technical knowledge of a PK3 professional is outlined in the PI4 rules designed by DPI. The rules can be thought of as specific content knowledge that must be gained by the prospective teacher in order to be deemed professional. The knowledge is assumed to be a valid measure of early childhood professionalism and all certified PK3 teachers are assumed to be in possession of this knowledge. The expert knowledge is assumed to be constant, unchanging, and valid regardless of who is in possession of it. In this way, the knowledge becomes disembedded from the local context of teaching. It doesn't matter who is in possession of the knowledge, when it was learned, or how it is applied to the various situations. For parents of children in preschool, it doesn't even matter exactly what constitutes this expert knowledge—it is enough to know that the PK3 teacher is certified by DPI and legitimized by the UW-Madison program. Through certification, the PK3 teacher is deemed a "professional" because they are presumed to possess expert knowledge determined by (the expertise of) DPI and the university.

There is a trust in this system of expertise that constructs the certified, professional, PK3 teacher. This type of trust is a form of confidence that the certified PK3 teacher possesses the expertise needed to teach young children. Trust of this type infers an exclusive quality of "faith" in society. It is specifically related to absence in time and space, as well as to ignorance. We have no need to trust someone who is constantly in view and whose activities can be directly monitored. High-trust positions, however, are those jobs performed largely outside the presence of management or supervisory staff. Although teachers are supervised and monitored from time to time, daily, consistent monitoring by the principal is largely absent. In reference to the expert system, this type of trust brackets the limited technical knowledge which most people possess about coded information (i.e., certification rules) which routinely affect their lives (Giddens, 1990, pp. 4–10). Trust of this sort reconstructs the teacher in terms of the codification rules and adds to the psychological security of individuals and groups. Parents trust that the teacher knows what they are doing because they are assumed to possess expert knowledge that is codified in terms of DPI certification standards.

The Historical Location of Expertise. The influence of professional ideology on the construction of the PK3 program has been investigated within a framework of governmentality. As such, a distinction can be made between the production of professional expertise and the creation of the professional. Professional expertise was examined for the ways in which it constructed knowledge in the university and how the expertise of the state (DPI) was used to determine programmatic content. The construction of the professional PK3 teacher was done through "standard" rules and codes determined by the state. Both of these constructions are linked historically to the governing of society.

The professionalization of knowledge is situated historically with the advent of specialized communities of professionals which developed after the Civil War (Popkewitz, 1987b). These professionals were given "expert" status to help guide the social reconstruction of society and to help establish meaning and tradition in America. Expertise of this sort was a type of authority arising out of a claim to knowledge, neutrality, and efficiency. The new professional expert helped to provide solutions to the governing of society. Over the second half of the nineteenth century "truths" produced and disseminated by the positive sciences of economics, statistics, sociology, medicine, biology, psychiatry, and psychology helped to mediate the governing struggle between the "needs of morality and order" and the "needs of liberty and economy" (Rose, 1996). The deployment of a new range of scientific and technical knowledges allowed the possibility of exercising social rule over time and space. Government analysis and decisions were now based on particular kinds of procedural and statistical expertise, generated by the "expert" professional. The scientist, the engineer, the civil servant, and the bureaucrat became the "expert" who determined the measuring stick of social norm for the needs of governing.

This type of expertise plays a part in translating society into an object of government. The authority of expertise is joined with the formal political apparatus of rule. Through the invention of rules, codes, and certification practices the state becomes a center that "governs at a distance" (Barry, Osborne, & Rose, 1996; Raab, 1994; Rose, 1996). Society is judged according to social norms set not by the government, but by professionals. Professionals became vested with authority to act as experts in the devices of social rule, and the subject of rule is reconceptualized through a type of moral normativity. These "specific" intellectuals are bestowed with a certain responsibility and power on the basis of their close association with "true" discourses (Simons, 1995). The citizen became a subject of needs, attitudes, and relationships governed through a nexus of cohesion and dependencies (Rose, 1996). The PK3 teacher, with their new professional status, would be given the authority to determine normalcy in society.

II. What examples of early childhood professional identities are represented in the text? How are they expressed through the discourses of science and child welfare?

Early Childhood Science. The "science" of professional early childhood education can be identified in early drafts of PI4 rules given to the faculty. The use of words such as cognitive, social, and emotional development indicated a strong propensity toward the science of psychology in defining early childhood professionalism. In December of 1988 the faculty was given a draft of the new rules that stated in part:

> PI 4.12 (2) The program shall require study of the characteristics of play and its contribution to the cognitive, social, and emotional development and learning of children birth through age 8. (Wisconsin Department of Public Instruction, 1992, draft given to faculty December 5, 1988)

In this rule, the "profession" of early childhood education is clearly linked with the "science" of psychology. Child development, as a method of organizing the curriculum of early learning, is unquestioned in the text.

As mentioned earlier, the historical influence of psychology on early childhood education has been particularly strong. Psychological criteria became the basis for scientific decision making in early childhood education during the first half of the twentieth century. The use of the words *cognitive*, *social*, and *emotional* in the early drafts of PI4 rules exemplify this link. Theoretical discussions about curricular goals in early childhood education are often predicated upon distinctions made within the psychological as opposed to the social, political or economic realm (Silin, 1987). Another example from an earlier draft of PI4 rules given to the faculty in the fall of 1986 shows an even stronger emphasis on psychology as child development and child study:

> PI 4.12 (1) The program shall require study of the principles and theories of child growth and development including a background in biological, cognitive, psychomotor, emotional, and social development and their relationship to learning.
> PI 4.12 (2) The program shall require study and experience in methods of child study. (Wisconsin Department of Public Instruction, 1989, draft given to faculty in the fall of 1986)

In both versions of PI4 rules, the historical influences of psychology can be seen by reference to child study and developmental psychology. Although there are acute distinctions between child study and child development, what is important to this examination is that both forms of study aimed to make the early childhood field more "professional" by emphasizing the science of psychology. In both sections there is an overarching emphasis on developmental aspects of learning through psychological categories (biological, cognitive, psychomotor, emotional, social) and through developmental research techniques (child study and child development theory).

Historical location of psychology: The use of psychological language has long been associated with education, particularly from the discipline of cognitive psychology. The school was a natural target for psychologists trying to "discover" internal mental processes, such as creativity, perception, thinking, problem solving, memory, and language (Rose, 1989). Educational usage of words such as "cognitive," "social," and "emotional" became commonplace in teacher lesson-plans and helped in the diagnosis of children who needed special attention. Teachers of young children in particular were encouraged to incorporate all aspects of mental ability into their lessons to ensure the well-balanced and integrated maturation of the child.

The emergence of the child study movement encouraged teachers and researchers to observe children to shed light upon human evolution and the characteristics distinguishing "man" from animals. Made popular largely through the efforts of psychologist G. Stanley Hall, the child study movement encouraged teachers to build curricula based upon observation (Bloch, 1987; Rose, 1989). Throughout the 1920s child study centers sprang up in universities across the country as a way to "make scientific" the education of young children. However, psychologists of the time, while acknowledging the contributions child study made, contested the belief that observation equated a "science" of maturation. By the early 1940s the normative studies of Arnold Gesell at Yale launched the beginning of a more "scientific" child development approach. It is Gesell who is credited with popularizing the notion that children pass through sequential, unfolding developmental stages (Braun & Edwards, 1972; Brennan, 1986; Cremin, 1988; Robinson & Hom, 1977).

What is important to recognize about these distinctions is that the faculty does not question the use of psychology in the minutes to determine course content in the early childhood program as defined in the PI4 rules document from the earliest drafts onward. Child study and child development are given as "scientific" methodologies to gain knowledge about the proper teaching of children. This emphasis on science and scientific methodology can be viewed historically, as part of the effort to professionalize the field.

Child Welfare

It is also interesting that it is only in the PK3 program rules that *play* is mentioned (rule PI 4.12 (2)). Although other certification programs list the importance of child growth and development as well as physiological aspects of education, none list play specifically. An emphasis on play is also mentioned in the university's expectations for the nursery/kindergarten teacher, as cited by the 1984 DPI program review:

> The institutional goal statements report expectations for the teacher of nursery/kindergarten children to be skilled in "setting up wholesome environments which include ample opportunities for play activities, music, dance, drama, art, and other means of self-expression and physical activity." (April 9, 1984, meeting minutes attachments)

Historical location of play: A historical interpretation of this emphasis links the emergence of early childhood education in America with the importance of play; seen as lacking in the homes of poor inner-city children. As nursery schools and kindergartens began to assume greater responsibilities for the "mental hygiene" of children in their care, the idea of "constructive play" became an important part of their curriculum (Bloch, 1987).[14] The importance of play in the early childhood curriculum also points to the influence of Fröebel and his belief that a child could be educated through play. Fröebel was among the first to link the play of the child with practical procedures and devices to achieve moral development.[15] Fröebel also emphasized the importance of having a female instructor for young children. He stressed the importance of the mother's role in preserving the inborn goodness of the child by creating a nurturing and home-like atmosphere in the classroom (Cremin, 1988). According to Fröebel, women were uniquely suited to create a classroom atmosphere that would encourage systematic play where children could learn in a natural way. This bias was probably due to Fröebel's contact with the philosophy of Rousseau and the methods of Pestalozzi (Richards, 1992). The importance of play and providing a nurturing environment is also linked to the child study movement in early childhood education history. By applying Darwinian principles of evolution to the study of childhood, G. Stanley Hall cultivated a view of child growth and development that affirmed Fröebelian beliefs in play in the early childhood classroom (Bloch, 1987).

The early drafts of PI4 rules also hinted at the welfare aspect of early childhood professional education through its emphasis on parental involvement and education:

> (6) The program shall require the study of and experiences designed to develop skills in promoting parent education and family involvement in the early childhood level program. (PI 4.12, specific rules, draft of December 1988 given to faculty)

As discussed earlier, nurturing and child welfare issues were an integral part of the first early childhood programs in America. The role of early childhood teacher as "parent educator" began in the first half of this century as psychologists began to apply their trade to avoid maladjusted children in society. Psychologists believed that parents needed help in raising well-adjusted children because of rapid and profound changes in society (Napoli, 1981). Early childhood teachers, already pulled by the identity of "nurturing social mother," began to adopt the idea that they, too, had a role in producing well-adjusted children. Prior to the creation of the PI4 rules, the nursery/kindergarten certification program also emphasized the importance of family and the home. The 1984 DPI program review highlighted this aspect:

> The unique institutional structure of this program provides students with the opportunity to gain information, attitudes, and skills necessary to synthesize the resources of both home and school environments as they influence the development of the very young child. (April 9, 1984, meeting minutes attachments)

The PI4 rules document outlines the role of the early childhood teacher as parent educator. None of the other certification programs outlined by DPI, neither drafts of PI4 rules nor early certification programs, required this role as part of the professional program for the training of teachers. It is found only in the PK3 and earlier nursery/kindergarten programs.

Both the "science" of early childhood education and its emphasis on child welfare can be contextualized as part of the way society is governed through the lens of professional knowledge. The use of psychology and psychological descriptions of children provide the means for the subjectification of the human soul. They enable "human powers" to be transformed into material that can provide the basis for calculation (Rose, 1989). By slicing human learning into cognitive, social, emotional, psychomotor, and biological development, techniques of examination are imposed upon the subject in question. The examining mechanisms of the psychological sciences provide a technique for rendering subjectivity into thought as a calculable force. The application of normalizing judgment makes the human subject visible and transcribes attributes into codified forms of documentation. The "soul" becomes thinkable in terms of psychology.

The use of psychological categories in descriptions of the PK3 program ensures certain techniques of organization will take place. Relations of hierarchy in human development epitomized in the use of child study and child development theories locates humans in space and time in order to achieve certain outcomes. The teaching of young children is to direct their conduct to meet certain predefined results. Using the principles of psychology, technologies of subjectivity are established that enable strategies of power to infiltrate the fissures of the human soul (Rose, 1989, p. 8).

The development and academic application of psychology also enables new forms of expertise in the "professional" social sciences. Armed with a "norm" of social behavior, the population can be scrutinized for deviance by the new professional. This sociopolitical approach emphasizes the welfare of the child in terms of a populational norm. Early childhood educators can examine children for their "normalcy" and act accordingly. Instruction in the synthesization of "home and school resources as they influence the development of the young child" ensures that the PK3 teacher will know how to use all available resources to protect the welfare of the child. The emphasis on parent education will also help to transmit psychological norms and pedagogic techniques into the home to ensure the best possible (maximum) development of the child. The new techniques help the private family to become a site where the production of a "normal" child takes form. The family uses the professional expertise of the PK3 teacher to examine and regulate their own behavior and apply specific techniques to produce a "normal" child.

The promotion of subjectivities relating the duties of parenthood with the production of "normal" children enables a mechanism of social control. By internalizing the psychological descriptions of normalcy, families become intensively governed. The technologies of family establish a way of viewing children psychologically in an effort to produce well-adjusted children. It is through the promotion of such subjectivities that the population at large is governed.

Summary

The purpose of this chapter was to explore the multiple effects of "professionalization" discourse during a ten-year span of time leading up to the construction of the PK3 program. A somewhat "classic" definition of professionalism was utilized for the analysis that assumed a specialized body of knowledge, juried entry to the field and a sense of social service. After examining the rather unique history of early childhood education as an emergent profession, two questions were pinpointed: (1) How is professional ideology and expertise distinguished in the text during the construction of the PK3 program? and (2) What examples of early childhood professional identities are represented in the text? How are they expressed through the discourses of science and child welfare? To help answer these questions, I examined the text for examples of how the new program was characterized as an emergent field of expertise, the technical and psychological descriptions of the program, the a priori assumptions of such language as being nonpolitical and ahistorical, and the ways in which the new program was placed in relationship to existing faculty standards.

It became clear that notions of professionalism did, in fact, influence the construction of the PK3 program in several ways. First, the influence of professional ideology and expertise was visible in the text. The prestige accorded UW-Madison was linked with the emerging recognition of early childhood education as a "certifiable" program. The reasons for offering a PK3 program were coupled with UW-Madison's historical prominence in teacher education. This highlighted the documented bond between professional ideology and prestige. Both the university and the state were positioned in the text as generating legitimate knowledges that attempted to guarantee a professional program by providing access to scientific knowledge during the program's creation. Professionalism was defined through a commitment to society and public need and job accountability through supervision and evaluation. This correlated with two of the three "benchmarks" of professionalism: specialized knowledge and a sense of social service. The expertise of the early childhood teacher was defined both by UW-Madison and DPI. Adequate preparation was used to determine and set parameters for the expert knowledge of each entity.

Both UW-Madison and DPI were positioned in the text as having specific expertise related to the professionalism of early childhood education. This can be viewed as an "expert system" which enables one to remove the social relationships from the immediacies of context. The university is positioned to use its expertise to interpret and augment state-defined rules and create a program for the students to pass through. This jointly created expert system splits time and space by deploying modes of technical knowledge which have validity independent of the practitioners and clients who make use of it. The technical or scientific knowledge of the certified "professional" early childhood teacher is disembedded from the local contexts of teaching through codification, rules, and descriptions of expert knowledge.

Second, a reliance on science and welfare was identified in early drafts of PI4 given to faculty, particularly through the use of psychological and developmental language. This can be viewed historically as part of the effort to professionalize the field of early childhood education. The faculty did not question this language to determine course content in the text. This correlates with the acceptance of such language as being ahistorical and nonjudgmental. Instruction in the importance of play was specifically mentioned as part of the early childhood teacher education program. This emphasis can be read as another historical link in early childhood professionalism which emphasizes child welfarism and family involvement.

The use of a social epistemology of educational reform guided the examination of historical constructions that governed the creation of the PK3 program. These included the historical influences of university prestige, expertise, psychology, and play. Seemingly apolitical, each of these constructions works to solidify part of an apparatus of power that shapes and manages individuals and populations by formulating the terms of "normality" and "expertise." Unlike more traditional forms of governing, this type of management governs people under the auspices of being more "professional."

For instance, both the university and DPI were seen in the text as having the expertise needed to determine how the PK3 program would be put together. Although "expertise" is generally interpreted as politically neutral (especially the autonomous university expertise) it is, nevertheless, part of the apparatus of rule. This occurs because of the truth claims of the experts determine norms of behavior to which individual members of the population are compared. Students in the PK3 program are taught how to determine "normal" child development and "normal" intellectual abilities in children. As future experts in their field, they are able to use their knowledge as a measuring stick and hold it up against their young charges to determine which need "correction" to become more "normal." This use of expertise forms a way to govern the population without the direct (i.e., visible) influence of the state.

Visualizing the construction of the PK3 program in terms of an expert system clarifies the ways in which the "professional" teacher becomes disembedded from the local contexts of teaching through codification, rules, and descriptions of expert knowledge. These rules and codes, such as the PI4 rules document that outlined the PK3 program, are seen as "valid" without regard for who is using them and how. It is both a trust in this system of expertise and the historical contexts from which this trust arose that has helped to create a "professional" PK3 teacher education program. This sort of trust reconstructs the teacher in terms of codification and rules and adds to the psychological security of society. There is a confidence that the professional PK3 teacher possesses the expertise needed to teach young children. I believe it is important to examine this trust and the codes and rules that define teacher education programs from a social-historical perspective. The decisions about what is "valid" knowledge in teacher education—or what a teacher needs to know to teach—needs careful consideration.

NOTES

[1] The faculty minutes, memos, and informational handouts chosen for study were specifically from the Elementary Education Area of the Department.

[2] Some of these arguments include the work of Gaston Bachelard, Georges Canguilem, Louis Althusser, and Jaques Derrida. Each theorist reinforced their own conceptions of the writing and study of history to produce meaning (For further discussion see, e.g., Bachelard, 1984; Baltas, 1989; Delaporte, 1994; Gottdiener, 1995; Kurzweil, 1980; Tiles, 1987; Young, 1990).

[3] Some of the general teacher education reform reports included: *The Reform of Teacher Education for the 21st Century: Project 30 Year One Report* (Murray & Fallon, 1989), The Holmes Group Reports (Holmes Group, 1986; Holmes Group, 1990, 1991a, 1991b; Holmes Group Forum, 1991), *A Nation at Risk: The Imperative for Education Reform* (National Commission on Excellence in Education, 1983), *A Call for Change in Teacher Education* (National Commission for Excellence in Teacher Education, 1985), *A Nation Prepared: Teachers for the 21st Century* (Carnegie Task Force on Teaching as a Profession, 1986),

Staffing the Nation's Schools: A National Emergency (Sanders, Benton, Kaagan, Simons & Teague, 1984), and John Goodlad's books: *A Place Called School* and *Teachers for Our Nation's Schools* (Goodlad, 1984, 1991). Reports critical of early childhood teacher education included: *Childhood Education's Guidelines for Teacher Preparation* (Association of Childhood Educational International, 1983), *Early Childhood Teacher Education Guidelines* (National Association for the Education of Young Children, 1982).

[4] The literature on professionalism generally acknowledges these traits, although some researchers argue for a more inclusive definition (e.g., Ade, 1982; Argyris & Schön, 1978; Katz, 1984; Mayhew, 1971; Morgan, 1994; Schön, 1983; Siegrist, 1994; Veale, 1991).

[5] It is important to recognize that during this same period the negative aspects of professionalism, such as fostering elitism and inequality, were also argued in the press. However, even those who spoke out against professionalization often believed that any movement toward "professional" status was better than no movement at all (Labaree, 1992b).

[6] Significant discussion of the issues surrounding teacher testing can be found in the books *Testing for Teacher Certification* (Gorth & Chernoff, 1985) and *Crisis in Teaching: Perspectives on Current Reforms* (Weis, Altbach, Kelly, Petrie, & Slaughter, 1989).

[7] Two reports not previously mentioned that argue for the construction of a pedagogical knowledge base include: *Restructuring the Education of Teachers* (Association of Teacher Educators, 1991) and *Standards, Procedures, and Policies for the Accreditation of Professional Education Units* (National Council for the Accreditation of Teacher Education, 1987). Significant discussion and support of this idea can be found in the earlier work of Lee Shulman, John Goodlad, and Linda Darling-Hammond (Darling-Hammond, 1986, 1987, 1988; Darling-Hammond & Berry, 1988; Goodlad, 1991; Meek, 1988; Shulman, 1987, 1988).

[8] This methodology is drawn heavily from Nikolas Rose (Rose, 1994, 1996).

[9] At this point the faculty believed they needed to create a new major instead of a concentration for the PK3 certification program.

[10] The final version of PI 4.12 (7) has slightly more emphasis on the management of early childhood programs. It reads: "The program shall require study of the administration and organization of early childhood level programs; program and staff development, supervision, and evaluation; financial management; accreditation and licensing; relationships with parents, advisory groups and community agencies; and the use of community resources" (Wisconsin Department of Public Instruction, 1992).

[11] The "split" over who's expertise would be used to determine the scope of the PK3 program correlates with the historical struggle for control over teacher education in Wisconsin as discussed by Prestine. Both DPI and the UW-Madison faculty felt it was their "right" to determine course and programmatic content for the teacher education program (see, e.g., Prestine, 1988, 1991, 1992).

[12] See, e.g., Barrow, 1990; Franklin, 1986; Ginsburg & Lindsay, 1995; Popkewitz, 1987a; Popkewitz, 1987b; Popkewitz, 1991; Popkewitz, 1995; Wittrock & Elzinga, 1985.

[13] This was before the discussion began on the PK3 program. The early childhood program DPI was critiquing in this quote referred to the nursery/kindergarten (NK) program in place at this time.

[14] Here, Bloch cites Elizabeth Peabody, who suggested that play was the critical element missing from earlier pedagogy and from the home environments of poor children (Bloch, 1987, p. 36).

[15] Rose (1989, p. 283) cites Fröbel's *The Education of Man*, New York: Appleton, 1906 (original work published in 1826).

Chapter 6

*Resisting the Norms of Elementary Education:
One Primary Teacher's Stories*
Lisa Goldstein

The primary grades are in a precarious position. Though bound by tradition and physical location to elementary schooling, they are also considered the capstone experience of early childhood education. Like the area between the two overlapping circles of a Venn diagram, the primary grades can be seen as an essential piece of elementary school as well as an essential component of early childhood education. But rather than being buttressed and supported by the strength of these two powerful domains, primary grade teachers often find themselves caught in the middle. Early childhood education and elementary education have distinctly different histories, norms, and traditions, different perspectives, expectations, and values, different standards, practices, and school cultures. Primary grade teachers are required to bridge these two disparate worlds, constantly mediating, negotiating, translating, and compromising.

Most primary teachers give up, and settle into the norms of elementary schooling. Other primary teachers emphasize their commitment to early childhood education by challenging and resisting the traditional practices of elementary schooling. These primary teachers can be thought of as "ECE-identified," a term which suggests their deliberate alliance with the values, principles, and practices of early childhood education. In this chapter I describe the practices of one ECE-identified primary grade teacher, Martha George, in order to explore the ways that she resists the professional paradigms of elementary schooling while teaching in an elementary school setting.

Elementary Schooling versus Early Childhood Education

The basic imperative of elementary schooling is "to manage large numbers of students who are forced to attend school and absorb certain knowledge in an orderly fashion" (Cuban, 1993, p. 17). This demand led to the development of a particular set of conventions and practices—organizational structures and instructional practices linked directly to the challenge of managing children—that have characterized elementary schooling for over a century and persist in the present time. These regularities of schooling—for example, an age-graded school with its self-contained classrooms, carefully leveled curriculum, penchant for ability grouping and for the division of academic content into discrete subject areas, and the pervasive commitment to rules such as hand raising, speaking only when recognized by a teacher, asking permission to leave the classroom, remaining seated while working, and not speaking while others are talking—are so prevalent that they have come to seem like a natural part of the education of the young. These characteristics are a direct result of elementary schooling's management-driven quest for efficiency, uniformity, standardization, and control of student behavior (Cremin, 1961; Callahan, 1962; Sirotnik, 1988; Cuban, 1993). Further, elementary schools serve as sites of socialization and the reproduction of the existing social order (Apple, 1979; Giroux, 1981; McLaren, 1989). Children are taught a set of values—punctuality, the work ethic, competitiveness, conformity—as a part of the schools' "crusade to eliminate diversity" (Apple, 1979, p. 66) and to maintain control.

Early childhood education, on the other hand, is a field centered around the developmental vicissitudes of young children, a field which rejects the "teaching as managing" model in favor of "teaching as paying attention" (Jones & Reynolds, 1992, p. 13). The early childhood education perspective emphasizes the treatment of children as individuals with the ability to make choices about their educational experiences. Children are given opportunities to learn through direct experience and hands-on explorations, and to engage in the types of problem-finding and problem-solving that lead to growth and development. Early childhood educational environments, in their ideal form, are responsive to the unique, particular needs, desires, abilities, and interests of the children involved.

These individualistic, child-oriented values blend fairly well with the values and the structure of many infant/toddler and preschool environments. However, these values are in fairly direct contrast to the rigid structure and the values of conformity, uniformity, and control (Apple, 1979; Callahan, 1962; Cremin, 1961; Cuban, 1993, Giroux, 1981; McLaren, 1989) that characterize elementary school environments. It seems, then, that there is a mismatch between the expectations of early childhood education and the traditional culture and expectations of elementary school. As a result, ECE-identified primary grade teachers are caught between a rock—the nationally recognized exemplars for high-quality education for the young children they teach—and a hard place—the norms, traditions, and expectations of the school settings in which they work.

In order to find out more about the contradictory experience of providing responsive, individualized, child-focused early childhood education within the confines of an elementary school setting, I engaged in a collaborative research study with Martha George, a primary grade teacher in a northern California suburb, spending over 150 hours in her multi-age primary grade classroom as both an observer and a participant (Goldstein, 1997). Though she works in a public elementary school setting, Martha's classroom is unlike traditional elementary classrooms. This is because of her commitment to engaging in ECE-identified practice. Rather than succumb to the "teaching as managing," control-centered practices typical of elementary education, Martha maintains a commitment to the child-oriented values of early childhood education.

Ann and Harold Berlak (1981, p. 135) developed a "dilemma language" to describe and explore schooling, outlining a series of sixteen dilemmas that highlight the tensions faced by teachers in their school settings. The concept of a dilemma language is particularly useful in discussing and analyzing Martha's experience of engaging in ECE-identified practice within the context of an elementary school educational environment because it draws attention to the conflict between the values and traditions of early childhood education and of elementary schooling. The dilemmas that characterize Martha's classroom life are: uniformity versus individuality, teacher direction versus child direction, content versus process, and commitment to academic disciplines versus commitment to children. In each of these binaries, Martha chooses to eschew the traditional elementary school responses—uniformity, teacher direction, emphasis on content, and commitment to academic disciplines—in favor of those representing an early childhood educational perspective—individuality, child direction, emphasis on process, and commitment to children. I will address the first of these dilemmas, uniformity versus individuality.

Uniformity versus Individuality

Martha plans five different activities for each morning's work session, all of which go on simultaneously at different locations in the classroom.

Martha describes each of the activities to the children during morning meeting, and when activity time begins, the children go to a station that Martha has selected for them. She explains how she makes these initial activity placements:

> It depends on what [activities] I've got out and who I think will work together well or not. And sometimes it's more because I've seen certain kids have an interest in each other and I'll pair them together. Sometimes I try to structure it so that there's a real heterogeneous group of ability in terms of kids who will be able to help each other, kids who are going to need support functioning at that station. And I also try to somewhat balance it for boys and girls.... Sometimes they fall out that way—certain activities attract more boys to them or more girls to them. I try to encourage kids who I think would not try certain things, because of, perhaps, those kinds of things, to try everything, to go everywhere.

Though it may seem odd that children are not offered a choice at this juncture, given the high regard for children's agency in ECE-identified practices, the close attention paid to the children as individuals and the sensitivity that characterizes the careful and deliberate nature of the placements are evidence of Martha's commitment to early childhood education. Organizational and administrative ease, in the shape of ability groupings or some other predetermined and unchanging working groups, clearly take a backseat to a focus on the children as individuals.

The children sitting on the rug at Martha's feet do not know about how carefully their needs, personalities, and desires are taken into consideration when these initial activity placement decisions are made. They just know that Martha has a tiny square of paper with the class list printed on it that tells who goes where, and that almost every morning meeting ends with Martha searching for her misplaced list. She finds it quickly this morning, and the children lean forward, eager to hear where they will be sent. Some even have their fingers crossed for good luck, hoping to be sent to the activity of their choice.

"At the round table," Martha says, pointing, "kids will be working on making their solar system puzzles. They need to be colored, glued, and then cut, just like I showed you. It needs to happen in that order, or else it will get very tricky." She reads the names of the children going to that station. "At the zigzag table," Martha continues, "Moon reports. Olders need to look in the books on the table and find three facts about the moon that you would like to include in your report. Youngers may pick up one of the sheets that I made and trace the words." She reads off the names, but does not specify who is an older and who is a younger. Second-graders are olders, kindergartners are youngers, for certain. But where do the first-graders fit? I asked Martha about this, and she replied:

> It depends. It is not cut and dried at all and it varies from situation to situation. I usually leave it up to the kids to decide (trails off). Well, that's not entirely true either. I expect the second-graders to do the more demanding option, and they know that. And I assume that most of the kinders will choose the simpler option. Though sometimes they surprise me, like Brian or Robert will choose to do the olders' page. And that's fine. The first-graders tend to (pause) well, some of the first graders, like Lauren or Eleanor, are very capable academically, and they'll always opt to do the harder page. And some of the first-graders who are just getting started with their writing skills, like Li Ping, for example, will take the easier page, and that's okay. And there are some first-graders who are capable but who don't want to put forth much effort.... They do the easier page too. And though that is not what I'd want for them academically, it tells me something about where they are at in other areas of their development. Sometimes I'll push those kids, and sometimes I won't. It depends.

Martha is unconcerned about the instability of her categories and the logistical complications of allowing children to level themselves: her approach to teaching is rooted in a commitment to each child as an individual. As she wrote in our dialogue journal: "It is very important to me that I respond to each child as an individual which means really knowing them, which means investing in them emotionally." Responding to children as individuals is one of the fundamental tenets of progressive education and of high-quality early childhood education; however, Martha takes this one step further. She is not content to stop at "really knowing them" in order to respond to their individual needs, but she also requires "investing in them emotionally" in order to do this type of work. Martha's enactment of ECE-identified practice emphasizes the important role played by interpersonal relationships in the education of young children. Martha not only thinks carefully about each child, but also cares deeply about each child, and about each child's experience in the classroom.

The room is a busy place as the children work. It feels a bit like Grand Central Station at rush hour, noisy, humming with activity. The children move around, bumping and jostling each other, determined to get where they are going. They are focused on their goals, their destinations. But Martha would not have it any other way. "It's hard," she admits. "But you know (pause), the alternative of having everybody doing the same thing (pause)—it doesn't really feel comfortable to me." The reasons for her discomfort reflect her deep commitment to the children as unique individuals. First, having a five-ring circus enables her to put out a variety of activities that cover different academic areas—writing, mathematics, art—and different types of learning modalities—aural, kinesthetic, visual. There is something for everybody here, and everyone has a chance to work in the ways that they like best. The children also have the chance to work in the ways they like least, and to grow as a result. Finally, Martha's classroom arrangement allows the children some flexibility. Martha says, "not everybody is at the point to do everything the same at any given time, and so, while I send them off to their activities to start with, if somebody wasn't ready to be there, like Carlos really wasn't ready to do his Halloween book, fine, he could go and do cutting." Children are welcome to make their own decisions, to do what feels right to them.

Backlash Against Martha's ECE-Identification

Martha's rejection of many of the norms of elementary schooling in favor of more ECE-identified practices feels comfortable and natural for her. Martha's views on the value of the individual, on the importance of process over content, on the capability of children to make choices about their education, and her belief that children will take from any classroom activity whatever it is that they need at a given moment are well-aligned with her conception of her classroom as an early childhood education setting.

However, some of the parents of Martha's students were concerned about what their children were experiencing. Their memories and their expectations of life in kindergarten, first and second grade were not matching up with their children's experiences in Martha's class.

Some of the parents' worries were communicated to Martha in backhanded ways. One mother laughed nervously and told Martha that her child had said that they never do any work at school. Another made a comment about her child only bringing home art projects in her work folder, and no "real work." Other parents were more direct. One mother told Martha that at the end of last year her daughter was able to add with regrouping and now she couldn't. She had concluded that it was because Martha's program didn't include any mathematics and that her daughter was losing all of her skills. Parents of kindergartners worried that the work was too hard; parents of second-graders worried that the work was too easy. It seemed like no one was happy.

Martha was not sure how to respond. The parents' criticism made her feel insecure and angry. She was operating within the norms of her school site and meeting nationally recognized standards for exemplary practice. Her ECE-identified style of teaching enables her to be keenly attentive to the particular experiences of each of the children in her class, an approach that, presumably, would be quite desirable and sought after by the demanding parents in this community. The situation is puzzling. How can a teacher who is succeeding so beautifully by the yardstick laid down by the profession be perceived by parents as failing so miserably?

The answer is simple: ECE-identified practice contradicts the traditional expectations and norms of elementary schooling. Though Martha departs from elementary school's traditional ways in manners that enhance the experience of children—moving away from uniformity toward flexibility, allowing for idiosyncrasy, developing confidence, agency, and judgment—it is the essential departure that threatens and unnerves parents.

Martha has had to wrestle with a variety of other issues related to the dilemma of providing ECE-identified practices in an elementary school setting. The concept of the age-graded school is so pervasive and strong that it is difficult to resist. Though Martha teaches an ungraded primary class, the school district has grade-level benchmarks and performance expectations for each grade, and prepares curricular materials and in-service events by grade level as well. The texts that are purchased for each school site are always age-graded: Martha's bookshelves are overflowing with virtually untouched teacher's guides, workbooks, and textbooks for kindergarten, first-grade, and second-grade reading, phonics, mathematics, health, science, spelling, social studies, and handwriting. Referrals for special education and reading remediation programs are made using grade-level scores, though the notion that a student is not reading at grade level makes little sense in a developmental, ECE-identified classroom. Despite this, the resource teacher continues to write "Classroom teacher reports that student is not reading at grade level" on the paperwork and forms she fills out for identified students in Martha's class. Martha herself has never reported such a thing when referring students for resource support, but still the terminology and mindset persist doggedly.

Parents, too, are caught up in thinking about their expectations for each grade level. Cursive handwriting and multiplication are taught in third grade, addition and subtraction with regrouping in second; parents either want to accelerate their children's experiences with these topics or try to keep these topics off-limits to ensure that their children won't be bored when they get to the "appropriate" grade level. Martha also sits through several springtime conferences each year with parents who are interested in holding their children back for a year or skipping them forward a grade, though retention and acceleration are unnecessary in a truly ECE-identified multi-age setting.

Moving beyond the types of difficulties highlighted here, there is surely a whole constellation of problems that Martha did not face, problems that complicate the lives of primary grade teachers at other school sites and in other districts as they attempt to engage in ECE-identified teaching in their kindergartens, and first-grade and second-grade classrooms. Report cards and standardized testing, mandates regarding instructional minutes and/or block scheduling, and forced adherence to commercially published curricula are a reality in the lives of many primary grade teachers, and are roadblocks to ECE-identified practice. In many cases primary grade teachers are evaluated for tenure and beyond using standards that reflect the values and expectations of elementary schooling: teachers engaging in ECE-identified practices may not meet the performance standards laid down by their districts, either because their practices are too unconventional or because their children have not been primed to score well on standardized tests. Finally, there are many primary teachers who lack the training and experience necessary to implement ECE-identified practice in their primary grade classrooms. As students in teacher training programs that focus specifically on elementary education, many aspiring primary grade teachers learn the methods, techniques, and perspectives of elementary schooling rather than early childhood education.

As this glimpse of Martha's ungraded primary classroom has illustrated, ECE-identified practice is a marked departure from the traditional shape of elementary teaching practice. Teachers centering their primary grade teaching around the values and perspectives of early childhood education will face challenges as they attempt to lay ECE-identified practices over the existing scripts for elementary school—coverage, accountability, uniformity of outcomes, and so on. Both in practice and in theory, the goals of early childhood education and elementary schooling seem mutually incompatible.

We are left with more questions than answers. How should we proceed to address the dilemmas facing primary grade teachers committed to providing exemplary early childhood education in their elementary school classrooms? Does elementary school need to change? Does early childhood education need to change? Can we expect that elementary schooling will change, given its robust nature and resistance to fundamental reforms of any kind? (Cuban, 1993; Sarason, 1991) Should the field of early childhood education redraw its boundaries and abandon kindergartners, first-graders and second-graders? Should elementary schools offer some kind of responsive, child-oriented teaching practices for their older students as well as for their primary graders? ECE-identified primary grade teachers will continue to struggle with competing and conflicting demands, expectations, and requirements until these tensions are addressed and resolved.

Note: An earlier version of this chapter was presented at the Sixth Annual Reconceptualizing Early Childhood Education in Research, Theory, and Practice Conference. Madison, WI, October 10–12, 1996.

Chapter 7

Eh, No Act!: The Power of Being on the Margin
Kerri-Ann Hewett

"Eh, no act!" This common phrase is usually followed by laughter, but can also be followed by tears. John D'Amato (1988), in his article entitled, "Acting": Hawaiian Children's Resistance to Teachers," notes "Hawaiian adults use the desist, 'No act,' to warn and to reprimand children whose behavior has the same appearance of defiance; they use the same desist to indicate affection, approval, and amusement when children's behavior is imaginatively and harmlessly mischievous" (p. 529). D'Amato was attempting to describe "acting" as a challenge to teacher authority by Hawaiian primary and preschool children.

However, there is more to "Eh, no act" than a warning or a reprimand; more than an indication of affection, approval, and amusement. While "Eh, no act" is more times than not the equivalent of "you're putting me on," or "you've got to be kidding!", it is actually a response to an act that is a form of resistance.

When I was growing up, my Aunty would say, "Eh, no act!" when I would compliment her about how nice she looked in her new dress or how pretty her hairstyle was. It was a response that I became accustomed to because I knew that although she appreciated my compliment she was "too shame," "too *hilahila*" or shy to accept it readily. In essence what she was doing was "acting" as a form of resistance to my verbal praise. Hawaiian tradition frowns upon verbal praise. Old Hawai'i did not openly praise because this might expose one, especially a child, to dangerous envy (Pukui, Haertig, & Lee, 1972, p. 262). It was also important to "be humble" in your good fortune, achievement, and success. Resistance to public acknowledgment of success was a way of respecting and upholding the *kupuna's* teaching of "When you achieve, do so with humility" (Pukui, Haertig, & Lee, 1972, p. 262).

"Eh, no act" is also a form of resistance to power. Lisa Delpit talks about the "Silenced Dialogue" in her book entitled *Other People's Children* (1995). She speaks of the way teachers of color stop disagreeing with white educators leaving those white educators with the idea that those teachers of color comply with their white authoritative logic. For example, here is the story of a black woman principal who is also a doctoral student at a well-known university on the West Coast. She is describing her university experiences, particularly about when a professor lectures on issues concerning black children:

> If you try to suggest that's not quite the way it is, they get defensive, then you get defensive, then they'll start reciting research.
> I try to give them my experiences, to explain. They just look and nod. The more I try to explain, they just look and nod, just keep looking and nodding. They don't really hear me.
> Then when it's time for class to be over, the professor tells me to come to his office to talk more. So I go. He asks for more examples of what I am talking about, and he looks and nods while I give them. Then he says that that's just my experience. It doesn't really apply to most black people.
> It becomes futile because they think they know everything about everybody. What you have to say about your life, your children, doesn't mean anything. They don't really want to hear what you have to say. They wear blinders and earplugs. They only want to go on research they've read that other white people have written.
> It doesn't make any sense to keep talking to them. (1995, p. 22)

When teachers of color stop disagreeing, they are showing resistance to white authority. They give themselves power by resisting the power of the authority. Of course by silencing themselves, the authority believes that those teachers of color are submissive to their power. After all, they stopped disagreeing, didn't they? (Delpit, 1995)

Another example of resistance to power comes through a personal experience I had several years ago. When my friend Roberta asked me to substitute (third-grade classroom) for her, I readily agreed because I felt happy to *kokua* her in her time of need. Having a baby is a blessed event, and the cooperation of family and friends is of the utmost importance. I agreed to substitute for her for approximately thirteen days during the month of May and into the first week of June. I was excited to meet her children and to get a "feel" for the progressive private school where she taught.

Of the small private schools in Honolulu, I had heard Roberta's school was very strong academically. Some folks say that this school is like Bingham Tract School with a great reputation for being a feeder school into other prominent private schools like Punahou and 'Iolani. As I reflected on the time I spent as a teacher at Bingham Tract, I could not help but think of both the positive and the negative aspects of that school.

I recall the tremendous parental support at Bingham Tract and I remember being told by a teacher-colleague, "these parents are going to be all over you because they pay big bucks to have their kids here." With that in mind, I accommodate every request and/or suggestions when a Bingham parent called me at home or stopped in to see me before or after school.

Anyway, I began my substitute experience for Roberta without any expectations. I was immediately reminded of Bingham Tract with the size of the school and the basic arrangement of the classrooms. The kids resembled Bingham kids; mostly *haole* and Asian kids, with a few Hawaiian kids here and there. The kids were basically very sweet and cheerful natured. They seemed very secure in their environment and I could tell that the majority of them were happy to be there.

It was on the third day of my second week when a *haole* woman walked into the classroom with a package. I smiled and said "Hello." She semi-smiled back and said, "Where can I leave this? It's Jane's lunch."

"You can leave it here," I said as I stood up and walked toward her.

"Is the teacher here?"

"I'm here for Roberta," I replied.

"You're the sub?"

"Yes," I responded.

"So, you're friends with Roberta?"

"Yes, Roberta and I go to school together."

"Oh, at UH?"

"Yah."

"So how do you like teaching?"

"I love it!"

"Have you subbed before?"

"Oh yes, many times."

"The kids are great!"

"Yes they are."

"Are you going to be subbing here next year?"

"No, I don't think so."

"So, you like teaching?"

"Yes, I love it!"

Are you planning to teach?"

"Well....I've been teaching for a while."

"Oh."

"Yes, elementary."

"What is your field of study?"

"Elementary education, teacher education."

"Oh, that's interesting."

I nod.

"Subbing is good experience," she says.

I nod again.

"Well, tell Steven (Roberta's teaching partner) that I came by to leave Jane's lunch."

"I will."

She walks out and I make a goofy face. Then I start to laugh. This whole scene was hilarious. It's funny because most *haole*, when they meet native (brown) people like me, they don't expect us to be in professional roles. They see me and they immediately wonder where the real "teacher" is. I feel like they think that I am the custodian, not that being a custodian isn't a respectable job. They don't perceive me to be a professional.

So I choose not to come right out and tell them who I really am at the start. Why should I? They're so smart. They're white and white people are the most intelligent people on this earth. Why wouldn't she know that I'm the sub? Why wouldn't she know that if I am the sub, I must be interested in teaching and qualified to be there in that room with her child and the other children. If I had told her that I was a doctoral student and that I was an experienced elementary school teacher, and that I come from a loving, secure, ambitious family, she would probably think that I was lying. See, expectations for native people are very low. So are the expectations that teachers hold for native children. Hawaiian children are supposed to be passive and learning disabled. We're supposed to be lazy, unambitious, and "at-risk" in everything we do at school. We're supposed to come from insecure, unstable, dysfunctional homes, and we're never supposed to be on time.

In my response to her questions, I was actually resisting her "*ho'oio*" attitude. By responding in a very limited way with short nonspecific answers, I was displaying my resistance to her power. I "passively" responded like a slave would in attempting to please the master. A form of resistance is when the colonized behaves in a manner that allows for the colonizer to feel that he/she has power over the colonized. By saying what they (colonizers) want to hear, the colonized has an opportunity to see the colonizer as the fool. It is funny to see people who think that they are smart, acting so *lolo* (stupid).

"Acting," both to come to combat and to come to terms with authority, is another more significant form of resistance for minorities. John Ogbu writes about "oppositional cultures" developed by minorities in reaction to a history of exploitation and oppression. These oppositional cultures are used to express group hostility against the majority culture. Haunani Trask, professor of Hawaiian Studies at the University of Hawai'i at Manoa, writes in length about this resistance and the process of oppositional cultures reacting to the majority culture. In her experiences at UH-Manoa as a Native Hawaiian professor, in what she describes as a "one of the few remaining institutions where no attempts have been made to add a little color to the visible white reality," displays resistance through the "act" of public activism and bold, verbal expression (Trask, 1993). Her role as leader in an oppositional culture group called Ka Lahui Hawai'i, a native initiative for self-government, reminds the majority culture that the native Hawaiian people are reacting to a history of unjust treatment.

She may be acting out her role as a Native Hawaiian activist, but she is living on the margin because she knows both worlds; she makes meaning in both the white world and the Hawaiian world. Skeptics, however, question her true desire to help the Hawaiian people because they see so many behaviors that are considered "un-Hawaiian"; for instance, the commonality of verbal resistance, the wearing of the pareo which is native to Tahitians, and the aggressive behavior and gestures displayed in public as a means of activism. In a big way, Haunani is using that power that she has in being on the margin and being a border crosser as an advantage in promoting change in the minds of native Hawaiians. Decolonization is her goal, and she will continue to "act" as a form of resistance to the Western world.

Acting is performance; the theater of postcolonialism with parts available to the Kanaka Maoli (Native people). Because Native Hawaiian people are a colonized people, definitions of Hawaiian people are numerous. We play out different roles and wear different masks as the result of colonialism.

1. *Role of Victim:* Hawaiians play out stereotypes placed upon them. Evidence of this role is revealed in statistics that name Hawaiians high (percentage) in the underachievement of students in school; in the number of homeless and families on welfare, in the number of inmates in

the prison system, and as the ethnic group with the poorest health conditions in the state of Hawai'i.

2. *Role of Mimic Man:* Hawaiians play the role of the mimic man/woman overly earnest to be *haole* (white). They have a willingness to become a part of the oppressive role white cultural imperialism has played and continues to play in Hawai'i. For example, their association centers around the elite with their ties to elite institutions such as Punahou School and the Outrigger Canoe Club.

3. *Role of Lolo (Stupid):* Hawaiians, in contrast, resist the role of the mimic man/woman by playing the role of the *lolo* or stupid. They pretend to not know and perform unintelligently out of fear that other Hawaiians may see them as acting white.

4. *Role of Living on the Margin:* Hawaiians play the role of what bell hooks describes as "living on the margin." The idea here is for the colonized to go along with, following through with the colonizer, performing to please the colonizer. While it is a form of resistance that gives us power to outsmart the colonizer, many Hawaiians find it a necessary role to play today.

5. *Role of the Rebel:* Hawaiians play the role of the rebel consumed in self-exotication. They rebel against the injustices suffered by the Hawaiian people as a result of colonization. Haunani Trask, as an example of this role, while studying at the University of Wisconsin-Madison, was exposed to the "Black Panthers." Since then, Trask has led the Hawaiian movement to rebel against the injustices and work to correct the wrongs done because of colonization. Describing herself as "an uppity Native woman," Trask shares in her recent book:

> Most Americans have come to believe that Hawai'i is as American as hot dogs and CNN News. Worse, Americans assume that if opportunity arises, they too may make the trip, following along after the empire into the sweet and sunny land of palm trees and hula hula girls. This predatory view of my Native land and culture is not only opposed by increasing numbers of us, it is angrily and resolutely defied. No matter what Americans believe, most of us in the colonies do not feel grateful that our country was stolen, along with our citizenship, our lands and our independent place among the family of nations. We are not happy natives. (1993, p. 2)

The power of living on the margin is an advantage to Native Hawaiians because we are Native Hawaiians living in a Western world. However, I must be cautious not to impose my definition of what constitutes who I am as a Hawaiian because of the many definitions of the Native Hawaiian, the roles we play, and the masks we wear as colonized people. We must find *pono* (balance) in our existence because we live with one foot in our native culture and one foot in the culture of the majority. The advantage for Native Hawaiians is that we are learning more about who we are, where we came from, where we want to go, and what we must do to function as Kanaka Maoli (Native people) in this society. In the process of learning about ourselves, we are learning that we are integrated into the culture of today. We must find *pono* in both worlds.

Part III: Resistance and Representation:

THE CURRICULUM

Chapter 8

Critical Perspectives on Social Studies in Early Childhood Education
Shirley A. Kessler

Introduction

Critical theory represents a significant shift in the way some early childhood educators think about research and practice with young children, and is a theoretical perspective worthy of exploration relevant to the history of early childhood education and curriculum. Applied to education, critical theorists argue that going to school does not provide equality of opportunity for all children to succeed if they put forth the effort, but the process of schooling itself contributes to the achievement gap which exists between various social, economic, and cultural groups in the U.S., inequalities which have been well-documented for decades (e.g, Children's Defense Fund, 1998). Critical theorists also acknowledge that low-income children, children of color, as well as women, are members of social groups which have different access to social and economic resources and which differ in terms of political influence and power, factors which effect their experiences of schooling. A critical perspective pays particular attention to the "official knowledge" of schools, that which is accumulated, legitimated, and unequally distributed through the formal, informal, and hidden curriculum (Apple, 1979, 1986), to examine the relationship between social class and school achievement. In this chapter critical theory is used as a lens to examine the history of social studies in early childhood education.

I chose to focus on the social studies because the primary purpose of this subject area is "citizenship education," a purpose relevant to the development of social and cultural beliefs and values related to the unequal social and economic relationships which exist in our society today. In this research I undertake a history of prescriptive theory (what educators call the purpose and proposed content of social studies) from, the date of the publication of the first curriculum developed especially for very young children,[1] Frederick Fröebel's *Education of Man*, to 1916, the date of the report of the NEA Committee on the Social Studies when the term "social studies" was officially adopted.

Early in the process of examining articles in journals such as *Kindergarten News* (1891–circa 1896) and *Kindergaten Review* (1897–1915), I was struck by the similarities between the social studies curriculum prescribed over ninety years ago and what I find in recently published social studies textbooks and in current teaching. I wondered how to explain the constancy of the so-called "expanding environments" curriculum in social studies and to what extent this formalized curriculum could help explain the continuing relationship between social class and unequal educational attainment. Since this approach to doing history is motivated by the desire to understand the persistence of inequality, discrimination, racism, and sexism in education, I count myself among the historians Finkelstein (1992) calls the "justice workers" (p. 270). Furthermore, this research is based on the perspectives of professional educators writing during that time and does not address the ideological struggles among social groups in specific cases. I agree with Finkelstein that to do so would be the next step in conducting the history of the early childhood curriculum.

Critical Historiography

The study of curriculum from an historical perspective is a relatively new area of inquiry. The first published account, *The Curriculum Field: Its Formative Years,* by Mary Louise Seguel, appeared in 1963.[2] This history represents what Lybarger (1991) calls the traditional, "celebratory" account, wherein historical change is seen as synonymous with social progress. "Most often, celebratory historians produce an account of the present as the happy result of past struggles…(and/or) …glorify a past hero or a golden age" (Lybarger, 1991, p. 3).

Critical historiographers, however, see little to celebrate in examining the history of education which in their view has always failed to serve well the children of the poor. As Katz (1971) put it, "Schools are not great democratic engines for identifying talent and matching it with opportunity" (p. xx). Instead, he characterized American education as universal, tax-supported, free, compulsory, bureaucratic, racist, and class-biased. "The children of the affluent by and large take the best marks and the best jobs" (Katz, 1971, p. xvii).

Furthermore, the achievement gap:

> cannot be explained either by genetics or by theories of cultural deprivation; it is the historical result of the combination of purpose and structure that has characterized American education for roughly the last hundred years. The purpose has been, basically, the inculcation of attitudes that reflect dominant social and industrial values; the structure has been bureaucracy. (Katz, 1971, p. viii)[3]

A critical history of education, therefore, would not be written as a "narrative of progress," given the persistence of the unequal outcomes of schooling. Instead, critical historians ask why is it that schools have failed to achieve successful educational programs for some women, children of the working poor, and people of color? What are the roots of this phenomenon? Furthermore, as Karier has argued, a critical history must attempt to uncover the intentions and motives of historic individuals, to "enter the 'level of belief' of the historic actor" (Karier, 1973, p. 13), rather than describe his/her actions behaviorally, without purposes, desires, ideas, and moral beliefs.

Lybarger (1991) situates critical histories of the curriculum within a "revisionist" or "radical" framework. A revisionist perspective chronicles the history of schooling by focusing on conflict among social groups and asks the question: "Who or what prevailed and why?" Herbert Kliebard's *The Struggle for the American Curriculum: 1893–1958* (Kliebard, 1995) represents a revisionist perspective. A radical account looks not only to political struggles for insight into this issue, but relates political ideologies to economic status. It begins with the premise that current educational phenomenon can be partially accounted for by examining social and/or economic factors, particularly conflict between social classes. Critical historians of the curriculum seek to understand the roots of educational inequality in the official curriculum, which emerged out of the political struggles and economic conditions of the past. Karier (1973) argues that prominent "schoolmen" (e.g., Horace Mann, Henry Barnard, and William Torrey Harris) embraced a "new liberal" ideology (Beyer & Bloch, 1996; Feinberg, 1975; Karier, 1973) and argued for a bureaucratic structure and form of administration for schools (Katz, 1971), consistent with the belief that schools should be agents of social control. I will discuss these ideas further in the conclusion of this chapter.

The first section of this chapter defines what is meant by the term, "social studies." The second section presents my interpretation of social studies as prescribed by Frederick Fröebel. Next, I present my interpretation of the social studies curriculum enacted in the late 1890s at the laboratory school developed by John Dewey at the University of Chicago. Finally, I revisit the five questions posed above and conclude with an analysis of the relationship between the early childhood social studies curriculum, the stated purposes of schooling, the bureaucratic structure of schools, and the ways in which education has produced and the legitimated cultural and ideological structures tied to the unequal outcomes of schooling.

Social Studies

In the last several decades social studies has been referred to as "social education" by early childhood researchers who have been more interested in studying the social development of young children than the formal or enacted social studies curriculum. This developmental orientation to early childhood research and curriculum analysis and evaluation has dominated research in early childhood for the past 100 years (Bloch, 1992). Descriptive research in social education/social studies has focused on "what is"—that is, what children are capable of learning (Bloch, 1987). The focus of study has been on examining the ways in which children can be taught the knowledge, skills, values, and attitudes that will enable them to function successfully in adult society.

Prescriptive theory examines social education/social studies from the perspective of "what should be" and raises questions such as, What should be taught in social studies? What is the purpose of schooling? What knowledge is of most worth? According to the most recent position paper of National Council for the Social Studies Task Force on Early Childhood/Elementary Social Studies (NCSS, 1989), the purpose of social studies is to provide children with the knowledge, skills, and attitudes they need to relate to others, solve problems, and to make decisions and thoughtful value judgments. "Above all, the social studies help students to integrate these skills and understandings into a framework for responsible citizen participation, whether in their play group, the school, the community, or the world" (NCSS, 1989, p. 15). Seefeldt (1989) maintains that social studies is a subject area which supports the primary purpose of education—the preparation of young children to become citizens of a democratic society. The subjects comprising the social studies are history, the social sciences (political science, economics, jurisprudence, and anthropology) and in some respects the humanities and science (Hinitz, in Seefeldt, 1989). Although there is not universal agreement as to the nature and preparation of the "good citizen" (Shaver, 1981), the concept "typically refers to informed and moral decision making about the political process—in voting, obeying the laws, expressing views on public affairs, (and) possibly running for public office. However, 'the uniting theme...is intelligent morality'" (Morrissett, 1981).

Traditionally, social studies for young children addressed four areas of learning: intellectual development and the teaching of concepts in the social sciences; socialization (learning the student role and the way society is organized); values and moral education; and self-awareness. There appears to be general agreement that in practice, these "elements" should not be taught as separate components, but integrated into broad topics or themes, with the socialization component usually receiving far greater emphasis than the other three, with a few exceptions. Intellectual development and concepts in the social sciences should include teaching the major principles in history, geography, and economics. Socialization is usually thought of as the process whereby one acquires the knowledge, skills, attitudes, and values necessary to perform adequately as adults in society (Goslin, 1969; Zigler & Child, 1969). In this way, education serves as one of the primary means whereby social cohesion and social stability are maintained and a society perpetuates itself.

History of Social Studies

Few "histories" of the social studies have been published and none has focused exclusively on the early childhood curriculum. As I mentioned earlier the term "social studies" was officially adopted in 1916 by the National Education Association Committee on the Social Studies and the American Historical Association. This date is used as a convenient marker for determining the beginning of the field, although the term had been used informally in the 1800s. Before 1916, what we now think of as the social studies was a collection of separate disciplines—history, geography, and civics. History dominated the social studies then and historians were the most vocal of the three groups in curriculum reform efforts during the early decades of the twentieth century.[4]

In adopting the term, "social studies" the committee further stated that the purpose of the social studies was to teach the skills and attitudes necessary for good citizenship. Thus, in 1916 the emphasis of the social studies shifted from a focus on knowledge within specific disciplines to a focus on using knowledge to develop good citizens. The critical questions are what "knowledge," what "attitudes," and what "skills" are thought to be necessary in developing good citizens. Whose knowledge is represented in under-theorized assumptions about the content of the early childhood curriculum? How are the objectives derived from a specific idea of citizenship education translated into programs and practices for young children?

When the NEA Committee on the Social Studies adopted the term social studies, it also outlined specific topics to be covered in grades seven through twelve. At the same time, a Bureau of Education publication issued in 1915 described topics to be taught in the curriculum for grades K through 8 (Morrissett, 1981). The recommended topics for the K through 12 curriculum are as follows (Jarolimek, 1981; Morrissett, 1981):

Kindergarten	Self, School, Community, Home
Grade 1	Families
Grade 2	Neighborhoods
Grade 3	Communities
Grade 4	State history, Geographic regions
Grade 5	United States history
Grade 6	World cultures, Western hemisphere
Grade 7	World geography
Grade 8	American history
Grade 9	Civics of World cultures
Grade 10	World history
Grade 11	American history
Grade 12	American government

This framework, the so-called "expanding environments" approach, prescribes a curriculum which focuses instruction in the early years on the self and family, expands to an examination of the neighborhood and community in the primary grades, broadens to a focus on the state and the nation in fourth and fifth grades, and world culture in the sixth. U. S. History was to be taught in the fifth, eighth and eleventh grades. First, the influx of immigrants, primarily from Eastern Europe, during this time led to the perceived need to socialize newcomers into the dominant culture—to "Americanize" them. Second, three cycles were developed so that children would be taught the basic concepts and principles in grades 1–6, after which many dropped out of school, and again in grades 7–9, when more students quit school. The same subjects were typically taught again in grades 10–12 (Morrissett, 1981).

The dominant pattern, or expanding environments approach, outlined at this time became firmly established in most schools by the 1920s and influenced the outline followed by curriculum planners. Two factors influenced the development of this pattern, the content of teacher education courses, and textbooks (Morrissett, 1981). To the consternation of most social studies educators, the pattern established then has changed very little, and continues to provide the organizational framework for the majority of social studies programs in the U.S. today. Recently, the NCSS recommended that the expanding environments approach be somewhat collapsed, so that the first three topics be taught in the kindergarten and first grade, thereby allowing teachers to take up more substantive subjects in grade 2 and beyond.

The origins of the "expanding environments" orientation in social studies education and early childhood education is difficult to ascertain with certainty. However, the curriculum advocated by Frederick Fröebel in 1826 looks remarkably similar to the expanding environments approach recommended today. Fröebel outlined a philosophy of education and set the stage for the establishment of the first kindergarten in Blankenburg, Germany, in 1836, and the first kindergarten in the U.S. in Watertown, Wisconsin, in 1856. One of the chief subjects included in the course of study he outlined was the study of "man and his surroundings" (Fröebel, 1887, p. 251), a topic realized in the expanding environments curriculum. Americans modified the Fröebelian curriculum in several interesting ways, and a few alternatives to social studies education were proposed during the first two decades of the twentieth century, when the Fröebelian curriculum was being reconstructed (Weber, 1969). For example, John Dewey proposed a curriculum the purpose of which was to teach children how to live in a democratic society. Patty Smith Hill, heavily influenced by the "scientists" of human behavior, such as Thorndike (Cremin, 1961), advocated a curriculum based on the formation of correct habits (Burke, 1923). Lucy Sprague Mitchell developed a program which emphasized the "here and now" experiences of young children and the teaching of geographical concepts (Mitchell, 1921). The so-called "romanticists" (Cremin, 1961) of this period, like Caroline Pratt (Pratt, 1924) developed schools which were to foster creativity and healthy psychosocial development. Naumberg believed one developed competent citizens by first developing psychologically healthy individuals.

However, none of the curricula proposed during these years supplanted the basic approach and framework set forth earlier, although aspects of the alternatives proposed are still visible in early childhood programs today. In other words, the content outlined by Fröebel over 150 years ago, with a few additions, has remained in place. Critical historians explain the persistence of this framework by pointing to the overarching "normative" theory that prescribes and justifies what should be taught, ideology of new liberalism (Feinberg, 1975; Karier, 1973). This ideology fostered belief in bureaucracy as a way to structure schools (Katz, 1971) which was solidified in the emergence and entrenchment of the "superintendancy" (Callahan, 1962). New liberal ideology and the bureaucratic structure of schools which it fostered and justified help to explain the constancy of the social studies curriculum in early childhood education over a century of time.

Social Studies in the Fröebelian Kindergarten

The curriculum theoretically evolves from one's philosophy of education, which includes one's beliefs as to the purpose of education. Fröebel (1887) believed that the ultimate aim of education was "the realization of a faithful, pure, inviolate, and hence holy life" (p. 4). He argued that to realize this aim, education should lead children to a knowledge of the inner essence of all things, in the natural and physical world, which would reveal a divine unity which in Fröebel's view was God. To accomplish this purpose, Fröebel described what he believed were the three chief subjects of instruction: religion, natural science and mathematics, and language. He further separated these three groups into sixteen particular topics and/or activities (e.g., physical education, poetry, handwork, colors, play, stories, etc.), one of which was the study of man and his surroundings. All of these topics were to be interspersed with the "ordinary occupations of home and school" (p. 236), or domestic duties.

The purpose of studying man and his surroundings was to aid in the discovery of the divine essence of humanity within and thus to bring the child to a knowledge of the eternal unity of all things and to knowledge of God. "The inner being, the divine essence of things and of man, is known by its outward manifestations" (p. 5). One way for children to discover this inner essence, divine unity, and God, was to examine the world around them beginning with the things in their immediate environment and proceeding outward.

> The knowledge of every thing, of its purpose and properties, is found most clearly and distinctly in its local conditions and in its relations to surrounding objects... These are the things of his nearest surroundings—the things of the sitting-room, the house, the garden, the farm, the village (or city), the meadow, the field, the forest, the plain. The sitting-room, then, furnishes the starting-point for this orderly study of nature and surroundings, which thus proceeds from the near and known to the less near and less known, and becomes for the purpose of orderly classification and subdivision a real subject of school instruction. (p. 251)

Instruction was to begin with an examination of the objects found in the home, such as the table and chair, and from there to parts of the room, such as the windows and doors. Reference was then made to the fact that "as the door, the window, etc. were parts of the room, so the room was a part of some greater whole" (p. 252)—the house. From an examination of the house, instruction proceeded to observations of the larger environment, the homestead, which was also a part of a greater whole, the village. At this time, geographical concepts, such as mountains, valleys, etc., became a part of instruction. Thus, "...in the observation of the outer world—the course of instruction resembles life closely" (p. 258).

Next, the "works of man" were similarly scrutinized (p. 259). First, man's works were enumerated: the house, the village, the road, the bridge, the wall, the plow, etc., examining their origins, materials, uses, and purposes. Then the child observed characteristics of villages and cities, the various buildings (stories, workshops, factories) and their various purposes and equipment. Finally, the child "ascends" from a study of the works of man to a study of the workman himself—"as from the study of nature he ascended to her creator, to God" (p. 260).

> He finds the names of the workmen in different kinds of workshops (carpenters, etc.) and classifies these workmen in accordance with the character of the place in which they work, the material on which they work, and the kind of work they do. (p. 260)
> As public buildings were considered, so were the names of the persons who worked there, as well as other occupations, such as hunter, fisherman, etc. (p. 260)

Lastly, the common features and the ultimate aim of all work are elicited..."and it is found that all men live together, grouped in a common relationship, that of the family" (p. 260).

> Thus the pupil in a great meandering circuit has returned to the home from which he started on his explorings of nature and the outer world, has returned to the center of all earthly endeavor; but with enlarged and keener powers of observation... He has found man in his various relations to the things of the outer world; he has found himself. (pp. 261–262)

The home and family life were of primary importance in Fröebel's vision of education. The beginnings of a truly religious spirit were found in the relationship between mother and child. The relationship between father and son was viewed as an expression of the relationship between God and Jesus..."the highest and most intimate relationship that man can know and comprehend" (p. 146). Further, it was in a loving family environment that children acquired "...a good heart and a thoughtful, gentle disposition in their full intensity and vigor" (p. 97). Likewise, a feeling of community first manifested itself in family relations, between parents and children, then among siblings.

To bring children into full realization of their holiness and oneness with God, Fröebel developed instructional materials, called "gifts" and "occupations", as well as songs, games, and "fingerplays" (dramatic play activities) about nature, family life, and community activities. Most of the ten gifts consisted of blocks, either one-inch cubes or small brick shaped blocks, which children manipulated according to specific directions, or "dictations," in order to create a symbol of or representation of an object or event in their environment, often a house or some type of building. The occupations—cardboard work, paper folding, weaving, drawing, stringing beads, perforating, etc.—were to reinforce the experience of manipulating the gifts and/or of engaging in various songs, games, and "plays." (p. 261)

Constructing representations of objects and events in the immediate environment had a spiritual significance. As Fröebel put it, "God created man in his own image; therefore, man should create and bring forth like God" (p. 31). It was through such work, therefore, that man became godlike, creating the inner in the outer, giving outward expression to inner sentiments and thereby coming to greater knowledge of the unity of all things. Fröebel's attitude toward work is instructive. He pointed out that the primary purpose of work was to lead to a greater awareness of

God, not to provide food and clothing. Material results, such as these, were "insignificant surplus" (p. 32). Fröebel had faith that with the correct attitude toward work, basic needs would be met. "The smallest effort cheerfully applied to work will secure bread, clothing, and shelter and respect" (p. 33). Therefore, one did not have to worry about the future welfare of children. In fact, he maintained, man's "intelligence" would help him during times of hardship find a way as well as "allay want by patient endurance" (p. 33). Further, without this religious component to his work, man was degraded "into a beast of burden, a machine" (p. 35).

In addition, Fröebel wanted domestic duties to be a part of the kindergarten program because it was natural for children to want to participate in such activities and gave them joy and delight (p. 102). In addition, domestic duties as well as "adventurous" activities allowed for the expression of the innermost life of the boy and the desire to control the destiny of things was expressed (pp. 102–103). The songs, "plays," and games were, likewise, infused with spiritual significance. The songs children learned enabled them to express their innermost feelings when words were not forthcoming, due to their lack of maturity. Songs dealt with such topics as the wonders and beauty of nature, ideal family relationships, and the importance of the labor of community members. Plays and games reinforced impressions made by the gifts and occupation work, as well as impressions by excursions. In addition, games provided an opportunity for character education. Through games children learned "justice, moderation, self-control, truthfulness, loyalty, brotherly love, and ...strict impartiality...courage, perseverance, resolution, prudence, together with the severe elimination of indolent indulgence" etc. (p. 113). Further, games help develop a spirit of community and respect for the laws of the community. "Thus, the games directly influence and educate the boy for life, awaken and cultivate many civil and moral virtues" (p. 114).

Discipline techniques were spelled out. Fröebel believed that man, created in God's image, was essentially good. Therefore, misbehavior was viewed as simply a "good tendency, only repressed, misunderstood, or misguided" (p. 122). Fröebel believed that sometimes teachers created discipline problems by focusing on the negative, and attributing evil motives to what the child did. The job of the parent or teacher was to "find the original good source and then foster this good side" (p. 122). Guidance, therefore, was to focus on the positive, what we promote today as a "catch them being good" technique.

In sum, the content of the Fröebelian social studies curriculum, much like the content today, focused on home and community life. Instruction began with the family and the home, then broadened to include the study of the community and other aspects of the child's surroundings. Children learned about history through stories, tales, and legends. Teachers were encouraged to take children on excursions, as well as engage them in songs, games, and plays. These activities were interspersed with gift and occupation work, which allowed children to express impressions gained from previous experiences in the environment, especially through the creation of symbols and representations. What we view as socialization and moral education took the form of religious instruction, character education, and the cultivation of a community spirit. Character education focused on developing virtuous qualities, under the gentle guidance of an adult. Knowledge of self, or self-understanding, was a spiritual activity, since knowledge of self revealed a divine unity which was God. The spiritual thrust of this curriculum deemphasized citizenship education as we think of it today, since the purpose of education was an awareness of the unity of all things and the creation of a religious way of life. Fröebel believed that the development of a religious self would promote harmonious living. Thus, the Fröebelian curriculum, despite all its rigidity in form and procedure, could represent one of the few social studies programs available to children in the U.S. where socialization was de-emphasized.

Social Studies in the American Fröebelian Kindergartens

Margaretha Shurz, daughter of a wealthy German family of liberal social views, opened the first kindergarten in the United States in 1856 in Watertown, Wisconsin. She and her husband immigrated to the U.S. for political reasons as a result of the German Revolution of 1848. The early kindergartens were created in the German-English academies established by other Germans who likewise emigrated after the revolution. Thus, the kindergarten was identified at the onset with liberal social views. In the U.S. the kindergarten received support from several influential individuals, among them Elizabeth Peabody, Henry Barnard, W. T. Harris, and Susan Blow, largely because of its ideological base in German Idealism, a branch of philosophy compatible with Transcendentalism, which thrived in New England at that time (Weber, 1969).

Most of the early kindergarten teachers, "kindergartners," had direct training from Fröebel himself, or from one of his disciples, such as

Baroness Bertha von Marenholtz-Bulow in Berlin. Her student, Louise Polluck, opened a kindergarten in West Newton, Massachusetts in 1864 and soon thereafter in Washington, D.C., where, in addition to a kindergarten, she opened a training school for teachers. Mrs. Polluck published several volumes on the kindergarten dealing with the songs and plays component of the curriculum, as well as one volume containing sample lessons, the *National Kindergarten Training Manual* (1889). The sample lessons in this manual give one an excellent idea of how Fröebel's principles were translated in the U.S., as well as suggestions for implementing the curriculum. The lessons also prescribe the way in which social studies in the Fröebelian kindergarten was to have been taught.[5]

Other interpretations of the Fröebelian curriculum can be inferred by examining early issues of newsletters and magazines published for kindergarten teachers. For example, *Kindergarten Review*, published between 1897 and 1915 (First called *Kindergarten News*, 1891–circa 1896), then later *Kindergarten and First Grade Magazine* (1916–1926) contains numerous articles offering teaching suggestions for each month of the year, as well as articles focusing on child guidance, parent education, issues in kindergarten education, proceedings from meetings of the International Kindergarten Union, songs and stories to be used in instructing children, etc. For example, articles in one volume suggested the following topics or themes for each month, topics which integrated instruction in terms of songs, games, stories, and gift and occupation work, and which bear remarkable resemblance to those found in early childhood programs today (Volume 8, September 1897–June, 1898):

October -	The change of seasons
November -	Thanksgiving
December -	Christmas
January -	Snow and The Trades, especially The Carpenter
February -	George Washington
March -	Transportation, Wind and Water
April -	Gardening
May -	Bees
June -	Grass mowing

The "expanding environments" orientation, where the content consisted of the child and his surroundings (the home, the school, and the community) as well as character and moral education, was transported to the United States with minor changes during the period leading up to the report of the NEA Committee on the Social Studies. As was pointed out earlier, this approach continues to dominate the early childhood social studies curriculum today. In translation, the Americans added what appears to be a new component or a new emphasis to character education—"socialization"—and new content—patriotism. Over the years the "dictated" lessons with the gifts were eliminated for more open-ended experiences with larger blocks. But the prescribed curriculum for social studies set forth by Fröebel and recommended to kindergartners between 1890 and 1910 seems to have changed very little. The parameters within which local programs developed social studies curricula were firmly in place at the turn of the century, and provided the main focus and framework for what was taught. Several alternatives to the expanding environments framework were proposed, however, through the 1920s, alternatives which continue to emerge from time to time and never completely disappear from the educational scene (e.g., Robison & Spodek, 1965). But the expanding environments approach has remained firmly intact.

Social Studies in the Dewey School

One alternative to the early kindergarten curriculum in the social studies was the curriculum recommended by John Dewey. Dewey's emerging philosophy of education was developed and tested in a laboratory school established and directed by him at the University of Chicago during 1896–1903. The sub-primary unit, the name given to the program for 4- and 5-year old children, opened in 1898 with 8 children. Several months later the enrollment increased to 20 and had an average daily attendance of 10 to 11 children. One teacher and 2 assistants, both graduates of the Free Kindergarten Association of the Armour Institute which was then under the direction of Anna Bryan taught in the sub-primary unit.

To accomplish the first goal Dewey maintained that the school itself should become a cooperative society on a small scale. Through participation in endeavors aimed at a common goal, parents, children, and staff would model appropriate attitudes and behaviors for children as well as create the ideal society in miniature. "Character" and "discipline" would be an outgrowth of a shared community life. Intellectual development and the acquisition of knowledge in the content areas would be achieved by the promotion of a scientific attitude (observation, hypothesizing, testing, concluding) combined with an opportunity for children to reconstruct knowledge as it had developed over the course of history, rather than expose children to subject matter in its highly evolved form.

The curriculum of the Dewey school which was developed to accomplish these goals was not organized around the usual subject areas but around Dewey's notion of "occupations," activities which had evolved over the course of human history to satisfy the basic needs of human life, such as the need for food, clothing, and shelter. It was in the satisfaction of these basic needs that man formed societies and learned cooperative behavior. Further, Dewey believed human intelligence and the forms of knowledge which exist today evolved out of these and other basic human activities. Rather than hand children this knowledge ready-made, the curriculum required children to reconstruct it for themselves. This approach allowed children the opportunity to develop the intellectual skills necessary for problem solving, to acquire greater depth of understanding in the content areas, and to practice the skills of social living.

The teacher's role was crucial in assuring that the spontaneous activity of children be directed toward the achievement of the aforementioned goals. This meant that she must neither require children to imitate the appropriate way to complete an activity—an obvious reference to some of the "dictated" lessons characteristic of the Fröebelian kindergarten—nor allow children to engage in haphazard, aimless experiences. Instead, the teacher must find some point between the two extremes, a middle-ground, whereby the child would initiate an activity based on his/her interests, and carry it forward in creative, unique ways, with the teacher's guidance. Suggestion and reinforcement were the primary means for providing this guidance. In this way the teacher was to help the child accomplish what is he/she wanted to do.

The study of home life furnished the initial point of instruction for the four- and five-year-olds, and at the beginning of the school year the morning talk focused on this subject. Children's attention would be drawn to the fact that others came from families where various members performed certain occupations and that all were dependent on individuals outside the home: the grocer, the milkman, the mailman, etc. From these initial discussions, and occasional excursions out into the community where the home life of the animal kingdom was observed and discussed, children "naturally" would be inclined to engage in imitative play when provided with the necessary props. Soon, seasonal changes would be observed, and with a suggestion from the teacher, children would be encouraged to enact the changes in the household brought on by the coming of winter. One typical lesson focused on the mother's need to prepare warm clothing for the family members. This requirement led to the creation of a dry goods store, where "mothers" would buy fabric, needles, thread, etc., with which to make winter clothing. Children next would often make a streetcar out of blocks and chairs, on which mothers would ride to the store. Children rotated the role of streetcar conductor and exchanged coins.

At some time during the school year, the children would build a playhouse with blocks. After constructing the basic framework of the house, children would add the necessary details: streets, sidewalks, lampposts, stepping-stones. Eventually, with a "hint" from the teacher, attention would be called to the interior of the house, and children would proceed to use blocks to make the necessary furniture, along with fabric for curtains, rugs, and upholstery. Some children represented houses with paper and drawing materials. Often these activities would be followed by a trip to the hardware store to see what tools a carpenter might use.

Teaching the basic skills of reading and arithmetic were to evolve out of activities such as these. Children learned reading and writing skills as they made store signs, for example, and numeration as they measured and cut fabric to upholster a "chair" for the playhouse. Preparation for the daily luncheon provided an opportunity for children to learn "one-to-one" correspondence, as they set the table, then later "set equivalency" as they learned to count the children and determine the correct number of napkins needed. Reading, writing, and arithmetic were not to be taught as separate subjects, but as the need arose in connection with constructive work.

Through activities such as these, children were required to interact socially and learn cooperative skills, problem-solving abilities, and a deeper understanding of basic social occupations from which subject matter evolved. Constructive activities also allowed for individual expression, the realization of inner motives, the urge to represent ideas.

Thus, in the Dewey social studies curriculum, as implemented at the University of Chicago laboratory school, the widening horizons approach prevailed. The home, and the occupations found therein, was the focus for all activities at the sub-primary level, with occasional excursions into the community to examine the occupations necessary to the maintenance of the home. Intellectual development was one of two primary goals of this curriculum, which stressed the development of a scientific attitude toward problems and the eventual comprehension of the content found within the organized bodies of knowledge. Socialization and citizenship education comprised the other major thrust of this program. The school itself, especially the social relations, therein, was to be organized as a miniature community where children would experience democracy in action. Moral education took the form of learning to function harmoniously in a group situation where the "good" was defined in terms of the group, not the individual. Self-development was also a focus in this program. The teaching method emphasized that instruction be based on the child's impulses to action, and through indirect approaches (suggestion and reinforcement) one would lead the child to accomplish what he/she was trying to do, as well as the attainment of the educational goals. Handwork, likewise, was thought to enhance the development of the self, since it provided for the individual expression of inner ideas. Self-development was also related to the group, since native impulses were best developed and expressed when applied to utilitarian ends.

Fröebel and Dewey compared: The curricula developed by Fröebel and Dewey differ in important ways, yet the expanding environments approach dominated. In terms of the goals of education, there were striking differences. For Fröebel, the purpose of schooling was what we might term religious or moral education, where education was to lead to the knowledge of the unity of all things and to God. For Dewey, the purposes of education were citizenship education and intellectual development. To Fröebel, moral education took the form of religious instruction, where virtue was stressed. For Dewey, what was right and good was determined by group needs; moral education and citizenship education were the same. For Fröebel, character education was derived from knowledge of self and of God. He thought that such understandings would lead to harmonious social relations. Children were taught to accept their surroundings and study them for a greater understanding of God's work. For Dewey, character education took the form of socialization. He stressed the importance of learning to function in a social group, and to solve problems using the scientific method.

Conclusion

Several arguments address the relationship between the constancy of the widening horizons curriculum in early childhood education. Some critics claim that during the nineteenth century the purpose of education was modified from what it was believed to be in colonial America—to prevent Satan's influence upon children and to promote individual salvation and the religious well-being of the colony. Over time the purpose of education for most Americans was to shape attitudes, dispositions, and beliefs compatible with concepts of citizenship, designed to support the new nation (Stevens & Wood, 1987). This emphasis strengthened with the immigration of thousands of economically poor Europeans, especially from southern and eastern Europe, and with the industrialization of the American economy. A major purpose of schooling then became the education of the "worker-citizen" (Stevens & Wood, 1987), as well as to prevent poverty, establish good work habits, and instill the American creed. The argument continues that because industrial production required that work be governed by the clock, schools were structured with a segmented day, a bureaucratic system of authority, and regimented drill. Stevens and Wood (1987) claim that the purpose of schooling again changed from the preparation of democratic citizens to the preparation of citizens who would accept their place in the emerging industrial order.

Along with this new purpose of education emerged a new form of liberal political thought. The "new liberal" claimed that the greater happiness for the greater number could only be achieved by the positive use of state power, through a "controlled economy, state planning, group thought, and managed change" (Karier, 1973). Isaiah Berlin claimed that the basic assumptions of this new "positive" form of liberalism assumed that "man's purpose was rational self-direction, and that when all men have been made rational, they will obey the rational laws of their own natures and be law-abiding and wholly free" (Karier, 1973).

This new form of liberalism expressed faith in the rational knowledge of the expert and rejected the irrationalism of the masses. In addition, there was a strong belief in the value of science as a way to solve social problems. Dewey was one of the chief proponents of this new liberal ideology of managed change, and Dewey, like all liberals, was interested in "improving" the social system, not radically challenging or altering significantly the social, economic, and political structures currently in place. Dewey viewed ethnic and religious differences as a threat to the survival of society which could be overcome through assimilation (Feinberg, 1975; Karier, 1973). Other historians argue that many prominent "schoolmen," such as W. T. Harris, Henry Bernard, and Horace Mann, held similar views (Curti, 1959; Katz, 1971).

The educational program Dewey established at the University of Chicago from 1894 to 1904 emphasized social unity, cooperative living, and the rational, orderly, progressive development of technology. From the spinning wheel to the modern industrial corporate society, we've witnessed an uncritical view of history, one which came to dominate much of the social studies curriculum. The bloody history of Native Americans, African Americans, as well as the conflicts between immigrant laborers and managers, a history "that eschewed conflict and violence and supported the organizational thinking of the new managerial class" (Karier, 1973), was not part of the "official knowledge" in social studies. The community Dewey visualized was one where social conflict was avoided through the application of scientific procedures in identifying social problems and by the intelligent use of education for social control (Karier, 1973).

Michael Katz (1971) agreed that "...schools were designed to reflect and confirm the social structure that erected them....Their main purpose is to make these children (the poor) orderly, industrious, law-abiding, and respectful of authority" (p. xviii). Katz further maintained that one of the chief purposes of early schooling was to counteract the unfavorable influence of the home and stated that "...schoolmen...argued that the primary purpose of early education was the formation of attitudes rather than the development of skills." This belief was also evident in the writings of W. T. Harris, founder of the first public school kindergarten in St. Louis and later U.S. Commissioner of Education, where he wielded significant influence over professional educators and school administrators (Curti, 1959).

> It was this emphasis on the relationship of early childhood education to social order that fed the kindergarten movement, in the same way, quite obviously, that widespread concern with crime and welfare expenses have given impetus to movements for preschool education today. (Katz, 1971, p. 122)

Katz (1971) maintained that while ideas as to the goals of education might be modified from time to time, as Kliebard (1995) documents, the overarching purpose of the schools to socialize the young so they acquire the necessary knowledge, skills, and attitudes to function as adults has not changed. The strong emphasis on socialization in the social studies curriculum is one way to realize this purpose since it teaches children to accept what they come to learn about their environment as appropriate, natural, and good even though that acceptance strengthens cultural values, beliefs, and ideologies which support and rationalize social inequality.

Thus, the roots of "official knowledge" which comprises the social studies curriculum can be found in the philosophy of Frederich Fröebel, and to some extent in the political struggles among the historians, geographers, and civic educators (Hertzberg, 1981). Government officials as well as members of the leadership within the National Educational Association likewise contributed to what became "official knowledge" in social studies when in 1916 they recommended specific topics for study, topics which formed the content of teacher education courses and textbooks, then as now. The voices of Eastern European immigrants, African Americans, American Indians, and women were absent when the social studies curriculum was articulated, legitimated, and made profitable through the sale of textbooks (Apple, 1986).[6]

Another explanation for the predominance of the widening horizons curriculum is the prevalence of developmental theory as the primary guide for curriculum development in early childhood education (Bloch, 1992). Developmental theory cannot address the most important question in curriculum planning, "What knowledge is of most worth?" (Kessler, 1991). In other words the emphasis of the early childhood curriculum has been on promoting the child's optimal development, and the question of content has not been addressed until recently. Today official knowledge in early childhood education is determined by the recommendations of professional organizations, such as the National Council for the Social Studies, whose guidelines are to be followed in creating a developmentally appropriate curriculum (Bredekamp, 1987).

Alternatives to the widening horizons curriculum were developed, however, which might have altered the emphasis on socialization embedded within the curriculum recommended in 1916, and it cannot be assumed that less visible and articulate groups accepted the socialization model without objection. For example, American socialists organized schools held on Sundays to teach their children an alternative perspective on industrialization and economic inequality, a curriculum which challenged the messages their children received in the public schools (Teitelbaum, 1995). The "socialist curriculum" attempted to "educate workers' children about the inadequacies of industrial capitalism, the nature of class struggle, and the potential benefits of socialism" (p. 138). Topics for lessons included: "Unemployment, Poverty and Drink," "Slums, Sweatshops, Sickness and Disease," and others which sought to portray industrial capitalism as contributing to the destruction of home life and the family. No doubt other immigrant and minority groups acted in ways to preserve their heritage and ethnic traditions. However, research has yet to examine forms of resistance to the official curriculum adopted in 1916. A critical examination would require historians to study the formal curriculum developed in diverse regions of our country, in urban and rural areas, as well as that experienced by individuals whose accounts are described in biographical and autobiographical works.

What can we learn by adopting a critical perspective on the history of the early childhood curriculum that might help us to address the unequal experiences of schooling among children today? A critical perspective provides us with a partial explanation for the constancy of the social studies curriculum over a century of time, and the process by which this curriculum was developed, implemented, and maintained. A social studies curriculum which intends to socialize and Americanize low-income and minority children, a curriculum which is not based on their cultural experiences, could be related to the continual low achievement of less privileged children today. How might we change the expanding environments framework in social studies and create possibilities for children which question current political, social, and cultural arrangements? Perhaps we can look to our history as Americans for visions of the way we want to live together in the future. These visions should guide curriculum planning, implementation, and evaluation (Beyer & Liston, 1996). Visions will take us only so far, however. Individual acts in one's everyday life as well as acts undertaken collectively in the larger political arena are means to achieving alternative perspectives on citizenship education and social studies education for young children.

NOTES

[1] Williams, in C. Seefeldt, *Early Childhood Curriculum*, 1989.

[2] Seguel traced the development of the field from 1890 when it consisted of a loose group of interested individuals to 1938, when it had developed its own professional organization, several respected journals, and the first department of curriculum at Teachers College, where Hollis Caswell was appointed professor.

[3] Katz (1971), Karier (1973), and others point to the well-documented research highlighting the relationship between educational attainment and family income and to the fact that the level of family income and educational attainment historically has been higher for whites, than for blacks, and people of Hispanic origin, findings reaffirmed in the most recent yearbook of the Children's Defense Fund (1998), *The State of America's Children*. During the 1960s, this "gap" in achievement was explained by situating the problem in the family or within a "culture of poverty" which included low parental expectations for school achievement and children's lack of motivation. In the 1980s and 1990s the problem has been partially accounted for in terms of lack of resources in schools serving poor children, such as poor facilities, inadequate equipment and supplies, and the lack of well-trained teachers. Others have explored the gap by examining differences between the culture of the school and the culture of the home, where the difference between the two cultures, especially in terms of language spoken, could explain the lower achievement of low-income children and children of color. However, research does not appear to support this conjecture.

[4] In his 1978 Presidential Address to the History of Education Society, Clarence Karier also called for a critical examination of the history of American education which arises out of "a consciousness of present reality"—one which would reexamine traditional interpretations in light of present conditions and which might help explain current reality.

[5] At the beginning of this volume, Mrs. Polluck suggested the activities for a typical week (Polluck, 1889, pp. 8–10). The study of the child and his/her surroundings was to provide the unifying topic around which daily lessons centered. Each day began with a conversation exercise, which introduced the topic. Next, some movement activity, usually accompanied by singing followed, related, sometimes rather loosely, to the topic. The next activity was usually followed by work with the Gifts, likewise related to the topic, work first directed by the teacher, and then by the child. Another movement activity followed, along with a story,

again integrated with the theme. Lastly, occupation work, in the form of paper folding, sewing, work with clay, ended the day. This activity also was integrated, though sometimes loosely, with the major topic for the day.

[6] Professors of civic education proposed a curriculum that would examine alternative forms of government (see Hertzberg, 1981). Because they were the least vocal of the three interest groups, social studies was not strongly influenced by their ideas.

Chapter 9

Pointed Noses and Yellow Hair: Deconstructing Children's Writing on Race and Ethnicity in Hawai'i

Julie Lokelani Kaomea

Several months ago a colleague of mine shared with me her sixth-grade students' written responses to an assignment that she had given them. She was preparing for a unit on multicultural literature and planned to use the assignment as a needs assessment to determine where she should begin her instruction. When she devised the assignment, she intended it to be very open ended. She simply listed several different races and ethnicities on a piece of paper and asked her students to honestly express what they know about or how they feel about each of these different groups. For a sample of their responses, see Figures 9.1–9.6 in the following pages.

My initial reactions to these students' responses were conflicted. On one hand, I found myself horrified by some of the students' comments. Several of their remarks contained chillingly negative stereotypes that caused me to look to these children's futures and worry about the racist adults that they will one day grow up to be.

However, on the other hand, I found other comments amusing. Perhaps this reaction was due to some combination of the shaky handwriting, invented spelling, and childish misconceptions that came out in the writing. Whatever the cause, I found at times when reading some of these responses that I couldn't help but crack a smile or laugh out loud. Such responses inevitably brought me back to my own childhood and I found myself laughing knowingly at the children's misguided remarks as I recalled saying similar things when I was young. Inevitably, this type of nostalgic reminiscing led me to conclude that these children's remarks were naive and innocent, and really nothing to be taken seriously.

Now, several months later, I realize that neither of my initial reactions was particularly useful. Both reactions view children as having lacks or deficits in comparison to adults. The horrified reaction constructs children as potential monsters in need of adult guidance and socialization. In a different way, the amused reaction also assumes a great distance between children and adults. This reaction constructs children as incapable of adult reasoning and emotions, and dismisses their responses as pure childish nonsense. Both reactions underestimate children and attach simplistic interpretations to their writing.

After spending several months studying these responses, I now believe that these texts are not as straightforward as they may at first seem, but instead are very rich and complex. In this chapter I suggest that there are more to these texts than initially meets the eye.

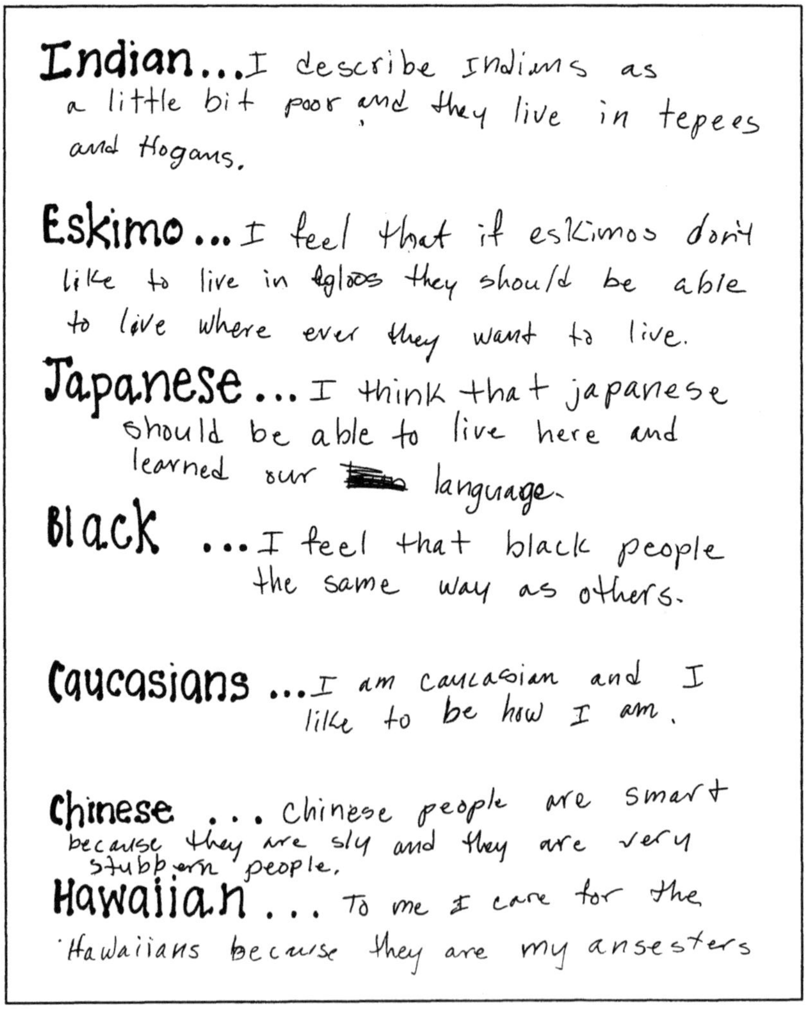

> **Indian**... I describe Indians as a little bit poor and they live in tepees and Hogans.
>
> **Eskimo**... I feel that if eskimos don't like to live in igloos they should be able to live where ever they want to live.
>
> **Japanese**... I think that japanese should be able to live here and learned our language.
>
> **Black** ... I feel that black people the same way as others.
>
> **Caucasians** ... I am caucasian and I like to be how I am.
>
> **Chinese** ... Chinese people are smart because they are sly and they are very stubborn people.
>
> **Hawaiian** ... To me I care for the Hawaiians because they are my ansesters

Figure 9.1: Student response 1.

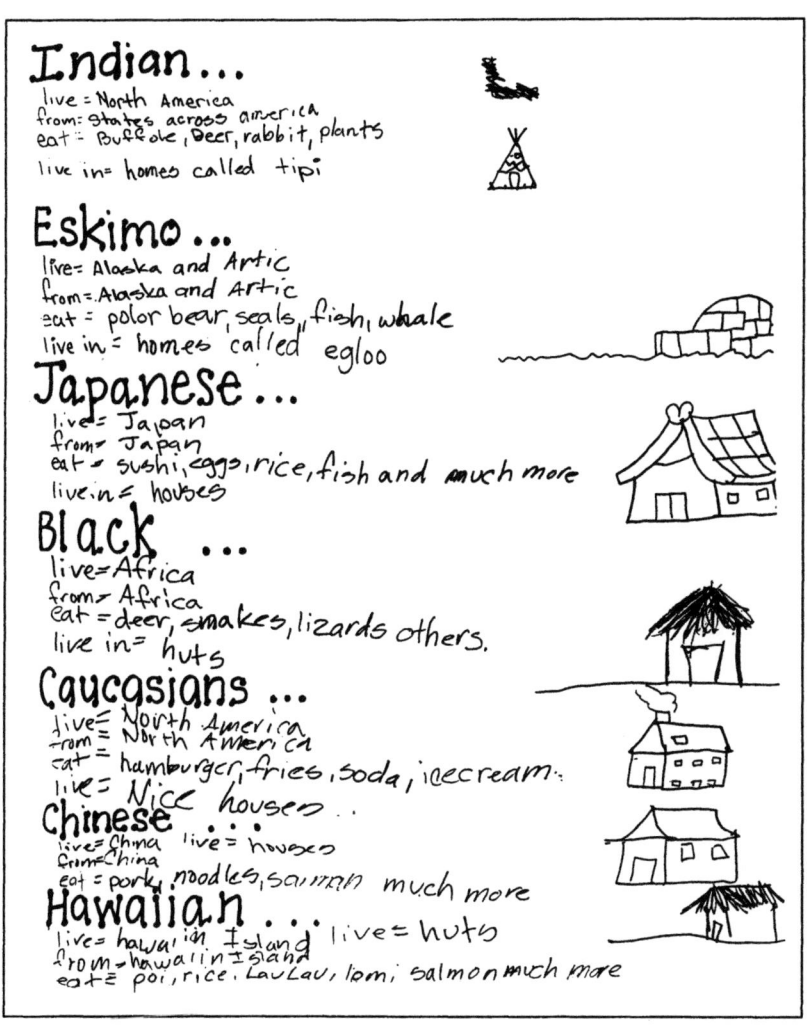

Figure 9.2: Student response 2.

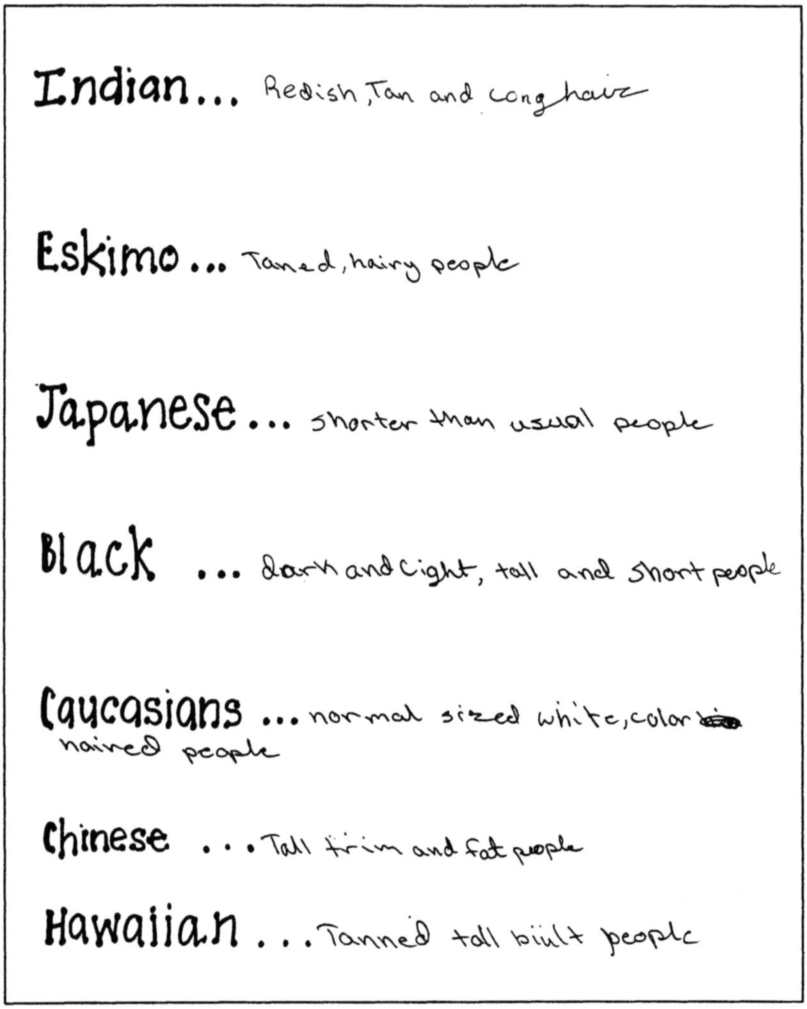

Indian... Redish, Tan and long hair

Eskimo... Tanned, hairy people

Japanese... shorter than usual people

Black ... dark and light, tall and short people

Caucasians ... normal sized white, color haired people

Chinese ... Tall tirim and fat people

Hawaiian... Tanned tall biult people

Figure 9.3: Student response 3.

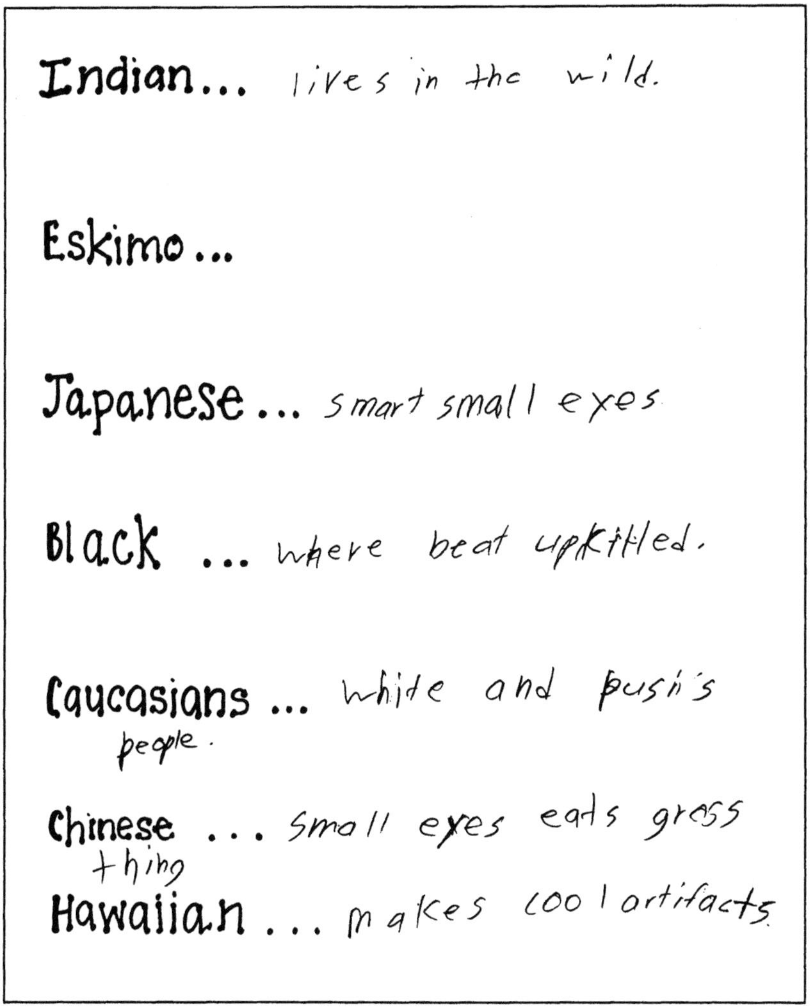

> Indian... lives in the wild.
>
> Eskimo...
>
> Japanese... smart small eyes
>
> Black ... where beat upkitted.
>
> Caucasians ... white and pusn's people.
>
> Chinese ... small eyes eats gross thing
>
> Hawaiian ... makes cool artifacts

Figure 9.4: Student response 4.

> Indian... Indian's look funny by the why they dress.
>
> Eskimo... They look ugly and they are canables.
>
> Japanese... Are bad turst.
>
> Black... Have bushy hair.
>
> Caucasians... Are strange strange people
>
> Chinese... Like to rip off people
>
> Hawaiian... Play nice music

Figure 9.5: Student response 5.

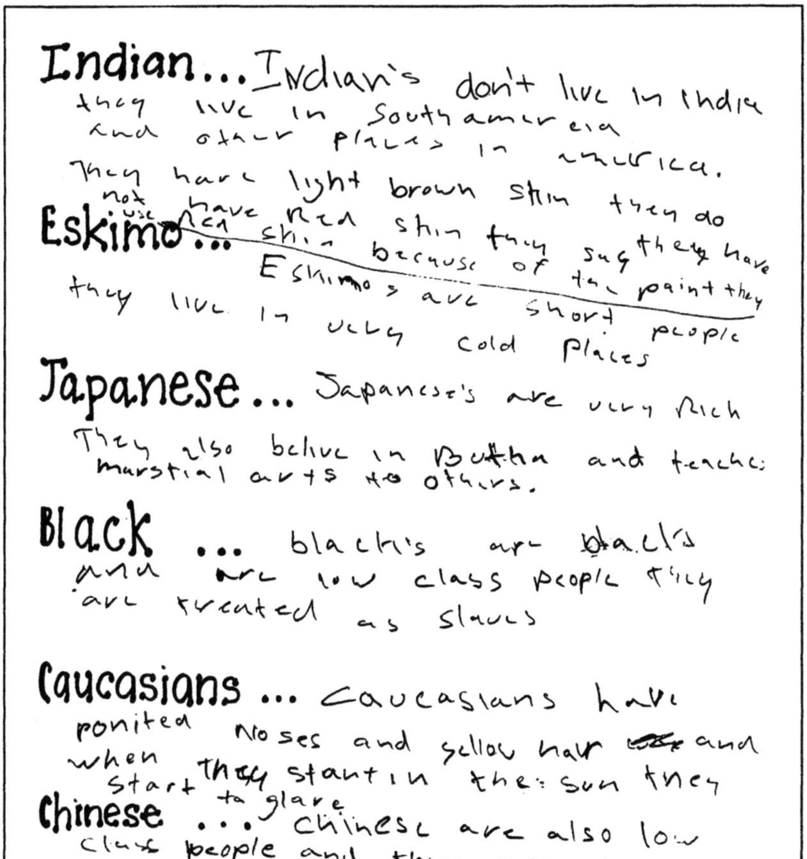

> **Indian...** Indian's don't live in India they live in South America and other places in America. They have light brown skin they do not have red skin they sug— they have red skin because of the paint they use
>
> **Eskimo...** Eskimos are short people they live in very cold places
>
> **Japanese...** Japanese's are very Rich They also believe in Buttha and teaches marstial arts to others.
>
> **Black...** black's are black's and are low class people they are treated as slaves
>
> **Caucasians...** Caucasians have pointed Noses and yellow hair and when they start in the sun they start to glare
>
> **Chinese...** Chinese are also low class people and they are very poor
>
> **Hawaiian...** Hawains are very poor and Nice

Figure 9.6: Student response 6.

This chapter takes you through the process that I went through over a period of months as I sought to make sense of these texts. It does this by focusing on particular points in the text that literary deconstructionists would refer to as aporia (Derrida, 1976). These are points in the text that open up doubts or contradictory readings. Aporia can be thought of as sites in a text that you might initially overlook or dismiss as uninteresting, but if you continue to study and tug at them you'll find that your initial reading begins to unravel and a slippage of meaning appears. For each of these aporia I explain my initial reading of the response and then show how this reading gradually unraveled or deconstructed, leaving me to question my earlier understanding.

While much has already been written on children's developing notions of ethnic prejudice and stereotypes (see Aboud, 1988), this study is unique in that it demonstrates how poststructural tools of analysis can give us a fresh perspective on this old educational problem. The majority of research in this area has typically been dominated by the perspectives of experimental psychology (Aboud, 1993; Bigler & Liben, 1993; Powlishta, Serbin, Doyle, & White, 1994). In contrast, the method of analysis for this particular study draws largely from the fields of literary studies and critical theory. Following in the tradition of Joseph Tobin (1995), this chapter applies interpretive techniques borrowed from literary and critical theory to the analysis of the writing of young children. It aims to study the words of these elementary school students with the same care and analytical respect with which a literary critic would study a canonical text.

My methodological analysis follows from an underlying assumption that meanings are often more complex than they at first seem and that there is often much more to a text (be it a great work or a child's response to a teacher's queries) than what appears on the surface. Drawing from Derrida's (1976) work in literary deconstruction, I use tools of literary and critical theory to move beyond the surface meanings of these texts in an effort to achieve a deeper level of understanding. I use Derrida's (1976) notion of aporia to focus on sites where the apparent coherence of the texts comes apart, and I apply Foucault's (1972) method of discourse genealogy, along with new historicism's technique of pairing a text with an unlikely partner from another genre, to denaturalize the children's stereotypical responses about various ethnic groups and expose their colonial, natural-historical, and anthropological underpinnings.

Kauʻi's Response: Facts and Figures or Field Guide?

I begin my analysis by taking another look at the response reproduced in Figure 9.2. This response was written by a girl named Kauʻi who identifies herself as part Hawaiian, part Chinese, and part Portuguese. It was a response that I had overlooked on my first few readings. Finding Kauʻi's comments to be objective, impersonal, and uninteresting, I dismissed them as a mere teacher-pleasing, formulaic student response.

The format of this response initially reminded me of a Facts and Figures chart that one would find at the beginning of an encyclopedic entry on a given country. For example, consider the following *Facts and Figures* chart that precedes *The New Book of Knowledge* (1992) entry on Japan (see Figure 9.7). In a format similar to Kauʻi's, the chart objectively describes Japan's location, its population, its capital city, and so forth.

While I initially considered Kauʻi's response to be of the *Facts and Figures* variety, as I looked more closely at the categories used in her response, I realized that it actually bears an even keener likeness to the type of classification system used to distinguish between different species of animals. In many ways Kauʻi's response resembles a chart that you might find in a field guide to mammals or birds.

To illustrate my point, in Figure 9.8 you will find a page taken from a children's field guide to endangered birds. While it is readily apparent that Kauʻi's response (in Figure 9.2) and the field guide page (in Figure 9.8) are strikingly similar in their general format and organization (virtually mirror images of one another), a closer look at the specific entries suggests further similarities in terms of the particular features discussed. For instance in Figure 9.9 we see that the Black and the Bali Mynah are both described in terms of where they live and where they're from (or their range), what they eat (or their diet), and what they live in (or their habitat).

It may seem odd for me to suggest that Kauʻi is somehow using a classification system that is typically used to distinguish between different species of animals to describe different races or ethnicities of people. But actually, this type of practice has been in use in Western cultures for over 200 years, since the beginning of the field of natural history.

FACTS AND FIGURES

JAPAN is the official name of the country. Its people call it Nippon or Nihon, meaning "base of the sun."

THE PEOPLE are known as Japanese.

LOCATION: Islands off the eastern coast of Asia.

AREA: 145,834 sq mi (377,708 km^2).

POPULATION: 121,500,000 (estimate).

CAPITAL AND LARGEST CITY: Tokyo.

MAJOR LANGUAGE: Japanese.

MAJOR RELIGIONS: Shinto, Buddhism.

GOVERNMENT: Constitutional monarchy. **Head of state**—emperor. **Head of government**—prime minister. **Legislature**—National Diet (consisting of the House of Councillors and the House of Representatives).

CHIEF PRODUCTS: Agricultural—rice, potatoes, wheat, barley, sweet potatoes, soybeans, tangerines and other fruits, tea, raw silk, livestock. **Manufactured**—iron and steel, motor vehicles, electrical machinery, ships, chemicals, textiles, electronic equipment, high-technology products (including computers and microchips), medicines. **Mineral**—coal, copper, lead.

MONETARY UNIT: Yen.

NATIONAL ANTHEM: *Kimigayo* ("The Reign of our Emperor").

Figure 9.7: Facts and Figures chart from an encyclopedic entry on Japan. From *The New Book of Knowledge*, 1992 Edition. Copyright 1992 by Grolier Incorporated. Reprinted by permission.

Natural History in the Eighteenth Century

The field of natural history began in the eighteenth century as a part of a project of the Enlightenment period. During this time of voyage and discovery the Europeans sought to describe, name, and classify every natural phenomenon that they encountered across remote areas of the globe. While the most obvious goal of voyages of conquest and discovery was to claim for the Crown lands and people, another closely related goal was to control information about these places (Tobin, 1996). Natural history was one means of achieving this latter end. Natural history classifications provided European voyagers with a method for naming and classifying each phenomenon that it encountered and locating it on a hierarchical grid.

According to the influential taxonomic system first developed by Swedish naturalist Carl Linne (also known as Carolus Linnaeus), every plant and animal could be identified and classified if specific attention was given to certain observable, typifying traits. In Linnaean botany, this system of classification focused on the number of pistils and stamens in a plant, and the shape and distribution of its flowers, leaves, and fruits (Regis, 1992). By focusing on these particular surface features one could determine the appropriate binomial label for the plant which designated both its unique species and its link to the Great Chain of Being. All other features of the plant, such as its inner workings or the climatic conditions it needs to survive, were dismissed as secondary to the effort to master the names of all forms of plants and obtain a comprehensive view of their place in the whole (Regis, 1992).

Linne also included man in his taxonomic system. According to Linnaean nomenclature, man resides at the top of the animal kingdom in close proximity to the ape. Regis (1992) argues that the lack of a boundary between *homo sapiens europaeus* and the apes was an unsettling idea for eighteenth-century Europeans, and spurred them to discover other inferior races or species of man that could "buffer" them from this "unpleasant propinquity to beasts." Thus, in addition to plants and animals, men also became objects of natural history scrutiny.

Bali Mynah
Leucospar rothschildi

Range: Bali, Indonesia
Habitat: Tropical forest
Diet: Fruit and insects
Size: 10–11 in. (25–27.5 cm) long
Reproduction: Average clutch: 2–4 eggs; incubation: 3 weeks
Threats: Habitat destruction and the pet trade

Least Tern
Sterna antillarum

Range: Coastal United States and interior river systems
Habitat: Open sandy areas along shores
Diet: Fish, aquatic invertebrates
Size: 8–9 in. (20–22.5 cm) long
Reproduction: Average clutch: 2–3 eggs; incubation: 20 days
Threats: Channelization, river damage, disruption of nesting sites, predation

Red-Cockaded Woodpecker
Picoides borealis

Range: Southeast United States
Habitat: Old-growth pine stands and open pine woodlands
Diet: Wood-boring insects
Size: 8–9 in. (20–22.5 cm) long
Reproduction: Average clutch: 2–5 eggs; incubation: 10–15 days
Threats: Habitat destruction

Figure 9.8: A page from a children's field guide to endangered birds.
From *Saving Endangered Birds* (p. 54), by T. Maynard, 1993, New York: Franklin Watts. Photographs by Ron Austing (top), Lawrence Wales (center), and Todd Engstrom (bottom). Copyright 1993 by the Zoological Society of Cincinnati, Inc. Reprinted by permission.

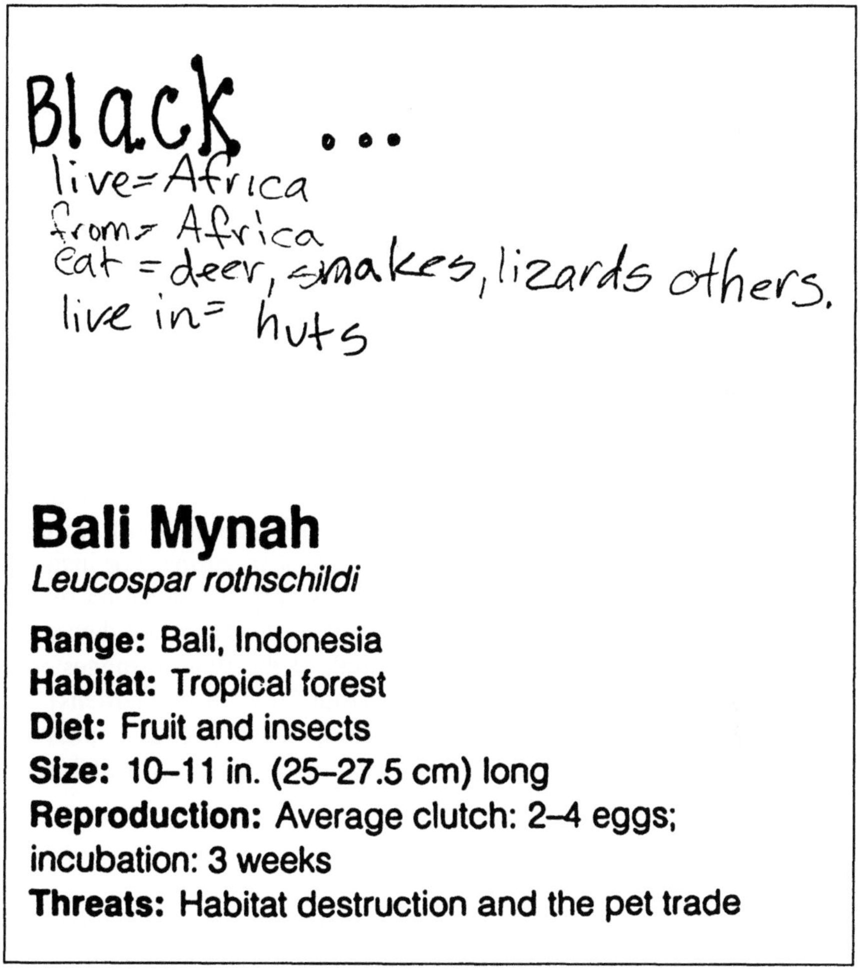

> Black...
> live = Africa
> from = Africa
> eat = deer, ~~snakes~~, lizards others.
> live in = huts

Bali Mynah
Leucospar rothschildi

Range: Bali, Indonesia
Habitat: Tropical forest
Diet: Fruit and insects
Size: 10–11 in. (25–27.5 cm) long
Reproduction: Average clutch: 2–4 eggs; incubation: 3 weeks
Threats: Habitat destruction and the pet trade

Figure 9.9: Close-up comparison of Kau'i's description of blacks and the children's field guide description of Bali Mynahs. From *Saving Endangered Birds* (p. 54), by T. Maynard, 1993, New York: Franklin Watts. Copyright 1993 by the Zoological Society of Cincinnati, Inc. Reprinted by permission.

The methods of exploration and description applied to the non-European man were similar to those applied to plants. Observers learned to recognize each group by a set of characteristics that are by definition shared with other individuals of the group, while overlooking qualities of particular individuals. Such depictions typically described non-European peoples in terms of various surface features such as their clothing, racial characteristics, dwellings, and diet (Regis, 1992). These features were then qualitatively compared and used to develop an ordered hierarchy of civilizations. The resulting European view of humankind arranged people of the world hierarchically, with Caucasians at the top, Asians next, then Native Americans, and Africans at the bottom (King, 1981).

Beth Fowkes Tobin (1996) argues that eighteenth-century British botany was part of a larger colonial discourse whose goal was to insist that there was only one legitimate order to the universe, and that this order was best understood by Europeans who were adept in managing this taxonomic system. She further contends that the Linnaean system of classification served imperial ambitions by encouraging British botanists to focus on those parts of the plant that would make possible its removal from its local environment and aid in its transfer and reproduction elsewhere. A similar argument could be made about proto-anthropological studies that also classified native peoples in terms of various features considered necessary for their transportation from place to place as slaves, laborers, servants, or European curios. For instance, while overseeing an eighteenth-century mass crop translocation project aimed at transferring breadfruit from Tahiti to the hurricane-devastated British West Indies, Admiral William Bligh of the Bounty suggested in his correspondence with Joseph Banks (founder of Kew Gardens) that because Polynesia, and in particular Tahiti, had a surplus population, they should consider sending some Polynesians to Australia, which at the time was empty (Mackaness, 1931).

Natural History Today
While the field of natural history was in its heyday in the eighteenth century, it would be misleading to suggest that it was restricted to that time period. In fact, the field of natural history has become a pervasive discourse that still holds great influence today. Foucault (1970) uses the term "discourse" to refer to the writings and dominant ideas of a specialized field of knowledge. He argues that these specialized or technical fields have had ever-increasing power over people, and their discourses have profoundly shaped the structure of our society. Similarly, I argue that this eighteenth-century natural history discourse still has significant influence over the way many groups of people are described and classified today.

For instance, consider the "Polar Eskimo" display case at the National Museum of Natural History in Washington, D.C. One in a series of exhibits devoted to America's native peoples, it consists of a painted background of an igloo built on an ice shelf with five dark-haired, brown-skinned mannequins dressed in fur parkas and mukluks standing in the forefront. The three adults and two children are accompanied by five stuffed sled dogs. The object of attention of both humans and canines is a small stuffed seal lying next to a hole painted on the bottom of the floor of the display case. The lifeless seal remains attached to the hands of one of the adults by a sturdy fishing line as the onlookers inspect this catch of the day (Regis, 1992). Typical of manner-and-customs descriptions of the natural history era, this display is static, frozen, and concerned strictly with the surfaces of people—their clothing, racial characteristics, dwellings, and diet (Regis, 1992).

Similar limitations are also evident in Kau'i's response (illustrated in Figure 9.2), which objectifies and typifies each group according to a set of predetermined surface characteristics and provides no room for individual differences, changes over time, or Kau'i's own personal comments and connections. While the author of this response, as I mentioned earlier, identifies herself as part Hawaiian, part Chinese, and part Portuguese, she makes no mention of this in her writing.

The Denial of Mixed-Race People

Oddly, Kau'i's response strangely depicts each group of people as still living in their place of origin. According to Kau'i, blacks live only in Africa (where they eat snakes and lizards), Hawaiians live exclusively in Hawai'i (where they eat *lomi* salmon and *poi*), Chinese live in China (where they eat pork and noodles), and so forth. Her response makes no allowance for migration or intermarriage between the groups, and implicitly denies her own existence as well as the existence of any person of mixed racial or ethnic heritage.

These features of Kau'i's response echo the denial of mixed-race people that has existed since the beginning of the eighteenth century. Spickard (1992) contends that the most important thing about races has always been the boundaries between them. If races were pure (or had once been), and if one were a member of the race at the top, then it was essential to maintain the boundaries that defined one's superiority, to keep people from the lower categories from "slipping surreptitiously upward" (Spickard, 1992).

Throughout history two basic strategies have been used to keep racial categories distinct and well defined (Nakashima, 1992). The first strategy was to discourage intermarriage and interbreeding through anti-miscegenation laws based upon the pseudoscientific argument that it is unnatural to mix the races (as it is unnatural to mix different species of animals). According to this argument, intermarriage "lowers" the biologically superior white race and produces people who are not only physically, morally, and mentally weak, but who are also forever tormented by their genetically divided selves.

The second strategy for keeping racial categories distinct was to flatly deny the existence of multiracial people through rules that rigidly forced multiracial individuals into one of the existing monoracial categories. The rule most typically followed in colonial America was the hypodescent or "one drop" rule that determined that all multiracial people should be regarded according to the most subordinate of their racial groups. According to this rule a person with one black ancestor (or "one drop of black blood") was defined as black, regardless of the proportion of black ancestry or the person's physical appearance (Davis, 1995). Through these rules of hypodescent the superordinate racial group is kept clearly defined and in complete political, economic, and social power (Omi & Winant, 1986).

Davis (1995) argues that Hawai'i may be the one place in America where this monoracial hegemony does not exist. He explains that racially and ethnically mixed people currently comprise the largest segment of Hawai'i's population (approximately one-third), and suggests that rather than being assigned membership in any one parent group, these people are perceived and respected as persons with roots in two or more ancestral groups. According to Davis, the *hapa* (or mixed) population in Hawai'i is increasing at such a rapid rate that ethnically and racially unmixed persons will be rare in a few more generations. In fact, Kau'i herself is one of these many *hapa* children. However, the familiar denial of multiracial people still lingers on in her response.

On Dwellings and Diet: A Hierarchy of Civilization
Another feature of Kau'i's response that is also typical of natural history classifications is the hierarchy of civilization that is implicit in her descriptions. Like the natural history museum's exhibit of the "Polar

Eskimo," Kauʻi's descriptions serve to reify some of the more indigenous cultures by freezing them in earlier times and causing them to look quite primitive in comparison to modern-day Asians and Caucasians. This dichotomizing of primitive and civilized can be seen in Kauʻi's descriptions of the shelters and eating habits of these various groups. Kauʻi's drawings and comments on the different living quarters of Indians, Eskimos, blacks, and Hawaiians depict these groups as living in "tipis," igloos, and huts—small, temporary shelters that offer minimal protection from the elements. In contrast to these more "primitive" groups, the Japanese, Chinese, and Caucasians are depicted as more advanced in gaining mastery over their environment. The Japanese and Chinese are described as living in more protective and more permanent "houses," while the Caucasians live in "nice (colonial style) houses" with two stories of rooms and a fireplace to regulate the interior temperature.

The dwellings of indigenous people have historically provided a basis of comparison for natural history comments on the progress of various civilizations. In *Observations Made during a Voyage Round the World*, a natural history account based on Forster's participation in Captain Cook's second nautical voyage, Forster (1996) draws a contrast between "comfortable European house(s)" and the "wretched hut(s)" of the "savages" of Tierra Del Fuego. He uses the Tierra Del Fuegians' "lack of civilization" (their nomadic type lifestyle of hunting and gathering) as an explanation for their "wretched hovels." He argues that their "rambling way of life in quest of food" obliges them to change their abode as often as the game becomes scarce and makes it not worth their while to build neat, large, and convenient houses. Instead, in every new place to which they move they erect temporary huts, just sufficient to screen them from the keen winds and frequent showers of rain, snow, and hail.

While Forster's descriptions of the Tierra Del Fuegians were written over 200 years ago, they are in many ways quite similar to Kauʻi's contemporary descriptions of Indians, Eskimos, blacks, and Hawaiians. By freezing these groups in this earlier time frame, Kauʻi implies that these people, like the Tierra Del Fuegians of long ago, continue to live as nomadic "savages, just removed one degree from animality" (Forster, 1996).

The Raw and the Cooked
In addition to studying the living quarters of various civilizations, Forster and other natural historians (Forster, 1996) also classified people

according to their methods of food procurement and preparation. Forster's (1996) chapter on "Remarks on the Human Species in the South Sea Isles" includes an entire section dedicated exclusively to "Food, and the Method of Procuring It." Many anthropologists and natural historians alike argue that what really separates people from animals is that animals eat raw foods while people eat cooked foods. Levi-Strauss (1970) highlights the salience of this difference between the raw and the cooked:

> Unlike the deer, the Tarahumara does not eat grass, but he interposes between the grass and his animal hunger a complicated cultural cycle involving the care and the use of domestic animals. . . . Nor like the coyote does the Tarahumara avail himself of meat torn from a scarcely dead animal and eaten raw. The Tarahumara interposes between his meat and his hunger a cultural system of cooking. (Zingg, 1942, p. 82)

Kau'i makes a similar distinction in her own response. According to Kau'i, Japanese, Chinese, and Caucasians eat prepared foods like sushi, noodles and hamburgers, while Indians, Eskimos, and blacks subsist on a diet of plants, deer, seals, and lizards. By neglecting to mention any method of cooking or food preparation when describing the diet of the latter groups, Kau'i seems to be suggesting that these groups, like animals, eat their foods raw.

When taken together, Kau'i's descriptions of the shelters and eating habits of these different groups imply a hierarchy of sophistication or civilization that is quite typical of natural history classifications. According to Kau'i's taxonomy, blacks, Indians, Eskimos, and Hawaiians (with their temporary, primitive shelters and/or unprepared foods) assume a position at the bottom of the hierarchy; the Japanese and Chinese (with their sturdy, permanent houses and prepared foods) occupy the middle tier; and Caucasians (with their two-story colonial homes and extremely processed foods) reign at the top.

Kau'i's implicit taxonomy closely resembles the previously mentioned eighteenth-century European hierarchy of civilizations which placed the Africans at the bottom (closest to the apes), the Native Americans one step above, the Asians next, and the Caucasians at the pinnacle (Spickard, 1992). While participating in this type of proto-anthropological classification of people, Kau'i's response can be seen to comply with the natural history assumptions that these groupings are fixed, natural, and timeless categories, while simultaneously denying the fact that all cultures are continually interacting and changing. She reifies the Indians, Eskimos, blacks, and Hawaiians in a more primitive time and thereby sentences them to the lowest positions on the civilization hierarchy.

Skin Color, Hair Type, and Other Identifying Traits

Several other students' responses are also influenced by this natural history classification system. One other example can be found in Figure 9.3. This response was written by a young man named Edward who identifies himself as Japanese, Chinese, Hawaiian, German, Portuguese, and Indian. In his response Edward focuses strictly on describing people by highlighting certain identifying or paradigmatic traits. In the same way that a field guide to birds can help us identify a particular species by directing our attention to the color of the bird's crest or the shape of its bill, Edward's response suggests that we can distinguish between people of different races or ethnicities if we simply focus on the color of their skin, the color of their hair, and the shape and size of their bodies.

This typological view of races was actually quite common in the nineteenth century when races were seen as distinct types. According to this paradigm, there were supposedly, at some time in the past, four or five utterly distinct and pure races, with physical features, gene pools, and character qualities that diverged entirely one from another (Spickard, 1992). While over the millennia there may have been some mixing at the margins, successors in this tradition contend that an observer can still distinguish a Caucasian type (with light skin, blue eyes, fine sandy hair, a high-bridged nose, and thin lips) from a Negroid type (with dark brown skin, brown eyes, tightly curled black hair, a broad flat nose, and thick lips) or an Asian type and so on. Although scientists have begun to take exception to this typological view of races by arguing that the genetic variability within supposed racial populations is greater than the variability between them (King, 1981), these ideas are still in common circulation and continue to hold great influence today. For instance, consider the following summary of the "Colour of Skin" map found in the 1982 edition of the Bartholomew *World Atlas*.

Light Skin Color (Leocodermi)
  Indo-European: White skin, straight to wavy hair
  Indo-European: Light brown skin, wavy hair

Hamitic-Semitic: Reddish brown skin, wavy hair
   Polynesian: Light brown skin, wavy hair
Yellow Skin Color (Xanthodermi)
   Asiatic or Mongolian: Yellow skin, straight hair
   Indonesian: Yellow brown skin, straight hair
   American Indian: Reddish yellow skin, straight hair
Dark Skin Color (Melanodermi)
   African Negro: Dark brown skin, kinky hair
   Pigmy Negro: Brown skin, kinky hair
   Melanesian: Dark brown skin, kinky hair
   Australo-Dravidian: Brown to black skin, wavy to kinky hair

In a format quite similar to Edward's, the map divides people of the world by skin color and hair type. According to the map, Indo-Europeans have "white (or "light brown") skin" and "straight to wavy hair," while American Indians have "reddish yellow skin" and "straight hair." When read alongside Edward's descriptions of "white color hair(ed)" Caucasians and "redish tan, long hair(ed)" Indians, these superficial, typological descriptions begin to sound quite familiar.

Ideal Types and Caucasian Normativity
Another interesting feature of Edward's response is that it once again suggests an implicit hierarchy which presents Caucasians as the ideal type or the assumed standard to which all other groups should be compared. Edward describes Caucasians as being "normal sized, white color haired people," and Japanese as being "shorter than usual (Caucasian) people." Even when he avoids such direct comparisons, the relative terms that he uses (tall, short, fat, trim, dark, light) all imply a certain Caucasian standard.

Once again a look into history suggests that Edward's implicit hierarchy is not at all surprising. As was suggested earlier, one of the essential features of this typological view of races was that it made it possible for European colonizers to arrange people of the world hierarchically. There were actually two ways of conceiving this hierarchy, depending on which side of the Darwinian divide one inhabited (King, 1981). Pre-Darwinians thought of Adam and Eve as Caucasians, with Asians, Africans, and Native Americans representing degenerated descendants in separate lines. Post-Darwinians who embraced the evolutionary view conceived of the human races as part of a continuum of ever-improving species and races, with great apes succeeded by chimpanzees, then by Africans, Asians, and Caucasians. According to both views Caucasians were seen as the ideal race, the most complex and perfect of nature's products.

Remnants of this perspective remain with us today. One such example is the "Cephalic Index" map in the same 1982 edition of the Bartholomew *World Atlas*. This map classifies people of the world according to the ratio of the breadth of the head to its length:

Dolichocephalic (Long-headed)	Primarily the peoples of Africa, Arabia, India, and Australia
Mesocephalic (Medium-headed)	Northwest Europe, North America, China, Japan, Persia
Brachycephalic (Broad-headed)	Rest of Europe, Latin America, rest of Asia
Hyperbrachycephalic (Very broad-headed)	Russia

While it is not entirely clear what exactly these mapmakers imagined they were measuring by this process, it is quite apparent that the classification is based upon an underlying assumption of Caucasian normality. Once again the northwestern Europeans and the North Americans are the implicit norm to which all other groups are compared. People with cephalic dimensions similar to these "normal" groups are classified as "medium-headed," while those with heads that happen to be thinner or wider than this arbitrary ideal are classified as "long-headed" or "broad-headed" (or "very broad-headed"), respectively. While this classification system may seem scientific and objective on the surface, it is actually extremely subjective and is based upon old, familiar notions of Caucasian superiority.

While I initially interpreted Kau'i and Edward's responses as evidence of deficits that these particular students have in their understandings of race and ethnicity, I now view them instead as evidence of the pervasive power of this natural history discourse and classification system. The dominant assumptions of this discourse reach children through school books such as encyclopedias and atlases, through many well-intended multicultural units of study, and through assignments such as the one I am analyzing here. When faced with these arbitrary categories and asked to write down everything one knows about these types of people in such a small space, a student is almost forced to treat the categories as natural and respond with typifying traits that emphasize within group similarities and between group differences.

Artifacts, Ancestors, and Hawaiians of Old

Once I realized that some of these students' responses may have been influenced by the dominant ideas of this natural history discourse, other lines that I previously had overlooked began to take on new meaning for me. For example, take another look at Figure 9.4, written by Jonathan who is Hawaiian, Chinese, Portuguese, German, and English. The final comment of Jonathan's response reads: "Hawaiian makes cool artifacts."

After passing over this line several times, it suddenly struck me that the word "artifacts" is an unusual word for a child of this age to use. It isn't a typical part of most elementary students' everyday vocabularies. However, the more I studied the line, the more I realized that there was something else odd about it, and that was the tense in which it is written. Why a present tense verb ("makes") with a direct object ("artifacts") which implies something made in the past?

There are several different ways in which we could read this phrase. "Hawaiian makes cool artifacts" could be read deconstructively as a sentence with an inherent tension or contradiction (makes/artifacts) which collapses in or breaks apart on its own, suggesting a fundamental social tension. According to this deconstructive reading, the phrase can be taken to reveal a deep social tension surrounding the Hawaiian people's struggle to live in the present. "Hawaiian makes cool artifacts" could also be read as suggesting that Hawaiians now produce artifacts for the tourist industry, or that they themselves are living artifacts.

Yet another way to read the phrase would be to treat it as if it were intended to read "Hawaiians made cool artifacts." In this case, the phrase would be disturbing in a different way. "Hawaiians made cool artifacts" makes no mistake about being situated in the past. It clearly harks back to times of long ago and thereby presents the Hawaiian race as a people already gone or extinct.

This comment on Hawaiian artifacts made me reconsider another response that I had overlooked initially—the response reproduced in Figure 9.1. The final comment on this page reads: "To me I care for the Hawaiians because they are my ancestors."

When I first read this response, I was optimistic about it. I viewed it as one of those rare occasions in which a child was actually making personal connections between the assignment categories and her own life situation. However, as I studied the response more closely, my initial reading of it gradually began to unravel.

I was first drawn to look more carefully at the line, when I once again noticed something odd about it—the word "ancestors" (like the word "artifacts") is not a word commonly used by most elementary school children. As I then pondered the child's choice of words, I began to ask myself: If this child was really making personal connections with these categories, as I had originally hypothesized, why would she choose to speak of her *ancestors*?

When commenting on Caucasians, she writes, "I am Caucasian and I like to be how I am." Why then when commenting on Hawaiians does she speak of generations so far removed? If this child has Hawaiian ancestors, then she is Hawaiian herself, and quite likely has at least one Hawaiian parent, grandparent, uncle or aunt, brother, sister, or cousin. However, none of this is ever mentioned in her response. Instead of focusing on Hawaiians she knows of today, she chooses to focus on Hawaiians of a more remote or primitive time.

The Primitivist Discourse

These students' comments on Hawaiian artifacts and ancestors are reminiscent of Kau'i's natural history description in which she depicts Hawaiians as living in grass huts and subsisting on traditional foods such as *poi, laulau,* and *lomilomi* salmon. Again, while such responses may be expected of children living in the United States mainland, they are particularly surprising when coming from Hawaiian children living in the state of Hawai'i. Instead of commenting on their own experiences as contemporary Hawaiians, these students seem to be articulating dominant Western views of Hawaiians and participating in a discourse of native Hawaiian primitivism.

Primitivism is closely intertwined with the natural history discourse that was discussed earlier. It constructs natives of non-European lands as static or frozen in some earlier, primitive time and places them in an antithetical relationship to modernity (Thomas, 1994). According to Torgovnick (1990), the primitivist discourse has long been a discourse fundamental to the Western sense of self and Other. In colonial times Europeans used this discourse to distinguish themselves from other "primitive" cultures in order to justify their dominance over these "backwards" people. If the colonizers viewed themselves as civilized, the primitive was viewed as savage. If they considered themselves to be rightly Christian, the primitive was considered heathen. While many of these "primitive" civilizations have experienced tremendous changes over the past 200 years, the dominant assumptions about them have not. To this day, Westerners still continue to construct and use the image of the primitive for their own ends.

Preserved in some earlier time, the primitive continues to function as the embodiment of everything the Westerner is not. According to this discourse, primitives will always be the white man's past persisting in the present. Primitives exist at the "lowest cultural levels" while the Westerners occupy the "highest." Primitives are the Westerners' untamed selves, their ids—libidinous, irrational, violent, dangerous, but also free, mystical, and in tune with nature.

Similar primitivist tropes were found among several other students' descriptions of native Hawaiians. Many of these students, Hawaiians and non-Hawaiians alike, described Hawaiians as exotic, nature-loving primitives, and ignored the fact that these descriptions are inconsistent with the conditions of the many Hawaiians that they know today. Generally, these students portrayed Hawaiians as "old people" who "use herd [herbs] and other nature to eat and make clothes" and "who know how to survive in the wild."

While I was originally shocked by these students' seemingly misguided remarks, I later began to realize that their comments are actually a direct reflection of our schools' Hawaiian studies curriculum which is largely influenced by this type of primitivist discourse. Developed in response to a 1978 state constitutional amendment requiring Hawai'i's public school system to promote the study of Hawaiian culture, history, and language, our state's Hawaiian studies program provides Hawaiian studies instruction for all of Hawai'i's public school children from kindergarten through grade 12. The Hawaiian studies taught at the elementary level typically focuses on Hawaiians of old, or Hawaiians as they are depicted in Hawaiian history and legends. Rarely in the curriculum is there ever any mention of contemporary Hawaiians.

Typical books used in our elementary school Hawaiian studies curriculum include Caroline Curtis's (1970) *Life in Old Hawai'i*, Betty Dunford's (1980) *The Hawaiians of Old*, and Dorothy Hazama's (1974)

The Ancient Hawaiians. These outdated books are supplemented by weekly visits from *kūpuna* or elders in the Hawaiian community who are brought in to share with the children Hawaiian stories of days long passed. In essence, these *kūpuna* are viewed as the embodiment of ancient Hawai'i—the last living specimens of a dying civilization. These Hawaiians are not valued for their ability to comment on contemporary situations facing Hawaiians of today, but instead are valued as a link to an exotic past.

In this respect, then, I suppose the students' primitivist descriptions of Hawaiians are actually not at all surprising. After all, when our curriculum is built around outdated books depicting the experiences of pre-contact Hawaiians and the earliest memories of the oldest Hawaiians around, what else can we expect? These students' shocking remarks are actually the natural result of yet another colonial discourse that continues to have significant influence on both contemporary society and our school curriculum alike.

Caucasians Are Strange, Strange People

While many of these students seemed to replicate dominant Western views by defining Caucasians as the familiar, ideal type to be contrasted with the exotic, primitive Hawaiian type, there were also incidents in which students overturned this racial hierarchy by making the familiar (Caucasian) seem exotic and the exotic (Hawaiian) seem familiar. For one such example let's now turn our attention to Figure 9.5. This response was written by a young man named Chris. Chris is part Japanese, part Chinese, and part German.

As I'm sure you may have noticed, Chris's response is filled with stereotypical remarks that are brief, unequivocal, and chillingly negative. He is able to sum up each race or ethnicity in eight words or less and really has nothing positive to say about anyone, except maybe the Hawaiians, who he says "play nice music." Chris says Eskimos "look ugly and they are canables," Japanese "are bad turst [tourists]," and Caucasians "are strange, strange people."

The Uncanny

While at one level I was disturbed by Chris's comments, at another level, something about his response struck me as uncanny. Freud (1958) uses the term "uncanny" to refer to something that is simultaneously both strange and familiar. He suggests that the eerie feeling that accompanies the uncanny is the result of the reappearance of something that previously has been repressed.

The part of Chris's response that seemed uncanny to me was the line about Caucasians. On one hand, the line struck me as strange. The phrasing seems un-childlike. I found myself wondering why Chris chose to repeat the adjective and say, "Caucasians are strange, strange people," when perhaps to say, "Caucasians are strange people" would have sufficed. On the other hand, however, the phrase seemed familiar. It had a catchy poetic ring to it, and I had a nagging feeling that I heard it somewhere before.

As I said the phrase over and over in my mind, it then came to me that I indeed had heard it before. It was part of a catchy tune performed by one of Hawai'i's local comedians, Frank DeLima. DeLima is a popular and controversial comedian in Hawai'i whose repertoire focuses almost exclusively on racial jokes, impersonations, and gag songs. While some understandably feel that DeLima's ethnic humor is in bad taste, he argues that he is an equal opportunity comedian, one who makes fun of all ethnicities equally.

DeLima's recently published joke book (DeLima, 1991b) is unashamedly divided into chapters by ethnicity. The first chapter, entitled "Da Portagee," consists of over 100 jokes that teasingly present Portuguese as intellectually challenged, smelly, and overly talkative. The second chapter, entitled "Da Blallah & Da Tidah" (translated: The Hawaiian Male and The Hawaiian Female), pokes fun at Hawaiians, and the third chapter (entitled "Da Buddha Head") takes on the Japanese, and so on.

The chapter on "The Haole" (or The Caucasian) opens with the following lyrics to DeLima's popular song entitled "Caucasians Are Strange People" which he sings to the tune of "Short People" recorded by Randy Newman in 1978:

> Caucasians are strange people
> Caucasians are strange, strange people
> Caucasians are not like you and me
> They got pointed noses and yellow hair
> When they stand in the sun they start to glare
> They name their daughters Sue and their sons Brad
> They got funny little expressions like "egad"
> Don't want no Caucasians, don't want no Caucasians
> Don't want no Caucasians around here (DeLima, 1991, p. 85).

After reading through the different chapters of DeLima's joke book and listening to his most recent audiotape (DeLima, 1991a), Chris's remarks about "strange, strange people," his comments on Japanese tourists and Chinese businessmen, and the "pointed noses and yellow hair" comment from another student's response reproduced in Figure 9.6, all began to have a familiar ring.

When viewed from this perspective, the apparent coherence of Chris's text begins to unravel or deconstruct before our eyes, leaving us unsure of how to interpret it. Once we realize that many of Chris's phrases have quite likely been appropriated from ethnic joke comedians like Frank DeLima, we are left to wonder what to make of all of this.

The Carnivalesque
While some may argue that Chris's use of DeLima's words is evidence of how a child can be interpellated into racism by a racist adult, others might contend that DeLima and Chris are not necessarily racist, but instead are challenging the expected forms of behavior and acting in ways that are consistent with Bakhtin's (1984) description of the carnivalesque. Bakhtin describes the world of the carnival in the middle ages as a time when all rank, privileges, norms, and prohibitions were suspended and participants enjoyed a temporary liberation from the prevailing truth of the established order. It was a time when authority was temporarily resisted and the status quo decentralized, all in the spirit of laughter. Guha (1983) contends that such ritual inversions continue to exist in various socially stratified societies throughout the world today.

I now view Chris's appropriations of DeLima's words as one of many instances in which the students employed various carnivalesque techniques to temporarily overturn the established racial hierarchy and simultaneously have fun with or playfully resist this assignment. While there is always some potential for students to show playful resistance to any school task, this particular assignment is especially open to various features of the carnivalesque, such as the parodic, the horrific, the grotesque, the fantastic, the forbidden, and the scatological (Bakhtin, 1984).

This assignment gives students an opening to talk about bodies that come in different sizes and appearances. It allows them to discuss grotesqueries such snakes, lizards, and other yucky foods. It gives them an opportunity to be outrageously prejudicial, and provides them with a rare opportunity to perform ethnic joke humor in the midst of a school assignment.

Conclusion

This study began as a needs assessment aimed at determining how we as educators can best assist children in developing their understanding of race and ethnicity. However, the children's responses proved to be both more and less than we had originally bargained for.

Through their writing, the children seemed to be performing scripts that allowed them to render themselves both transparent and opaque. Some responses were playfully resistant or carnivalesque, and with a little effort we found that we could trace back many of the students' words to ethnic joke comedians and other individuals from Hawai'i's popular culture.

When tracing the source of other shocking remarks, we sometimes found that the search took us full circle, and ultimately brought us back to our own schools and classrooms. Instead of giving us a look into the minds of these children, many of these students' responses held up a mirror to ourselves, and gave us as educators a glimpse of our own curricular deficiencies.

For instance, consider once again the students' comments on Hawaiian artifacts and ancestors. While I was initially shocked that students living in Hawai'i would describe Hawaiians in such primitivist terms, I now realize that such descriptions are a likely result of our schools' Hawaiian studies curriculum. As I imagine is the case with many other area studies, our Hawaiian studies instruction at the elementary level tends to focus on how great a tragedy it is that the Hawaiian culture was destroyed, and rarely if ever does it discuss Hawaiians of today. Such a curriculum implies that the good things about Hawaiians are what they once were. Seldom is there any mention of any contemporary good. This research has led me to question the focus of Hawaiian and other area studies and has caused me to wonder if these studies should instead focus on more contemporary situations.

Furthermore, this chapter has caused me to question the categories that we use when discussing race and ethnicity. I've suggested that several of these students responded to the assignment with natural history–type classifications and seemed to write themselves entirely out of the assignment. While I initially viewed these responses as indicative of certain deficits on the part of these particular children, I now think such responses suggest that many of these *"hapa"* children who are of mixed racial or ethnic backgrounds found the assignment's distinct categories difficult to relate to.

Many of my colleagues who have offered thoughtful critiques of this study have commented that the racial and ethnic categories that the teacher chose to use in this assignment are arbitrary and lack a certain parallel structure. (Some argued that the black and Caucasian categories are more general than all the rest, while others suggested that an additional Filipino category was necessary to make the list more representative of our state population.) While these points are well taken, I would also extend the critique and argue that all ethnic or racial categories are arbitrary social constructions that we have come to treat as natural.

Today social scientists agree that race is a socially constructed, as opposed to a biologically concrete concept (Fields, 1982; Omi & Winant, 1986; Spickard, 1992). Spickard (1992) contends that the so-called races are not biological categories at all; rather, they are primarily social divisions that rely on physical markers such as skin color to identify group membership. This sociopolitical construct is a means by which powerful people draw distinctions between themselves and others and thereby maintain and extend their own power. Putting simple, neat racial labels on dominated peoples, and creating myths about the physical and moral qualities of those peoples, makes it easier for the dominators to ignore the individual humanity of their victims and eases the guilt of oppression.

But what happens when individuals or groups of individuals subvert these categories by their very existence? Just as people who are transsexual, homosexual, and bisexual have upset and challenged the general understanding of gender and sexuality in mainstream American society, people who are multiracial and multiethnic are beginning to challenge our accepted understanding of race and ethnicity. Students such as these who do not neatly fit into a single, clearly defined racial or ethnic category force us to rethink the historical foundations of these categorizations and cause us to wonder if perhaps we need to "queer up" our notions of race and ethnicity as Butler (1990) does for gender. In the same way that Butler denaturalizes the illusions of continuity between sex, gender, and desire, we should also denaturalize the illusions of continuity between skin pigment, genealogy, race, ethnicity, character, behavior, ability, aspirations, dispositions, and so forth (Shrage, 1995).

I now realize that the multicultural activities that we conduct in school when we ask our students to bring in a national food, trace their lineage on a map, or complete assignments such as this one, however well meaning, may actually end up making race or ethnicity seem more fixed or unitary than it really is. And while there may be times when it is strategic or useful for subordinate people to invoke these racial or ethnic categories, perhaps we need to heed the advice of Stuart Hall (1991) who talks of using race and culture strategically and carefully.

Note: Portions of this chapter were presented at the Reconceptualizing Early Childhood Education: Research, Theory and Practice 6th Interdisciplinary Conference, Madison, Wisconsin, October 1996. I am grateful for comments and assistance from Joseph Tobin, Gail Boldt, Richard Johnson, Jacqueline Miwa, Neil Pateman, Miriam Sharma, Beth Fowkes Tobin, Lois Yamauchi, and Joseph Zilliox.

Chapter 10

What Does a Child Deserve in a Book? Harlan Quist and the Politics of Childhood Knowledge

Nicholas Paley

In 1966, Harlin Quist, a book editor with a background in acting and the theater, began publishing a number of curious, imaginative books for children. Quist's decision to become involved in the world of children's literature was inspired by the then current state of American children's book production as he saw it. Apart from the occasional book of distinction, Quist found most American picture books dominated by "the predictable: conventional concepts, weak illustration, unimaginative art and design, careless production" (Quist 1967, p. 272). Determined to remedy this state of affairs, Quist borrowed one hundred dollars and established his own company with the explicit intent of creating a radically new, stimulating series of picture books—books which, according to Quist, would honor young readers' true intelligence, potential, and judgment.

From 1966–1978, over 100 of these new, stimulating children's books issued from Quist's publishing houses in New York and Paris (where Quist, in 1968, founded a publishing corporation with Francois Ruy-Vidal, a young drama teacher who was also interested in children's books), and many of them aggressively challenged numerous long-held assumptions about the kinds of texts, images, and meanings that were suitable for young children. Producing books about happy little bunnies, garden picnics, and hills alive with the sound of music was not exactly the focus of Quist's publication agenda. As he put it:

> I believe mostly what a child deserves in a book is a very simple thing: the unexpected. I think if a child has a controlled experience with a book, which is to say if he can read it once (if it bores him the first time around and if it's nothing that he chooses to return to, then whatever value the book has, it's a limited value), that a book has to be something large and more-dimensioned....I'm not interested in the book which is going to be read to a child at night to put the child to sleep. My point is to wake the child up, to

start him thinking, to stimulate him, to provoke him, and sometimes to *torment* [original italics] him. He is not going to be in control of his life early or *ever* [original italics], as none of us is. And I think it's not so bad if he learns very early on, even in the fact of a book, that there are things that he does not understand, that there are things he does not control, that there are other dimensions to imagination, other fantasies that are possible to him that can enrich his person and his life. (Quist, 1978, pp. 36–37)

On either side of the Atlantic, Quist books were hard to miss on a book dealer's shelf. Visually, their distinctive, often surreal, artwork contrasted sharply with many other picture books of the day, and their impressive physical elegance was unusually seductive for a children's book. Equally unique were the textual elements of Quist books; many of their narratives advanced themes not generally addressed in the preschool or primary grades—death and sensuality, questions of education and power, issues of autonomy and authority, representation and identity. These kinds of themes, moreover, were frequently explored in Quist books by authors who were more well known for their work at the vanguard of contemporary adult literature than for their contributions to children's writing: Eugene Ionesco, Margeurite Duras, Shirley Jackson, Mark Van Doren, Francois Mallet-Joris, Robert Graves, and Robert Hughes were among some of the writers who published children's books under the Quist imprint.

Response to Quist books in America was sharply divided. While many of his books were admired in the graphic and fine arts communities (and were named to numerous book award lists), most of them met with categorical dismissal from his primary marketplace: school and library personnel whose purchases at that time accounted for 85 to 90 percent of all children's book sales. Many of these educators found Quist's textual politics unsuitable for their young readers, repeatedly warning that his books were, among other things, "frightening," "surreal," "disturbing," and "not to be put in the hands of children." This consistently negative assessment on the part of Quist's primary marketplace was a major factor in an interlocking series of factors contributing to the decline and eventual disappearance of Quist books from the literary landscape during the 1970s. In 1978, Quist closed his publishing houses, and by the 1980s his books were almost impossible to find except by chance, or in the most specialized of library collections devoted to research in children's literature.

I mention this background as a prologue to the question: Is it now time, thirty years after their initial publication, to assess Quist's contribution to the politics of childhood? His revolutionary concepts of what kinds of knowledge were suitable for young children, in what forms such knowledge might be presented, and his books' resistance to the dominant cultural institutions of the day (the conventional ideologies of children's book-making, the children's book publishing industry, the formal educational establishment, etc.) functioned as a powerful cultural critique. I am aware, of course, that such an analytic position already plunges into dense territory since the word "contribution" is a weighted term, but by reflecting on the phenomenon of Harlin Quist from this critical perspective, the extent of his challenge and the power of his reconceptualizations can better emerge.

* * *

Open any one of Quist's books and be prepared to leap into another thinking space. The best of Quist books challenge the primary systems that organize a substantial part of childhood experience: the family, language, ways of learning and knowing, human relationships. Consider the following examples:

Story Number 1, Story Number 2, Story Number 3, Story Number 4 by Eugene Ionesco. Pictures by Etienne Delessert (*Story Number 1* and *2*), Philippe Corentin (*Story Number 3*), and Jean Michel Nicollet (*Story Number 4*).

These books (published 1967–1974) were initially written by Eugene Ionesco for his daughter. Quist and Francois Ruy-Vidal persuaded Ionesco to have them reworked in picture book format and published under the Quist imprint for a wider reading audience. More than any other book, it was the publication of this series that catapulted Quist to the forefront of the children's book industry as the publisher of radical material for very young children. (The first two Ionesco stories' subtitles, for instance, explicitly directed them to children *under* 3 years of age.)

In each of these stories, the opening paragraphs introduce us to Josette, a three-year-old girl, as she opens the door to her parents' bedroom in the morning. In three of these books she pesters her father to tell her a story. Sparkling with the sophisticated vocabulary and witty grammatic structures characteristic of Ionesco's dramatic work, these introductions (and subsequent anti-narratives) reveal why Ionesco's books found themselves at the epicenter of considerable controversy. In the first story, Josette's father lies in bed with a hangover from a night of overindulgence; in the fourth, he awakes in bed alone, wondering to himself if his wife really told the truth when she said she would be spending the night at her mother's house.

Story Number 2, however, finds Josette's father in somewhat better spirits. Its opening reads:

> One morning, Josette's papa got up early. He had slept well because he had not gone to a restaurant the night before to eat sauerkraut. He had not gone to the theater either, or to a nightclub, or to a puppet show. He had not gone to the fair to eat onion soup. He had not even eaten sauerkraut at home. The doctor had warned him not to. Papa is on a diet. He was very hungry last night, so he went to bed very early—because, as the saying goes, a good sleep is a meal in itself.

Papa's prudence puts him in good form to then take Josette on a series of critical examinations of the discursive systems that structure and organize daily life. Functioning as a kind of poet-teacher, Josette's father sees it as his responsibility to reveal the "real" world to her—the one (of artistic—and ethical?—truth) that lies hidden, buried beneath the heaps of objective definitions. One lengthy episode in *Story Number 2* is especially illustrative of how this instruction occurs. It is the central motif in the book and it comprises a series of pages in which Josette's father subverts conventional reality by teaching her the "real" meaning of words. In doing so, he first challenges the assumptions that structure language for instrumental use, overturning functionalist definitions (a chair is a window; windows are pens; a head is a rear, etc.). Ionesco then turns "objective" language against itself through the repetitions of trivial statements in order to explore the ways discursive practices often teeter on the edge of absurdity, practices which, in turn, structure much of social interaction. This is the concluding page of the episode:

> Josette is doubtful about one thing. "What are pictures called?" she asks.
> "Pictures?" says papa. "What are pictures called? One mustn't say *pictures*! One must say *pictures*."
> At this moment Jacqueline [the maid] comes in. Josette races toward her and says to her: "You know, Jacqueline, pictures aren't pictures. Pictures are pictures."
> "Ah," Jacqueline says, "more of her father's foolishness. But of course, my dear, pictures aren't called pictures. They're called pictures."
> Then papa tells Jacqueline, "What Josette says to you is right."
> "No," Jacqueline replies. "She says the opposite."

"No," says papa to Jacqueline. "You're the one who says the opposite."
"No. It's you."
"No. It's you."
"You're both saying the same thing," Josette tells them.

The books that Ionesco wrote under the Quist imprint question many of the events that shape and pervade childhood experience. What we can know, the forms in which such knowledge is represented, and the ways we consider how we know—are all transformed, through Ionesco's "stories," from certainties to be uncritically "learned," into processes which are always open to question and examination, reorganization and reinvention—if and as needed.

Shhh! by Patrick Couratin (1973)

From many points of view, *Shhh!* extends the multiple critiques of Ionesco's books, and, in so doing, dispenses with the most of the conventions associated with children's books altogether. The "story" "begins" in this way:

For some unknown reason,
Gladys,
an apple rotten to the core,
wanted to communicate
with Jules and Francis,
shoes,
born of a Javanese father
and a Hungarian mother,
each usually occupied by a foot,
each foot usually covered by a stocking.
But, instead,
Gladys communicated
with Janice,
a cow,
daughter of a steak,
future steak.

Here, the first two "story" sentences immediately situate the reader in quirky time, emphasizing the undefined ("For some unknown reason"); the ambiguous ("Gladys, an apple rotten to the core"; "Jules and Francis shoes"); and the oblique ("born of Javanese father and a Hungarian mother, each usually occupied by a foot, each foot covered by a stocking"). These initial statements, in addition to resisting narrative conventions, are underscored by the ironizing device that connects the "story characters" together: their attempts to communicate which result in repeated *mis*communication ("But, instead, Gladys communicated with Janice").

The "story" of *Shhh!* continues much in the same way on the following pages with the introduction of Hector, a rhinoceros; an anonymous hand; Mr. Milhous, a rich man; and Stanislas and Dwayne, ducks of strange origin, all of whom become involved in Couratin's account of obsessive, repetitive, frustrated verbal desire. Finally, the narrative "ends" (or runs out of pages?) as oddly and unexpectedly as it began—on a note of uncertainty and contradiction—and with an admonition to the reader which challenges authorial power: "Don't believe everything you see. Or read. Or hear."

Book and anti-book, *Shhh!* could easily pass for a Surrealist "ABC." Textually, one can check off many of the themes and motifs favored by the Surrealist writers and poets: the random alignment of polar images, contextual contrasts (light and dark, dream and reality), linear ambiguity, the sytematic disordering of conventional reality, and so on. Visually, many of Couratin's pictures are also a Surrealist gloss: ambiguous, yet visually precise, they reconfirm the narrative's improbable circumstances by uniting fundamentally unrelated elements: ducks have human hands for heads, a man's legs end (or begin) as a pair of rhinoceri, etc. These visual subversions dominate the picture page, and by centering his illustrations in an eerily empty landscape against a darkening sky, Couratin creates a theatrical series of mystifying effects that are suggestive of the paintings of Magritte. In fact, several of Couratin's illustrations are appropriations of Magritte's *The Bowler Hatted Man*, an image that the Belgian Surrealist repeatedly explored in the 1960s. In many ways, *Shhh!* reveals the daringness of Quist's publishing vision—as well as the irony that jeopardized the power of his critique. After only a few years of his imprint's existence, Quist was already obsoleting his position by producing the kinds of books that children's libraries had absolutely no interest in building shelves for.

Crazy Days by Ed Leander. Pictures by Keleck (1975)

In 1975, Quist initiated an innovative line of quality paper cover picture books in pocket-size format—a production decision that suggests an attempt to democratize the accessibility of his unique books by making them more economically available to a broader audience. One of these releases was *Crazy Days*. In free verse, the book begins by asking the reader:

> Did you happen
> to live
> in the crazy days?
> Or did anyone
> tell you the tale
> of a time
> when our planet
> went loopety-loop
> and the doings
> made people
> turn pale?

These doings "started with gentlemen's heads popping off and floating there quite disconnected," bullets wizzing by on human legs, shoes carried along in the breeze, and people appearing with animal heads. This "craziness doubled and tripled" to include other improbable events: "a zebra-striped man with a hat on his head prancing merrily under the stars"; and "men from the past and cars flying fast and all kinds of other mistakes."

Most of this zaniness can be considered ordinary stuff in the world of picture books, nothing special here; it's the visual representations of these events that are startling. On the cover, for example, a leopard in a Rousseauian junglescape snarls (in anger? in pain? at the reader? at convention?), its teeth flashing. And in the first double-page picture, two animal-headed people (represented by man as leopard, woman as hare) are shown partially clothed, in a stylized boxing pose in a jungle setting that's intensified by a fire-orange sky. The entire image pulses with issues of power and control, struggle and survival. These issues are reinforced by many of the image's specific visual motifs: the jungle setting which suggests a primordial environment where power and force seem to be the only authority; the provocative, tight-fitting leopard skin costumes of the man (in black wristbands) and the woman (in a black half-bra and black, full-length latex gloves) which direct a particular kind of attention to the body; and the combatative posing which suggests subject relations of struggle/dominance. Taken together, these representational devices charge the artwork with the electricity of violence and eroticism—elements traditionally considered subversive since they define an order of experience traditionally denied by powerful cultural sanctions to adults, and certainly prohibited by most social conventions to children. These themes were partially repeated in several other single- and double-page illustrations and tended to overwhelm more lighthearted pictures of the story's madcap events, and its satisfying conclusion ("and then all was well: the crazy days ended as suddenly as they had started"), lending *Crazy Days* an especially problematic distinctiveness when compared to the range of Quist's other publications.

* * *

Not all Quist books presented young readers with such aggressive, challenging experiences, and not all were of such sharp insistence. Many other Quist books treated more conventional themes—adventure, humor, and ABC's—less problematically. And some Quist books missed their mark altogether. But the best of them were extremely effective. They advanced—with great verve and provocativeness—ideas that the world can be otherwise, in fact, that it *is* otherwise; that knowledge is more complex, deeply textured, and contradictory than frequently represented; that there are things in life which may be deeply felt, but never fully comprehended; and that the aesthetic dimension is an especially powerful political and "sublime means to express the problematic aspects of...human existence" (Escobar, 1995, p. 51).

Most boys and girls who lived during the years Quist books were published were probably educated without them—as were perhaps most of their parents and teachers. What a loss, since most of these publications opened up so many new avenues for meaning-making, knowing, and reading. They reflected aspects of Pop Culture (*Mitkey Astromouse, Andromedar SR1, Le Chat de Simulombula*); animation art and the cinema (*Alala: The Teletrips of Alala*); mass media (*Go, Go, Go, Grabote*); and Surrealism (*Number 24, Shhh!*). They referenced major western artists (Pieter Brueghel in Etienne Delessert's pictures for *Story Number 1* and Rene Magritte in Couratin's *Shhh!*). They explored approaches to collaborative illustration (*Here's Looking at You!, The 14th Dragon, People Papers*). There were books made by children for children (*Hubert the Caterpillar Who Thought He Was a Moustache*). There was artwork to puzzle out (*Test Your Wits (Or Lose Them) with a Book of A-Maze-Ments, Here's Looking at You!*) and pictures to literally deconstruct and reassemble (*Manipules 1*).

Quist books also reflected Quist's own passionate interest in the formal qualities of the picture book itself—its physical appearance, its "feel," its material structure. Conceptualizing the children's picture book this way suggested its possibilities as a multidimensioned experience; that is, more than just a medium for instruction or entertainment. For Quist, picture books also functioned as art objects. A self-admitted "monster" when it came to ensuring the integrity and material structure of his books, Quist repeatedly lavished—much to his economic detriment as a small, independent publisher of experimental books—careful attention to paper stock, type, inks, binding, and printing, "the kinds of things," Quist observed, "that important publishers scrimp on" (Quist, in Glueck, 1971, p. 39). The result? Picture books for children in hard and soft cover of startling design and presentation, superb craftwork, superior materials, and polished production.

By producing such objects for children, Quist advanced the idea that the picture book could be much more than just a container for pictures and story—that the book could be (and should be) something more than simply another object of consumption where the reader merely consumes "the story" and then throws it away only to reproduce this process by consuming another again and again. By challenging the explicit and implicit connections of the book as an object of commodification, Quist probed even deeper into the possibilities of the literary experience for young readers—reinventing its form and repositioning the experience of reading beyond commodity-logic *per se* and beyond the commodity-logic of the strictly cognitive. The tactile, physical power of Quist books invited children to enter a different reading space where they could experience the act of reading as a uniquely *sensual* or *aesthetic* activity. "Reading" a Quist book could be pure touch or absolute sight. Or it could mean encountering any one of a number of nameless pleasures (and puzzling satisfactions) sparked by encountering endpapers that gleamed with intensely saturated color, or by seeing deliciously dark inks, or by touching embossed covers of surprising texture, or by taking in the luxurious spread of richly coated paper—all this apart from ever experiencing the flow of narrative, the structure of story. These kinds of ambiguous yet startlingly singular pleasures awaited all children who managed to come in contact with Quist books, whether or not they had the ability to decode words and construe meaning from text.

An actual example of this kind of experience took place many years ago when I had the opportunity to discuss Quist books with a colleague when I was completing my doctoral dissertation at the University of Wisconsin. One evening, I had brought over several of Quist's books to her house to show her what I was working on. Her daughter, Emily, who was three years old at that time, happened to pick up a copy of one of the books—*The Damp and Daffy Doings of a Daring Pirate Ship* by Guillermo Mordillo. In addition to its inventive graphics, this book was notable for its intensely saturated endpapers of the deepest, most sensuous purple-blue color. What happened that night was this: Emily opened the cover of Mordillo's book, but only just wide enough so she could place her tiny hand into the space between the endpapers. She then proceeded to rub her fingers into the endpapers in a series of widening, concentric circles, almost as if to impress the intensity of the papers' colors into her fingertips—but also leaving the book sufficiently closed so that the color (or this remarkable literary moment?) wouldn't escape. Emily then put the barely opened book close to her ears "to hear what the color was saying" (as she told us later). When we finally asked her what she was doing, Emily looked at both of us as if we knew absolutely nothing about the aesthetics of literary experiences and replied: "I'm *reading* a *book*!"

* * *

Before the emergence of the important theoretical discourse outlining the pedogogical imperatives of providing "imaginative activity for picturing difference" (Apple, 1986, p. 178) and of creating "counter-texts" that engage students in the different ways in which "knowledge can be remapped, reterritorialized, and decentered" (Aronowitz & Giroux, 1991, p. 114), Quist was already producing his bold, revolutionary books for children. By providing the opportunities for a rich and diverse group of artists to target one of the primary emblems of childhood civilization—the picture book—with their differently constructed interrogations and re-imaginations of cultural processes and relations, Quist served as a catalyst for the picture book to be turned inside-out, upside-down. What tumbled out of that experimentation was an extravaganza of surprises that confronted American audiences with a more radical, expanded sense of what the texts, images, and meanings of childhood could be. As Quist books zoomed beyond traditional boundaries and penetrated ever deeper into unexplored zones of literary, artistic, and cultural expression, they created a lively dialogue among those publishers, librarians, educators, and parents who were concerned about understanding the complex intersections among children's books, representation, authority, and reading practices. Over the years, this discussion may well have generated an increased appreciation and acceptance of not just a more sophisticated picture book aesthetic, but also an increased sensitivity to the relational politics of childhood knowledge—that is, how criteria are formulated to determine which textual and visual forms and idioms are suitable for young audiences; how some interests are served by these criteria and others marginalized or excluded; and how these processes are always grounded in the ideologies and practices of cultural power.

* * *

April 28, 1998. Returning to my office this morning after a departmental meeting, I see a UPS package on my desk. Looking more closely, I notice it's from Quist in Paris. I cut the plastic envelope and find four books inside. An enclosed letter tells me the books are from his new line released just this spring.

One year ago in early April, during a visit with Quist in his studio on Boulevard Menilmontant just across from the cemetery Pere Lachaise, Quist discussed some of his plans for returning to the world of children's book publishing after a twenty-year absence. There would be reissues of several of his earlier books, with a new line being readied for fall release. There was going to be an extravaganza in Paris highlighting Quist books at an international conference of children's literature sponsored by the Salon du Livre de Jeunesse de Montreuil in early December. There would be negotiations to develop Quist books' distribution to most European countries.

I pick up the books that Quist has sent—two are reissues—and page though them. Time past suddenly collapses into time present. And why not? We're all different selves at different points in this life. Still I can't help but wonder what the future will hold for this reprise. How, for example, will Quist's new publications function in the increasingly luminous cyberspaces of children's contemporary life? What understandings will these new books express in (and of) this increasingly vital culture? What politics? How will they operate—will they operate—as they did decades ago—in creating the kinds of "fracture areas" that Michel Foucault (1988) has analyzed as essential to opening up "the space of freedom . . . of possible transformation" (pp. 37, 36)? What will these transformations tell us about the place of the book as we read culture across difference? What will they tell us about us?

Note: I am deeply indebted to Professors Gertrude Herman and John M. Kean (University of Wisconsin-Madison) for their generous assistance and thoughtful suggestions on an earlier version of this essay, which appeared as "Picture Books That Specialized in Breaking Boundaries: Recalling the Books of Harlin Quist," *Journal of Youth Services in Libraries*, Volume 4, Number 1, 1990. Thanks also to Professor Linda Mauro (George Washington University) for her particular suggestions on this essay.

Chapter 11

If You Think You're Naked, You Are!
Mary Jane Fox

As a *re yapisashe*, a white American, and by definition a member of the colonizers, what *can* be, or *should* be, my role in the decolonization of education in the Pacific? I have struggled with this question since accepting the challenge to both facilitate and document the development of "culturally relevant" curriculum for Yap State, Micronesia.

I am not Yapese, nor am I a *re imetawe* from the outer islands of Woleai, Satawal, or Ulithi. After living in Yap State for four years I have some understanding of local custom, some understanding of the differences between the four cultures which have developed there, and a great respect for the leaders who are forward looking in their resolve to keep their past. But I am very much aware that I am an outsider, both educated and trained in Western thinking and educational practices. How then can I, a *re yapisashe*, support the efforts of these communities to transmit their past to their young in the midst of the ever more persistent pressures from the West. And at the same time, how can I accurately document and analyze the process they are using to decolonize their schooling so that others who are moving toward more culturally relevant curriculum may benefit by their experiences?

In 1993 I experienced one of those cross-cultural dilemmas which made this issue more poignant. On that September morning, as I gazed out the window of the eight-passenger PMA island hopper, the pure undiluted blues and emerald greens of Woleai rose from the Pacific in welcome. I anticipated with joy my return "home" to my sponsor family and friends on Falalop Woleai after spending the summer in the capital teaching classes for the University of Guam.

The two and a half-hour flight had given me ample time to reflect on my first year as a Peace Corps volunteer. My students were extraordinary and my project as teacher trainer was well defined. During the school year I supervised outer island teacher interns and taught college-level writing and literature courses on Woleai Atoll. And during the summer recess, I taught similar university courses in Colonia, Yap.

As always I had learned more from my students than they learned from me. They often challenged my assumptions through rich narrative descriptions of island life and thoughtful expository analyses of colonial issues in the capital. I learned quickly to make no assumptions.

As I was about to step out of the plane, the uniformed American pilot rounded the wing and called to me. "Oh, Mary Jane, I forgot to tell you. Yesterday the Woleai Conference decided that no one may wear tops on Falalop unless they are working in the taro patches or fishing."

"Sure they did," I replied sarcastically. He was always teasing me and I thought he was teasing me now.

"No, honest to God," he said. "Just look around." As I peered out the door I saw sixty people and not one tee shirt!

I made a hasty retreat inside the plane, put down my basket, and slowly pulled off my sleeveless cotton tee shirt. As I was removing my bra a young Yapese pilot, having completed his final check of the cockpit, turned around and gasped, "What are you doing!"

Without thinking I snapped, "I may have to go topless for a year, but I don't have to undress in public!" After my partial disrobing was complete, I clutched my basket in front of me, climbed into the back of the truck with my luggage, and rode through the village to my sponsor family's compound.

When I arrived "home" the family welcomed me with freshly woven flower *mwar-mwars* (head wreaths and leis) and specially prepared food. We had a summer full of news to share, mine from family members in Yap and theirs from the recently ended Woleai Conference—a conference held every five years to review traditional issues important to the five inhabited islands of the atoll. The issue of dress, I subsequently learned, had been the subject of hot debate!

Forty-five minutes later, a young Peace Corps volunteer from Wottegai strolled into the compound to welcome me back. After drinking coconuts and discussing the state of affairs on the atoll, we left my compound to join our families at a local funeral. As we neared the funeral compound this young woman offered some profound advice. "Remember, Mary Jane, if you feel like you are naked, you are!"

As I pictured this skinny, gray-haired Caucasian, dressed only in a lava-lava and *zories* I burst into laughter. What a sight I must have been. Yet the young woman's comment carried me through the events of the next few days. Whenever my Western sense of propriety overwhelmed me, I remembered our discussion and laughed anew.

However, having made my debut at the funeral, I arose the next morning with some misgivings. Could I actually do this? Could I, a mid-Western school teacher from Long Island, New York, fulfill my contract as an educational professional in this state of dress (or undress, as the case may be)? As I struggled with these thoughts, I prepared to attend the eight o'clock mass with the rest of the islanders.

During that weekend I realized that I had a choice to make. I could put on my shirt and board the ship leaving Monday for the capital, or I could remain topless for a year and complete the task I had started. I chose to stay.

The text of the breast became a kind of primer for my future work in Yap State. Through my deconstruction of the tale I have just told I came to appreciate the significance of the Woleaian concept of respect and its function as a cultural underpinning for those who live on the islands. Through this understanding I saw the possibility for constructive facilitation of culturally relevant curriculum development and research on Woleai Atoll.

I began this deconstruction by attempting to read my own decision to remain on Woleai. This decision was very much embedded in my family's belief in the Protestant Work Ethic. Once you start something you have got to finish it. How often I had heard my parents proclaim this commandment. For me the voices in the text of the breast were those of my own family and culture.

Although the Work Ethic was the most prominent voice, there was a crescendo of counterpoint to be heard as well. From our Western perspective, the breast is erotic and must at all times be covered and hidden from view. Breasts are both envied and degraded. Females are encouraged to use liposuction and implants to shrink and enlarge these mammary glands while at the same time women must hide them and disguise them with clothing. Although the breast is sustenance for the newborn child, it is seen as immoral when seen in public. Why else, as Shapely (1999) notes, have there been such objections to state legislatures "decriminalizing breast feeding in public and requiring employers to accommodate their breast-feeding workers?" (p. B1). In spite of the radical sixties, the voices of our Victorian forefathers prevail it seems.

These same voices were heard in the reactions of American friends to the story I have just told. "Did you really go for a year without a top?" one friend asked incredulously. "I could never do that." "Why not," I quipped, "it was ninety-seven degrees with ninety percent humidity most of the time I was on Woleai. It was more comfortable than wearing a tee-shirt sopping with sweat all day." But she could not hear what I was saying.

An eighty-year-old friend, and retired American missionary, received a sketch of my bare-breasted story in my monthly letter. Upon receipt of the letter she threatened to write to the president. "Americans should not have to endure such disgraceful conditions when serving in another country," she wrote back. Fortunately, I got the letter when I was still in the capital and could use the telephone to dissuade her from writing her letter and shortening my tenure in the Peace Corps.

The reactions of most American males, however, were quite different. "What I wouldn't give to see all those breasts! I would love to come and visit," were the first words out of their mouths. It seems that the eighteenth-century romanticized myth of the Pacific is still believed in my culture. The exotic is still rendered erotic, as Margaret Jolly (1997) argues so well in her article "From Point Venus to Bali Ha'i: Eroticism and Exoticism in Representations of the Pacific."

But what of the other players in this little melodrama? Why had the American pilot waited so long to tell me about the Woleai Conference decision? He may have simply forgotten and remembered only after landing on Woleai. Bare breasts were a common sight as he flew his scheduled flights through the outer islands. Or, he may have purposely waited to see my reaction. We had previously discussed the fact that the young Peace Corp volunteer had been required to go topless from the time she first landed on her site. During that discussion the American pilot had remarked that his wife, a nurse, said she could never go topless and she was definitely not squeamish about most things. But they both lived in the expatriate community where their Work Ethic could flourish without contesting the Puritan propriety of their ancestors.

And what of the Yapese pilot who seemed so shocked when I removed my tee shirt? In his village, as in many others on the Yap Islands, women commonly went without tops when they were working around their compounds. I think it was the fact that I am a white American that made the difference. Americans, especially "mature" Americans, were supposed to be fully clothed. This was the understood rule and I was breaking this basic tenet.

The young American volunteer who became my close friend and tutor read the text of the breast quite differently. It was a matter of respect. She lived with a chiefly family, and it would have been disrespectful for her to have dressed otherwise when she was on the atoll.

The concept of respect in a cross-cultural setting is a significant issue. From our Western perspective, respect is an internal state. One either has feelings of respect for another or does not, and it is an individual choice as to what one does with those feelings. But our actions are not necessarily a reflection of our feelings. We may act respectfully by making appropriate eye contact, dressing appropriately, giving the "best" chair to a person of higher status, or arriving on time for a scheduled appointment. But this does not necessarily mean we have feelings of respect for that person. It may mean only that it is to our advantage to act respectfully in that situation. Respect behavior in Western cultures is specifically situated and individual in nature.

Respect in much of the rest of the world, however, is not an internal state, but is instead a set of prescribed actions. Anthropologists call this "respect behaviors" and publish long treatises on such topics. Respect in many non-Western cultures is also understood in terms of the extended family and not the individual. What you do and how you do it is a reflection on your clan, and your behavior, or misbehavior, has a greater impact upon them than on you as an individual. Misbehavior is seen as their lack of instruction, not as a statement of your individual thoughts. The young volunteer understood this and crossed the two cultures to show her feelings of respect for her sponsor family by emulating respectful behavior. Her words of wisdom were a warning to a neophyte white *re yapisashe* professional.

It was in the role of professional that another American most shocked me. Upon my return to the States I had sought the advice of a well-known anthropologist concerning my proposed research project in Yap. I was uncertain about the efficacy of my data gathering strategies and described to her my proposed research design. She commented that I would probably run into local politics when trying to design a curriculum based upon four different sets of locally defined priorities. I agreed that politics seemed to be inherent in all cultures and started to relate my bare-breasted story. When I voiced the pilot's news that no one could wear tops on Woleai she interjected, "You, of course, did not have to take off your shirt. You're an American!" I was speechless. Of all people, I was sure she would understand the implications of the situation. But I was wrong.

I see her interpretation of the text of the breast as a broader reflection of my own culture and, unfortunately, of most *re yapisashe, haole,* or *pakeha* professionals studying or working in non-Western settings (be they educators, anthropologists, or foreign aid specialists). They fear that "locals" will not respect them if they reveal themselves as ordinary people—flaws, blemishes, and imperfections.

On the other hand, what of the ordinary people of Woleai? How can their reading of the text of the breast be understood? "When you see them all the time, they are not much to look at," my male colleagues assured me. "In our culture, the erotic part of the body is the thigh." So I had learned during my Peace Corps preservice training. We had been told by our culture trainers to keep our thighs covered at all times, and I obediently adhered to the dress code, in spite of my long legs, by making sure my lava-lava hung to my knees.

However, one day in the presence of a group of elderly clan women I was trying to negotiate the capricious lava-lava while attempting to sit on a coconut. As I sat down I fell backwards off the coconut, onto the ground, with my knees in the air. The gasp of horror was resounding! After that mishap I was very careful to sit lightly on coconuts while clutching the lava-lava between my knees. You should try it sometime. It is not an easy thing to do.

Upon the unveiling of my breasts, the islanders, on the whole, were very solicitous. The women were concerned about my getting sunburned. And indeed I did suffer five days of very tender skin which had never been exposed to the elements. They were also concerned that I should feel comfortable in my new state of undress. The Woleaians knew that Westerners did not go about with their breasts uncovered. And the women had endured the ogling of tourists in the capital when, due to their cultural status, they were forced to wear traditional dress. They did not wish me to feel the same embarrassment.

The men of my host family were also extremely supportive, and said they were proud that I was willing to abide by the recent ruling of the Woleai Conference. It was at this point that I began to understand that my behavior reflected profoundly upon them.

This is not to say that the men were not curious. During my "coming out" at the funeral, while most islanders avoided eye contact with my chest, two very elderly men peaked unabashedly around a pole to confront those two white orbs which had been hidden from their eyes for a year. And as I began my fall classes, all student eyes (most of them belonging to men) were busily studying the surfaces of the desks, since you know what was directly at eye level. However, as the semester progressed, my breasts lost their mystery for the students as well, regular eye contact was resumed, and the rest of the school year progressed quite uneventfully.

But can the actions of the island leaders be understood through the text of the breast? Why had they agreed that all residents and visitors alike must go topless on their island? To understand this issue one must realize that electricity had come to Falalop Woleai only three years before I arrived. With it came the ubiquitous VCR. Until its arrival life on the island had continued much as it had for hundreds of years. Respect behaviors were taught, children learned through observation, and those who broke the rules were punished by payment of tribute to the offended party or expulsion from the island.

But with the coming of electricity and the invasion of the West through TV, life on the island was changing. Young islanders were emulating the people they saw on the TV screen. I heard there had been a rash of young "ninjas" just prior to my coming! But this had been halted by chiefly proclamation that no videotapes showing ninjas could be shown on the island.

However, children being children, they turned to a different method of showing their understanding of Western culture. Students started wearing tee shirts. Boys and girls in the high school were "styling" their newly acquired attire by cutting them and redesigning their shape. This expression of individuality was the antithesis of a culture that had survived for centuries through cooperation and uniformity.

And community cooperation was deteriorating. Families who could share a salary bought freezers, and the traditional distribution of sea catches among all members of the community was declining. Fishermen were freezing their catches for later use by their own clans.

It is within these parameters that the local communities struggled with the issue of dress at the Woleai Conference. With the installation of electricity and the advent of TV the process of assimilation had speeded up at an alarming rate and was penetrating the very roots of the culture. There were beginning to be "haves" and "have nots" and the cult of the individual was erupting in full force. Tee shirts became the symbol of Western intrusion, and the institution of a dress code was a way of controlling the outward signs of change while assessing the damage and forming new strategies to manage the corrosive effects of Western contact.

So what have I learned from the text of the breast? How does this text apply to my role in the decolonization of education in the Pacific? In the context of work in any non-Western culture, I, as a white American, will always be naked. I cannot hide my "whiteness," no matter how hard I may try. In the process of cultural negotiation I come with my own set of assumptions and must constantly struggle respectfully to understand the other.

It is in the context of respect that most Westerners miss the boat. Or leave on it, as the case may be. If we respect (in the Western sense of the word) the non-Western peoples with whom we work, we will act respectfully, whatever that takes. If we do not understand respect behavior, then we must learn as they learn, through watching and not asking direct questions.

Americans are known for their intrusive and persistent questions. They ask and give little in return. In the traditional world of Yap State's outer islands, knowledge is power and is not given up lightly. To ask direct questions, unless you know the person well, is an affront and tantamount to stealing. We Westerners appear to be thieves much of the time.

This is not to say that I never asked questions. Both my training family in the capital and my sponsor family on Falalop Woleai were familiar with Western ways, and as my teachers they patiently answered my cultural questions. They wanted me to understand so my actions would be culturally appropriate while living on the island. They had assumed responsibility for me, and my actions reflected upon the clan. That is why my sponsor expressed pride in my willingness to remove my top when the leaders requested it. I was demonstrating appropriate respect behavior in their culture.

But is respect behavior enough? We have all heard stories of anthropologists, and Peace Corps volunteers for that matter, who had "gone native" to get access to the culture for their own gain. They regale their audiences with stories of how they duped the locals into giving them secret knowledge, often sexual in nature, never told to another Westerner. (I doubt that very seriously.) As I gained the islanders' confidence, they regaled me with stories of invented tales told to unsuspecting Westerners who asked too many questions! And they were very angry when such tales were printed as the "truth" a few years later (see Thomas, 1987).

No, respect behavior is not enough. It is a necessary, but insufficient part of successful living, working, and doing research in a non-Western culture. To be an effective agent of change I must first have a clearly defined set of ethical priorities. (I do not accept the position of cultural relativity.) But within the parameters of my own beliefs I must be flexible in my responses to cultural dilemmas. In the process of cultural negotiation there are usually culturally acceptable ways of negotiating such dilemmas and it is up to me to figure them out. If after careful investigation a tenable process of negotiation cannot be found, then I should leave because my effectiveness will be, at the least, minimal, and more probably counterproductive.

I also began to understand that, in spite of my honest efforts to understand the "other," I must recognize that I approach most situations with my own set of assumptions. I learned that I must put these assumptions aside and look anew at the world around me because those assumptions may not be correct in the new context. Above all I must not join the long line of Western intellectuals Gayatri Spivak criticizes so severely (Spivak, 1988). I must not impose my Western perspective on the analyses of non-Western subjects. I must try to locate the agent of change in the "subaltern," not merely those with Western education. And I must be tenacious in my efforts to hear all indigenous voices in the texts I analyze.

If all texts, as Bakhtin (1981) claims, are "half ours and half theirs" (p. 152), the heteroglosia inherent in the multicultural texts I choose for analysis will be resounding. And as I analyze those texts I must constantly keep in mind the following warning voiced by Bakhtin (1981):

Each text is individual, its reading is semelfactive (this rendering illusory...) and nevertheless woven entirely with citations, references, echoes, cultural languages (what language is not?), antecedent or contemporary, which cut across it through and through in a vast sterophony. (p. 159)

I now understand that I must continually struggle to hear the nuances of the spoken and unspoken word and reflect on which interpretation of those texts is mine and which is theirs. Only through reflective analysis and respect can one effectively support the efforts of non-Western communities to decolonize their schooling and through this struggle escape becoming another *re yapisashe* who covers her breasts and takes the safe ship home.

Part IV: Resistance and Representation:

SOCIETY

Chapter 12

"*The Proof of the Home Is the Nursery*": *An American Proverb Revisited*
Larry Prochner

In an essay on qualitative research, Joseph Tobin (1995) observed that early childhood education (ECE) researchers "are stuck in time, too often failing to engage with emerging theory in the humanities and social sciences" (p. 224). In particular, he noted the absence of a body of research incorporating poststructural perspectives. However, the problem may not be that the field is stuck in the past. The history of early education theory and practice contains a number of examples that taken together point to the eagerness of the field to experiment with new trends and ideas. In their time, transcendentalism, the child study movement, behaviorism, and psychoanalysis had a profound impact on the development of the infant school, kindergarten, and nursery school. In each case, the engagement of old ideas in early education with new theories and ideas resulted in changes in programs and practices that added to, but did not replace, the previously existing ones. If the field of early education is stuck in time, it is stuck in a reconstruction of the past that reflects present needs. In other words, ECE lacks both a critical historical awareness and a futures orientation (Page, 1991), creating a situation where ECE is stuck in the present.

While history is always a reconstruction of the past told as stories, there is no tradition of revisionist history in ECE that has revealed them as such. In this respect, the historiography of ECE lags behind other areas of social history, including the history of schooling. Anthony Platt's comments on the history of crime in the 1970s are apt in the case of early education today: the "myths and propaganda of earlier generations have become implicitly incorporated into the work of contemporary scholars" (1971, p. vii). Yet the myths are not static, nor are they meant to be misleading. They contain cultural images (Smith, 1978) of the past that are a "version of actual historical events or situations…[and] the principal form in which knowledge of the past is really current in the society" (p. 33). Because they hold some current meaning or relevance, interrogating the images can reveal essential themes in early education (Singer, 1992). Thus, historical analysis can be used to explore practices of representation in early education. In this chapter I draw on a variety of evidence to examine the images of home in daycare history. The chapter is organized into two parts. In the first, I describe the way that the homes and childrearing abilities of poor parents were defined as inadequate from the point of view of charities and benevolent organizations involved in childcare work. Childcare institutions were constructed as alternate day homes for children within this discourse. In part two, I consider visual images (woodcuts, photographs, paintings) of childcare in institutions to explore ways in which one of the central activities of childrearing in the home—feeding children—was restructured in childcare institutions. Feeding children was an ongoing problem for poor families, and a central area of criticism of poor families by charity workers, and later, by nutrition experts. The visual images of feeding children in institutions indicate that mealtime was variously organized as a survival, nutritional, moral, and child management issue.

The Image of Home in Day Nurseries

The images of children's institutions—as school, clinic, or home—are mainly supported through evidence from providers of the services. This is particularly true of the image of daycare as home, because it takes its power from a critique of poverty homes as childrearing environments. The image of the day nursery was contrasted with one of poverty homes headed by uncaring, overworked, or incompetent parents. Thus, the images discussed in this chapter do not reflect the beliefs about homes or daycare held by wage-earning mothers. Nor does it consider children's own understanding of home.

Some images belong primarily to the culture of daycare professionals or researchers. The image of daycare as a school (kindergarten or nursery school), a combination care and learning facility, or as a healing place for children at risk, fits this image. Others are embedded in popular culture, for example, the image of daycare as a hurting place, in which children are placed at risk by their attendance. Although this image has been bolstered by a stream of scientific literature from the research culture that claims that daycare is harmful to the developmental well-being of young children, it has a much longer history. It stems in part from the problems of foundling homes mentioned earlier. It is also derived from smaller scale baby farms and boarding homes, some of which were notorious as places for disposing unwanted infants.

The images associated with early care and education have often been strengthened by the use of metaphors. For example, the infant school promoters of the 1830s made use of a horticultural metaphor (Clarke, 1985, p. 76) that was continued by Fröebel in his naming of the kindergarten. Images and their associated metaphors have been different in the realm of childcare in contrast with education. Infant care in particular has been dominated by an image of the public nursery as a place of refuge in a cruel world. Adelaide de Pastoret's nursery for the children of wage-earning mothers, that she established in Paris in 1801, was called an *asile* for this reason. The precedent for Pastoret's urban experiment in nursery care was the success in a rural setting of John Frederic Oberlin's "knitting schools" for young children established in the 1770s in the Alsace. Oberlin was a young Lutheran minister assigned to a parish in an impoverished and remote area of France in 1767. He was a devoutly religious man who was raised and educated in the city of Strasbourg, and he was distressed by the rough and unruly lives of his parishioners. In particular, Oberlin was struck with the lack of civility in the children's home lives. As a result of his observations, he was moved to take over part of the responsibility for the upbringing of the children. In his search for a teacher for his school, he became aware of a young woman named Sara Banzét in one of the parish villages, who was informally teaching knitting to local girls. He arranged to employ her as both a servant in his home and a teacher. In time, other women were similarly employed as servants and teachers in Oberlin's mission school for poor children. Because one of the activities of the schools was knitting, a practical skill in a cold climate, Oberlin called his establishments "knitting schools." The popular name for them, however, was *poêles*, meaning "rooms with a stove" in the local patois. The two names, knitting school and *poêle*, indicated an important difference in understanding of the function of the institution between Oberlin and his parishioners. Parents saw them as places in which their children could receive physical and perhaps emotional warmth, while Oberlin emphasized skill training and social and moral development. The re-making of care within a system of higher order goals can be seen to have begun.

Pastoret's nursery for infants was inspired by her chance encounter with the small children of a wage-earning mother. The story was fictionalized by Maria Edgeworth (1809) in her novella *Madame de Fleury*. According to Edgeworth, as de Fleury was passing by a house in Paris she heard a child's cry. When she climbed the stairs of the tenement she discovered three children locked in an apartment during their mother's absence. One child had fallen and injured an arm, which was the cause of the cry. de Fleury waited in the apartment with the children until their mother returned. Upon her return, their mother explained to de Fleury that she could not afford to provide for the children's care while she was employed in day labour. In the spirit of charity that was her social duty, de Fleury organized an infant nursery for the children of day laborers.

Nineteenth- and early twentieth-century accounts of the need for institutional daycare, all related by providers or philanthropists, are filled with references to children who suffered from this sort of temporary abandonment. Babies were reportedly tethered to bedposts, left in the care of an older sister, or under the eye of an elderly and infirm neighbor woman. In outlining the origins of the day nursery at Hull House in Chicago, Jane Addams (1910/1960) told of one child who "had a curved spine due to the fact that for three years he had been tied all day long to the leg of the kitchen table" (p. 127) while his mother was at work. Older children, aged four or five, were locked out of their homes and spent their days on the street. The image of the street as a nursery for criminals was a companion to the image of the poverty home as inadequate to the task of childrearing. Beginning with Pastoret's original *asile*, the day nursery was constructed as a rational alternative to the disorganized homes and lives of the poor.

Pastoret's *asile* closed after a few years for unknown reasons. A more lasting institution was founded at mid-century (1844) in Paris by Marbeau. Marbeau choose the name *crèche* to invoke the image of the Christ Child resting in the shelter of the manger. He believed that the safety and salvation of the *crèche* should be available to all children. The *crèche* was based on Marbeau's Social Catholic views that stressed, in part, the importance of applying Christian principles to social problems. He argued that it promoted contact between the rich and poor, and ensured the sanctity of the mother's role within the family. He argued against the popular Malthusian view that a nation can support only a limited population at an adequate standard of living. By providing public assistance to the poor, a population increased beyond its natural limit. The problem for Malthus was "how to provide for those who are in want, in such a manner as to prevent a continual increase of their numbers, and of the proportion which they bear to the whole society" (Malthus, 1803/1990, p. 302). The short answer was to let them perish as a result of their own folly. Marbeau (1845) believed that a growing population could be "controlled" through "industry and intelligence" (p. 27). If every citizen had useful work, there would be no poverty. He reasoned that the number of poor in Paris had decreased since the eighteenth century, despite an increase in the population and in the amount of charity. The *crèche* would help mother to help themselves, by becoming "efficiently employed" (p. 27).

Beginning in the Progressive era, the *crèche* was credited with being the model for nurseries in the United States. When Maria Love (1897) gave her talk on the "Physical Care of Children in the Fitch (Buffalo) Crèche" at the Conference of Day Nurseries in 1897, she observed: "We have adopted the French word *crèche* in Buffalo, signifying manger, in preference to day nursery, defining the work we are striving to do typical of the spirit of the Christ-Child, and feeling it wise and right that spirit should permeate our whole undertaking" (p. 79). Love continued her talk by reflecting on the history of daycare and looking to the future:

> From the mid of the 19th century the growth and propagation of knowledge [of early education] was slow; but through its cumulative form its progress from the mid of the 19th to the mid of the 20th century promises to sweep all barriers before it, *leaving only the wreck of old-time systems behind* [emphasis added], and a new growth which shall lead to a higher and nobler plane of life. Here, then, is the pulse of the body politic of the *crèche*, or day nursery, organized in this country within the latter half of the century, though of a much earlier existence in France. (p. 79)

As Love described it, the managers of the Buffalo Crèche adopted the image of the *crèche* in the original spiritual form proposed by Marbeau. However, she also made it clear that the "old time system" of childcare was past, meaning the large-scale orphanages and foundlings homes established as part of the asylum movement in the first half of the nineteenth century. By the second half of the century, institutions were recognized as creating their own set of problems. Thus, the day nurseries of the 1880s and 1890s grew out of a spirit of anti-institutionalism, and supporters promoted the image of "home away from home."

The *crèche* gained status in North American daycare historiography as an example of the benevolence of a nation toward its less fortunate. Unlike the mid-nineteenth-century nurseries established in New York and Toronto (Prochner, 1996), *crèche* was even a popular name for daycare facilities in the Progressive era. Day nursery supporters used the link to the *crèche* to counter criticism of their small but growing movement. In the early 1900s, day nurseries were attacked by social workers as a cause of family breakdown. They charged that nurseries encouraged mothers to leave their home and children for waged employment. Day nursery supporters countered that their services kept families together by preventing children from being sent to a more permanent care facility such as an orphanage. The day nursery movement was also vulnerable to criticism that out-of-home childcare caused damage to the mother-child relationship. In the 1870s, Mary DuBois, founder of the Nursery for the Children of Poor Women in New York City, vowed that the nursery would never disrupt the "sacred tie of mother and child" (Nursery & Child's Hospital, 1874, p. 9). At Pastoret's original *asile* in Paris, Edgeworth (1802/1979) reported that children were sent home at night because Pastoret did not want to "destroy the tie of natural affection" (p. 39).

Thus, the reference to the *crèche* aligned Progressive-era day nurseries with a successful and relatively nonthreatening foreign model of child welfare. By the early twentieth century, the *crèche* had been valorized by most child welfare historians as an agency dedicated to improving the lives of mothers and children. The renewed high profile of the *crèche* in France was partly due to its role in the Third Republic's national campaign for public health in the late nineteenth century (LaBerge, 1991). By invoking the story of the *crèche*, the Progressive-era nursery was favorably compared to a child welfare service dedicated to the goal of maternal and child health, and only secondarily to the support of maternal employment.

However, there is a growing body of evidence that the origins of daycare are far more varied than the history favored in the Progressive era would suggest. Influences included the orphanage, the poorhouse, the kindergarten, and the hospital, in addition to the *crèche* (Michel, 1999; Prochner, 1994). The evidence goes against the common view that programs for poor children were purely custodial, "with scant attention to the needs of the child" (Jones, 1989, p. v), by pointing to the blurred distinction between the care and education of poor children. Kindergartens often operated full days for the express purpose of providing childcare, while day nurseries gradually developed kindergarten programs for older children. The development of daycare at the Troy Day Home in Troy, New York, is a good example of the successive layering of child welfare and educational ideas. The Day Home began as an Industrial School and only later expanded to include day nursery work. It was modeled on the Industrial School located in the nearby city of Albany ("Meeting at Mrs. Hale's," 1858). The distinction between day home and day nursery was made on the basis of the age group served and the professed function of the service. The Home offered an educational program for school-aged children, while the Nursery provided care for the younger children of wage-earning mothers. There was, however, a crossover between the two services as children graduated from the nursery to the school. The relatively smooth introduction of nursery education into day nurseries in the 1920s, and the transition of many day nurseries in the 1950s from daycare to treatment centers, is further evidence of the multiple meanings contained in the daycare idea (Prochner, 1997). Daycare embodied a number of ideas regarding philanthropy, social welfare, psychiatry, mothers and work, poor parents, and the care and education of very young children. It drew its inspiration not from one particular model, but from a variety of contemporary institutions including the orphanage, the baby farm, and even the private homes of the middle and upper classes.

The idea of day nurseries as segregated play and living spaces for children originated in private homes. Domestic nurseries began as separate sleeping quarters and only later were used as *day* nurseries for children's play. Calvert (1992) observed that by the late nineteenth century, "parents believed the secluded and controlled environment of the nursery protected children's innocent natures and physical well-being and provided them an enclosed area in which they learned the discipline of regular habits" (p. 134). "The proof of the home is the nursery" surfaced as an American proverb at this time. The term *day nursery*, which was the common name for group daycare centers from the 1890s until World War II, was therefore borrowed from the privileged world of upper-class philanthropists. However, the influence of the private home on daycare went far beyond a name. Principles of the new domestic science guided the organization of staff, and the relationships of management, staff, parents, and children. Nurseries in private homes influenced the nursery school as well as public day nurseries. In practice, the two performed a similar function. Margaret MacMillan (1919) believed that the nursery school was "the private Nursery enlarged, and adapted to the average family's needs; and there is no reason at all why it should not rival any private Nursery in its homelikeness and efficiency.... Nursery schools provide for the working family what the rich man has at home" (p. 23). Maria Montessori considered the phenomenon of private nurseries to be yet another sign of the general lack of understanding of adults of the actual needs of children. She believed that "only rich and fortunate children have even a room of their own, more or less a place of exile" (Montessori, 1965b, p. 17). In contrast, poor children were free to roam the streets to the detriment of their social and moral development, and Casa dei Bambini were developed as alternate day homes for children. In 1910 the urban planner Edoardo Talamo invited Montessori to manage such children's houses in his housing project in Rome called Casa Moderna (Stevens, 1913, p. 6). While the Casa dei Bambini offered mandatory parent education as part of its program, its main clients were children. In this way, Montessori's Casa were distinct from North American day nurseries that aimed to meet the often contradictory needs of children and their parents (Prochner, 1996). Montessori (1965a) maintained that

> the special characteristic of the equipment of these houses [the Casa dei Bambini] is that it is adapted for children and not adults. They contain not only didactic material specially fitted for the intellectual development of the child, but also a complete equipment for the management of the miniature family. (p. 38)

While poverty was a characteristic of all families who used the Casa, it was not the fundamental criteria for admission. Children attended them as a right of childhood. In contrast, day nurseries were seen by both supporters and detractors as a stopgap solution to the problem created by wage-earning mothers.

The originator of the concept of children's houses in Italy was a contemporary of Montessori's, the educator Rosa Agazzi (Lombardo-Radice, 1934). A largely neglected figure in English language histories of early education, Agazzi established a nursery school in Mompiano in 1902, eight years before Montessori opened her first Casa in Rome. Her school was an experiment in creating a community of children, in which teachers were assigned the role of interested observers. The structure for the day was provided by the participation of all children in the "everyday jobs" (Lomardo-Radice, 1934, p. 35) of housekeeping, gardening, and carpentry, and the routines of meals and sleep. The activities were designed to foster responsibility and initiative, and to serve as basic training in modern and hygienic domestic practices. This latter point was considered particularly important due to the "home conditions of her working class children" (Lombardo-Radice, 1934, p. 39).

Visual Images of Feeding Time

In the preceding section I outlined a historical trend from an early focus on daycare as a shelter for young children, to the later notion of the day home as an independent children's universe. Both versions of home—supplement or substitute—were designed to offer children a refuge of sorts, whether from the evils of the street or the injustice of an adult-centered world. As well, staff in each necessarily took on responsibility for caring for children's routine needs. The way the tasks were structured is the focus of the final section of this chapter, in which I look at a series of visual images of feeding routines in different forms of daycare from the 1840s to the 1920s, as historical texts. With the exception of the painting by Albert Anker (1890, see Figure 12.3), and the photograph of children in the *crèche* operated by the Grey Nuns in Montreal (Figure 12.2), all of the images are taken from publications that promoted daycare. In this sense they are likely an idealized view of life in daycare in the nineteenth and early twentieth centuries.

One of the most difficult aspects of caring for groups of young children in the nineteenth century was feeding. Residence in one of the many large-scale foundling hospitals almost always resulted in death for infants. Many of these deaths resulted from artificial feeding. The use of wet-nurses was the only solution to the problem of infant feeding prior to advances in the understanding of germ theory and the development of pasteurization. Day nurseries shared the problem of infant feeding with large-scale institutions. In the original *crèche* in France it was mandatory for mothers to return to feed their infant during the day. However, this was rarely practical and the rule was not strictly enforced.

Along with playing and sleeping, eating was a central organizing feature of nursery life. For example, staff were distinguished as wet nurses or dry nurses, depending on their ability to breast-feed. Older children presented different kinds of problems than did infants. Feeding large numbers of children with only a few staff was a problem of efficient management in addition to health and nutrition. The first illustration represents one solution.

Figure 12.1: La Pouponnière. Thomas Fischer Rare Books, University of Toronto.

Figure 12.2: Crèche D'Youville, Montreal, 1920s.

Figure 12.1 is taken from a book published in 1845 promoting the *crèche* movement in France (Delbruck, 1846). It is one of a series of woodcuts in the publication that portrayed an idealized and even fanciful version of nursery care. The kidney-shaped tables were designed to maximize efficiency for feeding and supervising large numbers of similarly aged children. Children who finished eating or who were waiting their turn walked about in the circular pen. While seated at the tables, children were separated from one another by wooden rods. Children were not provided with individual eating utensils; all seemed to be fed by the nurse. Whether or not such a feeding station existed in any actual *crèche*, the woodcut does provides evidence of a change in thinking about the technology of group childcare. The design, which incorporated the principles of Jeremy Bentham's panopticon, restricted social exchange and managed the interaction of both the adults and children. Figure 12.2 is a photograph of children in a *crèche* operated by the Grey Nuns (Crèche D'Youville) in Montreal in the 1920s. It shows a similar technology on a much larger scale, and it demonstrates the continued use of the *pouponnière* in a facility that aimed to provide modern childcare in a clinical-therapeutic mode.

Figure 12.3: Die Kinderkrippe. Albert Anker, 1890.

By 1890, the *crèche* was an established part of child welfare in Europe. In Anker's (1890) painting a single nurse was responsible for feeding thirteen children. A large tureen of soup sits on the table. One child is asleep at the table, and another, for reasons unknown, is sitting alone by the door. The youngest children are seated nearest to the nurse, with older children on the far side. The nurse has adapted the seating style on the bench to the needs of the youngest children, by having them turn around and use the back of the bench as a prop or restraint. The result echoes the feeding station in Figure 12.1. However, there are at least two important differences. The first is the greater age range of the children, which in modern terminology is called a family grouping. The second is that some of the children are facing one another. In the first image, of those children seated, none are looking at any figure other than the nurse. In *Die Kinderkrippe* (Anker, 1890) the two older children on the left can be imagined to be having a conversation.

Figure 12.4: Dining Room, East End Day Nursery Toronto, 1902–03. Metropolitan Toronto Reference Library.

The photograph (Figure 12.4) of the dining room in the East End Day Nursery, Toronto, was included in the agencies annual report for several years beginning in the early 1900s. The photograph reflected a desire on the part of the day nursery administrators to promote its home-like mealtime to financial supporters and the community. The children were also moved across class and social boundaries into the dining room of an upper-middle-class family. Although some Progressive-era day nurseries were established in churches and storefronts, many others were in grand houses in formerly exclusive neighborhoods. This was the case at the East End Day Nursery. Domestic staff or nurses posed behind the children, and the table was set with a formal arrangement of plates and cutlery. The children are of fairly similar age, which was consistent with the trend in child-grouping practices in day nurseries in the early 1900s. No staff sit with the children at the table.

The arrangement was grounded in the perception that children in day nurseries needed experiences in proper mealtime behavior. Ethel Beer (1943), who was a longtime consultant with the New York–based Child Welfare League, believed that the problem rested in the childrearing practices of poor parents.

> In many poor families they scarcely ever have a sit-down meal. Very often the children do not eat in their own home but on the street where they are playing. It is not an unusual sight to see a mother carrying a bowl and spoon downstairs to the street, and there feeding the child like a baby. Sometimes the child in these families does not learn to feed itself before it is six years old. Even worse, up to four and five years of age, many of these children still take bottles. No wonder the Day Nursery has such great difficulty to instill good eating habits in them. (Beer, 1943, p. 54)

Mealtime in day nurseries therefore had the higher order goals of civilizing the children and instilling the virtues of independence and self-effort. It was also a form of indirect parent education, in which new manners would ideally be transferred to the home.

Figure 12.5: The Meal Hour in the Franciscan Nunnery on the Via Giusti.

Figure 12.5 was included in a book by Dorothy Canfield Fisher (1912) describing her visit to a Montessori school in Rome. Fisher was one of Montessori's earliest North American supporters, and the photographs were included to help readers understand the novelty and genius of her method. In Figure 12.5, the children sit at tables of three arranged in rows facing the front. Soup is placed in a container on the table in the foreground, and children serve themselves and return with their bowl to the table. The most striking aspect of the mealtime is the absence of adults. Children were given responsibility for serving the food, as well as feeding themselves. Although the following excerpt from Lombardo-Radice's *NurserySchools in Italy* described his visit to an Agazzi school, the principles were shared by Montessori.

> Dinner is like a meal in the fairy-tale world of the Seven Dwarfs. The masters of the house are little men and women, who serve and pour out and clear away for those who are smaller still, tie their bibs and break their bread for them. Afterwards, they hang out the table cloths and napkins to air and clear ways the crumbs. It is all done *without help* [orig. emphasis]. (Lombardo-Radice, 1934, p. 30)

Lombardo-Radice went on to quote Pasquali (1910), who noted that the "teacher merely looks on; and after the first few months she is not needed" (cited in Lombardo-Radice, 1934, p. 36). Mealtime in the Italian nursery school looked completely different from that depicted in the preceding figure. However, it had a similar meaning. In the Montessori school, the custodial function of feeding was subsumed within a vague moral curriculum that aimed to give children a more authentic life experience than they would have in their own homes. Similarly, mealtime at the East End Day Nursery was constructed as educational opportunity. In Figures 12.1 and 12.2, the custodial aspects of feeding—including the labor of the caregivers—was central.

Figure 12.6: Dinner Time, Handsworth Day Nursery, Birmingham.

The final figure was taken from a study of child and maternal welfare in Britain during World War I (Campbell, 1917). The kidney-shaped feeding-stations are reminiscent of those in the French *crèche* (Figure 12.1). The two nurses have taken positions at the back of the table, presumably for the purposes of the photograph. The 10 children in their care included an infant held by one nurse. Each of the children at the table had their own bowl and they are feeding themselves with their hands. Three toys lie in the foreground. The presence of the toys in a photograph of "Dinner Time" points to a difference in attitude from the austere or formal mealtimes in the other images. The only plaything visible in Figure 12.1, a rattle, sits on the ground out of the reach of the children in the promenade. The toys also indicate that the room was used for a variety of purposes. The ritual of mealtime was constructed in a corner of a multi-purpose room using such props as the kidney-shaped table and tiny chairs. At sleeptime, cots were laid out and the room was transformed into a resting place.

Conclusion

The rational division of the daycare schedule into micro-periods of activity was an essential part of the nursery education curriculum (Varga, 1993, 1997). One result was the development of highly ritualized feeding routines and strict rest-time practices. Eating and sleeping were adopted as part of the curriculum as nursery education took on its new role as a form of child guidance and habit training. Nursery schools of the 1920s and 1930s typically served a noon meal and had an enforced sleep time. Meals were occasions to foster self-effort and responsibility, social exchange, language development, and rehearsal of mealtime manners, and snacks were transformed into nutrition activities. More recently, the cognitive aspect of mealtimes and "nutrition breaks" has been stressed, as described by Vera Hildebrand (1997) in her popular textbook.

Hildebrand, explaining how teachers should design meaningful "food experiences" for children, noted that teachers should "allow children to eat their food products as soon after preparing them as possible for [the] most effective learning" (p. 387). Nonetheless, the moral dimension of feeding children in institutions has not been lost. Hildebrand pointed out that "children can also assist in cleaning up the tables following the meal. *This training is good for all children but may be especially beneficial to children whose home routines appear inadequate* [emphasis added]" (p. 395). The power of snack as a tool for behavior change is also sometimes exploited. Valerie Polakow's (1993) description of a teacher "disciplining by means of food deprivation" (p. 127) in a preschool attended by children who come to school hungry shatters the image of institutional nursery as a benevolent day home.

This chapter has described the historical construction of an image of poverty homes as bad for children, and the co-construction of an image of institutional childcare as a superior day home for poor children. One of the central problems of poor families was feeding their children. The visual images presented in the final section indicate that the meaning and practice of feeding children adapted to constraints of institutions. While children's basic physical needs were always met by daycare staff with varying degrees of success, they took on new meaning as ideas from social work, psychology, and nursery education gained influence. One way of explaining the changes in images is as a kind of evolution in which new and better ideas replaced the old and outmoded ones. This has proven to be the favored view of the history of ECE from the perspective of those within the field itself. In the words of Maria Love (1897), cited earlier, we have apparently left the "wreck of the old time systems behind." However, new conceptions of daycare did not necessarily replace the earlier versions. A different view is that new images are layered upon the old in the fashion of a palimpsest. Thus, the image of daycare as a school or a learning place was written upon the image of the daycare as home, but the earlier image was not erased. There has been some effort to resurrect the primacy of the image of home in infant care settings, and even in school age daycare (Silvern, 1988). Others have argued that home and school are fundamentally different places, and that it is a mistake to think otherwise (Clarke-Stewart, 1991). It is important to stress, however, that images of daycare do not shift around other images that remain stable, for example, those of the private home, children, family, and wage-earning mothers. If daycare reflects an image of home, it is an image that has changed its meaning over the past 200 years. The meaning of caregiving activities associated with very young children have also shifted focus. This has partly been due to decreased rates of infant mortality. The question "How can we help children survive?" has been replaced by "What shall we do with the majority of children who do survive?" (Myers, 1995). One answer has been to formulate cognitive, moral, and social curricula around basic caregiving activities such as feeding, and the labor involved in keeping house, as in Montessori's utopic children's world.

Chapter 13

Beating Mom: How to Win the Power Game
Susan Grieshaber

This chapter uses case study data to show how Robert, aged five years, employed various techniques of power and resistance when playing computer games with his mother. The data are drawn from a larger study that investigated parent and child conflict. In the study, video recording was used to capture everyday family interactions and routines occurring in the course of daily domesticity. Using a feminist poststructuralist analysis, the chapter shows the interplay between Robert and Bev, his mother. They continually challenge each other to occupy more powerful positions, resulting in rapid changes in the balance of power. Transcription extracts of the data demonstrate how throughout the game, Robert's mother used sensitive mothering strategies in response to Robert's more powerful masculine positioning. Although his mother actually won the computer game, Robert's constant contestation, resistance, and consistent use of the more powerful (male) discursive position of hegemonic (or dominant) masculinity ensured Bev lost the contest for power. Conversely, Robert lost the computer game but won the power game.

The chapter begins with a discussion of specific discourses on parenting such as sensitive mothering, authoritarian practices, and permissive parenting. The analysis shows how Bev operates as a mother within the frame of sensitive mothering, but draws on other discourses in an attempt to regulate Robert's behavior. In relying primarily on the discourse of sensitive mothering to deal with the conflict during the computer game, Bev is continuing to constitute Robert as successfully adopting the more powerful discursive position of hegemonic masculinity.

Discourses on Parenting

Contemporary Western culture supports a multimillion dollar child-advice industry composed of child psychiatrists, psychologists, pediatricians, social workers, teachers, support organizations, and a host of media publications (Willis, 1991). In this context, parents are searching continually for more effective ways to handle childrearing and, more specifically, parent-child conflict. The everyday realities of domestic life are fraught with problematic constructions of the child: the bedwetter, the child who eats too little, the arguer, the disobedient child, the nagger, the child who has temper outbursts, the hitter/fighter, the child who back answers, the constant attention seeker, and the child who resists going to bed, to mention just a few (Grieshaber, 1993). Advice regarding the resolution of problems comes from the application of research based on psychological theory, from the "professionals" to parents. Professional advice notwithstanding, in the everyday interaction of domestic life, conflict and resistance persists.

The large volume of information available to parents concerning child-rearing practices demonstrates that parenting, and more particularly mothering, has become professionalized. Institutional texts such as books and popular magazines, and television and radio programs that advise parents about every aspect of childhood from conception to adolescence, are central to the generation and exchange of meanings about the child. These texts promulgate normalized versions of the child and the role of the parent, implying that such professional views, opinions, and beliefs should be unquestionably accepted by parents as "the way it is" and "the way it should be done." Such institutional practices then become accepted as normal and "natural" behavior for parents and young children. Through this process of normalization, particular psychological discourses such as sensitive mothering have become taken-for-granted elements of child rearing. Sensitive mothering is the preferred version of parenting endorsed by discourses of parent-child conflict within the paradigm of developmental psychology.

The chapter now examines three discourses of parenting: sensitive mothering, authoritarian practices, and permissiveness. A brief description of each discourse is given, and the discourses of authoritarian practices and permissiveness are critiqued from a sensitive mothering perspective.

Sensitive Mothering

Discourses on developmental psychology place significant emphasis on "correct" models of socialization that provide specific details of how mother-child interactions should occur. For example, ethological discourse positions children as being predisposed to compliant behavior, and parents as valuing child compliance (Marion, 1983). The ethological model emphasizes the relationship between adult sensitivity and supportiveness and the level of child compliance. The discourse places an enormous burden on parents as they are held responsible for demonstrating those adult behaviors that are deemed necessary to support the development of compliance. This means that parents must demonstrate sensitive patterns of adult behavior as part of the general emotional climate or environment that is required in the home. Parents must also show sensitivity to the needs of the child and communicate expectations to the child in a way that will ensure the child will want to comply.

In another approach to sensitive parenting, Robinson, Mandleco, Olsen, and Hart (1995) have defined empirically the behavioral/communicative components of Baumrind's (1971, 1988) well-known taxonomy of parenting styles. Their preferred version of parenting, the authoritative style, incorporates parental features such as warmth and responsiveness, induction (reasoning), democratic participation, and good natured or easygoing parent-child interactions (such as patiently responding to the child's demands, joking and playing with a child). In the authoritative style, significance is attached to effective use of reasoning. In a feminist poststructuralist study of mother and daughter interaction, Walkerdine and Lucey (1989) found that sensitive mothers frequently utilized reasoning with their daughters and were able to make educational games of domestic chores. They found that these sensitive mothers were inevitably middle class, and that they reflected the type of mothering characteristics endorsed by psychologists and teachers to covertly regulate children. Covert regulation ensures that there is no visible form of mother-power operating, meaning that these middle-class mothers were able to effectively structure situations so that the girls wanted to comply.

Walkerdine and Lucey (1989) have argued that the discourse of the ideal, sensitive mother regulates children through an illusion of autonomy. Part of the illusion is achieved through the use of reasoning, where reasoning is understood as subverting conflict and as being situated in specific historical, cultural, and social circumstances (of the sort experienced from the postwar period to the late 1980s). As such, reasoning functions to covertly produce and control specific types of persons (Walkerdine, 1992b). These are persons who are successfully encultured into society, making sensitive mothering and reasoning a dominant and influential discourse on parenting.

Authoritarian Practices

Authoritarian parenting practices often incorporate behaviorist approaches, where children are seen as passive organisms responding to environmental changes. Such approaches are not the preferred versions of parenting in the discourse of developmental psychology. According to Robinson et al. (1995), authoritarian practices of parenting consist of power-assertive or coercive forms of verbal hostility, corporal punishment, non-reasoned punitive strategies, and directiveness.

Relatedly, research within ethological discourse has shown that noncompliant child behavior can result from coercive adult attempts to have children comply (Lytton & Zwirner, 1975). Coercive measures include adult use of criticism, threat, and the expression of displeasure in an effort to achieve compliance. Parenting can be regulated, limited, or controlled by such discourses because of the implicit threats or future implications about what can happen if parents fail to demonstrate the necessary sensitivity. Parents may feel bound to be sensitive for fear of what may happen if they do not. Lack of sensitivity, then, exists outside the boundaries of what good mothers do. Woollett and Phoenix (1991) contend that use of criticism, threats, and so on "would be viewed [within the sensitive mother discourse] as pathological and having a negative impact on children's development" (p. 35). The implication, then, is that insensitivity can threaten children's normal development. The implicit threat is that parents risk the normal development of their children if they employ insensitive techniques. Examining the work of Hart, Olsen, Robinson, and Mandleco (1996) suggests that such ideas are not only implicit, as they state that consistent authoritarian interaction with children diminishes

> Children's emotional functioning skills (e.g., encoding emotional signals and decoding others' emotional states) and cognitive representational processes (e.g., less attention to relevant social cues, more misattributions of hostile intent, less adaptive solutions generated for interpersonal conflict, and greater expectations of positive consequences for hostile behavior). (p. 16)

The development of these emotional skills and social-cognitive processes appears to coincide with aggressive and disruptive interactions with and rejection by peers (Hart, De Wolf, & Burts, 1993; Parke et al., in Hart et al., 1996, p. 16). Characteristics such as aggression and disruptive behavior are not revered qualities in the discourse on sensitive mothering.

Permissiveness

Permissiveness involves a lack of follow-through, ignoring misbehavior and, according to Hart et al. (1996), is associated with a lack of self-confidence in parenting. Like authoritarian approaches, permissiveness is not a preferred version of parenting within the discourse of developmental psychology as it fails to produce children who have been successfully enculturated. In addition to the aggressive and disruptive behavior resulting from permissive parenting, nonconforming, delinquent, and deviant behavior also appears to result from such approaches (Hart et al., 1996; Maccoby & Martin, 1983).

According to Hart et al. (1996), permissive parents are classified as having failed to manage the behavior of the child. Refusal to conform to the ordinary rules and conventions of society threatens the social and moral order because such children continually challenge society's positioning of adults as authority figures. Children are positioned as minors without access to authority and as being problematic if adult authority is challenged on a regular basis. Regular challenges to adult authority are seen as lack of conformity to social rules. Children demonstrating such behavior can be classified as at-risk or potential socialization failures because they are not conforming to social and moral mores. Remedying the behavior of these children is necessary to stop them from challenging adults, defined as authority figures. Permissive parenting is therefore a potential threat to the established social and moral order of society. Accordingly, preferred versions of parenting, or what is considered effective child discipline within developmental psychology, are ways of regulating children and parents and, hence, the social and moral order.

Correct Models of Parenting

Establishing "correct" models of socialization (such as the sensitive mothering discourse) that promulgate preferred ways of interacting with children produce normalized conceptions of mothering (Walkerdine, 1992a). This has the effect of pathologizing a significant proportion of parents (mothers). To Walkerdine (1992a), a normalized ideal has emerged in the regulation of mothering: "one merely had to look at the mother, the mothering practices or the child, and as a result, mothers and children were either exalted or pathologized" (p. 12). The home environment must therefore be the "right" one to ensure that things are done correctly, and those considered at risk in providing the right home environment were white and black working class mothers (Walkerdine, 1992a).

Within developmental psychology, preferred models of handling parent-child conflict aim to produce particular types of children/persons, and there are in-built penalties for dealing with those who do not measure up to the model. For parents (mothers) who are at risk of producing antisocial children, contemporary Western culture has its own mechanisms of control:

> Society demands that mothers be in control, blames them when they are not, and has the power to remove children from their care if they consider that mothers' control is insufficient. (Woollett & Phoenix, 1991, p. 37)

The discourses on parenting (mothering) available in developmental psychology preclude an understanding of power relations that operate between parents and children. Using understandings of parenting from a developmental psychology perspective ensures that any such power relations remain obscured, as the paradigm is unable to address the micro and macro relationships of power that operate in contemporary Western culture. The aim here is to move some way toward theorizing the links and relationships between the forces of power operating at the micro and macro levels of contemporary Western culture, with a specific focus on parent-child conflict. Such a perspective would remove the focus from the individual child or parent and seek an understanding of parent-child conflict as the product of a complex interplay of macro and micro forces operating in society. Analysis of the following transcript provides an insight into how discourses on parenting (mothering) available in developmental psychology can be re-read to understand power relations operating in episodes of parent-child conflict.

The Computer Game

Robert, an only child, frequently exhibited a particular type of verbal and physical behavior toward his mother that was not as evident when his father was present. On these occasions, Bev was subjected to both verbal and physical abuse from Robert that included shouting, swearing, hitting, crying, name calling, threats, attempted bribery, and fully blown temper tantrums. Although such behavior occasionally occurred in the father's presence, it was more pronounced in his absence.

In response, Bev utilized a variety of discursive positions, including the sensitive mother discourse, where she encouraged, supported, and reminded Robert about desired behavior. She also modeled the favored behavior and preferred utterances. Bev invoked aspects of authoritarian discourse when she threatened Robert and signaled aspects of behavior that were unacceptable (for example, swearing). She used overt power strategies to carry out threats, smack, and to invoke the last resort of rationalist discourse, "time out." In addition, Bev also used aspects of permissiveness by allowing Robert to express his impulses without imposing authoritative or authoritarian controls (Maccoby & Martin, 1983). Conflicts involving mother and son were long; the pace at which they occurred was swift and successful bids for power changed rapidly how each person was positioned.

On one particular Saturday morning, Bev and Robert were engaged in computer games for approximately two hours. They were seated next to each other facing the computer screen and shared the mouse, although Robert had possession of the mouse longer than Bev. The family lived in a semi-industrial suburb on a major access road. Robert's father is approximately twenty years older than his mother. The following episode is drawn from the longer transcript and is illustrative of the nature, length, and pace of the conflict. The transcript notation is as follows:

...	material deleted;
( )	word(s) spoken but not audible;
(( ))	transcriber's description;
yes	normal speaking voice;
yes	raised speaking voice, or with emphasis;
YES	loud speaking voice with emphasis;
YES	extremely loud speaking voice with emphasis;
[	two speakers, turns overlap at this point;
[[	more than two speakers, turns overlap at this point;
=	no interval between turns;

Robert	Shut up! Shut up! ((Robert has the mouse))
Bev	Don't be cheeky.
Robert	Ah shit!

Bev	Shivers. ((Bev provides the model of what Robert "should" have said))
Robert	Here we go. Ah, doodle. *Get lost! Boss. You're a pain in the arse! Lah, get lost bosses.* ((referring to a character in the computer game))
Bev	No, don't be cheeky, Robert. I'll turn it off.
Robert	**OH YOU, YOU!**
Robert	*Oh damn! damn!*
Robert	*Oh, see what you made me do!* ((Robert made a mistake and blamed Bev))
Bev	Oh, I'm sorry.
Robert	You turnip head, hen head!
Robert	Oh shivers!
Bev	Oh!
Robert	**BLOODY!** ((slaps hand in air))
Bev	Uh! ((voice used as a regulatory mechanism)) Oh there y'are Robert! There you are!
Robert	*No you!* Can't do it.
Bev	Do you want me to do the first one?
Robert	((nods)) It's too hard. ((Bev put her hand over Robert's and guided Robert's hand while it was on the mouse))
Robert	*Oh see what you made me do!*
Bev	Oh, I'm sorry.
Robert	You turnip head, hen head. *Oh look at this, oh that, look at that!*
Bev	Oh I'm sorry.
Robert	*You're beating me!* ((Robert had a lower score than Bev for the game so far))

In this transcript, there is evidence of the processes and relationships through which boys and girls conduct gendered lives within the family unit. The institution of the family is substantively gendered (Connell, 1995; Grieshaber, 1998; Wearing, 1996), and the continual negotiation of gender and the process of gendering is embedded in everyday interaction and practice. Davies (1989a) explains how this occurs: "By basing our interactions with children on the assumption that they are in some unitary and bipolar sense male or female, we teach them the discursive practices through which they can constitute themselves in that way" (p. x). Parents have been shown to construct infants as gendered identities from the time the sex of the infant is known, either from birth, or from the gestation age of approximately three months when the sex can be known using ultrasound equipment (Grieshaber, 1998).

Wearing (1996, p. ix) has argued that in late twentieth-century Australia, difference between the genders "is obvious at all levels of society from individual perceptions to macrosocial structures." In addition, Wearing (1996) contends that men and women "construct different realities in their everyday lives concerning their clothing, their families, their jobs, their ambitions, even their definition of happiness" (p. ix). Thus the work of men and women is to construct gendered practices and activities; in this sense, they are said to be "doing gender" (West & Zimmerman, 1991) in everyday situations. The competence of women, men, and children as gendered beings is judged in accordance with how well they demonstrate those characteristics that have come to be associated with femaleness and maleness. It is at a very young age that girls and boys learn what they can do. For example, the young boys in Walkerdine's (1981) study of nursery schools demonstrated an oppressive form of hegemonic masculinity when they constructed their female teacher as the object of their continued sexist discourse. In a similar manner, the following analysis shows how gendered existences are co-constructed for mother and son (aged five years) as they engage in a computer game. Identifying Robert's masculine discourse and practices shows how the process of gendering is embedded in everyday domestic interaction.

This transcript demonstrates how Robert participated in the influential discourse of hegemonic (or dominant) masculinity (Connell, 1995, 1996; Davies, 1996) as it is constructed in the social relations of his family. In this understanding, dominant discourses of masculinity are used to position men more powerfully than women and girls. The culturally dominant form of hegemonic masculinity is "an expression of the *privilege* men collectively have over women" (Connell, 1996, p. 209). Robert, then, participated in the relations of dominant masculinity known to him, practicing ways of "doing masculinity" by occupying a position that is institutionally more powerful than that of his mother.

Hollway (1984) argues the importance of identifying what is at stake when persons adopt preferred gender positions, as she believes there is some recompense involved when aligned in particular ways. For Robert, the recompense is huge, as invoking aspects of dominant masculinity locates him instantly in a more powerful position than his mother. Davies (1989a) has argued that because of the obligation of each child to be identifiable as male or female, boys must "...at least in part position themselves as masculine through oppressive acts of domination and control of their environment and non-masculine others" (p. 89). This means, for instance, that Robert can blame his mother for his failures (turns 7, 9, 19) in the game. It also means that he can shout and swear at his mother (turns 3, 5, 8, 11, 14, 21) and attack her physically by hitting her (turns 41, 47, 49). Through dominating and controlling his environment, Robert consistently utilizes hegemonic masculinity to oppress his mother, a non-masculine other, in various ways.

By her actions and talk Bev also affirmed the dominant masculine position that Robert adopted. In turn 4, Bev provided the model of the preferred utterance ("Shivers") for what Robert should have said instead of "Ah shit" (turn 3). Robert's use of the term "shit" positioned him as in control of the game, and allowed him to ignore the model provided by Bev and to continue with the game. After providing the model and then being ignored, Bev made no effort to pursue the matter further. Because she took no further action, Bev affirmed Robert's position as dominant male, able to be in control of what he said, when he said it, and to whom. This example shows how Bev has participated unknowingly in positioning Robert to adopt the discourse of hegemonic masculinity.

In this extract of the transcript Bev used "cheeky" twice (turns 2 and 6). On both occasions Robert appeared to cross the boundaries of what children are supposed to say to their parents, thereby challenging adult authority. Bev dismissed behavior such as telling your mother to "Shut up! Shut up!" (turn 1) and calling a character in the computer game "a pain in the arse" (turn 5) as being "cheeky." Bev's use of *cheeky* occurred as an attempt to regulate Robert's speech and manner, but it had little effect on his behavior. By identifying the behavior as *cheeky*, Bev dismissed it as playful and therefore as insignificant. Being aware of this, Robert immediately retorted with "Ah shit" (turn 3). Dismissing the behavior as cheeky could be seen as sensitive mothering within the ethological discourse (Marion, 1983). But within this discourse, children are also seen as being predisposed to compliance, and there is little in this transcript to indicate Robert is predisposed toward compliance.

Bev's sensitive mothering approach takes a battering in this incident because this discourse provides no refuge from the privileged version of masculinity that Robert continued to adopt. In short, she has nowhere to go. Robert's successful seizure of power is evidenced by the number of times that Bev apologizes to Robert for *his* failures in the game (turns 10, 20, 22). As part of the sensitive mother discourse, Bev was nurturing and demonstrated that she was aware of Robert's feelings by apologizing for her success (turn 10). Bev made a sympathetic response when he did not succeed (turn 13), and then helped Robert by deliberately failing on her turn (turn 15). She made it a little easier for him by offering to complete the more difficult turn for him (turn 17), and boosted his confidence even at her own expense when she failed (turn 15). Despite much encouragement and deliberate losing, Bev still won this particular game (turn 23). However, Bev's sensitive mothering approach was instrumental in continually positioning Robert within the discourse of dominant masculinity and therefore in a more powerful position than herself.

As the next section of the transcript shows, things do not improve:

Bev	You're wiping out there. ((Robert's character in the game is off the track and he has therefore lost points))
Robert	Oh, I'm wiping out.
Bev	That's ok.
Robert	Nup, not gonna make it, *damn meself!*
Bev	Don't think so, not this time.
Robert	((at further wipe out)) *Oh, bloody! Wipe!*
Bev	Have patience.
Robert	((hits Bev)) **OH, SHUT UP!**
Bev	Uh, uh, uh, uh ((voice used as a regulatory mechanism))
Robert	**YOU JUST WANT TO MAKE ME DONKEY! YOU PIG!**
Bev	Hey, if you're gonna talk like that, I won't play. I'll do this first part and you get ready.
Robert	[I didn't get it ...
Robert	**[I AM READY!**
Bev	Well don't get upset otherwise we'll have to turn it off ...

	((At each wipe out, Bev assures Robert that he has more time and is very encouraging. She mentions again the difficulty of the game. Approximately three minutes pass.))
Robert	((at wipe out)) It sinked me. *That dickhead!*
Bev	Hey, don't be cheeky. I don't like that.
Bev	Are you gonna do it yourself this time?
Robert	((shakes head for no)) You go first.
Bev	Oh mommy do the first one? I think you go faster in the first one than mommy does.
Robert	OK I'll do it.
Bev	OK do you think you can do it all?
Robert	((nods))
Bev	That's better, then you can say you got the whole way yourself.
Robert	**OH, NO! DAMN!** ((hits Bev))
Bev	Uh, uh, uh! ((voice used as regulatory mechanism)) You hit me, and I'll hit you back.
Robert	((hits Bev again)) **DON'T TELL ME TO HIT ME BACK OR I'LL HIT YOU BACK!**

Bev continued the sensitive mother discourse, supporting Robert by encouraging him (turns 26, 30, 44, 46). She even told him how difficult the game was (turn 37) and boosted his confidence by indicating that he is faster than she is (turn 42).

In her responses to Robert during episodes of conflict, Bev remained quietly spoken, stayed on her seat, and showed few signs of movement. She showed no active and violent emotions and managed to sustain aspects of the sensitive mother discourse at most times. In contrast to Bev, Robert was positioned as active, violent, and oppressive throughout the computer game. Walkerdine and Lucey (1989) argue that in the production of nurturant femininity, women are "denied active and violent emotions," which is also a "denial of power and oppression" (p. 128). This is an example of how the idea of what it is to be male (Robert) is constructed in opposition to the idea of femaleness (Bev) (Davies, 1989a).

Beside sensitive mothering and nurturant femininity, Bev did draw upon discourses of authoritarianism and permissiveness. In regard to authoritarianism, she threatened not to play (turn 34), to turn the computer off (turns 6, 37), and that she would hit Robert if he hit her (turn 48). Following the understanding of authoritarian parenting practices (Robinson et al., 1995), threats such as these would be seen as authoritarian and coercive measures used in an attempt to achieve compliance with the desired behavior. Similarly, the expression of displeasure is seen as a coercive measure (Lytton & Zwirner, 1975). Bev expressed displeasure on a number of occasions. For instance, in turn 39, she indicated that she did not like the term that Robert had just used ("dickhead"). She also used her voice as a regulatory mechanism indicating displeasure through saying "Uh!" after Robert had shouted "BLOODY!" (turn 15), after he had hit Bev and told her "Oh shut up!" (turn 32), and again after Robert had used another profanity and hit her once more (turn 48).

In the understanding of permissiveness advanced by Hart et al. (1996), Bev could be classified as a permissive parent on a number of counts. She did not follow through on the threats that she made to turn off the computer (turns 5, 37) and the threat that she would not play (turn 34). She also ignored several instances of what could be called misbehavior. Robert challenged Bev's authority as an adult by telling her to "Shut up!" (turns 1, 31), calling her a "turnip head, hen head" (turns 11, 21) and a "pig" (turn 33). He ignored the desired expressions that Bev wanted him to use instead of the profanities, and he challenged her authority again as an adult when he hit her on three occasions (turns 31, 47, 49). On all these accounts, Bev could be seen to have failed to manage Robert's behavior. Robert continually challenged his mother's authority as an adult, positioned as an authority figure by society. Regular challenges to adult authority are seen as a lack of conformity to social rules, and such children are often considered threats to the social and moral order.

This particular struggle lasted for approximately two hours and the conflict escalated considerably following the above episodes, culminating in Robert being smacked and sent to his bedroom for "time out." This was achieved through the use of reasoning (which is highly valued in the sensitive mother discourse) about Robert's behavior throughout the morning. Bev provided reasons for smacking Robert and reasons for his confinement to the bedroom for a period of time.

Robert had difficulty accepting that his mother won the game. He acted as if he had to win, but it is hard to cheat a computer. On other occasions when playing card and board games Bev had adopted contradictory positions about cheating. She had both playfully allowed Robert to "win" through cheating and also disallowed it. So this time, when it appeared to Robert that his mother had not allowed him to "win," he slapped her. Simply put, the sensitive, nurturant mother discourse was not working in this episode. Robert would not play the game and suppress the conflict, frustration, and anger because he adopted a much more powerful position than his mother did (cf. Walkerdine, 1981). This powerful position allowed Robert to say almost what he liked to Bev. The consequences of this seizure of power are considerable. Robert is constructed as successfully able to position his mother the powerless object of his dominant male discourse. The effect of such power is the control and regulation of his mother. This power came at seemingly little cost to Robert but at huge costs to his mother. Bev's use of the discourse of sensitive mothering was instrumental in continually positioning Robert within the discourse of dominant masculinity and therefore as more powerful than her.

There are many different ways of being a mother, and Bev has access to and used the discourses of sensitive mothering, permissiveness, and authoritarian parenting. Bev's access to other ways of being a mother that exist outside these discourses (cf. Phoenix & Woollett, 1991) is limited or nonexistent. Because the discursive resources are so few, persons such as Bev become entrapped in those available.

The normalizing and regulative discourses of mothering (parenting) available within developmental psychology offer a limited range of alternatives and few options to those responsible for mothering (parenting). This means that mothers such as Bev are restricted to selecting options from available discourses because they have no access to powerful discursive resources that are necessary to generate alternative practices. There are few ways to access understandings of parent-child tension and conflict other than those promulgated by the discourses of developmental psychology. The transcript analysis here shows how in daily domestic conflict, processes of normalization operate to produce certain types of persons. Bev, desirous of the sensitive mother discourse, unknowingly co-constructs her son in ways that are detrimental to her own position as mother and woman.

Conclusion

Many discourses of developmental psychology construe good mothers as those who are able to avert the possibility of conflict occurring because of the way in which they structure the environment. For instance, the warm, supportive, and nurturing atmosphere created by the sensitive mother will entice the child into compliance with adult requests. If conflict does eventuate, the good mother is able to rationalize it, to reason with the child and therefore gain compliance through the ability to make the child see the reason behind requests. In developmental psychology, skill in fostering what is considered good child development rests on the proficiency of the sensitive mother to use the technique of reasoning to avert and resolve conflict.

The above transcript has demonstrated the contradictory nature of mothering. Significant differences exist between this analysis and the ideas about mothering found in childcare and parenting manuals (Marshall, 1991) and psychological views on mothering (Phoenix & Woollet, 1991). Despite wanting to be a sensitive mother, Bev drew upon authoritarian and permissive discourses in an effort to position herself more powerfully in relation to Robert's ongoing and oppressive version of hegemonic masculinity. Individual parents are thus not defined by singular discourses. Instead, they act as agents reading, misreading, restating, ignoring and, in instances, resisting the multiple connecting and complementary discourses available in mass mediated, multi-textual cultures. However, the discourses on mothering examined here provide no opportunities for alternative conceptions of dealing effectively with dominant expressions of masculinity as lived in daily life. Support has therefore been gathered for Mac Naughton's (1992) claim that child development is "fundamentally sexist" (p. 225). Preferred versions of mothering (such as sensitive mothering) and those versions in less powerful positions within developmental psychology cannot offer any substantive practices which are able to thwart the recompense Robert receives from doing masculinity in this powerful way. Alternative conceptions of mothering that exist outside the dominant paradigm of sensitive mothering and nurturant femininity are required to deal with situations of dominant masculinity of the type related here. Continued reliance on the idealized discourse on mothering perpetuated in developmental psychology ensures mothers will be denied opportunities for positioning themselves more powerfully when faced with dominant masculinity in the course of daily domestic interaction and practice.

Note: The names of parents and children have been changed.

Chapter 14

Who's Making These Policies Anyway?: How Head Start Staff Interpret Official Policies

Deborah Ceglowski

As I prepare for an upcoming training session for bus riders and drivers, Ruth, the Wood River Head Start bus rider, tells me she'd heard that the children aren't supposed to have anything in their hands during the hour-long bus ride to and from the center. Ruth asks what she is supposed to do with the children on the bus if they can't have playthings.

I call the administrating agency, Hoover Community Action Corporation, for clarification about the "empty hands on the bus" policy. The transportation coordinator says that the policy was established to prevent child injury. She tells me that the bus riders can sing and read to keep the children occupied.

Judy, the Wood River Head Start teacher and site-based manager, upon hearing the empty hands on the bus policy tells Ruth and me: "Who is making these policies anyway? Are they the people who are riding the bus? I will tell you what I think. I think that it should be up to the bus driver and rider. They should make the decision. If it works for them, then it is OK."

Judy's comment, "I think that it should be up to the bus driver and rider" captures the tension that Wood River Head Start staff express when describing many official policies and procedures. Official policies emanate from policymakers who may have little working knowledge of the daily activities of program staff and local staff, who, when faced with the realities of riding the bus for four hours a day, make other decisions about what is most feasible. Tension between central authority and local control is most evident when Wood River staff describe what the administrating agency requires and how the staff envisions handling situations. As Johnson (1994) writes, "Most teachers think of educational policy as a nuisance or a threat devised by 'Them'—the policy-makers who work in the Central office...to control the work of 'Us'—the people who really know kids and classrooms" (p. 15).

From September 1993 to May 1995, I joined the four-member Wood River staff as a volunteer to study how policies and mandates are enacted in the day-to-day lives of Head Start staff. I utilized interpretive research methods that included field notes, collecting and analyzing written policies, talking with staff, children, and parents, writing stories about the mundane and extraordinary occurrences, and participating in the daily events at the program. As a volunteer and staff substitute, I supervised the boys' restroom, set up art activities, read stories, wrote accident reports, led children's games, rode the bus, served lunch, washed dishes, cleaned the kitchen, emptied the trash, and accompanied the children and staff on field trips. At the staff's invitation, I attended monthly parent meetings and staff meetings.

Wood River Head Start, located in Wood River, a rural community in the Midwest, is like thousands of other Head Start programs across the United States and territories. Administered by the Hoover Community Action Corporation (Hoover CAC), its mission is to serve families whose incomes fall below the federal poverty guidelines. Judy Roberts, the teacher, Susan Jensen, the assistant teacher, Ruth Donalds, the site aide, and Gary Nielson, the bus driver, provide center-based services to seventeen income-eligible three-and four-year-olds and their families four days per week. Services include health and dental care, meals, preschool program, social services, and parent involvement.

In this chapter I describe how the Wood River Head Start staff define and implement official policies. I begin by briefly reviewing Head Start history, defining official policies, and explaining why Head Start policies have become more prescriptive in nature. Following a review of the research examining the relationship between policies and program quality, I explain how staffs' interpretations of Head Start policy can augment our current understanding of policy practice. I then describe how I use vantage point analyses to examine stories about the mundane and special occurrences at Wood River Head Start.

A Brief Review of Head Start History

The War on Poverty focused national attention on the needs and troubles of economically disadvantaged families. In 1965, Congress responded to societal demands to eradicate poverty by legislating new policies. These policies resulted in the creation of new programs like Head Start. By the end of the 1960s society's attention had shifted from the War on Poverty to the war in Vietnam (Brown, 1985; Peters, 1980). During this shift, funding and support for Head Start waned (Zigler & Muenchow, 1992). From 1969 to 1978, Head Start programs continued to operate. There were slight increases in annual budgets, but often the increases were less than the rate of inflation. In the 1970s the Head Start Bureau, under the leadership of Edward Zigler, developed new policies and procedures aimed at upgrading the quality of local programs. These policies included the development of national Performance Standards, annual program self-assessment, and on-site federal validation team visits (Collins & Kinney, 1989). In the 1980s Head Start's fortune changed. Republican and Democratic leadership supported the program and voted in substantial funding increases.

Expansion efforts stem from two sources. First research studies like those of the High Scope Foundation (Barnett & Escobar, 1987; Berruta-Clement, Schweinhart, Barnett, Epstein, & Weikart, 1984; Schweinhart, Barnes, & Weikart, 1993; Schweinhart & Koshel, 1986; Schweinhart, Koshel, & Bridgman, 1987; Schweinhart & Weikart, 1993) found that quality early childhood programs have significant and long-term impact on the lives of young children. Such programs provide a seven-dollar return for each dollar invested in preschool programs.

Second, the National Governors Association's recommendations (U.S. Department of Education, 1991) for educational improvement focused attention on the importance of school readiness. The first national education goal, "By the year 2000, all children in America will start school ready to learn" (U.S. Department of Education, 1991, p. 5) spurred new interest in and support for Head Start.

Attention to Head Start has resulted in two major outcomes. First, commissions were appointed to study the current status of Head Start and make recommendations for program growth and expansion. Second, administrating agencies received substantial funding increases. As indicated in the Advisory Committee Report on Head Start Quality and Expansion (U.S. Department of Health and Human Services [U.S. DHHS], 1993) and the National Head Start Association's Silver Ribbon Panel's report (1990) there is variance in the quality of Head Start programs. Both the committee and panel recommended that program quality be the top priority in Head Start funding.

The Head Start budget doubled from $1.95 billion dollars in 1991 to $3.98 billion in 1997. The Head Start Bureau has issued new policy mandates, is revising existing policies, and formulating procedures to terminate poorly performing Head Start programs. The implicit assumption is that more policies and better management will result in higher quality programs.

Official Policies

A public policy is an "authoritative determination by a governing authority" (Downey, 1988, p. 10) for those institutions that fall under the policy's jurisdiction. Policies dictate to those who work in such institutions what the institutional goals are and how these goals are to be achieved (Rich, 1974). It is the responsibility of those who work in institutions to make any structural and programmatic changes necessary to comply with the policy. Public policies cover a span of service agencies including health, education, transportation, and social services.

Head Start policy is generally viewed as hierarchical, developed at a higher level of authority and then imposed at a lower level of practice. Head Start policy implementation means compliance (Rich, 1974) with standards imposed by external forces such as the U.S. Department of Health and Human Services, state childcare licensing board, and the local administrating agency. The hierarchical nature of Head Start organization reflects historical and cultural trends (Tyack & Tobin, 1994). Historical influence is evident in how policies are developed, described, and interpreted as either limiting or expanding individual and/or program opportunities. For instance, Head Start, founded during the Civil Rights movement era, is organized as a federal-local program partnership. This organizational structure reflects the 1960s distrust of state governments to guarantee basic rights, such as educational services. Head Start programs by and large are autonomous and not well integrated with other early childhood programs in the community (Besharov, 1993; Grubb, 1991; U.S. DHHS, 1993; Zigler & Muenchow, 1992).

Prescriptive Policies

Cohen and Spillane (1992) argue that in federally funded programs like Head Start, the federal regulatory system is weak and that local administrative structures, such as Hoover CAC, are quite autonomous. The federal response to this loose structure is to impose more and more prescriptive policies upon local agencies. Agencies administrating Head Start programs are subject to a "vast regulatory enterprise" (Timar, 1994, p. 53). As this enterprise grows, "rules became increasingly narrow and prescriptive" (Timar, 1994, p. 53). These rules are based on the dual premises of limiting the risk factors in program operation and increasing program quality through prescriptive policies. As agencies orient toward rule compliance, they become "wary of straying from procedural mandates" (Timar, 1994, p. 53). Narrow and prescriptive policies funnel down from the federal level to the local programs that in turn develop prescriptive policies for Head Start staff. Prescriptive policies require that program administrators and staff follow certain prescriptions (Pauly, 1991) to meet stated goals and objectives. These policies are "rooted in distrust of the motives and capacity of local and school officials" (Kirp, 1986, p. 3). Prescriptive policies are based on the premise that centralized decision making and monitoring are essential to standardize certain characteristics of local programs, including services provided and staff qualifications (Weiler, 1990).

As programs attend to rule adherence they focus more on following stated rules and procedures and less on local options that might best serve children and families. This rule adherence changes the nature and scope of the program by simultaneously limiting the roles and responsibilities of program staff and increasing the amount of paperwork and documentation required to insure that programs are in compliance.

When staff complete the required paperwork they signal to the program administrators that they are following the rules and regulations. The paperwork may not reflect the events at the program but is a procedural display to the administrators that Wood River staff are in compliance. "The phrase 'procedural engagement' refers to how local staff orient themselves toward the requirements to follow the rules and regulations established by program administrators with the aim of maintaining uniformity in policy compliance" (Ceglowski, 1998, p. 55).

Policy and Program Quality

What, then, is known about the connection between policies and program quality? Head Start research and policy analysis consists of three phases (Collins & Kinney, 1989). During Phase I, researchers answered the question: Does Head Start work? The goal of Phase I studies was to determine the effectiveness of Head Start as measured by children's performance in elementary school (Brown, 1978; Datta, McHale, & Mitchell, 1976; Hubell, 1983; Lazar, Darlington, Murray, Royce, & Snipper, 1982; McKey, Condelli, Ganson, Barrett, & McConkey, 1986; Westinghouse Learning Corporation, 1969; Zigler & Valentine, 1979). Phase I studies were critical to justify continued and expanded funding of the Head Start program (Brown, 1985; Hymes, 1991; Washington & Oyemade, 1987; Zigler & Muenchow, 1992; Zigler & Valentine, 1979).

During Phase II, Head Start policy analysis focused upon various curricula and service delivery models to determine which are most effective in producing significant and long-lasting gains for Head Start children and their families (Bissell, 1971; Collins, 1980; Coulson, 1972; Love, Nauta, Coelen, Hewlett, & Ruopp, 1976; Lukas, 1975; Nauta & Travers, 1982; Smith, 1973; Stanford Research Institute,

1971; Travers, Nauta, & Irwin, 1982). The Head Start Planned Variation Studies found that a variety of curricula and service delivery models are effective in eliciting favorable child outcomes (Datta, 1972; Smith, 1973).

During Phases I and II of Head Start policy research, policymakers assume a relatively direct relationship between federal policy inputs, local responses, and program outputs (McLaughlin, 1990). While programs that implement policy may be diverse, the goal of policy implementation is that these programs will produce similar, measurable results. Successful policies are those in which the outcomes are closely aligned to the original intent of the policymakers. The goal in such a policy model is for consistency in measured outcomes. In traditional Head Start policy analysis, evident in Phase I and II studies:

> Many members of the policy-making community are embracing a view of teacher knowledge and skill that represents a limited epistemological perspective on what teachers should know and be able to do. This perspective is classified ...as the formal perspective. (Fenstermacher, 1994, p. 4)

Schön (1983, 1987, 1991) names this type of knowledge technical rationality, which is defined as the "application of conventional social science to the problems and tasks of everyday professional practice" (Fenstermacher, 1994, p. 12). The basic premise of technical rationality is that those who study teaching and school systems systematically, rather than those who work in these systems, are best suited to determine educational policy. From the technical rational perspective, practitioners are "consumed by the day-to-dayness of school: of finding ways to meet the challenges from one's students, the needs of one's colleagues and the demands of one's supervisors" (Cook, 1994, p. 48), not policy-making. Technical rationality's top-down approach reflects the current view of the policy-making structure. Policy is governmental governance and practice is defined by the activities conducted within classrooms. Policy and practice, as Cohen and Spillane (1992) illustrate in their question, "What are the relations between policy and practice?" (p. 8), are viewed as interrelated but separate entities.

The current research focus in Phase III:

> Explores ingredients and indicators of program quality [that]...includes an emphasis on individualization of services to children and families based on unique needs and characteristics, attention to variations in program services, the role of parents, teacher characteristics and behaviors and the use of

classroom and home observational techniques. (Collins & Kinney, 1989, p. 30)

Collins and Kinney (1989) list several reasons why Head Start policy analysis shifted in Phase III. First, the input-output model of policy analysis did not produce "meaningful insights into major program and policy questions" (p. 30) because it is now recognized that program climate is an essential component of policy interpretation. Policymakers now are suspicious of one-shot evaluation studies that provide a comprehensive analysis of the program and are more interested in comprehensive, longitudinal studies. In addition, most policymakers and researchers believe that early intervention programs like Head Start produce short-term and long-term gains for children living in poverty and that "any well designed and well implemented curriculum...can produce meaningful gains for high risk children" (p. 31).

All phases of Head Start research, including Phase III, have relied primarily on large-scale national studies that measure how certain variables affect children's performance and program quality. Head Start programs participating in these studies are geographically, programmatically, and organizationally distinct. Within such a structural framework, local programs vary in orientation and outcomes. Research studies thus blur the distinctive characteristics of Head Start programs. These studies ignore how staff develop and maintain daily services to families and young children. Yet it is precisely these distinct differences that determine how each program interprets and implements official policies. It is "local capacity and will" (McLaughlin, 1990, p. 12) that determine how policies are negotiated at local sites.

Recognizing that studies have not focused on local capacity, the Head Start Committee on Head Start Quality and Expansion (U.S. DHHS, 1993) recommended that Head Start research include studies of local sites because

> The way programs interpret these [Head Start Program Performance] standards to meet the needs of a diverse population under various local conditions can provide a rich source of data regarding how to define and implement comprehensive child development and family support programs. (p. 38)

In current educational policy analysis, cultural climate is recognized as the major factor in how policies are implemented in local institutions (McLaughlin, 1990; Mintrop & Weiler, 1994; Mirel, 1994; Ogawa, 1994; Weiss & Cambone, 1994). At the center of this implementation approach is careful consideration of local factors and climate. In this approach, policy, regardless of its level, is viewed as negotiated within various local contexts (McLaughlin, 1990). Given the diverse climates and resources of these local institutions, it is impossible to accurately predict policy implementation in any given setting.

Additionally, states McLaughlin, local staff may view the policy structure differently than policymakers and analysts.

> Our research and analysis took the policy system for granted.... [We] assumed that the structure most relevant to teachers was the policy structure-the federal, state, and local policies.... Had we made those assumptions problematic, rather than taking them as givens, we would have seen that although we as policy analysts were chiefly concerned with the policy system, it was not always relevant to many teachers on a day-to-day basis. (p. 14)

What then are the structures most relevant to staff on a day-to-day basis? How could McLaughlin's finding be applied to Head Start policy analysis? How would bottom-up studies of policy contribute to our current understanding of policy development, implementation, and evaluation? If studies focus on the various local conditions, then the locus of study changes from the examination of "official policy-making bodies, including Congress, state legislatures, state school boards, and local boards of education" to the local and "unofficial policy environment" (Ogawa, 1994, p. 545).

By focusing on staff's daily activities, we can understand those forces and structures most relevant to the operation of a program. In-depth studies are needed to understand how staff both interpret and implement official policies (Palank & Burch, 1992) and create local policies. In examining policy from the perspective of local staff, we might also understand the taken-for-granted nature of the policy process. It is probable that staffs' interpretations might lead to different models of policy development and implementation.

Vantage Point Analyses

A vantage point, or viewing position, draws attention to certain policy processes. In moving the vantage point from one position to another, the policy processes look different. The move from one vantage point is similar to focusing a camera lens from a distant to close object; the indistinct foreground comes into clear view. Top-down vantage point analyses are the traditional methodology used by policy analysts. In top-down analysis, local staff are viewed primarily as policy implementers. Top-down vantage point analyses describe how local staff implement official policies. Official policies define the program and program's characteristics: determining the program clientele, staffing pattern, and program components. Traditional top-down analysis does not focus on policy from the perspective of local staff (McLaughlin, 1990; Mintrop & Weiler, 1994; Pauly, 1991) or question whether the existing policy structure is the one most relevant to staff (McLaughlin, 1990).

In my study, top-down vantage point analyses describe how local staff interpret, negotiate and implement official policies. When staff talk about policy from a top-down perspective, they generally describe agency policies, how administrators enforce those policies during site visits, and how they comply with mandated paperwork and record keeping. The Wood River staff usually do not distinguish between the various layers of policy—federal, state, or agency but refer to all policy as Hoover CAC policy. There are several reasons for this. First, as Gary, the bus driver, recalls, there was a time when there were few policies. Under the direction of the Head Start director, Hoover CAC developed a policy manual. Second, staff learn about policies from Hoover CAC administrators at staff meetings, during phone conversations, and through agency memos.

Staff recognize both the value of and need for official policies. Gary describes how different bus driving was before transportation policies were developed and enforced. During the pre-policy days, some children sat on the floor of the van, and when parents were not there to greet their children, Gary brought the children home with him. At that time, Gary and other bus drivers were fed up with the lack of policy and approached the Head Start director. The director, with assistance from bus drivers, developed transportation policies. Since the inception of bus policies, all children ride in car seats or seat belts. When parents are not home, the child is brought to a person listed on an emergency contact sheet.

At Wood River policy talk is connected to the daily events at the program. It is during breakfast, lunch, before and after school, on the bus and on the playground that Judy, Susan, Ruth, Gary, and I talk about policies. Staff interpret and implement official policies in the context of local conditions, their understanding of the children and families they serve, and the available human and material resources. Shaped by "individual voices in dialogue" (Howard, 1994, p. 302), the Wood River staff develop a community-based understanding of what a policy means within the local context. From this perspective, how a policy is defined

Is situational; it is open-ended; it is ambiguous; it is ad hoc. It is defined differently by different people depending upon their relationship to what is going on. It's inevitably local and subject to multiple interpretations. (Denzin, personal communication, June 9, 1994)

The Wood River staff interpret and define the empty hands on the bus policy differently depending upon the audience and context. Prior to the bus staff training session, Ruth asks me if she should bring up the empty hands on the bus policy for discussion. During the training session for bus riders and drivers, Ruth and Gary, like other Hoover CAC Head Start bus staff, do not question administrators when they describe the policy. Yet at Wood River, Ruth, supported by Judy, decides that the empty hands on the bus policy interpretation includes allowing children to look at magazines and hold stuffed animals on the bus ride. Ruth, like other Hoover CAC bus riders who provides playthings for children, defines the policy in two ways: as an official policy and working policy. The official policy definition, constructed by agency administrators, reflects local, state, and federal policies and procedures. The working policy entails the Wood River staff's definition of how the official policy will be implemented in the daily program.

One explanation for the difference between staffs' and administrators' interpretations of policies is that administrators are removed from the daily operation of the program, and when they do visit programs, they focus on completing evaluations and checklists. Focusing on monitoring and compliance limits administrators in their understanding of how local programs operate. Gary suggests that instead of coming out and monitoring staff, that the administrators should "spend several days or real time riding the bus to get a feel for what it is really like."

Why would Hoover CAC develop the empty hands on the bus policy when it seems that local staff, familiar with the bus route, are more aware of the children's needs? One explanation for this discrepancy is that central authority structures are "prone to delegate tasks, but they are not inclined to delegate power" (Malen, 1994, p. 250). Though Hoover CAC vests Judy with the power and authority of site-based manager of Wood River Head Start, her power and authority to make decisions relevant to the everyday operation of the program are limited.

Federal and Hoover CAC Head Start policies are predicated on the dual aims of local control and central authority. Federal Head Start Performance Standards require that local agencies develop and operate programs sensitive to local conditions and needs and simultaneously adhere to an expanding array of Head Start policies. Likewise administrating agencies appoint local staff to site-based positions and at the same time monitor staff and require documentation of numerous prescriptive policies. These authoritative structures have "a dual interest: ensuring effectiveness and maintaining control, on the one hand" (Weiler, 1993, p. 55) and granting a certain level of autonomy to programs within their jurisdiction. This dual interest gives the illusion that local agencies are empowered to make significant decisions and at the same time significantly limits the types of decisions local personnel can make.

Discussion

Wood River Head Start has unique characteristics that distinguish it from other local, regional, and national programs. Studying the unique events at Wood River can lead to a broader understanding of the social processes that Head Start staff employ to interpret and implement official policies. What connects Wood River to other programs are the historical, cultural, and economic forces that shape all Head Start programs. While the same events are enacted differently at other Head Start centers, the types of events are bounded by the general framework of Head Start.

If Head Start staff are viewed as active participants in the policy process, then the nature and scope of many prescriptive policies are problematic because they ignore teachers' and students' knowledge and ideas (Pauly, 1991). As Ayers (1989) states,

> Prescriptions for the schools are too often of the quick-fix variety and come in the form of proclamations from above with little appreciation for the contexts and needs of particular children.... Neither do they address the real-life concerns of specific families and teachers. When this happens, the policy-making, managerial perspective overwhelms the messy, idiosyncratic nature of children and teachers in schools and the truth of nuance and subtlety is lost in the interest of smooth formal problem solving. (p. 2)

Prescriptive policies ignore Head Start staffs' knowledge of their own strengths and weaknesses and downplay the complexity and messiness of daily life. Moreover, prescriptive policies are premised on the assumption that standardized practices will result in standardized outcomes for children and staff.

How, then, could investigations of local policy influence the development and analysis of Head Start policy? Studies of local staffs' interpretations of policy may redefine program quality and effectiveness. Staffs' working knowledge of communities and resources could result in local definitions of quality and effectiveness. Building on teachers', children's, and parent's choices turns the present policy-making system upside down. Instead of prescriptive policies dictating local practice, local choice would influence the formation of policies. Any shift to a local approach to program quality would necessarily require that the current emphasis on procedural compliance be altered.

Timar (1994) suggests that if the nature and scope of federal policy shifted to an evaluation system that focuses more on the intent of policies than procedural compliance, then local agencies would follow suit with local programs. In this model, federal evaluation would focus on local conditions and needs and how program administrators and staff address those needs within the broad parameters of Head Start. If local Head Start administrators shift from a monitoring to a facilitating role, they would focus on how they could provide the support and resources necessary for local staff to achieve a local definition of quality and effectiveness. Administrators would "provide support for a diversity of problem-solving responses tailored to the needs and strengths of those affected by the problems at hand" (Pauly, 1991, pp. 126–7).

At the heart of this policy discussion is a belief that local knowledge is a key element in quality programming. If administrators provide information on policy reform efforts, teachers, assistant teachers, bus drivers, and aides, might work collaboratively within individual programs and across program staffs to envision how to develop a range of program options. This would mark a dynamic change in the current system where the "teacher's [and other staff's] primary task is coping with change rather than enacting" (Mintrop & Weiler, 1994, p. 272). In creating this unofficial policy environment, local solutions, not policy mandates, would become the mainstay of the discussion.

Conclusion

In the wake of substantial increases in Head Start funding and the historical loose coupling with administrating agencies, policy-makers have developed new directives and monitoring procedures for Head Start programs. The implicit assumptions are that these policies and monitoring will produce higher-quality services to families and children.

Traditionally Head Start policy analysis relies upon an input-output model that analyzes how policy directives impact services to families and children. This model does not include studies of how Head Start staff interpret and implement official policies within the context of the specific children and families served.

My study, which investigated how the Wood River staff interpret and implement official policies, found that the staff recognize the importance of official policies and the impracticability of implementing certain policies within the realities of the program. Staff discuss policies in the context of ongoing problems or dilemmas. Through these discussions staff determine how to interpret and implement policies. Staff hold multiple viewpoints about the same policy that include an official definition emanating from Hoover CAC. Staff also define a working policy that describes how staff implement a specific policy within the context of the Wood River program.

Chapter 15

Restructuring Governing in Eastern Europe: Constructing New Needs for Families, Children, and Child Care

Marianne N. Bloch

Introduction

In 1993 and in 1995, I had the opportunity to examine changes in family, educational, and, specifically, childcare policy in three Eastern and Central European countries during the early stages of the post-Soviet transition away from Communism and toward a market economy. My principle interest was to understand how individual countries as well as the group of countries in Eastern and Central Europe, faced with a similar and sudden need for change, would choose to restructure their family and educational policies, especially in relation to women, family, and childcare for young children. As a Western educational researcher, I had understood that childcare provision in Eastern and Central Europe as well as the former Soviet Union was substantial and I had wondered how a transition toward Western economic, social, and political ideas would transform policies, practices, and lives for the better or for the worse. Using a Foucaultian theoretical perspective (e.g., see Barry, Osborne, & Rose, 1996; Burchell, Gordon, & Miller, 1991; Foucault, 1980, 1991), this chapter examines *the changing governmentalities* in Eastern and Central Europe that I saw that were affecting the lives of families, mothers, and their young children.[1]

Introducing the Subject

The collapse of the Soviet Union's hegemony over its satellites since the late 1980s and early 1990s resulted in enormous and varied changes in the former Soviet- and Soviet-bloc countries, including those of Eastern and Central Europe. Among the significant changes that have been occurring, some of the most important have related to the changing nature of discourse related to the education and care of citizens. This chapter is focused on discursive language and practices that give a window into the ways in which the new citizen is being represented and constructed since the transition away from Communism started in 1990. This chapter results from research done in 1993 and 1995 in three representative Eastern and Central European countries: Bulgaria, Hungary, and Poland. While the discursive changes that will be discussed will be presented briefly here, they should be viewed as a way to imagine the complexity and dynamic nature of changes that are occurring, as well as representing new theoretical ways to look at change.

The ways in which different countries moving from one political/economic regime to another conceive of changes in the education of their youngest citizens is rarely discussed in the literature related to the transitions that are occurring in East/Central Europe today. While some have written about educational reform, and some have studied changing social/family policies in this region, there has been very little examination of the complex ways in which discourses circulate to create new imaginations of what citizens should be like or should become, how families should act differently, ways in which schooling and childcare for children is changing (Anderson, 1991). In contrast, in this chapter, I focus on the ways in which complex discourses at global, regional, national, local, and individual levels intermingle in the formation of new ways to reason about the ways children, their parents, and their teachers should act as they reconstruct life and education for children and for the adults of the next generation.

I try to illustrate how reforms related to families and the care and educational systems organized for young children represent new conceptions, new ways of reasoning about national, family, and individual "needs."[2] In addition, reforms taking place also embody selective images of liberalism, welfare, the market, democracy, and the role of the state and civil society in governance, including the care and education of the young child as citizen.

Governing in East/Central Europe

In examining recent reforms in East/Central Europe, it seemed critical to examine global as well as more localized discourses in order to begin to understand how these discourses come to govern through the new ways of reasoning about families, children, what the good parent, teacher, and child should become. The research that was conducted, therefore, in Bulgaria, Hungary, and Poland, was complemented by continuing examination of international economic reports, global reforms represented through different sources (media, international reports, transnational changes and debates). The research conducted, in conjunction with a variety of other documents that were examined, then allowed me to explore ways in which young children's education appeared to be changing in each country and, using these three countries as examples, within the East/Central European region, more generally. I focused on the reasoning created in new laws and policies, and the ways these discourses become immersed in new local practices and the language used to promote interests and beliefs by different groups and individuals within the state and civil society. In this chapter, I argue that the new patterns of governing affect the way state and non-state, public and private groups (businesses, schools, families), and individuals have come to act and reason about themselves and others.

Governance and Governmentality

Foucault's theoretical concept of governance and governmentality[3] provides a theoretical frame for this research. While Foucault also wrote within the context of Western Europe, his concepts of governance and governmentalities seem particularly useful when looking at the rapid changes related to new discourses about family, education, and care of young children in the post-Soviet transition.

Foucault used the concept of governance simultaneously in relation to *governance of others and governance of the self.* Governance refers to all those ways of reflecting and acting that aim to shape, guide, manage, or regulate the conduct and ways of reasoning embedded in institutions, groups, and individuals. In this conceptualization, governance has both macro-social forms as well as micro-governing patterns, including governing through the reasoning evidenced in the words of laws and policies, as well as governing private thoughts, conduct, or the soul (see Foucault, 1991; Rose, 1989).

Foucault proposed the notion of *governmentality* as a blurring of boundaries between the state and all quarters of civil society and blurring the boundaries between the self and the society. The governmentalized subject views him/her self not merely as a self-governed individual but also as "citizen." In Foucault's sense, governance is political—not through particular actions of the state, institutions, or particular actors (e.g., the state as a sovereign power)—but by the varieties of political reasoning that come to order the affairs of a territory and its population to ensure its well-being or welfare, and that construct and establish individuals' and group reasoning. The creation of ways to reason can result in natural divisions between the proper spheres of action of different types of authority; for example, the way we reason about the divisions in authority between state and other actors in civil society, or the state, schools and family, even divisions between public and private that we take as natural.[4] Foucault argues convincingly that the creation of artificial distinctions and dichotomies in the ways we learn to reason hides important governing strategies that are subtle, diffuse, and extremely complex.

The two ways of governance used by Foucault—governance of others and governance of oneself—both include the creation of what is called governmentalities as to who should govern and toward what end, which institutions have certain rights and responsibilities, and what the rights and responsibilities for action, participation and thought are for individuals and different groups. These ways of reasoning or governmentalities are a result of complex circulating discourses at global, national, and local levels that are filtered through different texts, regulations and policies, the media, statistics, what comes to be known as authoritative knowledge, social scientific and other educational expertise, pedagogical reforms, and through the ways we (parents, teachers, children) come to reflect and reason (self-govern) in our most private thoughts.

Power and Knowledge

The different reasoning that comes to be accepted involves the creation of new power/knowledge relationships with differential effects and opportunities to participate. Not everyone, in short, has the ability to participate equally in the construction of authoritative knowledge, what knowledge is taken as truth at a particular period or time (Foucault, 1980). In summary, in this chapter, I investigated new ways of reasoning or governmentalities that helped to construct new truths about conduct at public/private levels, new ways to think about the actions and interactions of parents, teachers, government, and children. Finally, I saw these new ways to reason as elements of power/knowledge relations, that include and simultaneously exclude, not as simply neutral shifts in reasoning with no effect.

Constructing Conceptions of Welfare in Eastern and Central Europe

Although the transition away from Communism is often linked to the Solidarity trade movement strikes in Poland in 1989 and to the fall of the Berlin wall, the transition was obviously more complex historically and was linked to a declining economy in the Soviet Union during the 1980s. In addition, there was continuing political unrest in the Soviet Union and in the East/Central European region, and, at least by the late 1980s, increasing communications between East and West that brought different images of citizenship and economic, social, and political rights to Soviet bloc citizens. Within this broader context of change, beginning (at least) in the 1980s, we can then turn toward the early 1990s, when international organizations, businesses and banks, Western media commentators, Western feminist groups and writers, educational reformers, and others began to rush in to support or discuss the transitions of diverse countries to more liberal market-oriented and/or "democratic" systems. Within the context of East/Central Europe, individuals, different groups within civil society (for example, women's groups, labor union representatives, teachers, academics), and government officials began to debate the wisdom of different discursive models for rebuilding the social, political, and economic institutions. They searched for their own way to define democracy or "market economy," searching for ways to define the way life should be in the newly reconstructed countries, or how future citizens should be educated or cared for. The urgency associated with dialogue and reform in all spheres, new opportunities (e.g., entry into NATO or the European Union) as well as the difficulties associated with rapid change led to quick policy changes and reversals, as well as new dialogues about what is possible within each country, and between countries in the region. In 1998, for example, new elections in Hungary resulted in a socialist government's replacement by a more liberal, market-oriented, pro-capitalist government. Different discourses provided different ways of reasoning as a foundation for dialogue within and across countries, with different actors and different texts generating temporary truths about which social, economic reforms or scenarios for a region or country might be best. These discursive ways of reasoning embodied different ways of reasoning about "good changes" for different interest groups, for the majority, for various minority groups, for short-term changes, and for longer-term changes; they also embodied power/knowledge relations such that different discursive practices appeared to be inclusive and "democratic," while, in their effects, favoring some groups over others, and, therefore, including and excluding at the same time. Thus, rapid disintegration and changes in policies, institutions, and practices that had been taken-for-granted for approximately forty years under Communist governments resulted in increased uncertainty. In addition, the transitions resulted in severe impoverishment for many and wealth for a minority, to new visions and opportunities. The governing discourses, thus, generated new possibilities for action for some, while at the same time, excluding possibilities for others, including some in reforms while excluding others from participation in reforms and debates, and other material possibilities.

Reasoning, Governance, and Early Childhood Care and Education prior to 1990

Families—especially women and children—were expected to be particularly vulnerable to the post-Soviet transition toward a market economy. Under a Communist scheme of welfare, governing reasoning prioritized collective welfare over individual opportunity, and care for all families, at least at minimum levels, over enhanced welfare and wealth for only some. Within these ways of reasoning, families were guaranteed minimum family incomes, universal health benefits, access to universal family allowances and childcare, and a variety of other entitlements and social benefits that ensured them at least minimum acceptable economic welfare. In addition, to try to ensure reasonable quality care and education for children at all levels, central control of childcare and schooling was mandated and enacted. Childcare and schooling were virtually free; they were highly standardized and regulated. Curriculum was centrally led and controlled and, in addition, to standardize skills and activities children would encounter, curriculum also promoted the social ideals of the (diverse) Communist governments.

Families were supported through a variety of intricate family allowances that were based upon the number of children in a family, age of child, and the premise that society needed to support care and education for preschool-age children while supporting (men's and) women's work outside the home. From birth to three years of age, care for children was guaranteed through maternal leave policies, family allowances that allowed mothers to stay at home with young children from one to three years with guaranteed jobs at the end of their leave, and nurseries/creches (while both the English and French words were used in translations into English, hereafter, I use the term "nursery"). Programs typically included full-day care and were administered by Ministries of Health and/or Social Welfare and were especially targeted toward families where mothers "needed" to work. After three years, children of mothers who (went back to) work attended state and factory-subsidized (also state) centrally controlled kindergarten centers. These were full-day programs and were administered by the Ministry of Education.

Changes in Mentalities and Governance since 1990

The political discourses that surrounded the conception of collective "cradle to grave" safety and welfare and gender equity in the workplace for women were never fulfilled and varied significantly both within and across countries of the former Communist bloc. There was less equity in the workplace than ideologically promised. While there was a minimum income provided to all, along with health care, etc., there were still wide resource variations, and political oppressions, for which the Soviet and Communist governments became (in)famous. New discussions of competition, freer markets, and democracy began to emerge in the late 1980s. With the change from Communist governments, Bulgaria, Hungary, and Poland began to shift toward conceptions of a free market, to try to compete, and to try to build forms of democracies; each country, however, had different ways of forming this imaginary community (Anderson, 1991). Some (individuals and countries) with greater resources moved quickly to consolidate opportunities, to position themselves within the market; for others, income disparities grew along with uncertainty for the many who lost jobs and other guarantees of minimum welfare for their families. The sense of collective welfare, within the framework of different governing discourses that encouraged/regulated the shifts, gave way to discourses that encouraged "individualism" that allowed some to be impoverished while others were able to benefit or become rich. The changing discourses also shifted reasoning so that long-term economic "growth" could be seen as the most important collective goal, with short-term poverty for many, including children, suddenly acceptable. In addition, the global, national, and local discursive environment presented a sense that "democratization" would allow for economic and political independence, new freedoms of speech and participation, recognition of individual rights and choices, and an ability to participate actively in civil society as voters and decision makers. The expectation was that the new possibilities would be all-inclusive in a way that socialist/communist governance failed to accomplish, especially once the long-term goals for economic development and modernization were accomplished. With new expectations came new policies and regulations, new patterns of governance that included ways of self-reflection and self-action. In the new discursive environment, independence, personal responsibility to oneself or one's own family, freedom, and choice appeared as important "signifiers" of the new good life, although "personal responsibility" was a problem for many who were increasingly impoverished and/or out of work. I argue these were new ways to reason about life and self—new governmentalities in a Foucaultian sense. As a way to fight against the control and centralization rampant in the Communist governments, and in response to global, national, and local discourses, reasoning that encompassed ideas of decentralization, privatization, and choice began to occur in the market and in educational and child care policy reforms.

The cases of Bulgaria, Hungary, and Poland provide a window into the ways in which a convergence of international, national, and local governmentalities have come to include new representations of words associated with the free market and democracy (e.g., decentralization, privatization, choice, flexibility, autonomy) and how these new ways of reasoning represent power/knowledge relations and their effects. I will also try to illustrate how the new ways of reasoning include some more than others, limit, divide, and create distinctions, often while claiming to be more inclusive and democratic.

Both Hungary and Poland were leaders in the move away from Communist governments and both, since 1990, have made significant economic "progress," according to international reports on "Countries in Transition" (see Bloch & Blessing, in press). In 1990, Bulgaria was more closely aligned with the Soviet Union and was geographically and economically further from the West and Western markets than Poland or Hungary. By 1998, Bulgaria also had made "progress" toward democracy and a market economy, though still at a slower pace than the other two countries. It was less "attractive" to outside Western firms searching for lower risk East/Central European partnerships, and had a slower start in the competitive market to attract outside investors. As a result of these differences, and others, in 1998 Hungary and Poland were approved as the first candidates (along with the Czech Republic) for entry into NATO and will be among the first accepted in the European Union when it is expanded. Bulgaria will be in a later group to be accepted into NATO and the European Union; to date (1998) no dates have been projected as to when it will be "ready."

While all three provide a glimpse of regional economic changes, the three also provide examples of ways to study how global discourses have presented pictures of different countries, pictures that come to govern the mentalities of others, as well as individuals' private self-reflections of country, family, and self. To illustrate these points, in the next section I discuss international discourses that were commonly used in international media and donor agency reports describing East/Central European countries' transition or progress. In addition, I use statistical patterns from selected international reports to show (1) which indicators are used within international reports to portray economic "progress," and (2) how differences in the countries, based upon statistics, are used to indicate problems and prospects in economic development during the transition from Soviet control: 1990–1995.

International Discourse Related to "Becoming a Free Market"
International banks and donors became important influences in East/Central Europe and the entire group of Newly Independent States (NIS) made up of the former Soviet Union by at least the early 1990s. Whereas under Soviet influence, economic stagnation or increased poverty was rarely discussed, by the late 1980s, the economic slowdown associated with the Soviet Union's command market and economy had affected all of the member nations, including those of East/Central Europe. Local black market entrepreneurial activity facilitated the transitions in each country, particularly in Poland. Therefore, new discourses within countries as well as from the outside to privatize, develop open markets, become "efficient" and "competitive" provided an important governing context that allowed East/Central European countries to become receptive to the terms, and to become receptive to Western multinational companies that wanted to form joint private/state partnerships or "joint ventures." During the early transition years, each of the former Soviet bloc countries competed for international donor funds and for multi-national companies to buy state factories or to develop joint venture schemes.

Neo-liberal market economic discourse—competition, choice, privatization, efficiency, and "free" markets—were circulating discourses—within the three countries, and in the European region, in general. By circulating, I mean circulating with no one point of origin, and no causal relationships involved, as though one could see capillaries that circulate within the biological body. In addition, the discourses of "freedom," "autonomy," "individualism," and "democracy" were linked with the concept that competition was good, open markets were needed and provided choice—even at the cost of social provisions for citizens.

To become "democratic" and "economically competitive," almost no matter what cost, came to be understood as normal and desirable; these governing discourses became important at the broad as well as at the local levels and in private self-governance in ways individuals spoke, the reasoning they used, and the actions they chose.

International Economic Reports: Statistics and Populational Reasoning

The reasoning was embedded in international reports that generally are accepted without question, yet the statistics and the reasoning within, for example, a World Bank report, portray what Hacking (1991) calls group or populational reasoning. "Populational reasoning" began in the early twentieth century in Western Europe and the United States as a manner of describing groups or individuals, and was used by social scientists in social policy development to describe groups in need of intervention. The human side of numbers or groups was erased as groups become classified by terms ("under the poverty line," "single parent"). By contrast, groupings also enabled classification where some groups were considered as normal, and by comparison, others were abnormal. Using the same idea with countries, we can see modern or developed countries, undeveloped countries, or those "in transition," where modern and developed becomes the unquestioned norm, that also defines what is good.

In the case of international discourse that describes the transitional period in East/Central Europe (and the former Soviet Union), international banks and donor agencies select labels and statistical indicators that represent progress toward goals characteristic of a healthy free-market, a "modern" and "developed" and a neo-liberal economic perspective and call such progress "normal" or "in transition" toward normality. The examples below illustrate how international texts contributed to the governing mentalities (governmentalities) that were present in East/Central Europe in the early 1990s and that created new ways to reason about continuing support for childcare.

Economic growth is represented internationally by Gross Domestic Product (GDP) figures (see Table 15.1 below for GDP figures for Bulgaria, Hungary, and Poland, 1990–1995), investment, and national debt. In addition, unemployment and poverty figures are commonly examined indicators of the economic and social health of a nation. The GDP figures (Table 15.1) indicate all three countries have been "progressing" economically. Investment and debt statistics also show there have been large increases in international monies coming into Hungary and Poland (with slower investment in Bulgaria).

Table 15.1: Annual Percentage Change in GDP, 1990-1995[5]

	1990	1991	1992	1993	1994	1995
Bulgaria	−9.1	−6.9	−5.7	−3.7	2.2	2.5
Hungary	−3.3	−11.9	−3.0	−0.8	2.9	2.0
Poland	−11.6	−7.0	2.6	3.8	5.0	7.0

As suggested earlier, international agency discourse typically praised foreign investment. In the early years of the East/Central European transition, foreign investors were being enticed into countries with a variety of low-cost incentives, including the ability to disregard traditional welfare guarantees such as childcare. Therefore, the complex ways in which economic progress was entangled with the "need" for outside investment, privatization, and need for budgetary "efficiency" pushed each country in the region to market itself as a modern (i.e., open, free-market) economy, and to look aside when traditional social guarantees, such as childcare, that had earlier been accepted as normal were ignored or shut down by foreign companies. The relation between investment and social benefit maintenance or provision was best represented by a comment recorded during my 1993 visit to Hungary. A young male American international consultant at an international firm charged with privatizing companies and attracting foreign investors stated that the Hungarian firms were being urged to get rid of all of their "social assets" as quickly as possible (including nurseries, kindergartens, etc.) as these only detracted from the firm's or factory's value, were cumbersome and costly, and not typical of Western business benefits to employees. This mentality discursively played into the development of social policy reforms during the transition period that, in all three countries, undermined the taken-for-granted status and desirability of nursery and kindergarten provision.

International banks and donor agencies not only provided resources for occurring, emerging, and emergency needs, but "guided" policy development with strict rules, regulations, incentives, and threats, in return for loans. While adding to external debt, international donor requirements to reduce internal debt stimulated many countries in East/Central Europe and the Newly Independent States (NIS) of the former Soviet Union to be concerned with the amount of social benefits and services they were providing as these services and benefits contributed to high costs, especially when the economy was slowing down, and factories were closing or unable to pay wages. In addition, universal social benefits were not provided by many Western firms or many Western economies (particularly the U.S.) that were considered to be the market-oriented models promoted by international donors for the transition countries. Finally, Western European countries were under pressure to reduce their own social costs in order to unite their currencies in the Euro; France, a country with significant social benefits, including virtually universal and inexpensive childcare, had relatively successful labor strikes in 1998 that kept the government from major cuts in "social expenditures." As East/Central European countries also were constructing a need to join the European Union, different actors pushed to trim social benefits that were costly and increased debt. The result of these discourses in reports, the media, external and internal discussions was that by 1995 social benefits, including childcare and other family allowances, were being cut or proposed for reduction in Bulgaria, Hungary, and Poland. While Bulgaria was the most in debt, Poland and Hungary were under continuous pressure to take international loans, while reducing internal debt and social programs, including nurseries and kindergartens for 0–6's.

Unemployment, Professional Mothers, and the Discourse of Choice
Unemployment rates and changes in unemployment policies also were part of the discursive environment in the transition away from Communist governments. Communist government policies supported a discourse of universal entitlements to jobs, income, health, social safety, including childcare; therefore, the very emergence, acceptance, and naturalness of statistics documenting employment and unemployment as well as poverty reflected important discursive shifts in reasoning. As important were the debates that were occurring about reductions in social expenditures except for those "in need," those who were unemployed, those "in poverty," these policy debates moved Bulgaria, Hungary, and Poland, by 1995, toward a liberal welfare philosophy, encouraged by the international (Anglo- and U.S.-) models that would provide social supports to the "needy" and the unemployed rather than as universal entitlements to all.

A new category of description, *unemployment* did increase during the first years of the transition. The rise in unemployment (see Table 15.2 below) was, in part, created by the transition from the command economy of the Soviet period when factories lost markets, were sold, reduced, and/or closed.

Table 15.2: Unemployment Rates, 1990–1994

	1990	1991	1992	1993	1994,[6]
Bulgaria	1.7	11.1	15.3	16.4	13.3
Hungary	1.7	8.5	12.3	12.1	11.0
Poland	3.5	9.7	13.3	15.7	16.9

But who were the needy and unemployed? What were their "needs"? Between 1989 and 1992, for example, female employment participation was reported to have fallen from 93% to 66% in Bulgaria, from 78% to 66% in Hungary, and from 70% to 60% in Poland.[7] While female/male unemployment rates did not indicate sharp differences in the three countries, industry by industry rates varied (e.g., textile factories had high female unemployment; mining industries had higher male unemployment). With industries and factories closing, being sold or privatized, many were suddenly unemployed. Many women were encouraged to take childcare leave; women and men were also told to take "involuntary vacation." In addition, women were told they finally had a choice to not work outside the home, that they could return home to be with young children, to enjoy becoming "professional mothers," to take advantage of opportunities to become more involved in their children at home and at school. These statements were expressed in the media, in Eastern women/feminist writings, by labor ministry officials, and were part of the post-Communist self-governing reflections of parents interviewed during the research conducted in 1993, and to a lesser extent in 1995 (Einhorn, 1993; Fernandez & Bloch, 1993; Funk & Mueller, 1993).

Although the statistics suggested male/female unemployment was similar, registration for unemployment (the statistical indicator most heavily used in international reports for unemployment) did not include unemployment when on childcare leave, nor when women or men were on "involuntary vacation." Women were by far the largest childcare leave takers, of course, and were often not given a "choice" as to whether to take leave, to be on "involuntary vacation," or whether they wished to become or were able to become "professional mothers"; in addition, while women and families considered most "in need" continued to receive low parental leave allowances under new social reforms for their time at home with children, other women were given no subsidies for childcare leave time, nor to help pay fees for childcare if they were employed. Moreover, if women took childcare leave, they were officially employed and received no unemployment benefits. Increasingly, in addition, the laws that guaranteed a return to employment after childcare leaves of three years, for example, could not be upheld, as factories were restructuring and, at times, closing down completely. Women who were discursively still employed while on childcare leave being "professional mothers" were ineligible for job retraining opportunities, and were often employed part-time and/or without benefits upon returning to work outside the home. Thus, the maintenance and, at times, augmentation of maternity leave allowances or leave time, at low cost to governments and factories, presented a picture of relatively low female unemployment, while at the same time offered the government and industries opportunities to save money by eliminating a portion of the workforce during the transition period.[8] With more women at home, or out of regular employment, there was less money to pay fees for childcare, and more opportunities to cut social costs of childcare provision. The complex discursive formations that supported the logic of the changes described above, including international, national, and local patterns, statistics, texts, regulations, media, were part of power/knowledge relations that appeared inclusive and democratic, while, in fact, they were highly exclusionary.

Childcare, Kindergartens, and Education
Decreasing Enrollment and Provision of Programs

As suggested earlier, full provision of either paid maternity leave or nurseries for 0–3-year-olds and provision of kindergarten places for 3–6 or 3–7-year-old children had been a part of the discourse of universal entitlement in all of the former Soviet bloc countries, including Bulgaria, Hungary, and Poland. In the post-communist transition period, proposals for extensions of time for maternity leave and reductions in maternity leave subsidization as well as other social subsidies and services were made; reductions in services to which families were discursively, at least, entitled in Bulgaria, Hungary, and Poland included nurseries and kindergartens.

Nursery enrollment and programs for 0–3-year-olds as well as in kindergartens for 3–6-year-olds declined in the years immediately following 1990 (Bloch & Blessing, in press; Fernandez & Bloch, 1993). Nonetheless, there were important differences among the three countries even before 1990 and important changes in provisions across the region and within countries since 1990. These are represented in Table 15.3 (empty cells reflect my difficulty in getting comparable statistics across the three countries).

As Table 15.3 and follow-up interviews with ministry officials suggested, since 1990 nurseries and kindergartens decreased in all countries, except Hungary.[13] In Hungary, nurseries decreased somewhat and also combined children into fewer programs, but the proportion of children enrolled in or "covered by" kindergartens remained fairly constant (see tables for further discussion). A close examination of Table 15.3 shows that kindergartens and nurseries also began closing before 1990 in most countries, with significantly greater coverage of children in 1980 and even in 1985 than in 1990. In Bulgaria and Poland, nursery coverage has declined proportionately more than kindergarten enrollment, though these have also decreased fairly rapidly. In Hungary, the 1995 Bokros Amendment related to extensions of maternity leave led nursery educators and Ministry of Health officials to predict significant declines in nursery availability for 0–3-year-olds. Kindergartens closed in Poland as a response to rising unemployment, lower fertility, and fees for kindergarten, and because the Polish Ministry of Education stressed that coverage during a child's sixth year, the year prior to primary school, was most crucial for continued coverage. In Bulgaria, kindergarten coverage declined because of unemployment, lower fertility, fee inflation, and in response to a discourse that appeared to favor privatization. In both countries, the factors were even more complex than stated here, and were certainly difficult to disentangle. In contrast, relatively few kindergartens were closed in Hungary compared to the other two countries because Ministry of Education legislation was changed to include kindergartens for 3–6-year-olds as the first stage or step of public schooling, a discursive step that made it more difficult to close kindergartens (see Bloch & Blessing, in press, for further discussion of this point).

Table 15.3: Nursery and Kindergarten Coverage (%), 1980, 1985, 1990–1994

	1980	1985	1990	1993	1994
Bulgaria					
Nurseries: 0–3			11.7	9.2[9]	
Kindergartens-3–6		100	93	67–80	60–82[10]
Hungary					
Nurseries-0–3	14.8	1	1.1	11.1	11.2[11]
Kindergartens-3–6	96	91	84.9	86.6	86.3[12]
Final Yr. Kind-5 yrs.				95%	
Poland					
Nurseries-0–3		5.2	5.1	4.2	4
Kindergartens-3–6	55	51	47.1	42.6	42.7
Zero class-6 yrs.			96		

Discourses Concerning Childcare and Early Education

Many factors account for the described changes in provision for and attendance in nursery and kindergarten programs in the three countries. These include falling birth rates, increasing fees for childcare at the same time as unemployment (especially female) and poverty were increasing, and a differential history of provision at the nursery/creche and kindergarten levels. In addition, as I have tried to show in earlier sections already, international and regional discourses—from varying sources—promoted the conception that women might choose to stay at home, especially with young children, and that it was no longer necessary for the country to pay for centrally administered, extensive, and expensive social benefits including nurseries and kindergarten childcare. In the next section, I look at ways different actors at international, regional, national, and local levels developed arguments, policies and responses to new regulations—showing the possibilities for complex debate, local actions, meanings, and resistance. Several examples from the research on Hungarian regulations about kindergarten, women's groups in Russe, Bulgaria, or policy implementors in local communities that kept these "social assets" represent the importance of looking at local meaning and action.

Local Meanings: The Language of Reform Policies

In kindergartens for 3–6-year-olds, which were administered and supervised in special preschool units in Ministries of Education from the beginning of the twentieth century in all three countries, there was a historical discourse associating, and at the same time *dis*associating, young 3–6-year-old children's care and education with the formation of schools and schooling. For example, while primary schooling was mandatory, kindergarten attendance was not mandatory for children in any of the countries. Nonetheless, unlike nursery schools for 0–3-year-old children, it was regulated that governments provide kindergarten centers and places for parents who requested or needed it. Coupling this with full employment policies and a discourse supporting universal provision, the majority of parents wanted kindergartens and governments had to respond. In fact, in Bulgaria and Hungary, with long historical traditions of educational experimentation with kindergartens that predated the Communist period, the policies requiring kindergartens for all children resulted in 80–90% of the 3–6-year-old children having places in kindergartens in both countries by the 1980s. In Poland, a much larger, more rural, and more politically and religiously traditional country than the other two, finances were never made available to fully enact the policy of providing kindergartens for all 3–6-year-olds; therefore, kindergarten provision reached only 55–60% of the 3–6 year olds, even at the peak of provision in the 1970s, with greater coverage in the Zero Class—a class for 6-year-olds—preceding entry into primary school.[14]

While the historical differences are very important, they also manifested themselves in different transitional policies during the 1990–1995 period. In all three countries, new regulations and policies were passed during this period that supported the continuation of maternity leave and other allowances for 0–3-year-old children (and in Hungary by 1995 the proposed law to provide leave only for mothers with 0–1-year-old children) and legislation that supported the desirability but not the necessity of providing "places" in creches or nurseries for 0–3-year-old children; the choice of providing nursery places would be left to local governments. In contrast, in all three countries, new regulations were passed that reinforced the state mandate to provide kindergartens for those who wanted them. However, again, local governments were to put these regulations into place. In Poland and Bulgaria, the mandates were written into regulations in the strongest form for the year prior to primary school, "that communities must provide kindergarten for [the six-year-old] zero class, the year preceding entry into the public school...", with slightly weaker language for kindergarten provision for 3- and 4-year-old children.

In Hungary, in contrast, Ministry of Education officials in the preschool section charged with policy related to kindergarten education lobbied for and helped to pass legislation mandating that communities had to provide kindergartens for all 3–6-year-old children as kindergartens were the first step of publicly provided "school." By associating kindergartens with public school, the Hungarian officials merged kindergarten into general and accepted discourse on "schooling" rather than the more flexible, disposable, and separate/separatable early education, preschool, or kindergarten schooling. The result of the shift in language used in the legislation was to force communities to maintain kindergartens for 3–6-year-old children in Hungary, while in Bulgaria and Poland, the protection was only for the final pre-public school year. In the case of nurseries, the legislative wording was even weaker in all three countries, providing *choice* to economically strapped communities as to whether to continue to keep nurseries open for families who requested space.

The Language of Regulation: Decentralization and Choice

The subtlety of the shifts and differences in ways laws and regulations referred to the need to provide nursery/creche or kindergarten care (openings) for families signals the ways in which subtle shifts in reform discourse enact broader discourses (e.g., that of choice). The case, for example, of Hungarian policy changes also shows that discourses are not determining or "totalizing" but that local, contingent histories and actions are important. The new regulations were also being formed as a response to discourses of "democracy"—decentralization, local control, and autonomy. While the state continued to provide broad "steering" and maintained some control of finances, prioritization of needs and specific financial allocations were shifted to local municipalities, in part because neither the central nor the local governments had enough money to finance all prior services. They were also a response to discourse supporting the desirability of privatization, and a response to the broad international and regional discourses concerned with local autonomy, choice, and democracy.[15]

In the 1980s, state factories were among the earliest to see a financial need to shift childcare (nurseries and/or kindergartens) from their own budgets to those of local municipalities which were also responsible for providing state nurseries and kindergartens; the first major changes in kindergarten/nursery provision, then, was in who was in nominal control at local levels, while the government maintained central control of curriculum and finance. The second major change occurred in the early 1990s, when partial financing and decision making was handed over by the central governments to local municipalities in new laws related to local municipality control. This change, combined with the changes in the wording of regulations about providing nursery and kindergarten places for children, allowed some municipalities to keep existing nurseries or kindergartens open, while others didn't—they closed or sold buildings, or reduced the number of children who had access to public programs.

One vice-mayor of a district in Budapest described some of the ways in which the financing and decentralization policies as well as the new regulations on nurseries and kindergartens resulted in a discourse that appeared to give greater "choice" and local control to families, women and men, and communities, while at the same time regulating and reducing "choice," autonomy, and control.

> Before the transition, they (the government) thought there was no need for creches, but (its) just the opposite. There's unemployment of men and women who want to keep jobs and so they want children in creches. But the creches aren't growing. We thought we could give an allowance for mothers to stay at home, but it's not enough. Social insurance, 5,000 Forints for each mother to stay at home, but (its) not enough, so mothers are still trying to go to work.
>
> ...[T]he state gives subsidies for Kindergartens, roads, or whatever a municipality needs; but they just give money. It's not obligatory how municipalities should do the task—Greatest stress is the subsidy, (but its) not enough to cover tasks...especially in poorer communities. Start with creches—no specific subsidies are set aside for creches—so we have to find sources for this: All costs—energy, operating costs are theirs (the municipalities) now...If we wanted to hold a vote, we can't because we do not have enough money, so (we) cannot hold a vote.[16]

Discourse and Acts of Privatization

New privatization laws restored state-owned property to their pre-Communist-era owners, allowed state-owned companies to be sold along with their *"social asset"* (including kindergartens/nurseries), and allowed municipalities to sell their buildings, including all those connected with social services, if they chose to do so. Many of these initiatives were stimulated by market discourses—that privatized companies were more efficient and productive than state companies; many sales were instituted by economic need or difficult choices by poorer municipalities with too many services and needs to pay for (see the vice-mayor's points above). The restitution of private property returned many state kindergarten or nursery buildings to earlier owners, who often converted the buildings from kindergartens to houses or other businesses. While one of the bigger previous owners, the church, often chose to keep kindergartens open for educational purposes, when restored to the church, they were now non-state, private, and included a sectarian education; in other words, they were no longer universal, public, or accessible to everyone.

In Bulgaria, in 1995, an interview with a government consultant concerning the number of kindergarten buildings that had been sold or closed down resulted in the following report that showed (in the first example) local sites of resistance to sale, closing, or privatizing kindergartens, as well as the importance of local contexts that forced cutbacks.

> (Recently there was a) Strike by mothers in one city when a kindergarten was sold and was to be used as a business. The population was so shocked that the structure was closed, although their children were probably changed to another kindergarten. Also there were other initiatives of other private entrepreneurs to open other kindergartens. (The strike was) Shown on TV and in the news and probably no other mayors (in other districts of Bulgaria) will sell kindergartens. The kindergartens are under municipal ownership and they should keep them. Probably the mayor was corrupt and this was the problem.

A Discourse of Pedagogical Individualization, Democracy, and the "Whole" Child

Church-owned or church-sponsored kindergartens were also evidence of *an* enactment of the discourse of both choice of ideas, decentralized decisions and participatory patterns, and "democracy," here meaning freedom for diverse ideas and pedagogies. These discourses were positively contrasted with former Communist regulations that required central control, standard and uniform quality. In the new transition period, local control and participation, diversity of ideas and experience, enhanced parental choice, including the availability of sectarian or private schooling, and individualization, differentiation of experience, and creativity were positioned as important for the new "imagined community" of the post-communist, democratic, and market-oriented Eastern and Central European citizens (again, see Anderson, 1991).

These discourses were exemplified in all three countries most directly in changes in the legislation for schools that gave choices of old as well as newly developed curricula to kindergartens and schools, by encouraging more municipality and teacher control of pedagogy, by encouraging more parental involvement in choosing schools *and* through paying for some "special classes" (e.g., English, gymnastics) offered in schools (another way to decentralize and cope with a decreasing budget). The choices and autonomy offered by the central government were offered in the name of creating a new type of a "good teacher" and "good parent," where the good teacher is more "democratic," more "autonomous" and flexible, one who can collaborate with the good parent, who has time, money, and motivation to become "involved," to choose his/her children's schools, and to contribute. Finally, these new skills and conceptions would be instilled in the subjectivities of the teacher, parent, and, through them, in the new Eastern/Central European child.

Conclusion

I end this chapter by focusing on ways in which the discursive "environment" globally, nationally, and locally framed the construction of experience in different localities for regions, nations, and different members of civil society including teachers, families, parents, and young children. In earlier sections, I tried to show how global trends and discursive practices provided a complex context in which competition, economic efficiency, individualization, autonomy, and "personal choice," to select some examples, provided frames for governance patterns that shift from a center or centralized locality toward a more decentered governance process in which local government actors assume it is "right" and good to take on more decision making and that local financing (including by parents) is part of that "good" direction. Similarly, the construct of "choice" for women, most prevalent in our interviews with different ministry officials, in the discourse of Eastern women and feminist writers and in government reform reports authorized women within families to assume the right to stay at home, the entitlement to take care of their own children, if possible. Finally, there were the voices of local municipality directors and teachers who encourage "parent involvement," choice to stay at home or to help to choose between the few newly privatized schools or public schools.

There are the voices of teachers who interpret changes in government curriculum to allow them the flexibility to autonomously choose new curricula, to encourage greater parental involvement with children at home, greater parental choice in paid variations in the school settings and that encouraged attention toward children as autonomous, creative, "developing" "whole" children. All of these, and other, discursive patterns reframed the mentalities of governance from a centralized conception of "sovereign" control or power to a more reflective, autonomous form of "self-governance" characterized by the internment of "truths" from the broader discursive environment.

In fact, there is governance and there are governmentalities in both the centralized and the decentered or decentralized forms of "government." The argument is not that new structures of governing are occurring now in East and Central Europe (or, for that matter, in the Newly Independent States of the former Soviet Union), but that the discourses that are circulating now are new ways of reasoning, different from those in the past. In addition, I argue that the new discourses are emerging from an amalgamation of global/international sources as well as from regional constructions and debates, discourses prevalent at national and local and individual levels. The central point is that these complex and circulating discourses across all levels must be understood as framing conduct, reflection, and reasoning that is different today from earlier periods.

In addition to the examination of the ways this discursive environment has changed ways to reason, I have emphasized that the new ways to reason, the new governmentalities, represent power/knowledge relations that, while appearing to be inclusive and participatory, in fact are inclusive for some while excluding others. The ways in which a neo-liberal discourse of "needs" relates to new conceptions of welfare state, as well as "choice," provide examples that illustrate the way power and knowledge are combined and infuse governing discourses that we come to take as normal, natural, or as truth. Similarly, I have tried through brief illustrative examples to show different meanings given to words such as "free" market or democracy that emanate from countries such as the U.S., but that are incorporated differently into other countries' discourses despite quite different histories and cultural settings despite the notion of "incorporation" just mentioned. However, I have also stressed the importance of local meanings as well as the possibilities of resistance. Finally, I am hopeful that this analysis will help us to reflect on the accepted goods of privatization, decentralization, flexibility, and choice in curriculum, local control, autonomy, and even community or parent involvement that are being examined and incorporated into discourses currently in East/Central Europe, as elsewhere.

In this chapter, I have had a particular focus on changes in social policies and practices related to young children's care and education in Bulgaria, Hungary, and Poland as representative countries facing similar discursive pressures in the transition from a Soviet bloc society to a "free market,, more "democratic" society. I have used a comparative strategy to examine these issues—three countries in Eastern and Central Europe, and an examination of selected discourses at international, regional, national, and local levels. Because of the broad scope I wanted to touch upon in this chapter, I have necessarily presented broad arguments about changing governmentalities, rather than an in-depth look at any country, or even the East/Central European region since 1990. Although this strategy has many pitfalls, not the least of which is to underemphasize the particularities of local and national culture and history, the chapter was meant to be illustrative and raise questions about the formation of social policy, and how this may be occurring currently in the Eastern/Central European region undergoing rapid transition and the impact of changing discourses on, particularly, poor families, women, and young children.

Throughout the analysis, there has been an emphasis on discourses that come to define and govern the actions of families, what men and women are to be and do, where and how children are to be cared for and educated, the formation of schools for different age children, and the role of governments for the well-being of private citizens, particularly, children. Through the illustrative examples provided in earlier parts of the chapter, I have tried to suggest how "choice" and discourses of professional motherhood have been used to redefine the positions and conduct, as well as self-governing reflections about families, women, men, and where and how young children should be cared for and educated. By constituting *"needs"* and *"choices"* as women's problems, or as some families' problems more than others (for example, the needs of families in poverty), we can see how the discursive shifts under a neo-liberal welfare state philosophy move the reasoning about care for children from a societal level more to an individual family or person's (especially women's) level. Within the conceptions of a liberal welfare state discourse, moving from the West to the East in complex ways (including through the choice of statistics and text presented in international reports), the chapter suggests the power of power/knowledge relationships that regulate and administer freedom, limiting and defining who is to be included and who to be excluded from participation. While the power/knowledge relations are productive in that they define how we think and act, they have negative effects through the exclusionary understandings we come to take as normal, through the divisions and differentiations we take as truth. I hope at least I have succeeded in convincing readers to look further at the interplay between what we do in the West and our actions and words in relation to new governing strategies in the East. I hope I have complicated the way we look at family and childcare policy formation and its representation and the opportunities for some to resist at individual reflective as well as at governmental and governance levels; if so the chapter is a success.

NOTES

[1] This chapter reflects research done during two relatively short visits to Bulgaria, Hungary, and Poland, the first in 1993 in a project funded by the U.S. Agency for International Development related to women and childcare (Fernandez & Bloch, 1993), the second, in 1995, as part of a research fellowship funded by the Land Tenure Center, University of Wisconsin-Madison while on sabbatical during the spring, 1995. While I was an outsider in each country and am representing issues by myself here, I acknowledge the many people who gave time to me for interviews and help while in Bulgaria, Hungary, and Poland. My principle collaborators in each country were: Ivan Dimitrov, University of Sofia in Bulgaria, Malgorzata Karwolska-Strucyk, University of Warsaw in Poland, Marta Korintus, National Institute of Nursery Education, and Maria Zam (currently with United Way) in Hungary. This chapter also draws from an earlier chapter (Bloch & Blessing, in press) in a volume edited by Tom Popkewitz; I want to thank him for help in thinking through ideas expressed here.

[2] The social construction of "need" and "dependency" has been examined by Nancy Fraser and Linda Gordon in several pieces; see Fraser (1989), Fraser and Gordon (1994). See a similar argument in Hungary in Haney (1997).

[3] See Foucault (1991), for a recent discussion.

[4] See Foucault (1991) and Hindess (1996).

[5] *World Employment 1995*, Table 15; also *World Economic and Social Survey, 1996*, p. 115.

[6] *World Employment 1995*, Table 18.

[7] See Evans (1995), Vol. I, p. 17.

[8] There are some indications that women are pushed toward "involuntary vacations" more often than men, but figures for the three countries are not only hard to find but generally believed to be inaccurate when cited.

[9] Sources for 1993: Bulgaria—National Statistics Institute 1991 Annual Report, Ministries of Education and Health; Poland—Central Statistics Office and UNICEF, Interviews Ministries of Education and Social Welfare; Cornia and Sipos (1991); Hungary—Central Office of Statistics, Interviews in Ministry of Education and Social Welfare; Fernandez and Bloch (1993).

[10] Sources used give varying estimates. See Evans (1995), Vol. 1, p. 20; *World Education Report: 1995*. Table 3, p. 129; Central Office of Statistics Annual Reports; Interviews (1993–1995) by M. Bloch with Ministry Officials.

[11] *Statistical Handbook of Hungary* (1995/1996), p. 83. Interview with Marte Korintus of the National Day Care Institute, who suggested that 1995 enrollments in nurseries was down to 8%, when the Bokros Proposal recommended reducing maternity leave from 3 to 1 year.

[12] *Statistical Handbook of Hungary* (1995), (1996), p. 108.

[13] The *International Herald Tribute* of May 27, 1998, reconfirmed a sharp drop in kindergartens through 1998.

[14] See Fernandez and Bloch (1993) for further detailed discussion of this history.

[15] See Popkewitz (1996).

[16] Vice-Mayor District in Budapest, 1/15/95

Chapter 16

Resisting Normative Representation in the Pacific Islands: Domestic Enemies Meet over Coffee
Richard T. Johnson and Maria Gaiyabu

> *"What is made possible is the experience of something for the first time that at the same time seems to be already known, known before...Thus certain narrative elements are intensified so that their historical sense makes itself felt."*
> —Patricia Clough, *The End(s) of Ethnography: From Realism to Social Criticism*

Although the expansive Pacific now separates us for the time being, Maria and I have been reading and listening closely to each other's stories since we first met, some five years ago. In fact, it was a personalized story of colonization Maria shared with me that personally and professionally bound us together the moment we met. The stories we've shared, whether oral or written, have kept us connected personally and professionally. This collection of stories we share here allows our strong friendship to survive as we collectively theorize about issues that are important to us. The stories of resistance and representation presented are offered here as a collection of narratives representing our collective theorizing about issues which are important to us as early childhood educators. These stories are of personal importance to us and have implications for a further audience(s), for other "interpretive communities" (Fish, 1980) who care for children (e.g., teachers, child-care workers, future caregivers, mothers and fathers). Just as "the story has become recognized as one of the central roots we have into the continuing quest for understanding human meaning" (Plummer, 1995, p. 5), Maria and I chose to represent our individual and collective professional and personal identities here, through the telling of brief stories.

Story One: How Rich Reads a Menu

Three thousand miles from home I (Rich) craft this part of this collaborative piece in a hotel in Suva, Fiji. Why is it that my first night in a new place, while seeking out dinner in a town I don't know, I decide to eat at a restaurant named "The Bad Dog Cafe," instead of choosing to eat more local food served from a street vendor? My comfort in a more recognized name ("Bad Dog" is located on a corner near a bar named O'Reilly's and a pizza place) initially draws me to the front window of this restaurant, where I spy the menu. I only slept an hour or two on the plane last night, I'm very tired, and I don't have to think much to eat here—everything on the menu looks remarkably familiar. I'm pretty confident about what I'll be getting when I recognize menu items like hamburgers, chicken strips, and caesar salad on the menu. I order fish and chips. In this quick read and ready acceptance of the menu I realize I am excluding other restaurants of equal or better quality, places where I could learn what Fijian food is like, where I could learn new things about different ways of Pacific-island food preparation (while comparing Fijian to Pacific island food preparation in Hawaii), and where I could compare the taste of raw coconut-basted Fijian fish (*kokoda*) to the raw shoyu-basted Hawaiian fish (*poke*) I enjoy back home.

I share this brief story as it is no different than my comfort in browsing and choosing from other familiar menu items over the past twenty years, in this particular case professional menus which for me provided other forms of sustenance. I tasted and learned to like a limited number of items from a limited menu, and each time I ordered in the future I tended not to venture far from those items that I was most familiar with and which I liked the most after repeated consumption. Comparing the field of early childhood education (ECE) to my Fijian restaurant experiences, in my professional life as a teacher I typically consumed highly recognized (i.e., entré) menu items like Piaget, Montessori, Dewey, and Skinner to first help get me through my schooling and later help me get through the day as a teacher. As I well learned in my teacher education preparation programs, these were the items of choice for all those who entered the typical ECE restaurant. Just as I conservatively took to food, I took to my profession. I didn't stray far from those menu items I was taught to like through effective modeling techniques by my professors. I infrequently tried other items, and I always returned to and read from a limited Western menu, a limited Western theory. This limited menu is what strikes me as most important for this story. Restaurant ownership and names have changed, but the traditional, popular menu items have held true.

Thinking back many years to the time when I first enrolled in child development courses as an undergraduate and later as a graduate student, I realize that little has changed intellectually in the discipline I most closely professionally identified myself with over the past twenty years. Sure we're more concerned now about issues like childcare quality, affordability and teacher compensation, but **the** theory (i.e., menu) I studied then remains **THE** theory students (like me then) learn about today. Although the presentation of the food and the limited appetizer selection has changed over the years (i.e., in the 1990s Piaget meets Vygotsky in most popular early childhood texts), the normative nature of the theory remains quite familiar to our collective palates. By reviewing the latest world reknowned Italian "dish," all the way from Reggio Emilia, this particular story helps me stomach the field of early childhood education's overreliance on normative theories, even at a time when other disciplines are expanding their own boundaries and moving well beyond normative notions.

Normative Early Education Practices

Reggio Emilia preschools embellish what most well-qualified early childhood professionals would consider to be essential aspects of quality early educational programs around the world (New, 1994). The journal *Scholastic Pre-K Today* offers a broad description of the Reggio Emilia program as an

> *Approach (that) grows from the belief that children are rich, powerful people, full of the desire and ability to grow up and construct their own knowledge.* . . . [Here] *educators consider creativity and learning part of the same process. Children use the many languages of art, words, movement, etc., to communicate their own knowledge to themselves and others. Every part of Reggio schools, including design, furniture, and materials, is carefully planned to be safe, supportive, and wonderfully stimulating.* (Editorial, 1992, pp. 82–83)

Key elements of the Reggio Emilia program include the image of the child(ren) as "having potential, curiosity, and interest in constructing their learning;" the importance of children's relationships and interactions; the important role of parents; emergent curriculum; project approach to curriculum and allowance of "child time" to work through these projects; teachers as partners (Gandini, 1993). Exposure to and interaction with a multitude of art experiences is a cornerstone of the Reggio program (Schiller, 1995).

The types of theoretical concepts and practical concerns some of you, like me, address each semester at the university and that some of you dialogue about with your colleagues at your respective workplaces, are in concert with what Reggio offers (children viewed as "having potential, curiosity, and interest in constructing their learning;" importance of children's relationships and interactions; important role of parents; emergent curriculum and project approach to curriculum; and teachers as partners). These are the cornerstone features (Henniger, 1999; New, 1994) upon which early childhood education programs here and around the world have been built.

The popularity of Reggio Emilia has been phenomenal the world over, for as a program model it continues to be *the rage* in early childhood today. Intriguing as it is, well over 10,000 international educators have visited Reggio, early education conferences are devoted specifically to Reggio, and "Reggio Emilia" is now a thematic content strand in many national and international conferences (Schiller, 1995). I can't figure this phenomena out, and I'm intellectually intrigued by it. I really want to understand how/why Reggio became so overwhelmingly popular. What is it that seems to make Reggio so appealing? From all that I've read, heard, observed in the field, and reviewed here, Reggio does not necessarily bring any new or reconceptualized theory to the table.

In previous work, I've tried to analyze Reggio's popularity by positioning it against the theoretical anthropological works around cargo cult (e.g., Johnson, 1996, 1997). Cargo cult has been helpful as it allows me to begin to understand how I view early childhood education's approach of transporting Reggio (back) to America and the simplistic attempt to colonize the field of ECE with it's principles. Lindstrom's work (1993) assisted in this critique as he describes cargo cults in the following manner:

> *Cargo cults develop when primitive societies are exposed to the overpowering material wealth of the outside industrialized world. Not knowing where the foreigners' plentiful supplies come from, the natives believe they were sent from the spirit world. They build makeshift piers and airstrips and perform magical rites to summon well-stocked foreign ships and planes . . . the faithful still expect the Americans to arrive soon, bringing with them lots of chocolates, radios and motorcycles.* (Lindstrom, 1993, p. 1)

Much of Lindstrom's critical work (e.g., *Cargo Cult: Strange Stories of Desire from Melanesia and Beyond,* 1993) further captures the essence of the relationship between cargo cult and Reggio Emilia.

Normative Desire

Is it the exotic, "strange stories of desire" about Reggio that intrigue us the most and make us seek it out and bring it back to our own centers, incorporating "Reggio" into our own practices? Even though Reggio Emilia is close to 10,000 miles away from me in Hawaii, Reggio is not strange or exotic; it is highly familiar. In fact, early childhood education's understanding of Reggio (our fantasy world) is subject to the law that produced it (Mulvey, 1977, p. 26), and this is the traditional law of normative educational practices. Again, as I described it earlier, based on my interpretation of other interpretations, Reggio practices are much like those popular practices early childhood educators have been professing for many years. The very persons who typically construct and reconstruct the identity of our field (the privileged academics like myself who can afford to theorize) saw the potential of Reggio as a "new" construct. In the name of innovation those who could afford the travel/tourism went to Reggio and returned with a wealth of stories (a share of the precious cargo) to share with the rest of the early childhood field.

In other writing (Johnson, 1996, 1997) I've interrogated this common, authoritative practice, questioning who gets to go to Reggio to study and learn and how does the theory/practice then get transmitted back home to the common childcare workers? The tradition which pervades our profession today is very much a top-down process, as the privileged, powerful experts (again, those theoreticians like myself who colonize our field—the masters) go to Reggio and other far-off destinations and then bring back the valuable cultural capital (the different products and goods) to share with the marginalized masses (the servants). The power base remains in the hands of those who have access and ownership of this "new" Reggio knowledge—the opportunistic university professors, center directors, program administrators, and a few lucky teachers.

The power has always been located there, well away from the overworked, underpaid, oppressed "8–5" factory workers. Even the typical structure of our conferences, like the annual National Association for the Education of Young Children (NAEYC) conference, allow that model to thrive. As long as the "make and take" model remains popular in our field, we silence the masses by "training" de-skilled teachers to not question, to be obedient and respectful. They are "trained" to perform on Monday morning and not allowed to theorize much past that. This approach models closely what I would term a tourist approach to intellectual engagement. Like the latest photographic engineering, this point and click, "no think" approach is ideal for simplistic theorizing in ECE, and more importantly, for keeping power in the hands of those who have always controlled it.

(Re)Theorizing Our Collective Early Childhood Identity

I believe one reason Reggio has become so popular is because, as a field, as a discipline, we're very much afraid of our own collective identity as early childhood educators. Maybe, as Mulvey illustrates, we're afraid that by "analyzing pleasure, or beauty, [we] destroy(s) it" (1977, p. 24). But we pay a price by not critically analyzing key issues in our field. When we simplistically import Reggio back home and let it simplistically do the thinking for us, we don't theoretically engage many other critical issues in the field. This adaptive process doesn't push us to search out other truths, other representations of ourselves as early educators. When academics like myself intellectualize the field and our relationship with the field from the perspective of master—servant relationships, our participation in the field (e.g., accepted publications, paper presentations, and invited addresses) is marginalized at best. Yet this way of thinking, this type of theorizing, helps me politicize my colonial relationship with those preschool teachers and caregivers I work with.

When I see my academic role as the patriarchal master and my preschool teacher friends and colleagues as servants, I can more clearly observe the same power relationships evident in the larger field of ECE. Here I witness a small group of successful, proven academics (as their thick "refereed" CV's attest) devoted to the moralization of society (Fairchilds, 1984), professing singular truths (e.g., developmentally appropriate practices) at the expense of other ways of problematizing children and pedagogy in early schooling. The field of early education is bound together by "ties of duty and obedience" (p. 5) as together we (masters and servants) work for and serve a common cause (i.e., enhancing preschool quality; improving care options for parents who need childcare; keeping costs of childcare services affordable; helping poor children; going to Reggio for new ideas). The problem with this narrow-minded perspective is it makes all we do collectively seem natural and good because, in the end, as we so willingly say, it is "for the children." Maybe that end is true, but along the way certain expectations in a patriarchal relationship are common. Fairchilds's (1984) work reveals that according to patriarchalism,

> Wife and child owed respect and submission to their patriarchal husband/father; in return he provided for their material needs and watched over their moral and spiritual welfare. ...[S]ervants owed respect and obedience to their masters; in return, their employers were to care for them as a father would, providing, as one domestic manual put it, "not only temporal subsistence, but [also] instruction, good morality. (p. 5)

Looking at the field through the lenses of patriarchal theory (in this case master–servant relationships) I see an inherent political problem, clearly not just anyone can participate or is allowed to participate in the intellectual side of our field. And why would servants, who are dutifully obedient and who "owe respect and obedience" (Fairchilds, 1984), question their masters? The majority of our field are the marginalized masses of women making slightly better than minimum wage, with few benefits, little paid vacation time, and little money to travel to places like Reggio Emilia, Italy. I question then who speaks for this collective majority of our field, these servants? Who defines their subjectivity, their identity? Who has the right to define their subjectivity—certainly not me, the privileged male university professor, the master! I wonder, is it any of you? Is it any of the tourists to Reggio? What does tourism and Reggio Emilia have to do with the children in Head Start programs, with issues of school leavers and colonial curriculum in Nauru, and how is it related to the high teacher turnover rates in our childcare centers? I think the field of early childhood education has many more critical needs and questions that need addressing right here, right now. And yet our "Psychic desires are displaced in partial and vicarious participation in another set of relations (another place and time), and the self becomes realized as the hero of its own narrative of departure and return" (Robertson, Mash, Tickner, Bird, Curtis, & Putnam, 1994, pp. 5).

Story Two: Maria Resists Representation as a Pacific Islander
Sitting in a cool, open aired, spacious building supervising the first (but breezy) day of USP extension examinations for the next two weeks, four students, three women and a man, sit to fulfill the normative practices/requirements for two of our courses, "Communication & Study Skills"

(LLF11) and "Agriculture, Food & Nutrition in the Developing World" (GE202) for this semester—atypical institutionalized pedagogy!

A sudden gust of wind breezes through the room, ruffling papers and breaking the quietness and tense atmosphere. It must effect their collective train of thought and concentration but they appear undeterred, writing away, clinging onto their papers from the wind and racking their brains throughout the long three hours. I have never been good at exams but to some it is their flair—a piece of cake! I usually freak out and gaze into space, butterflies churning in my stomach, ogling at other students and the clock on the wall. The paper and pencil decides to write anything that comes to mind in the last hour or so. It is a wonder I have not gotten ulcers all these years. Imagine the trauma we put our children through as throughout their school lives we forcibly feed them without choice unpalatable menus—standardized testing and other unhealthy sustenance that does more damage than enrichment. These children unfortunately are branded for life with a trademark, determining their class groupings and "streaming" into A, B, C, D, etc. groups as they climb up and slide down the hierarchy of schooling. It is not surprising that the high failure rates, behavior problems, truancy, and dropout rates are the common symptoms plaguing our Nauruan children and many other children throughout the Pacific islands.

I cringed at the thought now as I revisited my own past, recollecting teaching days at the Nauru Primary School, teaching young children in Levels 3–4 (8–9 years) from 1978 to 1993. The Tate Oral English Course book was supposed to teach Nauruan children how to speak "proper" English. Children were drilled sentence patterns while merely parroting back to the teacher without meaning and comprehension in this choral response. The Pacific readers and workbooks too were the traditional menus of the curriculum in teaching how to read and write. Learning to read and write in the "prestige language" is a favorable flavor that most Nauruan parents desire for their children—the key to many opportunities—to gain education status overseas (mainly in Australia), white-collar jobs, to name but a few. The Nauruan language, songs, dances, and other such cultural/traditional dishes are not quite as appealing. These were considered "primitive," hence rarely exist on the school menu. The norm focused typically on an academically oriented curriculum, a curriculum imported from Australia, as were most other "goodies" like food, medicine, money, and so forth.

I sit, drinking in the open, fresh atmosphere, nature's surroundings are serene and peaceful, and a colorful playground for our children instead of being cooped up in classroom routines in learning centers. What rich learning experiences for our children?

Five female teacher trainees in Diploma in Early Childhood Education (DECE) sat their paper on "The Young Child in the South Pacific Family" for HU112 courses today, the second day of exams. Piaget is certainly not the main course for this particular course menu. A full share of Piaget was offered last semester in "Child Development" for HU111, a compulsory first course prerequisite! Clearly, the archetypal structure of progression on DECE course program appears to echo the sentiments of Piaget's logical sequential format. Students are channeled and shaped into a linear, Western thinking, as if Piaget's word is the only "gospel" to be consumed. What of Lev Vygotsky? Apparently his menu/theory is only a side dish not yet familiar to our liking, our taste!

A slight tinge of guilt surfaces at how we have manipulated our students with this ideology, as if they are "empty vessels," the very thing the constructivist early educators despise. How many times have we turned down students from enrolling in HU112 because they have not done HU111? Blinded strictly with aloof rules and regulations, we tend to undermine the invaluable and rich experiences (cultural, emotional, intellectual, social, etc.) of the students as adults, parents, and educators. What a rich array of experiences to add spice and food for thought to our ECE menus! Equally important, who other than the students themselves know more or better understand about the children in their society in this part of the Pacific region?

Is it really necessary that they be fed Piaget? Needless to say, but the benefit of the doubt in not totally Piaget. It is how we have easily come to crave and embrace Westernized educational menus as part of our daily nourishment, which never ceases to amaze me. Unbelievably, we seek afar for a "model" Early Childhood Program from Brisbane, Australia, at the advice of a special curriculum consultant (who was only here for a week). Certainly he was a great salesperson, for he scored an annual "market" from many infant teachers and of course the responsible minister for education at the time! Yet, in our own backyard our Pacific oriented ECE packages are "coconuts," hence not so palpable! These "domestic enemies"—the barriers in our culturally domesticated profession—have certainly not changed.

One of the students was quite disturbed by these so-called foreign theorists/experts (Piaget and the like) and "Western packages" that are so one-sided and made to fit the European child(ren). Viva Bella has hit the nail on the head! It is really encouraging to see these students "bloom" rather than swallowing everything the "experts" say. Is this the purpose of the course? Evidently the course materials are designed to involve the students in the learning process as active learners rather than passive readers of information: to think and question the arguments, theories, and many issues raised. Most of the students have indicated that the course is relevant and meaningful, as they can relate to it because they were studying, comparing their childhood experiences with the/their children in their society, in the Pacific as a whole and according to what other Pacific experts share. As one student shared in the discussion, "It all makes sense because it is us and about us in the Pacific. I see and understand myself and our children better." Another student who had wished to obtain a degree in Australia for "prestige" has changed her "mentality." She was peeved at how we continuously attempt to be "carbon copies" of Europeans when it is not culturally sustainable. "I would have been blind, ignorant and narrowly focused," she retrospectively commented.

A colleague commented jokingly how we should emphasize the proper sitting for exams as she nodded toward a huge student. Both knees propped on the long elongated seat of a huge gray wooden table at the far end of the room, bottom up in the air, the top of her body sprawled on top of the table, the left side of her face laid on her left clenched fist writing away comfortably. It is a pity we do not have the camera on hand to capture this moment, this ECE "relaxed and non-threatening" environment displayed right here in the examination room! Do we have to conform to traditional paradigms? This reminded me of my own attitude and expectations enforcing rules that children had to conform and abide by rigid, "straightjacket" regulations. Children are expected to follow directions, "Sit up straight," or "Be quite and do your work!", etc., as if they are "objects." The past seems to haunt us still. There appears to be a moral panic and nightmare of the deteriorating standards of education as indicative of the ills of society—children's loss of respect and value, bad behavior, etc.—that exists in the schools. As a result, teachers and children become the usual victims of the criticisms that "teachers/children are not as good as they used to be." Why? Are they resisting the dominant structure of an inherently dysfunctional system? How caring are we? How professional? How responsive are we to the dramatic sociological changes that have taken place over the past five decades in Nauru? "Are we doing our jobs?" is an insistent question that students are grappling with in the reality of lip service in education when it comes to the acid test—funding and budget cuts!

I pondered each of the student's life stories wearing various career masks, including fulltime teachers and mothers as well as juggling the challenge of studying at a distance for these various "distance-education courses." Amidst all of this are the problems of being isolated in the Pacific, isolation which influences the lack of qualified subject-area lecturers, lack of good facilities (e.g., tutorials via satellite, computers and so forth), and creates problems that hinder individual learning styles-each student with her/his own personal stories of struggle and hardship on top of these other issues. Also, we have the struggles to meet deadlines, not being able to find the right reference books, and burning the midnight oil as it is usually difficult to find peaceful, quiet study time in our extended family context. As well, many completed assignments are ripped into shreds, as angry spouses nag about time spent on the "books" while neglecting them. I commend these women for having to survive the various obstacles and harsh realities whilst studying. The challenge now is to overcome the domestic enemies of androcentric ideology—male chauvinistic, egotistical attitudes and ideas. What/whose knowledge is of most worth and who determines that? But I have no qualms in saying there is a ray of hope ahead with our promising students to voice the concerns and interests of women and children rather than being behind the scenes.

The exams have come to the end and so has my story, for now. Indeed it has drained me as I battled and struggled over what to say over the past two weeks heavily intoxicated by "domestic enemies meeting over too many cups of coffee."

Story Three: What of the "The Bad Dog Cafe"

I was intrigued to see those most famous of famous early childhood words "developmentally appropriate" (DAP) in a curriculum document I'm reviewing for my consultancy work next week here at the University of the South Pacific (USP). As has been repeated throughout the Pacific so many times in the past century(s), another "expert" Westerner probably consulted with early childhood officials at USP and helped bring DAP's normative discourse into this part of the Pacific. Or, maybe one of the USP faculty or a post-secondary Fijian education student went off-island to the university, traveling to Australia or New Zealand and learning other truths about children and child development, returning to Fiji clouded with these Western ways of seeing and knowing children, seeing and knowing the world.

It is my second day in this new town, Sunday morning, and the jet lag slowly dissipates. With great hunger I am disappointed to find no restaurants open early today as I make my way around the city, that is, until I round a corner and come upon imperialism's most common icon, McDonald's. The owners of this eatery, like the owner(s) of "The Bad Dog Cafe," realize their eatery will thrive as they cater to the needs and desires of the colonial appetite, like mine, the Western tourist wishing to see the world but never at the cost of completely giving up all that is Western. Alas, did I travel this far just to eat at McDonald's? How appropriate that it should be Sunday morning when I have to face this big moral dilemma! My appetite wins over, I enter the restaurant knowing full well that I can get hotcakes this early in the morning. Even if I'm 3,000 miles from home in another country, I retreat to what I know best—American food. My colonial, tourist appetite allows me to venture far from home in my desire to colonize, but I always quickly return to the comforts of home (hamburgers and fries) while on conquest. Like me, others will travel thousands of miles from home, and they too will retreat to their own colonial ways of knowing.

Story Four: Domestic Enemies Meet over Coffee
It is late Friday night, my last night in Suva, for Maria and I our last moments together for now. After having met over coffee, Maria, her sister-in-law Noté, and I walk the streets looking for a taxi to take them home. I notice that Noté disappears. Glancing to my right I soon see her off the road climbing a nearby fence. Maria suddenly says, "Tsk, tsk, such a waste," as she stares down at the ground. I look down and all I see is a single trampled, small green mango. By all accounts not much of a loss to me as the color, even in the dark, depicted its hard, unripe interior flesh. I add, "But it's not ripe." Maria responds to this, "That's how we (Nauruan's) like to eat them!" Noté, I now see, has climbed the fence so that she can reach more mangos for her and Maria to devour. Mangos. I adore the sight of a yellow mango, with traces of orange, a mango I know will be soft and ripe to the touch and to my taste. In Nauru the green mango is equally a delicacy worth climbing a fence for on a dark September night. Mangos, green or yellow.

Chapter 17

To Speak: Problematizing of the Use of Personal Stories in Early Childhood Research
Chelsea Bailey

A Somewhat Personal Introduction

I tell personal stories. I tell these stories in my research, theory, and classroom practice. I tell these stories in my writing, in my conference presentations, and in my teaching. I have believed for a long time that in order to survive psychically in a world beyond our comprehension that we must tell stories about our lives, to document our experience. This necessity of telling is articulated by Felman and Laub (1992) when they state that "there is...an imperative need to tell and thus come to know one's story" (p. 78). This chapter addresses what this telling might mean within the context of researching and theorizing early childhood education.

"Early childhood education" itself evokes images of children, under the protective care of adults, telling and being told stories. Fables, fictions, lies, and lessons fill conceptions of early childhood experiences. Indeed, children and their caregivers do make use of stories, both personal and abstracted, to contextualize and create a "knowing" of experience, but what of the researchers and theorists of this field? To what extent do stories of personal experience help these "scientists" make sense of their work and their world? What are the limitations and dangers of such practice? What do stories, particularly risky personal ones, offer the field and researcher?

After finishing one of my typically personal papers at a large research conference, the first response from the audience was something like: "what is the point of all this bloody personal drivel? It is self-indulgent and useless." Although all the authors presenting on the panel that morning explored personal themes in their writing, indeed the panel itself identified a concern with personal accounts of experience, the audience member's statement rang with impact. The power of this statement lay in its familiarity. For those of us who draw on personal accounts for our social scientific writing, this is a predictable critique.

This critique is born out of an understanding of inquiry that relies on rationalist definitions of truth and knowledge. Within this framework, truth may be known through generalized accounts of experience. Local, individualized accounts, therefore, cannot represent "truth" in this sense. This audience member's critique represents the position that the work of social scientists is to identify these generalized truths rather than tell their own local stories of experience. Although we as a panel had, at that moment, more influence over the room than a single audience member, her perspective represents a predominant understanding of the use of stories.

We are currently living with the legacy of thought that sought to organize stories of experience in particular ways. With the rise of rationalist thought, dichotomies were created between mind and body, subjectivity and objectivity, personal and professional, public and private. Through the creation of these hierarchized dichotomies, particular ways of telling stories became more highly valued then others.[1] Systems of understanding that rely on objective constructions of observational practices put forward the idea that these rational, objective stories were more accurate and therefore, more true.

Contemporarily, we have created elaborate systems of separating truths from non-truths and systems for understanding and organizing our experience around rationalism and logic. It is my contention that these distinctions are a construction. Fiction and truth, autobiography and objective observation are made of the same stuff (Gilmore, 1994). Is it possible that even the most objective scientist is creating autobiographical texts in her stories about atoms?

A "Crisis of Representation"

As researchers and theoreticians of human experience, scholars within the field of education have found themselves in the midst of an intense debate over the political and ethical implications of their work. In an attempt to respond to the questions raised concerning our research practices, we have drawn on discussions taking place in other fields within the arts, social sciences, and philosophy. Resonating within all of the discussions is a critical examination of the ways in which "science" particularly organizes knowledge and the (political, economic) effects of that organization on the representation of human experience. There is currently, within the arts and sciences, a virtual "crisis of representation" which has critically problematized the innocent interpretation and representation of experience.

Brenda Marshall (1991), drawing on the work of Fredric Jameson, argues that "representation is based on an essentially realistic epistemology; it 'projects a mirror theory of knowledge and art, whose fundamental evaluative categories are those of adequacy, accuracy, and Truth itself'" (p. 49). These assumptions about the nature of the "knowable" have shaped the fundamental ontological structures of Western thought and discourse. Representational practices are a reflection of these structures. Postmodernism has given rise to a questioning of the stability of these categories and to the possibilities for imagining representation differently. Peggy Phelan's (1993) argument that "representation...always conveys more than it intends and...is never totalizing" (p. 2) poses a problematic, always failing relationship between experience and representation. This failure, she argues, takes place on the both physical and psychic levels. Neither the "eye" nor the "I" are able to comprehend the totality or complexity of the physical and psychic world. Empiricism, however, is dependent on the "eye" as its primary tool for recording and verifying "the real." This is troubled by Peggy Phelan's reminder that "when Newton discovered the prismatic properties of light the human eye became a poor creature, an organ whose limitations define its properties more than its powers. Unable to see, to perceive the full range of color inherent in light, the human eye is physiologically falsifying" (p. 14). This leaves the recognition of "the real" dependent on the inadequate technology of the human eye.

Rather than questioning the limitations of vision (and, consequently the limitations of our knowledge of "the real") the response of the scientific community was to develop visualizing technologies to supplement to the limitations of the eye. Donna Haraway (1990) calls these technologies an "unregulated (technological) gluttony...mythically about the god trick of seeing everything from nowhere" (p. 581). These efforts to maintain and extend the myth of a visible real signify not just a commitment to "vision," but to the empirical subject. Brenda Marshall (1991) contends that the "empirical subject" "believes in the objectivity of his/her own perceptions, and thus, seeks methods which prove, objectively, his/her hypothesis" (p. 50). And I would add that the objectivity of these perceptions is dependent on the singularly objective subjectivity of the observer.

A critique of the relationship between unified subjectivity and perceptual objectivity is crucial to an examination of representation. The notion of the unified subject was born out of Cartesian rationalist thought. The premise, "I think, therefore I am" created a link between knowledge and existence which has fundamentally shaped Western thought. Postmodernism has provided an important critique of the ways this premise has come to determine ontology and epistemology of contemporary culture. Judith Butler (1992) explains the postmodern investigation of the subject: "The critique of the subject is not a negation or repudiation of the subject, rather, a way of interrogating its construction as a pre-given or foundational premise" (p. 9). This means that through the examination of assumptions about subjectivity (that an unproblematic subject may know an unproblematic reality), we may also question the foundations of knowledge and the construction truth.

Peggy Phelan (1993) argues that "the 'I' cannot be witnessed by the 'eye'" (p. 5). This is important in that it points to the impossibility of verifying the existence of the "self" as a definable entity.[i] If the self is unrecognizable, therefore undefinable, how is it that it is the basis of objective understanding? Coupled with the limitation of actual vision, it becomes increasingly difficult to argue for the certainty of a knowable real. We must return then to Donna Haraway's notion of the "god trick" in order to explore how and why truth circulates in the ways that it does. That "way," contemporarily, is in the form of essential, generalizable, noncontradictory explanations of the physical and psychic experience and phenomena, the laws of nature and "man." The invention of Truth has shifted the burden of "the real" from individuals to institutions of science and culture. If Truth, as a universal constant, is an invention, constructed through the myths of the seeing "eye" and knowing "I," why do the scientific and cultural institutions continue to structure themselves around the search for certainty?

Michel Foucault (1980) has argued that power and knowledge are not only related to one another, but function as the discursive same. Truth, in so much that it functions as knowledge, is explicitly implicated in his examination of the workings of power. Foucault wrote, "'Truth' is linked in a circular relation with systems of power which produce and sustain it, and to effects of power which it induces and which extend it. A 'regime' of truth" (p. 144). This reading of the relationship between truth and power situates truth directly in the center of struggles of understanding. Truth is both a product and an impetus of that struggle. Unlike relativist readings of truth which argue that individuals, through personal interpretation of experience, create their own reality, Foucault is proposing a truth which is mediated by the desire to advocate and sustain particular understandings of "the real."

To locate Truth within complex social, political, and economic power structures is to recognize Truth as vulnerable to the desires of individuals and institutions to garner and maintain positions of power and influence, to understand that Truths are stories of "the real" generated to serve particular interests, and to locate representation within a particular construction of reality. Representation, like other fictive stories of "the real," can only ever be a partial, thoroughly constructed, contingent reality.

The question that arises for me as a researcher and theorist of early childhood education is the following: given the limitations of representation and the fact that personal stories are widely used in a variety of manners despite critiques, what are the usefulness and the problematics of such research practices?

The Problem with Stories
Part 1: Dry, Empty Vessels

In order to consider what it means to use personal stories within research, I believe that we must begin by exploring the effects an absolutist view of truth has had on the imperative to tell. I believe the effect has been to severely handicap our efforts to document experience outside a limited scientific framework. Clearly there have always been poets, and writers, and artists. However, pushed into one corner of the subjectivity/objectivity binary, the stories they tell are not given the same attention or support (financially or culturally) as the work "objective" recorders of experience. And for those of us who fall between, or more often, move between these broad categories of artist and scientist (but make our living largely within a rationalist academy), we have a problem. My first concern, then, is that we are untrained to tell our stories because these dichotomies fail us and our experience(s).

In the academic incarnation of the field of education, there are many of us who cannot tell the stories we need within the dichotomies created between truth and fiction. We are pushing and questioning. Unfortunately, many of us, rejecting hard numbers, have embraced "stories" unproblematically, our own stories as well as the stories of others. I believe that there are dangers to this unproblematic embracing of stories. First, I believe that most academics are, for the most part, unprepared to tell our own stories in ways that speak to others who have not shared our experiences. Because we are rarely educated (professionally or culturally) to locate our experiences in relation to broader or relational notions of truth, we rely on conventional narrative constructions in relating our stories. These stories, stripped of the complicated dynamics rationalism has sought to eliminate, are dry, empty vessels, hollow and limited in scope and metaphor. As we cling to our attempts to tell the most literal, if not empirical versions of our experience, we lose the richness of experience. The effort to speak those moments which are beyond description and comprehension are what offer a bridge of understanding for those with whom we share our stories as they seek to find a vehicle for their own impossible stories. However, absent of this excess of the unrelatable, our stories are indeed self-indulgent, confessional, and navel-gazing, if you will. For if we are unable to situate our experience through and beyond the confines of our own limited scope of reality, the meanings and usefulness of any account are quite limited as well.

Part 2: A Colonization of Stories

My second concern about the recent embracing of stories is the ways in which we, as teachers and researchers, have begun to ask our students and research participants to tell their stories. In classrooms and in the field, we are asking these people to tell the "truth" of their lives, most often in the linear, progressive, narrative style I expressed concern about earlier. I would make the same arguments here about the limitations and dangers of stripping stories of their uncertainties as I did earlier. However, the stakes are higher when you begin to mess with stories that aren't your own. Not only do you limit the success of the story telling experience by assuming what formats are most appropriate or even most true, but you also run the risk of taking over authorship of the stories and colonizing the very voices you supposedly seek to represent.[3]

What I mean by this is the following: as you seek to elicit particular stories about the experiences of others, you insert your own agenda into the telling of the story. You have, in essence, created a story that would not have existed without your presence; you have now become the moment of origin for someone else's story. Additionally, as you make choices about what you will do with these stories, your authorship further permeates the text of another's story. The deeper your involvement, the more total your colonization. The stories become part of your terrain of experience and power. Returning to Foucault's interpretation of the relationship between knowledge and power I discussed above, a concern arises about the inherent dangers of giving up one's story to someone with a greater ability to produce knowledge in the public arena.

Certainly, exploitative research and teaching relationships are a concern and not an inevitability with or without the use of stories. I am not arguing here against using other's stories in our teaching and research, only for a more careful use of this methodology. I am arguing for a suspicious use of stories, a suspect vision of the places that stories take people. Acknowledging the relationship between power and truth and the exploitative capacities of knowledge producing institutions, perhaps we should ask ourselves before we ask others to share their stories: Where do I want your story to take me (and my research or teaching)? and second: Am I willing to go elsewhere before I ask you to begin speaking? These questions cannot resolve the concerns I raise here, but perhaps they can reposition the researcher in relation to these concerns.

Taken together, these two concerns constitute major questions about the use of personal stories in early childhood research. However, despite these concerns, I remain passionate about telling and hearing stories of personal experience. In this next section, I will discuss the ways I have learned to work despite and because of the limitations I have outlined.

Making Use of Stories through Power, Truth, and Excess

Clearly, I have not given up on the use of personal stories in my academic (or everyday) work, but what makes those tellings possible are a particular set of understandings and uses of my own stories and stories in general. These understandings and uses are stories themselves, situated within my life experiences in academia. The first story is about the birth of my speaking voice, the power of that voice, and the sense of community I share with the feminist articulators of women's experience who modeled that voice for me.

Power

When it became clear to me early in my graduate work that I was going to tell stories about myself, I began to look to the work of other women who had done the same thing. I found tremendous resources of women's work and words that put biography and autobiography in professional contexts. Clearly, in literary genres like memoir, biography, autobiography, and fiction women have always told their stories, and, I would argue, these works have had a respected and successful literary life. Increasingly within the social sciences and natural sciences, women are telling stories that contextualize their disciplinary concerns in relation to personal and political experience (Abu-Lughod, 1993; Behar, 1993, 1996; Haraway, 1991; Harding, 1991; Tsing, 1993).

As I sought out discussions of feminist methodologies, I found that feminist scholars, particularly within sociology and anthropology, disciplines which are already concerned with "stories," have worked hard to create the space for the kinds of personal narratives that more traditionally have been part of a feminist literary tradition. And, of course, these women are not just doing memoir, autobiography, biography, and fiction. They have been creating whatever spaces are necessary for telling the feminist, activist, queer, postcolonial stories they need to tell. (Abu-Lughod, 1993; Anzaldua, 1990; Behar, 1996; Flax, 1993; hooks, 1990; Jipson, 1995; Tsing, 1993; Visweswaran, 1994). The literacy, academic, storied spaces include ethnographic texts, literary criticism, and studies of early childhood spaces. All this creating of space through speaking and acting for things that are crucial to our survival is about voice, presence, and pleasure inasmuch as these elements are critically linked to the production of meaningful stories. In the power of these stories, I recognize and conceive of the power of my own speaking. I feel different when I speak, but that difference is engendered by the situatedness of my speaking in relation to a community of other women who speak before, with, and after me, and who speak for and about the issues which make their lives both meaningful and impossible.

Truth.

But, it is not that simple. Never do I simply "speak." The time, location, subject of my telling, my mood, and my motivation always mediate my speaking. Speaking, in so much as it is subject to the limits of the failure of representation, can never be the performance of truth. It can only ever be the failure to tell truth (Phelan, 1993).

I want to suggest now that although all stories fail to account for the complexity of experience, it is how we chose to address that failure in our stories that continues to make the stories useful. I think of my stories, particularly the public ones, as performative. The "performative" is a key concept here because it provides a way to make use of personal stories while at the same troubling rationalist constructions of truth. Peggy Phelan (1993) describes performance in the following way:

> Performance's only life is in the present. Performance cannot be saved, recorded, documented, or otherwise participate in the circulation of

representations of representations: once it does so, it becomes something other than performance. To the degree that performance attempts to enter the economy of reproduction, it betrays and lessens the promise of its own ontology. Performance's being, like the ontology of subjectivity proposed here, becomes itself through disappearance. (p. 146)

The notion of "performance" allows for the "real" to give way to contingent realities and slippery identities. I always doubted the ability of my stories to express a lasting truth. Translating experience into language feels like I am "making it up as I go along," and I am sure that I am. Somehow, however, the possibility of my "lying" even as I attempt to tell the "truth" makes the process both more fearful and safe. There is the fear of both my lies and truths being discovered, and simultaneously, a safety in the knowledge that no matter what I tell, I cannot be "known" because I am not even certain of my own "truths." Part of what motivates me to tell and keep telling is both the excitement of being afraid of disclosure (perhaps an emotional exhibitionism) and the safety/strength of speaking at all, making myself present—politically, personally, etc. (perhaps an emotional activism).

Performative stories that blur the line between personal fact and fiction can create spaces that engage truth differently, therefore situating both the teller and the listener differently within the truth/power dynamic. You can tell a story that is your story, but the details can be borrowed or made up. You can consciously highlight those elements that are relevant and leave out things that don't add to the story. This performative element of telling personal stories is not only an effect of the impossibility of telling, it is also a powerful tool in resisting the efforts of others to coop and rewrite our stories in disingenuous and dangerous ways.

Excess

In my opening paragraphs, I talked about the ways in which rationalist discourses of truth and representation have come to dominate the ways that stories are told. I would add that this orientation to truth also dominates the ways that stories are interpreted as well. Therefore, when I tell a story, I must assume that it is being rewritten by dominant notions of truth and reality, made something it was not intended to be. There are, however, modes of resistant speaking and telling that I believe we all engage in.

Returning to the notion of the purposeful confusing of performance and personal narrative, I believe that by acknowledging and working with the excessive and uncontrollable elements of personal narrative, there is less for the spin doctors of rationalist discourse to work with. Put another way, stories of experience do not automatically or easily fit into categories. It is not until after they are trimmed and re-imagined (sometimes with much effort) that these stories will fit into the categories that have been created to explain experience. These oppressive categories leave out the parts of stories (and often entire people's themselves) that challenge the racist, sexist, classist, homophobic mandate of this society. As storytellers, we can choose to tell the far-out, difficult to spin parts of stories to make that rewriting harder and to keep present and speaking the counter-stories we all need to tell.

One way of imaging what I mean by excessive stories are stories that embrace or enhance the fears about human experience that our society makes efforts to wipe out. These are stories of identities in flux, politicized sexualities, children with power, angry women, angry people of color, angry people with disabilities, and other threats of disruption. Examples of this are Queer Nation's slogan: "We're here, we're queer, we want everything;" the Lesbian Avenger's slogan: "We recruit;" the literary work of James Baldwin (1985), Richard Wright (1940/1998) Ishmael Reed (1996), Toni Morrison (1994), bell hooks (1994), Kathy Acker (1993), Virgina Woolf (1993), Nancy Mairs (1994), the art of Jean Michel Basquait, Karen Finley, Manuel Ocampo, Holly Hughes, Annie Sprinkle, Bob Flanagan, Tim Miller.

In academia, again because we are not sanctioned to speak freely in the ways that artists (or activists) are because our speech is marked as too valuable, there are fewer examples of radically excessive stories here. bell hooks (1990) has crossed the line between artist and academic, keeping her radical, personal voice strong, as has Nancy Mairs (1994). Other examples are Gloria Anzaldua (1990) and Henry Louis Gates (1996) work on race and gender. Judith Butler (1993), Peggy Phelan (1993), and Elizabeth Grosz (1995) have each disrupted sexist and heterosexist imagery at work in philosophy and performance studies.

More locally, in a disciplinary sense, I am continually moved by work of several people in my field. Vivian Paley (1992), Jan Jipson (1995), and Jonathan Silin (1995) all make stories dangerously central to their work. Paley, in the first moment, writes about children (and herself) in ways that disrupt dominant notions of power relations between teachers and young children, and in the second moment speaks about children in ways that construct them as powerful agents of their own understanding and action. Jipson risks structure and voice to speak about (and rework) teacher education and feminist research from decidedly personal and narrative locations. Silin speaks the powerful stories that have shaped his life and his work as a gay man, teacher educator, and researcher. My own work (1998a, 1998b) blends personal experience and reflection with stories of children's dangerous physicalities in classroom to challenge dominant notions of children's sexuality and corporeal learning.

These are all stories of risk. And what all of these works and the stories they tell have in common is that not only do they challenge dominant constructions of ability, race, sexuality, gender, etc., but they, in their excesses, exceed the domains of their own disciplines to shake up the truth structures and strictures in unpredictable and powerful ways. In resisting the boundaries of truth makers, these stories tellers open up spaces for others' complex and excessive stories as well.

Considerations on Silence

Through these three reworking of stories, power, truth, and excess, I have been able to make sense and make use of my own personal narratives in my scholarly work. But before I leave you to celebrate the wonder of stories, I want to introduce and explore questions about the limitations and necessities of silence. One of the assumptions many proponents of stories make is that silence represents psychic death and political disenfranchisement.

In speaking about silence, I consider the silences in my own public stories. What I am not willing to risk in my telling? I have stories that are simply too scary, too dangerous, too uncontrollable to release to the public, even as performance. Some of these stories mark critical junctures of understanding and misunderstanding in my research, theory, and teaching but remain unspoken. As a researcher and teacher, I must regularly navigate the choices about my telling, lest I put others and myself in danger in ways that I cannot predict. Storytelling becomes, in this sense, a careful negotiation between the contingent "real" of my fictive tellings and the "real" dangers and responsibilities of jobs and relationships.

Silence, just as storytelling, functions as a vehicle for negotiating public space and identity. But, silence can also be perceived as a location of power and resistance. At times, one's only power is the power not to participate in one's own potential misrepresentation. Silence may act as a guard against testifying against oneself; to remain silent is to maintain one's cogent sense of self. Too often as teachers and researchers, we are quick to interpret silence as an indicator of indifference, ignorance, or disempowerment. Consider that this silence may be a choice, an active refusal to participate in your agenda, as helpful as it may be intended.

Speaking about women's silence and speaking in feminist ethnography, Kamala Visweswaran (1994) writes,

> ...feminist ethnography cannot assume the willingness of women to talk...(however) one avenue open to (ethnography) is to investigate when and why women do talk; to assess the strictures placed on their speech; the avenues of creativity they have appropriated; the degrees of freedom they possess. Perhaps then, a feminist ethnography can take the silences among women as the central site for the analysis of power between them. We can begin to shape a notion of agency that, while it privileges speaking, is not reducible to it. My aim is to theorize a kind of agency in which resistance can be framed by silence, a refusal to speak. In this my is partly...one on measuring silences. (p. 51)

Perhaps, then, speaking is not the only response to oppressive misrepresentations. Strategic and purposeful silence must be acknowledged as a mode and method of response. We cannot, however, ignore these misrepresentations and enforced silences of dominating cultures. We must remain critical of the stories and the silences that we hold onto, share, elicit, and become audience for.

Conclusion

I have offered to you multifarious and, at times, contradictory images and meanings of speaking and silence. If stories are to be thought of as both useful and dangerous, empowering and vehicles for oppression, what can we conclude about the use of personal stories in the research, theory, and practice of early childhood education? If we are to begin to reconceptualize the field, how we use personal stories must be part of that discussion. Through the notions of power, truth, and excess, I would suggest that personal narratives, mediated by silence, can put into play powerful stories of survival and pleasure in and around the early childhood classroom. These stories can help to open up opportunities for complex and challenging counter-narratives of theory and research with and about children.

Moreover, I for the consideration of researchers and theorists of the field, I would make the following points.

For those of us concerned with social change, stories create more ways (and more pleasurable ways) to address and rewrite social, political, and cultural inequities.

For those of us who can't teach or research without stories, the critical use of personal stories creates a reason and a way to participate professionally, personally, and critically in our field.

A radical use of personal stories requires an active commitment to risk and disclosure.

Deploying stories in response to totalizing narratives is risky and dangerous and will always scare you when you do it or you're not doing it right.

Finally, as much as we might risk in the process, we have the opportunity to create in our research, our teaching, and all parts of our lives, spaces that stretch and bend the dominant and dominating images that cramp and restrict knowledge and experience.

My task, like yours, is to document the uncanny and unrelatable experiences of my life. As an academic, I must make sense of these experiences in relation to my field. For years now every time I have stood to speak at a conference, I have passionately told stories from my life that help me to understand the work I do about and for children. I have told stories of teaching, stories of my childhood, and recently, stories of my young daughter. They are raw, personal, and always told in such a way as to engage my audience provocatively. This chapter is both an invitation and a warning to other tellers and solicitors of the personal to tell and to hear and to use stories with a careful attention to the power and vulnerability of fragile truths.

NOTES

[1] See Foucault (1970) for in depth analysis of the rise of modernist and scientific thought.

[2] The two fields that are explicitly concerned about the nature of "the self" are psychology and psychoanalysis. Interestingly, they take very different perspectives on the issue. Much work with psychology is interested, locating that which defines human behavior/nature through experimental empirically based research. I gave a lengthy critique of the effect of empiricist psychology on the lives of young children in my

unpublished master's thesis, "Radical Theories of Voice, Power, and Desire in Preschool" (1993). Psychoanalysis, founded on the work of Freud, views the subject as only partially knowable. Current postmodern interpretations of this construction of the subject have been explicit in their critique of the unified subject. The work of Jacques Lacan (1977) and Julia Kristeva (1980) stand out in this area of thought.

[3] I use colonization here to mean the act of asserting ownership over people and property not your own in ways that exploit the value of these assets to your own benefit. See Ashcroft, Griffiths, and Tiffin (1995) for an overview of discussions on postcolonialism.

Epilogue

Reconceptualization as Interruption, Interrogative Punctuation, and Opening
Richard T. Johnson

At this point the finite and close consolation once associated with the presumed uniqueness of a community can either withdraw into the dead husk of blind cultural conceits or else fruitfully fragment and remake itself under the weight of a multiple inheritance.
  —Iain Chambers, *Migrancy, Culture, Identity*

As teachers of a new historical criticism, our first task must be to disabuse students of the notion that history is what's over and done with; to convince them that, on the contrary, history is always now.
  —Marina Leslie, *Renaissance Utopias and the Problem of History*

In concert with Jan's opening chapter, I too want to first share a conference story. Last year a friend of mine received a "rejection" notice which disallowed her from presenting a paper for the Child Development/Early Childhood Special Interest Group (SIG) at AERA's annual meeting. Commenting on the merits of her submitted proposal, one of the three "external" reviewers stated, "What does feminism have to do with early childhood education?" At this same conference I was awarded space for a roundtable presentation. I was really looking forward to deliberating with other early childhood professionals about some recent baseline research findings. In my presentation I planned on arguing that even while critical issues of sexuality continue to present themselves in one form or another to our early childhood education field, my findings revealed that "the popular discourse around childhood sexuality is a discourse focused not on teaching about sexuality, but on teaching *around* sexuality—a process of erasure" (Johnson, 1998). Thinking these findings would be interesting to my colleagues, I presented a paper entitled "Erasure of Sexuality in the Care of Young Children," a paper which drew absolutely no respondents.

With no other people to talk with (aside from one or two friends who stopped by to chat as they clearly felt sorry seeing me sitting by myself),

I now had plenty of time to observe other interactions in this large conference room. As demoralized as I was about the number of uninterested colleagues in attendance, this whole session surrealistically played out the concluding section of my paper (non)presentation. It couldn't have been performed any better had I planned it with my colleagues across the room who were discussing developmentally appropriate practices. My "sexuality" paper concluded by arguing that at a time when we should be enlarging the spaces for intellectual deliberations about sexuality to be heard, we have instead reduced the dialogue on sexuality. Even while we pretend sexuality is not an important issue, that it doesn't exist for children and for the field of early childhood education, our ignorance protects us and keeps us theoretically safe. Early childhood education remains ignorant and silent at a time when sexuality has shifted from the margins to the center in many disciplines highly familiar and interrelated to most of our own work.

People chose not to come to my session for various reasons. Maybe my title was misleading or uninteresting; other more interesting, topically relevant people were presenting at the same time; possibly they went sailing or to the beach; or, because they instead wanted to critically engage, once again, developmentally appropriate practices. No matter the reason, the fact remains, at this particular point in this particular conference nobody wanted to critically engage this particular topic, this particular theory. I left the session thinking I didn't get a chance to present, feeling very much like I was silenced at this professional conference. In retrospect my (non)presentation became the classic *virtual* [italics added] performative piece for the field of early education. Just as the title implied, as the non-attendance by my colleagues implied, once again sexuality was *erased* from our collective consciousness. Sexuality was silenced.

Moving Out of a Silence

Normalcy and safety are the thematic issues traditionally adhered to throughout the field of early childhood education. This occurs while more radical perspectives remain mostly silenced. The authors here actively move against this trend, a traditional movement that certainly continues valorizing conservative, singular, humanist perspectives on children and their developmental progression, and which "enables certain normative discourse (i.e., child development as staged-based, "universal" phenomena; "normal behavior," "child as innocent") to emerge and be sustained" (Haywood, 1996; Madus, 1995; Tobin, 1997; Wagener,

1998). In this collection a group of professionals let all of their "own complexities, viewpoints, hesitations, dreams and passions—and their vulnerable aspects too—become apparent" (Kozol, 1981, p. 12) as they partake in their own individual and collective acts of intellectual resistance and representation.

The interrogative, emancipatory works offered throughout this book do not offer a utopian future but rather "work to open up new public spaces by contesting the core assumptions and values of discourses of modern democracy" (Yeatman, 1994, p. x). Engaging narratives which are historically passed over in silence, the authors in this collection help the field of early education move out of other silences, not by simply telling new stories of ECE as much as by involving themselves and all who read in the "retelling of our critical genealogy" (Kay, 1993, p. 69). As a form of excavation work, critical work which involves "discovery and recovery of the many texts that are still lost or undervalued...as well as in the work of encouraging new voices to come to speech through writing" (Hedges & Fishkin, 1994, p. 13), this collection helps us actively move away from traditional normative discourse as we speak to new issues, re-theorize traditional issues, and problematize the many other concerns we face every day of our personal and professional lives.

These theoretical approaches to the study of children and childhood were once highly transgressive, attempted by only a few theorists who were typically people who wouldn't define themselves as early childhood educators (e.g., Rose, 1989; Stainton Rogers & Stainton Rogers, 1992; Walkerdine, 1984). As is evidenced here, new spaces of intellectual engagement are opening up and are becoming more popular as theorists are willing to engage the field in different ways. That different theorists are more willing now to participate in this transgressive movement is evidenced by the wide variety of contributions presented here. Taking a critical stance against many of the long-standing traditions in the field, they are willing to "fruitfully fragment and remake...under the weight of a multiple inheritance" (Chambers, 1994, p. 71) and move the field forward in an intellectually stimulating manner.

"What Does Feminism Have to Do with Early Childhood Education?"

Gloria Bird, in her work, "Towards a Decolon0ization of the Mind and

Text 1," serves us well by challenging us to rethink ourselves,

> *In order to move out of colonizing instances of interiorized oppression, we first have to identify those moments in which we reinforce those useless paradigms and search for new approaches to the way we speak of ourselves in relation to our histories and stories. To **imagine** a future.* (1993, p. 6)

Revisiting my opening story here, I think this volume reveals, among many other things, feminism has much to do with early childhood education, as does critical theory, historicism, postcolonial study, and poststructuralism. In the recent past most of my intellectual work in early education (e.g., critiques of Reggio Emilia and child sexuality) has moved forward only through the adaption of theoretical perspectives far afield from my early education-influenced, traditional past. Included here are the valuable usage of critical theory, queer theory, cultural studies, and sociology. While involved in these projects, with each new "read" I felt invigorated, refreshed, and stimulated intellectually in a manner I hadn't experienced in many years. But, more and more I felt I was "reading" myself out of the field of early education and this felt uncomfortable.

Like bell hooks, I too believe if our minds are to be sites of resistance, only the imagination can make it so. To imagine, then, is to begin the process of transforming reality. All that we cannot imagine will never come into being (1994, p. 53). The authors present in this text, in this performance, help me realize that in fact I'm not "reading" myself out of the field of early childhood education at all. As this text witnesses, our individual and collective imaginations, our individual and collective work realize new opportunities as the field is being creatively redefined, unsilenced, and reconceptualized. Just as Chambers shared in my opening, the authors in this collection "fruitfully fragment and remake itself [the field of ECE] under the weight of a multiple inheritance" (Chambers, 1994, p. 71). These theorists push the present theoretical limitations of early education and write well beyond the current field as they theoretically delve into "space as spaciousness, as the unbounded, the area of total possibility" (Lewis, 1955, as cited in Jarvis, 1998). The variety of trajectories these authors choose to (re)read the early childhood landscape is exciting. It is because of the critical contributions from the many reconceptualists present and represented in this text that I can have and share hope with my colleagues while continuing to "imagine a future" for myself and for the field of early childhood education.

References

Aboud, F. (1988). *Children and prejudice.* Oxford, U.K.: Blackwell.

Aboud, F. (1993). The developmental psychology of racial prejudice. *Transcultural Psychiatric Research Review, 30,* 229–242.

Abu-Lughod, L. (1993). *Writing women's worlds: Bedouin stories.* Berkeley: University of California Press.

Acker, K. (1993/1990). *In memoriam to identity.* London: Flamingo Press.

Addams, J. (1960). *Twenty years at Hull-House.* New York: New American Library. (Original work published 1910)

Ade, W. (1982). Professionalization and its implications for the field of early childhood education. *Young Children, 37*(3), 25–32.

Alloway, N. (1995a). The wearing of the badge: Discourses of early childhood education and the possibilities of gender reform. Paper presented to staff of the deLissa Institute.

Alloway, N. (1995b). *Foundation stones: The construction of gender in early childhood.* Carlton: Curriculum Corporation.

Anderson, B. R. (1991). *Imagined communities: Reflections on the origin and spread of nationalism.* New York: Verso Press.

Anzaldua, G. (Ed.). (1990). *Making face, making soul: Creative and critical perspectives by women of color.* San Francisco: Aunt Lute Foundation Book.

Apple, M. W. (1979). *Ideology and curriculum.* London: Routledge and Kegan Paul.

Apple, M. (1986). *Teachers and texts: A political economy of class and gender relations in education.* New York: Routledge.

Argyris, C., & Schön, D. A. (1978). *Theory in practice: Increasing professional effectiveness.* San Francisco: Jossey-Bass Publishers.

Aries, P. (1962). *Centuries of childhood.* New York: Vintage Books.

Aronowitz, S., & Giroux, H. (1985). *Education under siege: The conservative, liberal and radical debate over schooling.* South Hadley, MA: Begin and Garvey.

Aronowitz, S., & Giroux, H. (1991). *Postmodern education: Politics, culture, and social criticism.* Minneapolis: University of Minnesota Press.

Arthur, L., Beecher, B., Dockett, S., Farmer, S., & Richards. E. (1993). *Programming and planning in early childhood settings*. Marackville, NSW: Harcourt Brace Jovanovich.

Ashcroft, B., Griffiths, G., & Tiffin, H. (Eds.). (1995). *The post-colonial studies reader*. London: Routledge.

Association of Childhood Education International. (1983). *Childhood education's guidelines for teacher preparation*. Washington, DC: Author.

Association of Teacher Educators. (1991). *Restructuring the education of teachers*. Washington, DC: Commission on the Education of Teachers into the 21st Century.

Ayers, W. (1989). *The good preschool teacher*. New York: Teachers College Press.

Azhar, R. (January, 1998). *Children: A cost-benefit analysis*. Paper presented at the International Conference on Reconceptualizing Early Childhood Education. Honolulu, Hawaii.

Bachelard, G. (1984). *The new scientific spirit* (A. Goldhammer, Trans.). Boston: Beacon Press. (Original work published 1934)

Bailey, C. (1993). *Radical theories of voice, power, and desire in preschool*. Unpublished master's thesis, University of Wisconsin-Madison.

Bailey, C. (1998a). *Excess, intimacy, and discipline: Curriculum of the body in the early childhood classroom*. Unpublished doctoral dissertation. University of Wisconsin-Madison.

Bailey, C. (1998b). Writing home: Stories of a feminist self. In M. Hauser & J. Jipson (Eds.), *Intersections: Feminisms/Early childhoods* (pp. 37–47). New York: Peter Lang Publishing.

Baird, J., Jones, J., Sharpe, F., Payne, C., & MacNaughton, G. (1992, July 2–3.). Never too early. *The GEN*.

Baker, S. (1991). Reflection, doubt, and the place of rhetoric in postmodern social theory. *Sociological Theory*, 232–245.

Bakhtin, M. M. (1981). Discourse in the novel. (C. Emerson & M. Holquist, Trans.). In M. Holquist (Ed.), *The dialogic imagination: Four essays by M. M. Bakhtin* (pp. 146–161). Austin, TX: University of Texas Press.

Bakhtin, M. M. (1984). *Rabelais and his world*. (H. Iswolsky, Trans.). Bloomington: Indiana University Press.

Ball, S. (Ed.). (1990). *Foucault and education: Disciplines and knowledge*. London: Routledge.

Baldwin, J. (1985). *Evidence of things not seen*. Cutchogue, NY: Buccaneer Press.

Baltas, A. (1989). Louis Althusser and Joseph D. Sneed: A strange encounter in philosophy of science? In K. Gavroglu, Y. Goudaroulis, & P. Nicolacopoulos (Eds.), *Imre Lakatos and theories of scientific change* (pp. 269–286). Dordrecht, Netherlands: Kluwer Academic Publishers.

Barnett, W. S., & Escobar, C. M. (1987). The economics of early educational intervention: A review. *Review of Educational Research*, *57*(4), 387–414.

Barrow, C. W. (1990). *Universities and the capitalist state: Corporate liberalism and the reconstruction of American higher education, 1894–1928*. Madison, WI: University of Wisconsin Press.

Barry, A., Osborne, T., & Rose, N. (1996). Introduction. In A. Barry, T. Osborne, & N. Rose (Eds.), *Foucault and political reason: Liberalism, neo-liberalism and rationalities of government* (pp. 1–18). Chicago: University of Chicago Press.

Barry, A., Osborne, T., & Rose, N. (1996). *Foucault and political reason: Liberalism, neo-liberalism and rationalities of government*. Chicago: University of Chicago Press.

Bartholomew, J. (1982). *World atlas* (12th ed.). Edinburgh: Bartholomew.

Baumrind, D. (1971). Current patterns of parental authority. *Developmental Psychology Monographs*, *4*, 1–103.

Baumrind, D. (1988). Rearing competent children. In W. Damon (Ed.), *Child development today and tomorrow*. San Francisco: Jossey Bass.

Bazerman, C. (1992). The interpretation of disciplinary writing. In R. H. Brown (Ed.), *Writing the social text: Poetics and politics in social science discourse* (pp. 31–38). New York: Walter DeGryuter, Inc.

Beaty, J. (1992). *Preschool appropriate practice*. New York: Harcourt Brace Jovanovich College Publishers.

Beer, E. (1943). *The day nursery*. New York: Whiteside and Morrow.

Behar, R. (1993). *Translated woman: Crossing the border with Esperanza'a story*. Boston: Beacon Press.

Behar, R. (1996). *The vulnerable observer: Anthropology that breaks your heart*. Boston: Beacon Press.

Berlak, A., & Berlak, H. (1981). *Dilemmas of schooling*. London: Methuen.

Berruta-Clement, J. R., Schweinhart, L. J., Barnett, S., Epstein, A., & Weikart, D. (1984). *Changed lives: The effects of the Perry Preschool Program on youths through age 19.* (Monographs of the High/Scope Educational Research Foundation, 8). Ypsilanti, MI: High/Scope Press.

Besharov, D. (1993, June 14). Fresh start. *The New Republic,* 14–16.

Beyer, L. E., & Bloch, M. (1996). Theory: An analysis (Part 1). *Advances in Early Education and Day Care, 8,* 39.

Beyer, L. E., & Liston, D. (1996). *Curriculum in conflict: Social visions, educational agendas, and progressive school reform.* New York: Teachers College Press.

Bigler, R. S., & Liben, L. S. (1993). A cognitive-developmental approach to racial stereotyping and reconstructive memory in Euro-American children. *Child Development, 64,* 1507–1518.

Bird, G. (1993). Towards a decolonization of the mind and text 1: Leslie Marmon Silko's "Ceremony." *WICAZO SA Review, 9,* 1–8.

Bissell, J. (1971). *Implementation of planned variation in Head Start I. Review and Summary of the Stanford Research Institute Interim Report: First Year of Evaluation* (Publication No. OCD-72-44). Washington, DC: U.S. Department of Health, Education, and Welfare.

Bloch, M. N. (1987). Becoming scientific and professional: An historical perspective on the aims and effects of early education. In T. S. Popkewitz (Ed.), *The formation of the school subjects: The struggle for creating an American institution* (pp. 25–62). New York: The Falmer Press.

Bloch, M. N. (1992). Critical perspectives on the historical relationship between child development and early childhood education research. In S. A. Kessler & B. B. Swadener (Eds.), *Reconceptualizing the early childhood curriculum: Beginning the dialogue* (pp. 3–20). New York: Teachers College Press.

Bloch, M. N., & Blessing, B. (in press). Restructuring the state in Eastern Europe: Women, child care, and early education. In T. Popkewitz, (Ed.), *Educational knowledge: Changing relationships between the state, civil society, and educational community.* Albany: State University of New York Press.

Block, A. A. (1995). "Its alright, ma (I'm only bleeding)": Education as the practice of social violence against the child *TABOO. Journal of Culture and Education, 1,* 121–142.

Bourdieu, P. (1991). *Language and symbolic power.* (G. Raymond & M. Adamson, Trans.). Cambridge: Harvard University Press.

Braun, S. J., & Edwards, E. P. (1972). *History and theory of early childhood education.* Worthington, OH: Charles A. Jones Publishing Company.

Bredekamp, S. (Ed.). (1987). *Developmentally appropriate practice in early childhood programs serving children from birth through age 8.* Washington, DC: NAEYC.

Bredekamp, S. (1992). Composing a profession. *Young Children, 47*(2), 52–54.

Bredekamp, S., & Willer, B. (1993). Professionalizing the field of early childhood education: Pros and cons. *Young Children, 48*(3), 82–84.

Brennan, J. F. (1986). *History and systems of psychology* (2nd ed.). Englewood Cliffs, NJ: Prentice-Hall.

Brown, B. (Ed.). (1978). *Found: Long-term gains from early intervention.* Boulder, CO: Westview Press.

Brown, B. (1985). Head Start: How research changed public policy. *Young Children, 40*(5), 9–13.

Brown, R. H. (1987). Reason as rhetorical: On relations among epistemology, discourse and practice. In J. S. Nelson, A. Megill, & D. N. McCloskey (Eds.), *The rhetoric of the human sciences: Language and argument in scholarship and public affairs* (pp. 184–197). Madison, WI: University of Wisconsin Press.

Brown, R. H. (1992a). From suspicion to affirmation: Postmodernism and the challenges of rhetorical analysis. In R. H. Brown (Ed.), *Writing the social text: Poetics and politics in social science discourse* (pp. 219–227). New York: Walter de Gruyter, Inc.

Brown, R. H. (1992b). Poetics, politics, and truth: An invitation to rhetorical analysis. In R. H. Brown (Ed.), *Writing the social text: Poetics and politics in social science discourse* (pp. 3–7). New York: Walter de Gryuter, Inc.

Bulgaria. *Statistical Yearbook 1994.* Sofia: National Statistical Institute.

Burchell, G., Gordon, C., & Miller, P. (1991). *The Foucault effect: Studies in governmentality.* Chicago: University of Chicago Press.

Burke, A. (1923). *A conduct curriculum for the kindergarten and first grade.* New York: Scribner's.

Burman, E. (1994). *Deconstructing developmental psychology.* New York: Routledge.

Butler, J. (1990). *Gender trouble: Feminism and the subversion of identity*. New York: Routledge.

Butler, J. (1992). Contingent foundations. In J. Butler & J. Scott (Eds.), *Feminists theorize the political*. New York: Routledge.

Butler, J. (1993). *Bodies that matter: On the discursive limits of "sex."* New York: Routledge.

Byrnes, D., & Kiger, G. (Eds.). (1992). *Common bonds: Anti-Bias teaching in a diverse society*. Wheaton, MD: Association of Childhood Education International.

Cahan, E., Mechling, J., Sutton-Smith, B., & White, S. H. (1993). The elusive historical child: Ways of knowing the child of history and psychology. In G. H. Elder, Jr., J. Model, & R. D. Parke (Eds.), *Children in time and place: Developmental and historical insights* (pp. 192–223). New York: Cambridge University Press.

Callahan, R. E. (1962). *Education and the cult of efficiency: A study of the social forces that have shaped the administration of the public schools*. Chicago: University of Chicago Press.

Calvert, K. (1992). *Children in the house: The material culture of early childhood, 1600–1900*. Boston: Northeastern University Press.

Campbell, J. (1917). *Report on the physical welfare of mothers and children* (Vol. II.). London: The Carnegie United Kingdom Trust.

Cannella, G. (1997). *Deconstructing early childhood education: Social justice and revolution*. New York: Peter Lang.

Carnegie Task Force on Teaching as a Profession. (1986). *A nation prepared: Teachers for the 21st century*. Washington, DC: Carnegie Forum on Education and the Economy.

Ceglowski, D. (1998). *Inside a Head Start center: Developing policies from practice*. New York: Teachers College Press.

Chambers, I. (1994). *Migrancy, culture, identity*. New York: Routledge.

Cherryholmes, C. H. (1990). *Reading research* [Unpublished Manuscript]: Michigan State University, Dept. of Political Science, East Lansing, MI.

Children's Defense Fund. (1998). *The state of America's children, Yearbook 1998*. Washington, DC: Author.

Clamp, P. G. (1990). Professionalism in education: A state of mind. *The Education Digest, 56*(2), 53–56.

Clarke, K. (1985). Public and private children: Infant education in the 1820s and 1930s. In C. Steedman, C. Urwin, & V. Walkerdine (Eds.), *Language, gender and childhood* (pp. 74–87). London: Routledge & Kegan Paul.

Clarke-Stewart, A. (1991). A home is not a school: The effects of environments on development. In M. Lewis & S. Feinman (Eds.), *Social influences and socialization in infancy* (pp. 41–62). New York: Plenum.

Clifford, G. J., & Guthrie, J. W. (1988). *Ed school: A brief for professional education.* Chicago: University of Chicago Press.

Clough, P. T. (1992). *The end(s) of ethnography: From realism to social criticism.* London: SAGE.

Cocks, J. (1989). *The oppositional imagination: Feminism, critique and political theory.* New York: Routledge.

Cohen, D.A., & Spillane, J. (1992). Policy and practice: The relations between governance and structure. In G. Grant (Ed.), *Review of research in education* (Vol. 18, pp. 3–49). Washington, DC: American Educational Research Association.

Collins, R. C. (1980). Home Start and its implications for family policy. *Children Today, 9*(2), 12–16.

Collins, R. C., & Kinney, P. F. (1989). *Head Start research and evaluation: Background and overview* (Report No. BBB19384). Washington, DC: U.S. Department of Health and Human Services.

Connell, R. W. (1995). *Masculinities.* Sydney: Allen and Unwin.

Connell, R. W. (1996). Teaching the boys: New research on masculinity, and gender strategies for schools. *Teachers College Record, 98*(2), 206–235.

Cook, A. (1994, January 19). Whose stories get told? *Education Week, 34*, 48.

Cornia, G. A., & Sipos, S. (Eds.). (1991). *Children and the transition to the market economy: Safety nets and social policies in Central and Eastern Europe.* Aldershot, England: Avebury.

Coulson, J. E. (1972). *Effects of different Head Start program approaches on children of different characteristics: Report of the analysis of data from the 1968–1969 National Evaluation* (Report No. HEW-08-70-166).Washington, DC: U.S. Department of Health and Human Services.

Couratin, P. (1973). *Shhh!* New York: Harlin Quist.

Cremin, L.A. (1961). *The transformation of the school: Progressivism in American education 1876–1957*. New York: Vintage Books.

Cremin, L. A. (1988). *American education: The metropolitan experience, 1876–1980*. New York: Harper & Row.

Cuban, L. (1993). *How teachers taught*. New York: Teachers College Press.

Curti, M. (1959). *The social ideas of American educators* (Rev. ed.). Totowa, NJ: Littlefield, Adams & Co.

Curti, M., & Carstensen, V. (1949). *The University of Wisconsin: A history 1848–1925* (Vol. One). Madison, WI: University of Wisconsin Press.

Curtis, C. (1970). *Life in old Hawaii*. Honolulu: Kamehameha Schools Press.

D'Amato, J. (1988). "Acting": Hawaiian children's resistance to teachers. *The Elementary School Journal, 88*, 529–543.

Darling-Hammond, L. (1986, Fall). Teaching knowledge: How do we test it? *American Educator*.

Darling-Hammond, L. (1987). Schools for tomorrow's teachers. In J. Soltis (Ed.), *Reforming teacher education* (pp. 44–48). New York: Teachers College Press.

Darling-Hammond, L. (1988). The futures of teaching. *Educational Leadership, 46*(3), 4–10.

Darling-Hammond, L., & Berry, B. (1988). *The evolution of teacher policy* (RAND/JRE-01): Center for Policy Research in Education, Center for the Study of the Teaching Profession.

Datta, L. (1972). *Planned variation: An evaluation of an evaluative research study*. Washington, DC: National Institute of Education.

Datta, L., McHale, C., & Mitchell, S. (1976). *The effects of the Head Start classroom experience on some aspects of child development: A summary report of national evaluations 1966–1969* (DHEW Publication No. 76-30088). Washington, DC: U.S. Government Printing Office.

Dau, E., & Creaser, B. (Eds.). (1995). *The anti-bias approach in early childhood*. Sydney: Harper Educational.

Davies, B. (1989a). *Frogs and snails and feminist tales*. Sydney: Allen and Unwin.

Davies, B. (1989b). The discursive production of the male/female dualism in school settings. *Oxford Review of Education, 5*(3), 229–241.

Davies, B. (1990a). Agency as a form of discursive practice. *British Journal of Sociology of Education, 11*(3), 341–361.

Davies, B. (1990b). Lived and imaginary narratives and their place in taking oneself up as a gendered being. *Australian Psychologist, 25*(3), 318–332.

Davies, B. (1991). *The concept of agency.* A feminist poststructuralist analysis. *Social Analysis. Special Issue on Postmodern Critical Theorising, 30*, 42–53.

Davies, B. (1993). *Shards of glass.* Sydney: Allen and Unwin.

Davies, B. (1996). *Power knowledge desire: Changing school organisation and management practices.* Canberra, ACT. DEETYA.

Davis, F. (1995). The Hawaiian alternative to the one-drop rule. In N. Zack (Ed.), *American mixed race: The culture of microdiversity* (pp. 115–132). Lanham, MD: Rowman & Littlefield.

Delaporte, F. (Ed.). (1994). *A vital rationalist: Selected writings from Georges Canguilhem.* New York: Zone Books.

Delbruck, J. (1846). *Visite a la crèche-modèle.* [A visit to a model crèche]. Paris: Paulin.

DeLima, F. (1991a). *The best of DeLima too.* Sound recording. Honolulu: Pocholinga Productions.

DeLima, F. (1991b). *Frank DeLima's joke book.* J. Hopkins (Ed.). Honolulu: Bess Press.

Delpit, L. (1995). *Other people's children: Cultural conflict in the classroom.* New York: The New Press.

de Mause, L. (1974). The evolution of childhood. In L. de Mause (Ed.), *The history of childhood* (pp. 1–73). New York: Psychohistory Press.

Denise, T. C., & Peterfreund, S. P. (1992). *Great traditions in ethics: The challenge of applied ethics* (Seventh edition). Belmont, CA: Wadsworth.

Densmore, K. (1987). Professionalism, proletarianization and teacher work. In T. Popkewitz (Ed.), *Critical studies in teacher education: Its folklore, theory and practice* (pp. 130–160). New York: The Falmer Press.

Dermon-Sparks, L., & The A.B.C. Task Force (1989). *Anti-Bias curriculum: Tools for empowering young children.* Washington, DC: NAEYC.

Derrida, J. (1976). *Of grammatology.* Baltimore: Johns Hopkins University Press.

Downey, L. W. (1988). *Policy analysis in education*. Calgary, Alberta: Detselig Enterprises Limited.

Dreyfus, H., & Rabinow, P. (Eds.). (1982). *Michel Foucault: Beyond structuralism and hermeneutics*. Chicago: University of Chicago Press.

Dunford, B. (1980). *The Hawaiians of old*. Honolulu: Bess Press.

Duryea, E. D. (1981). The university and the state: A historical overview. In P. G. Altbach & R. O. Berdahl (Eds.), *Higher education in American society* (pp. 17–38). Buffalo, NY: Prometheus Books.

East End Day Nursery. *Annual report*. Toronto: Author.

Edgeworth, M. (1809). *Madame de Fleury: Tales of a fashionable life: Tales and novels*. London: J. Johnson.

Edgeworth, M. (1979). Maria Edgeworth to Mrs. Ruxton, 1 December 1802. In C. Colvin (Ed.), *Maria Edgeworth in France and Switzerland: Selections from the Edgeworth family letters* (pp. 39–40). Oxford: Clarendon.

Einhorn, B. (1993). *Cinderella goes to market*. Boston: Verso Press.

Elkind, D. (1984). *All grown up and no place to go: Teenagers in crisis*. Reading, MA: Addison-Wesley

Escobar, E. (1995). The heuristic power of art. In C. Becker (Ed.), *The subversive imagination: Artists, society, and social responsibility* (pp. 35–54). New York: Routledge.

Evans, J. (1995). *Who is caring for the children? An exploratory survey conducted in Hungary, Poland, Bulgaria, and Romania*. Report to the World Bank, Parts I and II. Washington, DC: The World Bank.

Fairchilds, C. (1984). *Domestic enemies: Servants & their masters in old regime France*. Baltimore: Johns Hopkins University Press.

Feinberg, W. (1975). *Reason and rhetoric: The intellectual foundations of 20th century liberal educational policy*. New York: Wiley.

Felman, S., & Laub, D. (1992). *Testimony: Crisis in witnessing in literature, pychoanalysis, and history*. New York: Routledge.

Fenstermacher, G. (1994). The knower and the known: The nature of knowledge in research on teaching. In L. Darling-Hammond (Ed.), *Review of Research in Education, 20*, 3–56. Washington, DC: American Educational Research Association.

Fernandez, M., & Bloch, M. (1993). *Child care during the transition to a market economy: Focus on Bulgaria, Hungary, and Poland*. Washington, DC: Price Waterhouse International.

Fields, B. J. (1982). Ideology and race in American history. In J.

MacPherson & M. Kousser (Eds.), *Region, race and reconstruction* (pp. 143–177). New York: Oxford University Press.

Finkelstein, B. (1988). The revolt against selfishness: Women and the dilemmas of professionalism in early childhood education. In B. Spodek, O. N. Saracho, & D. L. Peters (Eds.), *Professionalism and the early childhood practitioner* (pp. 10–28). New York: Teachers College Press.

Fish, Stanley. (1980). *Is there a text in this class? The authority of interpretive communities.* Cambridge, MA: Harvard University Press.

Fisher, D. (1912). *A Montessori mother.* New York: Henry Holt.

Flax, J. (1993). *Disputed subjects: Essays on psychoanalysis, politics, and philosophy.* New York and London: Routledge.

Forster, J. (1996). *Observations made during a voyage round the world.* N. Thomas, H. Guest, & M. Dettelbach (Eds.). Honolulu: University of Hawaii Press.

Foucault, M. (1965). *Madness and civilization: A history of insanity in the age of reason.* New York: Pantheon.

Foucault, M. (1970). *The order of things: An archaeology of the human sciences.* (A. Sheridan, Trans.). New York: Pantheon.

Foucault, M. (1972). *The archaeology of knowledge and the discourse on language* (A. M. Sheridan Smith, Trans.). New York: Pantheon. (Original text published 1969)

Foucault, M. (1977a). Truth and power. In C. Gordon (Ed.), *Power/Knowledge: Selected interviews and other writings 1972–1977* (pp. 109–133). Sussex: The Harvester Press.

Foucault, M. (1977b). Two lectures. In C. Gordon (Ed.), *Power/Knowledge: Selected interviews and other writings 1972–1977* (pp. 78–108). Sussex: The Harvester Press.

Foucault, M. (1978). *The history of sexuality: Vols. I–III.* New York: Pantheon.

Foucault, M. (1980). *Power/Knowledge.* New York: Pantheon.

Foucault, M. (1982). The subject and power. In H. Dreyfus and P. Rabinow (Eds.), *Michel Foucault: Beyond structuralism and hermeneutics* (pp. 208–226). Chicago: University of Chicago Press.

Foucault, M. (1988). Critical theory/intellectual history. In L. Kritzman (Ed. and Trans.), *Politics, philosophy, culture: Interviews and other writings* (pp. 17–46). New York: Routledge.

Foucault, M. (1991). Governmentality. In G. Burchell, C. Gordon, & P. Miller (Eds.), *The Foucault effect: Studies in governmentality* (pp. 87–104). Chicago: University of Chicago Press.

Franklin, B. M. (1986). *Building the American community: The school curriculum and the search for social control* (Vol. 4). Philadelphia: The Falmer Press.

Fraser, N. (1989). *Unruly practices.* Minneapolis: University of Minnesota Press.

Fraser, N., & Gordon L. (1984). A genealogy of 'dependency': Tracing a keyword of the U.S. welfare state. *Signs, 19,* 309–336.

Fraser, N., & Gordon L. (1994). Dependency demystified: Inscriptions of power in a keyword of the welfare state. *Social Politics, 1*(1), 4–31.

Freud, S. (1958). The uncanny. In B. Nelson (Ed.), *On creativity and the unconscious: Papers on the psychology of art, literature, love, religion* (pp. 122–161). New York: Harper & Row.

Friere, P. (1990). *Pedagogy of the oppressed.* New York: Continuum.

Fröebel, F. (1887). *The education of man.* (W. M. Hailman, Trans.). New York: D. Appleton. (Original work published 1826)

Funk, N., & Mueller, M. (1993). *Gender politics and post-communism.* New York: Routledge.

Gandini, L. (1993). Fundamentals of the Reggio Emilia approach to early childhood education. *Young Children, 49,* 4–12.

Gates, H. L. (1996). *The future of race.* New York: A. A. Knopf (Distributed by Random House).

Geyl, P. (1958). *Debates with historians.* Cleveland, OH: World Publishing Company.

Giddens, A. (1990). *The consequences of modernity.* Stanford, CA: Stanford University Press.

Giddens, A. (1991). *Modernity and self-identity: Self and society in the late modern age.* Cambridge: Polity Press.

Gilmore, L. (1994). *Autobiographics: A feminist theory of women's self-representation.* Ithaca, NY: Cornell University Press.

Ginsburg, M. B., & Lindsay, B. (Eds.). (1995). *The political dimension in teacher education: Comparative perspectives on policy formation, socialization and society.* Bristol, PA: The Falmer Press.

Ginsburg, M. B., & Newman, K. K. (1985). Social inequalities, schooling and teacher education. *Journal of Teacher Education, 36*(2), 49–54.

Giroux, H. (1981). *Ideology, culture, and the process of schooling.* Philadelphia: Temple University Press.

Giroux, H. (1983). *Theory and resistance: A pedagogy for the opposition.* South Hadley, MA: Bergin and Garvey Publishers

Glueck, G. (1971, 2 May). No tame kiddy trader he. *The New York Times Book Review*, 7, 39.

Goldstein, L. (1994, April). *What's love got to do with it? Feminist theory and early childhood education.* Paper presented to the Annual Meeting of the American Educational Research Association, New Orleans, LA.

Goldstein, L. S. (1997). *Teaching with love: A feminist approach to early childhood education.* New York: Peter Lang.

Goodlad, J. (1984). *A place called school.* New York: McGraw-Hill.

Goodlad, J. I. (1991). *Teachers for our nation's schools.* San Francisco: Jossey-Bass Publishers.

Gordon, L. (1994). *Pitied but not entitled: Single mothers and the history of welfare.* New York: Free Press.

Gore, J. (1991). *Neglected practices: A Foucauldian critique of traditional and radical approaches to pedagogy.* Paper presented to The Liberating Curriculum Conference, University of Adelaide, Australia.

Gore, J. (1993). *The struggle for pedagogies: Critical and feminist discourses as regimes of truth.* London: Routledge.

Gorth, W. P., & Chernoff, M. L. (Eds.). (1985). *Testing for teacher certification.* Hillsdale, NJ: Lawrence Erlbaum Associates.

Goslin, D. A. (Ed.). (1969). *Handbook of socialization theory and research.* Chicago: Rand McNally.

Gottdiener, M. (1995). *Postmodern semiotics: Material culture and the forms of postmodern life.* Cambridge: Blackwell Publishers.

Grey Nuns. *Crèche D'Youville, 1920s* (photograph). Montreal: Grey Nuns Archives.

Grieshaber, S. J. (1993). *Parent and child conflict: A poststructuralist study of four families.* Unpublished PhD thesis. James Cook University of North Queensland.

Grieshaber, S. (1998). Constructing the gendered infant. In N. Yelland (Ed.), *Gender in early childhood* (pp. 15–35). London: Routledge.

Grosz, E. (1995). *Space, time and perversion: Essays on the politics of bodies.* New York: Routledge.

Grubb, W. (1991). Young children face the state: Issues and options for early childhood programs. *American Journal of Education, 97*(4), 378–397.

Guha, R. (1983). *Elementary aspects of peasant insurgency in colonial India.* Delhi: Oxford University Press.

Gutting, G. (1989). *Michael Foucault's archaeology of scientific reason.* Cambridge: Cambridge University Press.

Hacking, I. (1991). How should we do the history of statistics? In G. Burchell, G. Gordon, & R. Miller (Eds.), *The Foucault effect: Studies in governmentality* (pp. 181–196). Chicago: University of Chicago Press.

Hall, G. S. (1904). *Adolescence.* New York: Appleton.

Hall, S. (1991). Old and new identities, old and new ethnicities. In A. King (Ed.), *Culture, globalization and the world-system* (pp. 41–68). Binghamton, NY: State University of New York.

Haney, L. (1997). But we are still mothers: Gender and the construction of need in post-socialist Hungary. *Social Politics, 4*(2).

Haraway, D. (1990). Situated knowledges. *Feminist Studies, 14* (3).

Haraway, D. (1991). *Simians, cyborgs, and women: The reinvention of nature.* New York: Routledge.

Harding, S. (1991). *Whose science? Whose knowledge?: Thinking from women's lives.* Ithaca, NY: Cornell University Press.

Hart, C. H., De Wolf, M. D., & Burts, D. C. (1993). Parental disciplinary strategies and preschoolers play behavior. In C. H. Hart (Ed.), *Children on playgrounds: Research perspectives and applications* (pp. 271–313). Albany, NY: State University of New York Press.

Hart, C. H., Olsen, S. F., Robinson, C. C., & Mandleco, B. L. (1996). In B. R. Barleson (Ed.), *Communication yearbook 20.* International Communication Association (pp. 1–91). Thousand Oaks, CA: Sage.

Haywood, C. (1996). 'Out of the curriculum': Sex talking, talking sex. *Curriculum Studies, 4,* 229–249.

Hazama, D. (1974). *The ancient Hawaiians.* Honolulu: Hogarth Press.

Hedges, E., & Fishkin, S. F. (Eds). (1994). *Listening to silences: New essays in feminist criticism.* New York: Oxford University Press.

Hekman, S. J. (1995). *Moral voices, moral selves.* Cambridge: Polity Press.

Henniger, M. L. (1999). *Teaching young children: An introduction.* Columbus, OH: Merrill.

Hertzberg, H. W. (1981). *Social studies reform 1880–1980.* Boulder, CO: Social Science Education Consortium, Inc.

Hewes, D. (1976). NAEYC's first half century: 1926–1976. *Young Children, 31*(6), 461–476.

Hildebrand, V. (1997). *Introduction to early childhood education.* Upper Saddle River, NJ: Merrill.

Hindess, B. (1996). Liberalism, socialism and democracy: Variations on a governmental theme. In A. Barry, T. Osborne, & N. Rose (Eds.), *Foucault and political reason: Liberalism, neo-liberalism and rationalities of government* (pp. 65–80). Chicago: University of Chicago Press.

Holland, P. (1992). *What is a child? Popular images of childhood.* London: Virago

Hollway, W. (1984). Gender difference and the production of subjectivity. In J. Henriques, W. Hollway, C. Urwin, C. Venn, & V. Walkerdine (Eds.), *Changing the subject: Psychology, social regulation and subjectivity.* (pp. 227–263). London: Methuen.

Holmes Group. (1986). *Tomorrow's teachers: A report of the Holmes Group.* East Lansing, MI: The Holmes Group.

Holmes Group. (1990). *Tomorrow's schools: Principles for the design of professional development schools.* East Lansing, MI: The Holmes Group.

Holmes Group. (1991a). Midwest Equity Conference. *The Holmes Group Forum, 6*(1), 6–10.

Holmes Group. (1991b). *Toward a community of learning: The preparation and continuing education of teachers* (Occasional Paper 5): Michigan State University.

Holmes Group Forum. (1991). Regional conferences focus on multicultural issues and professional development schools. *The Holmes Group Forum, VI*(1), 6–10.

hooks, b. (1990). *Yearning: Race, gender, and cultural politics.* Boston: South End Press.

hooks, b. (1994). *Teaching to transgress: Education as the practice of freedom.* New York: Routledge.

Howard, M. (1994). The role of the communal voice in constructing meaning at the funeral of an infant child in a Quaker community in Costa Rica. *Symbolic Interaction, 17*(3), 295–308.

Hubbell, R. (1983). *A review of Head Start research since 1970.* Washington, DC: CSR, Inc.

Hungary. (1996). *Statistical Handbook of Hungary 1995.* Budapest: Hungarian Central Statistical Office.

Hunt, L. (1986). French history in the last twenty years: The rise and fall of the *Annales* paradigm. *Journal of Contemporary History, 21*(1), 209–224.

Hunt, L. (1989). Introduction: History, culture, and text. In L. Hunt (Ed.), *The New Cultural History* (pp. 1–24). Berkeley: University of California Press.

Hunter, I. (1990). Personality as a vocation: The political rationality of the humanities. *Economy and Society, 19*(4), 391–430.

Hymes, J. (1991). *Early childhood education: Twenty years in review.* Washington, DC: National Association for the Education of Young Children.

Ionesco, E. (1967). *Story Number 1.* New York: Harlin Quist.

Ionesco, E. (1970). *Story Number 2.* New York: Harlin Quist.

Ionesco, E. (1971). *Story Number 3.* New York: Harlin Quist.

Ionesco, E. (1974). *Story Number 4.* New York: Harlin Quist.

James, A. (1996). Learning to be friends. *Childhood: A Global Journal of Child Research, 3*(3), 313–329

James, A., Jenks, C., & Prout, A. (Eds.). (1998). *Theorizing childhood.* New York: Teachers College Press.

Jarolimek, J. J. (1981). The social studies: An overview. In H. D. Hehlinger & O. L. Davis, Jr. (Eds.), *The social studies: Eightieth yearbook of the National Society for the Study of Education, Part II* (pp. 3–18). Chicago: University of Chicago Press.

Jarvis, B. (1998). *Postmodern cartographies.* New York: St. Martin's Press.

Jipson, J. (1991). Developmentally appropriate practice: Culture, curriculum, connections. *Early Education and Development, 2,* 120–136.

Jipson, J. (1992). The emergent curriculum: Contextualizing a feminist perspective. In S. Kessler & B. Swadener (Eds.), *Reconceptualizing the early childhood curriculum* (pp. 149–164). New York: Teachers College Press.

Jipson, J. (1995). *Repositioning feminism and education: Perspectives on educating for social change.* Westport, CT: Bergin & Garvey.

Jipson, J. (1999). The stealing of wonderful ideas: The politics of early childhood research. In L. De Soto (Ed.), *The politics of early childhood education.* New York: Peter Lang.

Jipson, J., & Munro, P. (1993) "What's real: Fictions of the maternal." *Journal of Curriculum Theorizing, 10*(2), 7–28.

Jipson, J., Munro, P., Victor, S., Froude Jones, K., & Freed-Rowland, G. (1995). *Repositioning feminism and education: Perspectives on educating for social change.* Westport, CT: Bergin & Garvey.

Jipson, J., & Paley, N. (Eds.). (1997). *Daredevil research: Re-Creating analytic practice.* New York: Peter Lang.

Johnson, R. T. (1996, October). *Reggio Emilia and cargo cults: Fact or fiction?* Paper presented at the Annual Reconceptualizing ECE Conference, Madison, WI.

Johnson, R. T. (1997, May). *Imperialism and cargo cults in early childhood education: Does Reggio Emilia really exist?* Paper presented at the Center for Applied Studies in Early Childhood, Queensland University of Technology, Brisbane, Australia.

Johnson, R. T. (1998, April). *Erasure of sexuality in the care of young children.* Paper presented the annual meeting of the American Educational Research Association, San Diego, CA.

Johnson, S. M. (1994). Teachers and policy makers. *Harvard Graduate School of Education Alumni Bulletin, 36*(3), 15–17.

Jolly, M. (1997). From Point Venus to Bali Ha'i: Eroticism and exoticism in representations of the Pacific. In L. Manderson & M. Jolly (Eds.), *Sites of desire, economics of pleasure: Sexualities in Asia and the Pacific* (pp. 99–122). Chicago: University of Chicago Press.

Jones, E., & Reynolds, G. (1992). *The play's the thing: Teachers' roles in children's play.* New York: Teachers College Press.

Jones, J. (1989). Preface. In E. D. Cahan (Ed.), *Past caring: A history of U.S. preschool care and education for the poor, 1820–1965.* New York: National Center for Children in Poverty, Columbia University.

Karier, C. J. (1973). Liberal ideology and the quest for orderly change. In C. J. Karier, P. C. Violas, & J. Spring (Eds.), *Roots of crisis: American education in the twentieth century* (pp. 84–107). Chicago: Rand McNally.

Katz, L. G. (1984). The professional early childhood teacher. *Young Children, 39*(5), 3–10.

Katz, M. B. (1971). *Class, bureaucracy, & schools: The illusion of educational change in America.* New York: Praeger.

Kay, S. (1993). Sexual knowledge: The once and future texts of the Romance of the Rose. In J. Still & M. Whorton (Eds.), *Textuality and sexuality: Reading theories and practices* (pp. 69–86). New York: St. Martin's Press.

Kennedy, D. (1988). Images of the young child in history: Enlightenment and romance. *Early Childhood Research Quarterly, 3,* 121–137.

Kenway, J., Willis, S., Blackmore, J., & Rennie, L. (1994). Making 'hope practical' rather than 'despair convincing': Feminist poststructuralism, gender reform and educational change. *British Journal of Sociology of Education, 15*(2), 187–210.

Kessen, W. (1993). A developmentalist's reflections. In G. H. Elder, Jr., J. Model, & R. D. Parke (Eds.), *Children in time and place: Developmental and historical insights* (pp. 226–229). New York: Cambridge University Press.

Kessler, S. A. (1991). Alternative perspectives on early childhood education. *Early Childhood Research Quarterly, 6,* 183–197.

Kessler, S., & Swadener, B. (Eds.). (1992). *Reconceptualizing the early childhood curriculum.* New York: Teachers College Press.

King, J. (1981). *The biology of race.* Berkeley: University of California Press.

Kirp, D. (1986). Introduction: The fourth R. In D. Kirp & D. Jensen (Eds.), *School days, rule days* (pp. 1–17). Philadelphia: The Falmer Press.

Klein, J. T. (1992). Text/context: The rhetoric of the social science. In R. H. Brown (Ed.), *Writing the social text: Poetics and politics in social science discourse* (pp. 9–27). New York: Walter de Gryuter, Inc.

Kliebard, H. M. (1992). *Forging the American curriculum: Essays in curriculum history and theory.* New York: Routledge.

Kliebard, H. M. (1995). *The struggle for the American curriculum: 1893–1958.* New York: Routledge.

Kozol, J. (1981). *On being a teacher.* New York: Continuum.

Kristeva, J. (1986). *The Kristeva reader* (T. Moi, Ed.). New York: Columbia University Press

Kurzweil, E. (1980). *The age of structuralism: Lévi-Strauss to Foucault.* New York: Columbia University Press.

Labaree, D. (1992a). Power, knowledge, and the rationalization of teaching: A genealogy of the movement to professionalize teaching. *Harvard Educational Review, 62*(2), 123–154.

Labaree, D. F. (1992b). Doing good, doing science: The Holmes Group Reports and the rhetorics of educational reform. *Teachers College Record, 93*(4), 628–640.

LaBerge, A. (1991). Medicalization and moralization: The crèches of nineteenth century Paris. *Social History, 25*(1), 65–87.

Lacan, J. (1977). *Ecrits: A selection.* New York: Norton.

Lazar, I., Darlington, R., Murray, H., Royce, J., & Snipper, A. (1982). Lasting effects of early education. *Monographs of the Society for Research in Child Development, 47* (2–3, Serial No. 195).

Leander, E. (1975). *Crazy days.* New York: Harlin Quist.

Lemert, C. C. (Ed.). (1981). *French sociology: Rupture and renewal since 1968.* New York: Columbia University Press.

Lerner, G. (1986). *The creation of patriarchy.* New York: Oxford University Press.

Lerner, G. (1993). *The creation of feminist consciousness: From the middle ages to eighteen-seventy.* New York: Oxford Univesity Press.

Leslie, M. (1998). *Renaissance utopias and the problem of history.* Ithica, NY: Cornell University Press.

Levine, R. (1994). *Child care and culture: Lessons from Africa.* Cambridge: Cambridge University Press.

Levi-Strauss, C. (1970). *The raw and the cooked.* (J. & D. Weightman, Trans.). New York: Harper & Row.

Lewis, J. (1995). *Critiques and alternatives to child development theories.* Unpublished manuscript.

Lindstrom, L. (1990). *Knowledge and power in a South Pacific society.* Honolulu, HI: University of Hawaii Press.

Lindstrom, L. (1993). *Cargo cult: Strange stories of desire from Melanesia and beyond.* Washington, DC: Smithsonian Institution Press.

Lombardo-Radice, G. (1934). *Nursery schools in Italy: The problem of infant education* (M. C. Glasgow, Trans.). London: George Allen.

Love, J., Nauta, M., Coelen, C., Hewlett, K., & Ruopp, R. (1976). *National Home Start final report: Findings and implications.* Cambridge, MA: Abt Associates.

Love, M. E. (1897). The physical care of children in the Fitch Crèche. In Federation of Day Nurseries, *The proceedings of the Conference of Day Nurseries*. New York: Federation of Day Nurseries.

Lukas, C. (1975). Problems in implementing Head Start Planned Variation Models. In A. M. Rivlin & P. M. Timpane (Eds.), *Planned variation in education: Should we give up or try harder?* Washington, DC: Brookings Institution.

Lybarger, M. B. (1991). The historiography of social studies: Retrospect, circumspect, and prospect. In J. P. Shaver (Ed.), *Handbook of research on social studies teaching and learning* (pp. 3–15). New York: Macmillan.

Lytton, H., & Zwirner, W. (1975). Compliance and its controlling stimuli observed in a natural setting. *Developmental Psychology, 11*(6), 769–779.

Maccoby, E. E., & Martin, J. A. (1983). Socialization in the context of the family: Parent-child interaction. In P. H. Muffen (Series Ed.), E. M. Hetherington (Vol. Ed.), *Handbook of child psychology: Vol. 4 Socialization, personality and social development* (pp. 1–102). New York: Wiley.

Mackaness, G. (1931). *The life of Vice-Admiral William Bligh*. New York: Farrar and Rinehart, Inc.

MacMillan, M. (1919). *The nursery school*. London: Dent.

MacNaughton, G. (1992). Equity challenges for the early childhood curriculum. *Children and Society, 6*(3), pp. 225–240.

MacNaughton, G. (1995). *Transforming gendering in early childhood settings: An action research project*. Unpublished doctoral thesis. Deakin University, Australia.

Madus, J. L. (1995). *Unstable bodies: Victorian representations of sexuality and maternity*. New York: St. Martin's Press.

Mairs, N. (1994). *Voice lessons: On becoming a (woman) writer*. Boston: Beacon Press.

Malen, B. (1994). Enacting site-based management: A political utilities analysis. *Educational Evaluation and Policy Analysis, 16*(3), 249–267.

Mallory, B., & New, R. (1994). *Diversity and developmentally appropriate practices: Challenges for early childhood education*. New York: Teachers College Press.

Malthus, R. (1990). *An essay on the principle of population; or a view of its past and present effects on human happiness; with an inquiry into our prospects respecting the future removal or mitigation of the evils which it occasions.* Selected and introduced by Donald Winch using the text of the 1803 edition as prepared by Patricia James for the Royal Economic Society, 1990, showing the additions and corrections made in the 1806, 1807, 1817, and 1826 editions. Cambridge: Cambridge University Press.

Marbeau, J. (1845). *Des crèches: Ou, Moyen de diminuer la misére en augmentant la population* [The crèche, or a way to reduce poverty by increasing the population], 2nd ed. Imprimeurs-Unis: Paris. Trans. by Vanessa Nicolai.

Marion, M. (1983). Child compliance: A review of the literature with implications for family life education. *Family Relations, 32,* 545–555.

Marshall, B. (1991). Teaching the postmodern: Fiction and theory. New York: Routledge.

Marshall, H. (1991). The social construction of motherhood: An analysis of childcare and parenting manuals. In A. Woollet, A. Phoenix, & E. Lloyd (Eds.), *Motherhood: Meanings, practices and ideologies* (pp. 66–85). London: Sage.

Mayhew, L. (1971). *Changing practices in education for the professions.* Atlanta, GA: SREB Research Monograph No. 17.

Maynard, T. (1993). *Saving endangered birds: Ensuring a future in the wild.* New York: Franklin Watts.

McKey, R., Condelli, L., Ganson, H., Barrett, B., & McConkey, C. (1986). *The impact of Head Start on families and communities. Final report of the Head Start evaluation, synthesis, and utilization project.* Washington, DC: CSR, Incorporated.

McLaren, P. (1989). *Life in schools: An introduction to critical pedagogy in the foundations of education.* New York: Longman.

McLaughlin, M. (1990). The Rand change agent study revisited: Macro perspectives and micro realities. *Educational Researcher, 19*(9), 11–16.

Meek, A. (1988). On teaching as a profession: A conversation with Linda Darling-Hammond. *Educational Leadership, 46*(3), 12–17.

Meeting at Mrs. Hale's for establishing a day home for destitute children. (1858, Oct. 30). *Troy Daily Times.*

Merleau-Ponty, M. (1964). *The primacy of perception.* Evanston, IL: Northwestern University Press.

Michel, S. (1999). *Children's interests/mothers' rights: A history of child care in America.* New Haven, CT: Yale University Press.

Mintrop, H., & Weiler, H. (1994). The relationship between educational policy and practice: The reconstitution of the college-preparatory gymnasium in East Germany. *Harvard Educational Review, 64*(3), 247–277.

Mirel, J. (1994). School reform unplugged: The Bensenville New American School Project. *American Educational Research Journal, 31*(3), 481–518.

Mitchell, L. S. (1921). *Young geographers.* New York: Bank Street College.

Montessori, M. (1912). *The Montessori method.* (trans. from the Italian by Anne E. George). London: William Heinemann.

Montessori, M. (1965a). *Dr. Montessori's own handbook.* New York: Schocken.

Montessori, M. (1965b). *Spontaneous activity in education.* New York: Shocken.

Morgan, D. F. (1994). The role of liberal arts in professional education. In C. M. Brody & J. Wallace (Eds.), *Ethical and social issues in professional education* (pp. 13–28). New York: State University of New York Press.

Morrison, T. (1994/1987). *Beloved: A novel.* New York: Random House.

Morrissett, I. (1981). The needs of the future and constraints of the past. In H. D. Hehlinger, & O. L. Davis, Jr. (Eds.), *The social studies: Eightieth Yearbook of the National Society for the Study of Education, Part II* (pp. 36–59). Chicago: University of Chicago Press.

Morrow, R., & Brown, D. (1994). *Critical theory and methodology.* Thousand Oaks, CA: Sage.

Mulvey, L. (1977). *The sexual subject: A Screen reader in sexuality.* New York: Routledge.

Murray, F. B., & Fallon, D. (1989). *The reform of teacher education for the 21st century: Project 30 year one report*: University of Delaware and Texas A & M University.

Myers, R. (1995). *The twelve who survive: Strengthening programmes of early childhood development in the third world.* London: Routledge & Kegan Paul.

Nakashima, C. (1992). An invisible monster: The creation and denial of mixed-race people in America. In M. Root (Ed.), *Racially mixed people in America* (pp. 162–178). Newbury Park, CA: Sage.

Napoli, D. S. (1981). *Architects of adjustment: The history of the psychological profession in the United States.* Port Washington, NY: National University Publications.

National Association for the Education of Young Children. (1982). *Early childhood teacher education guidelines.* Washington, DC: Author.

National Commission for Excellence in Teacher Education. (1985). *A Call for Change in Teacher Education.* Washington, DC: American Association of Colleges for Teacher Education.

National Commission on Excellence in Education. (1983). *A nation at risk: The imperative for educational reform.* Washington, DC: GPO.

National Council for the Accreditation of Teacher Education. (1987). *Standards, procedures, and policies for the accreditation of professional education units.* Washington, DC: Author.

National Council for the Social Studies. (1989). *Social studies for early childhood and elementary school children: Preparing for the 21st century.* Washington, DC: Author.

National Head Start Association. (1990). *Head Start: The nation's pride, a nation's challenge. Recommendations for Head Start in the 1990's. Report of the silver ribbon panel.* Alexandria, VA: Author.

Nauta, M., & Travers, J. (1982). *The effects of a social program: Executive summary of CFRP's infant-toddler component.* Cambridge, MA: Abt Associates.

New, R. (1994). Reggio Emilia: Its vision and its challenges for educators in the United States. In L. G. Katz, & B. Cesarone (Eds.), *Reflections on the Reggio Emilia approach* (pp. 33–40). Eric/EECE Monograph Series.

The new book of knowledge. (1992). Danbury, CT: Grolier.

Nsamenang, A. B. (1992). *Human development in cultural context: A third world perspective.* Newbury Park: Sage.

Nursery & Child's Hospital. (1874). *20th Annual Report.* New York: Author.

Ogawa, R. T. (1994). The institutional sources of educational reform: The case of school-based management. *American Educational Research Journal, 31*(3), 519–548.

Omi, M., & Winant, H. (1986). *Racial formation in the United States: From the 1960's to the 1980's.* New York: Routledge & Kegan Paul.

Orner, M. (1992). Interrupting the calls for student voice in "liberatory" education: A feminist poststructuralism perspective. In C.

Luke & J. Gore (Eds.), *Feminisms and critical pedagogy* (pp. 74–89). New York: Routledge.

Page, J. (1991). Critical futures studies: Rendering the early childhood curriculum responsive to the future needs of children. *Australian Journal of Early Childhood, 16*(4), 42–48.

Palank, A., & Burch, P. (1992). *Mapping the policy landscape: What federal and state governments are doing to promote family-school-community partnerships.* Baltimore, MD: Center on Families, Communities, Schools and Children's Learning.

Paley, N. (1995). *Finding arts place: Experiments in contemporary education and culture.* New York: Routledge.

Paley, V. (1992). *You can't say you can't play.* Cambridge, MA: Harvard University Press.

Pasquali, P. (1910). *Il nuovo spirito dell'Asilo.* [A new spirit in day care.] Milan: G. Merendi.

Pauly, E. (1991). *The classroom crucible: What really works, what doesn't, and why.* New York: Basic Books.

Peters, D. (1980). Social science and social policy and the care of young children: Head Start and after. *Journal of Applied Developmental Psychology, 1*(1), 7–27.

Phelan, P. (1993). *Unmarked: The politics of performance.* London: Routledge.

Phoenix, A., & Woollet, A. (1991). Introduction. In A. Phoenix, A. Woollet, & E. Lloyd, E. (Eds.), *Motherhood: Meanings, practices and ideologies* (pp. 1–12). London: Sage.

Platt, A. (1971). *History of child saving in the United States.* Montclair, NJ: Patterson Smith.

Plummer, K. (1995). *Telling sexual stories: Power, change and social worlds.* New York: Routledge.

Polakow, V. (1993). *Lives on the edge: Single mothers and their children in the other America.* Chicago: University of Chicago Press.

Poland. *Annual reports.* Central Office of Statistics.

Popkewitz, T. S. (1987a). The formation of school subjects and the political context of schooling. In T. S. Popkewitz (Ed.), *The formation of the school subjects: The struggle for creating an American institution* (pp. 1–24). New York: The Falmer Press.

Popkewitz, T. S. (1987b). Ideology and social formation in teacher education. In T. S. Popkewitz (Ed.), *Critical studies in teacher* education: Its folklore, theory and practice (pp. 2–34). New York: The Falmer Press.

Popkewitz, T. S. (1991). *A political sociology of educational reform: Power/knowledge in teaching, teacher education, and research.* New York: Teachers College Press.

Popkewitz, T. S. (1994). Professionalization in teaching and teacher education: Some notes on its history, ideology, and potential. *Teaching & Teacher Education, 10*(1), 1–14.

Popkewitz, T. S. (1995). Teacher education, reform and the politics of knowledge in the United States. In M. B. Ginsburg & B. Lindsay (Eds.), *The political dimension in teacher education: Comparative perspectives on policy formation, socialization and society* (pp. 54–75). Washington, DC: The Falmer Press.

Popkewitz, T. S. (1996). Rethinking decentralization and state/civil society distinctions: The state as a problematic of governing. *Journal of Educational Policy, 11*(2), 27–51.

Powlishta, K. K., Serbin, L. A., Doyle, A., & White, D. R. (1994). Gender, ethnic, and body type biases: The generality of prejudice in childhood. *Developmental Psychology, 30*(4), 526–536.

Pratt, C. (Ed.). (1924). *Experimental practice in the city and country school.* New York: E. P. Dutton.

Prestine, N. A. (1988). *Systems theory and the struggle for control of governance in teacher education: A case study.* Doctoral dissertation, University of Wisconsin-Madison.

Prestine, N. A. (1991). Political system theory as an explanatory paradigm for teacher education reform. *American Educational Research Journal, 28*(2), 237–274.

Prestine, N. A. (1992). The struggle for control of teacher education: The University of Wisconsin-Madison. In H. D. Gideonse (Ed.), *Teacher education policy: Narrative, stories, and cases* (pp. 159–180). New York: State University of New York Press.

Prochner, L. (1994). *Themes in the history of day care: A case study of the West End Crèche, Toronto, 1909–1939.* Unpublished doctoral dissertation, University of Toronto, Toronto, Ontario.

Prochner, L. (1996). Quality-of-care in historical perspective. *Early Childhood Research Quarterly, 11*(1), 5–18.

Prochner, L. (1997). The development of the Day Treatment Center for Emotionally Disturbed Children at the West End Crèche, Toronto. *Canadian Bulletin of Medical History, 14,* 1–25.

Pukui, M., Haertig, E., & Lee, C. (1972). *Nana I ke kumu*. Honolulu, HI: The Lili'uokalani Children's Center.

Quist, H. (1967). Children's book production in the U.S.A. *Graphis, 131*, 272–312.

Quist, H. (1978). Designing books for the delight of the child. In *Proceedings: Children's book international 3* (pp. 34–37). Boston: Boston Public Library.

Raab, C. D. (1994). Where we are now: Reflections on the sociology of education policy. In D. Halpin & B. Troyna (Eds.), *Researching education policy: Ethical and methodological issues* (pp. 17–30). Washington, DC: The Falmer Press.

Reed, I. (1996). *Mumbo jumbo*. New York: Simon and Schuster.

Regis, P. (1992). *Describing early America: Bartram, Jefferson, Crevecoeur, and the rhetoric of natural history*. DeKalb: Northern Illinois University Press.

Rich, J. M. (1974). *New directions in educational policy*. Lincoln, NE: Professional Educators' Publication.

Richards, G. (1992). *Mental machinery: The origins and consequences of psychological ideas, Part 1: 1600–1850*. Baltimore, MD: The Johns Hopkins University Press.

Robertson, G., Mash, M., Tickner, L., Bird, J., Curtis, B., & Putnam, T. (Eds.), (1994). *Travellers' tales: Narratives of home and displacement*. New York: Routledge.

Robinson, C. C., Mandleco, B. L., Olsen, S. F., & Hart, C. H. (1995). Authoritative, authoritarian and permissive parenting practices: Development of a new measure. *Psychological Reports, 77*, 819–830.

Robinson, P. A., & Hom, H. L., Jr. (1977). Child psychology and early childhood education. In P. A. Robinson & H. L. Hom Jr. (Eds.), *Psychological processes in early education* (pp. 23–36). New York: Academic Press.

Robison, H., & Spodek, B. (1965). *New directions in the kindergarten*. New York: Teachers College Press.

Rose, N. (1989). *Governing the soul: The shaping of the private self*. New York: Routledge.

Rose, N. (1994). Expertise and the government of conduct. *Studies in Law, Politics and Society, 14*, 359–397.

Rose, N. (1996). Governing "advanced" liberal democracies. In A. Barry, T. Osborne, & N. Rose (Eds.), *Foucault and political reason:*

Liberalism, neo-liberalism and rationalities of government (pp. 1–18). Chicago: University of Chicago Press.

Rose, N., & Miller, P. (1992). Political power beyond the state: Problematics of government. *British Journal of Sociology, 43*(2), 173–206.

Rueschemeyer, D., & Skocopol, T. (1996). *States social knowledge, and the origins of modern social policies.* Princeton, NJ: Princeton University Press.

Sanders, T., Benton, R., Kaagan, S., Simons, L., & Teague, W. (1984). *Staffing the nation's schools: A national emergency* (Ad Hoc Committee Report on Teacher Certification, Preparation and Accreditation): Council of Chief State School Officers.

Sarason, S. B. (1991). *The predictable failure of educational reform.* San Francisco: Jossey-Bass.

Schiller, M. (1995). Reggio Emilia: A focus on emergent curriculum and art. *Art Education, 48*, 45–50.

Scholastic Pre-K Today. (October, 1992). Reggio Emilia: A model in creativity.

Schön, D. (1983). *The reflective practitioner: How professionals think in action.* New York: Basic Books.

Schön, D. (1987). *Educating the reflective practitioner: Towards a new design for teaching and learning in the professions.* San Francisco: Jossey-Bass.

Schön, D. (Ed.). (1991). *The reflective turn.* New York: Teachers College Press.

Schweinhart, L., Barnes, H., & Weikart, D. (1993). *Significant benefits: The High/Scope Perry Preschool study through age 27.* Ypsilanti, MI: High/Scope Press.

Schweinhart, L., & Koshel, J. (1986). *Policy options for preschool programs.* Ypsilanti, MI: High/Scope Press.

Schweinhart, L., Koshel, J., & Bridgman, A. (1987). Policy options for preschool programs. *Phi Delta Kappan, 68*(7), 524–529.

Schweinhart, L., & Weikart, D. (1993). *A summary of significant benefits: The High/Scope Perry Preschool study through age 27.* Ypsilanti, MI: High/Scope Press.

Seefeldt, C. (1989). *Social studies for the preschool-primary child* (4th ed.). New York: Merrill.

Seifert, K. (1988). Men in early childhood education. In B. Spodek, O. N. Saracho, & D. L. Peters (Eds.), *Professionalism and the early childhood practitioner* (pp. 105–116). New York: Teachers College Press.

Sen, X. (1993). Motherhood and mothercraft: Gender and nationalism in Bengal. *Gender and History, 5*(2), 237.

Shapely, T. (1999, March 9). Breast-feeding moms seek decent facilities at work. *Seattle Post-Intellegencer,* B1, B4.

Shaver, J. P. (1981). Citizenship, values, and morality in social studies. In H. D. Hehlinger & O. L. Davis, Jr. (Eds.). *The social studies: Eightieth Yearbook of the National Society for the Study of Education, Part II* (pp. 105–125). Chicago: University of Chicago Press.

Shrage, L. (1995). Ethnic transgressions: Confessions of an assimilated Jew. In N. Zack (Ed.), *American mixed race: The culture of microdiversity* (pp. 287–296). Lanham, MD: Rowman and Littlefield Publishers, Inc.

Shulman, L. (1987). Knowledge and teaching: Foundations of the new reform. *Harvard Educational Review, 57*(1), 1–22.

Shulman, L. (1988). A union of insufficiencies: Strategies for teacher assessment in a period of educational reform. *Educational Leadership, 46*(3), 36–41.

Siegrist, H. (1994). The professions, state and government in theory and history. In T. Becher (Ed.), *Governments and professional education* (pp. 3–22). Buckingham, England: SHRE & Open University Press.

Silin, J. (1987). The early childhood educator's knowledge base: A reconsideration. In L. G. Katz (Ed.), *Current topics in early childhood education Vol. VII.* (pp. 17–31). Norwood, NJ: Ablex.

Silin, J. (1995). *Sex, death, and the education of children: Our passion for ignorance in the age of AIDS.* New York: Teachers College Press.

Silvern, S. B. (1988). Continuity/discontinuity between home and early childhood education environments. *Elementary School Journal, 89*(2), 147–159.

Simons, J. (1995). *Foucault & the political.* New York: Routledge.

Singer, E. (1992). *Child-care and the psychology of development.* New York: Routledge.

Siraj-Blatchford, J., & Siraj-Blatchford, I. (1995). *Educating the whole child: Cross curricular skills, themes and dimensions.* London: Open University Press.

Sirotnik, K. A. (1988). What goes on in classrooms? Is this the way we want it? In M. Apple and L. E. Beyer, (Eds.), *The curriculum*. Albany, NY: State University of New York Press.

Skocpol, T. (1995). *Social policy in the United States*. Princeton, NJ: Princeton University Press.

Smith, H. N. (1978). The West as an image of the American past. In R. E. Beringer (Ed.), *Historical analysis: Contemporary approaches to Clio's Craft*. Toronto: Wiley.

Smith, M. (1973). *Some short-term effects of Project Head Start: A preliminary report on the second year of Planned Variation—1970–71*. Cambridge, MA: Huron Institute.

Smith, P. K. (1980). Shared care for young children: Alternative models to monotropism. *Merrill Palmer Quarterly, 6*, 371–389.

Social Indicators of Development. (1996). Washington, DC: The World Bank.

Spickard, P. (1992). The illogic of American racial categories. In M. Root (Ed.), *Racially mixed people in America* (pp. 12–13). Newbury Park, CA: Sage Publications.

Spivak, G. C. (1988). Subaltern studies: Deconstructing historiography. In G. C. Spivak (Ed.), *Selected subaltern studies* (pp. 3–32). New York: Oxford University Press.

Spodek, B., Saracho, O. N., & Peters, D. L. (1988). Professionalism, semiprofessionalism, and craftsmanship. In B. Spodek, O. N. Saracho, & D. L. Peters (Eds.), *Professionalism and the early childhood practitioner* (pp. 3–9). New York: Teachers College Press.

Stainton Rogers, R., & Stainton Rogers, W. (1992). *Stories of childhood: Shifting concerns of child concern*. Toronto: University of Toronto Press.

Stanford Research Institute. (1971). *Implementation of planned variation in Head Start: Preliminary evaluations of planned variations in Head Start according to follow-through approaches (1969–1970)*. (Publication No. OCD 72–7).

Stevens, A. (1913). *A guide to the Montessori method*. New York: Frederick A. Stokes.

Stevens, E., Jr., & Wood, G. H. (1987). *Justice, ideology and education*. New York: Random House.

Swadener, B. (1995). *Children and families "at promise": Deconstructing the discourse of risk*. Albany: State University of New York Press.

Tallberg Broman, I. (1993). *When work was its own reward: A Swedish study from the perspective of women's history, of the kindergarten teacher as public educator* (Summary of doctoral thesis ERIC document ED366466): Malmö School of Education, University of Lund.

Teitelbaum, K. N. (1995). *Schooling for "good rebels": Socialization, American education, and the search for radical curriculum.* New York: Teachers College Press.

Thomas, N. (1994). *Colonialism's culture.* Princeton, NJ: Princeton University Press.

Thomas, S. D. (1987). *The last navigator.* New York: H. Holt.

Tiles, M. (1987). Epistemological history: The legacy of Bachelard and Canguilhem. In A. Griffiths (Ed.), *Contemporary French philosophy* (pp. 141–156). Cambridge, MA: Harvard University Press.

Timar, T. (1994). Federal education policy and practice: Building organizational capacity through Chapter 1. *Educational Evaluation and Policy Analysis, 16*(1), 51–66.

Tobin, B. F. (1996). Imperial designs: Botanical illustration and the British botanic empire. In S. Conger and J. Hayes (Eds.), *Studies in eighteenth-century culture, Vol. 25.* Baltimore: John Hopkins University Press.

Tobin, J. (1995). Post-structural research in early childhood education. In J. Amos Hatch (Ed.), *Qualitative research in early childhood settings* (pp. 223–242). Westport, CT: Greenwood.

Tobin, J. (Ed.). (1997). *Making a place for pleasure in early childhood education.* New Haven: Yale University Press.

Tong, R. (1993). *Feminine and feminist ethics.* Belmont, CA: Wadsworth.

Torgovnick, M. (1990). *Gone primitive: Savage intellects, modern lives.* Chicago: University of Chicago Press.

Trask, H. (1993). *From a Native daughter: Colonialism and sovereignty in Hawaii.* Maine: Common Courage Press.

Travers, J., Nauta, M., & Irwin, N. (1982). *The effects of a social program: Final report of the Child and Family Resource Program's infant-toddler component.* Cambridge, MA: Abt Associates.

Tronto, J. (1987). Beyond gender difference to a theory of care. *Signs: Journal of Women in Culture and Society, 12*(4), 644–663

Tsing, A. (1993). *In the realm of the diamond queen: Marginality in an out-of-the-way place*. Princeton, NJ: Princeton University Press.

Tyack, D., & Tobin, W. (1994). The "grammar" of schooling: Why has it been so hard to change? *American Educational Research Journal, 3*(1), 453–479.

United Nations Economic Commission for Europe. (1994). *Economic Bulletin for Europe*, 46.

U.S. Department of Education. (1991). *America 2000: An education strategy*. Washington, DC: Author.

U.S. Department of Health and Human Services. (1993). *Creating a 21st century Head Start: Final report of the advisory committee on Head Start quality and expansion* (DHHS publication No. 1994-517-593/80715). Washington, DC: U.S. Government Printing Office.

Varga, D. (1993). From a service for mothers to the developmental management of children: Day nursery care in Canada, 1890–1960. In *Advances in Early Education and Care*, Vol. 5 (pp. 115–143). Greenwich, CT: JAI Press.

Varga, D. (1997). *Constructing the child: A history of day care in Canada*. Toronto: James Lorimer.

Veale, A. (1991, September). *The emergent profession*. Paper presented at the Early Childhood Convention, Dunedin, New Zealand.

Visweswaran, K. (1994). *Fictions of feminist ethnography*. Minneapolis: University of Minnesota Press.

Wagener, J. R. (1998). The construction of the body through sex education discourse practices. In T. Popkewitz & M. Brennan (Eds.), *Foucault's challenge: Discourse, knowledge, and power in education* (pp. 144–169). New York: Teachers College Press.

Walkerdine, V. (1981). Sex power and pedagogy. *Screen Education, 38*, 14–21.

Walkerdine, V. (1984). Developmental psychology and the child-centered pedagogy. In J. Henriques, W. Hollway, C. Urwin, C. Venn, & V. Walkerdine (Eds.), *Changing the subject: Psychology and social regulation and subjectivity* (pp. 153–202). London: Methuen.

Walkerdine, V. (1988). *The mastery of reason: Cognitive development and the production of rationality*. London: Routledge.

Walkerdine, V. (1989). *Counting girls out*. London: Virago Press.

Walkerdine, V. (1990). *Schoolgirl fictions*. London: Verso Books.

Walkerdine, V. (1992a). Progressive pedagogy and political struggle. In C. Luke and J. Gore (Eds.), *Feminisms and critical pedagogy* (pp. 15–24). London: Routledge.

Walkerdine, V. (1992b). *Reasoning in a post-modern age.* Paper delivered at the 5th International Conference on Thinking. Townsville: Queensland, Australia.

Walkerdine, V., & Lucey, H. (1989). *Democracy in the kitchen: Regulating mothers and socializing daughters.* London: Virago.

Washington, V., & Oyemade, U. (1987). *Project Head Start: Past, present, and future trends in the context of family needs.* New York: Garland.

Wearing, B. (1996). *Gender: The pain and pleasure of difference.* Melbourne: Longman.

Weber, E. (1969). *The kindergarten: Its encounter with educational thought in America.* New York: Teachers College Press.

Weber, E. (1984). *Ideas influencing early childhood education: A theoretical analysis.* New York: Teachers College Press.

Weedon, C. (1987). *Feminist practice and poststructualist theory.* Oxford: Basil Blackwell.

Weiler, H. (1990). Comparative perspectives on educational decentralization: An exercise in contradiction? *Educational Evaluation and Policy Analysis, 12*(4), 433–488.

Weiler, H. (1993). Control versus legitimation: The politics of ambivalence. In J. Hannaway & M. Carnoy (Eds.), *Decentralization and school improvement: Can we fulfill the promise?* San Francisco: Jossey-Bass Publishers.

Weiner, M. (Ed.). (1966). *Modernization: The dynamics of growth.* New York: Basic Books.

Weis, L., Altbach, P. G., Kelly, G. P., Petrie, H. G., & Slaughter, S. (Eds.). (1989). *Crisis in teaching: Perspectives on current reforms.* Albany: State University of New York Press.

Weiss, C., & Cambone, J. (1994). Principals, shared decision making, and school reform. *Educational Evaluation and Policy Analysis, 16*(3), 287–301.

West, C., & Zimmerman, D. H. (1991). Doing gender. In J. Lorber & S. A. Farrell (Eds.), *The social construction of gender* (pp. 13–37). London: Sage.

Westinghouse Learning Corporation. (1969). *The impact of Head Start: An evaluation of the effects of Head Start on children's affective and cognitive development: Vol.1. Text and appendices A–E.* Washington, DC: Clearinghouse Federal Scientific and Technical Information. (ERIC Document Reproduction Service No. ED 036321).

White, H. (1978). Introduction: Tropology, discourse and the modes of human consciousness. In *Tropics of discourse* (pp. 1–25). Washington, DC: Johns Hopkins University Press.

Willer, B., & Bredekamp, S. (1993). A "new" paradigm of early childhood professional development. *Young Children, 48*(4), 63–66.

Willis, P. (1977). *Learning to labor.* Lexington: D.C. Heath.

Willis, S. (1991). *A primer for daily life.* London: Routledge.

Wisconsin Department of Public Instruction. (1989). *Teacher education program approval rules and appeal procedure PI4.* Madison: Wisconsin Department of Public Instruction.

Wisconsin Department of Public Instruction. (1992). *Teacher education program approval rules and appeal procedure PI4.* Madison: Wisconsin Department of Public Instruction.

Wittrock, B., & Elzinga, A. (Eds.). (1985). *The university research system: Public policies of the home of scientists.* Stockholm, Sweden: Novapress, Lund., Almqvist & Wiksell, International.

Woodhead, M. (1990). Psychology and the cultural construction of children's needs. In A. James & A. Prout (Eds.), *Constructing and reconstructing childhood* (pp. 60–78). New York: The Falmer Press.

Woodrow, C. (1996, May). *Images of childhood: Some ethical issues.* Keynote address to the North Queensland Early Childhood Conference, Townsville and Cairns.

Woolf, V. (1993). *Orlando.* London: Bloomsbury.

Woollet, A., & Phoenix, A. (1991). Psychological views of mothering. In A. Phoenix, A. Woollet, & E. Lloyd (Eds.), *Motherhood: Meanings, practices and ideologies* (pp. 28–46). London: Sage.

World Economic Outlook. (1997). Washington, DC: International Monetary Fund.

World Economic and Social Survey. (1996). New York: United Nations.

World Education Report. (1995). New York: UNESCO and Oxford Publishing Co.

World Employment. (1995). Geneva: International Labour Organization.

Wright, R., (1998/1940). *Native son.* New York: Harper Perennial.

Yearbook of Labour Statistics. (1995, 1996). Geneva: International Labour Organization.

Yeatman, A. (1994). *Postmodern revisionings of the political.* New York: Routledge & Kegan Paul.

Young, I. M. (1990). *Justice and the politics of difference.* Princeton, NJ: Princeton University Press.

Young, R. (1990). *White mythologies: Writing history and the west.* New York: Routledge.

Zigler, E., & Child, I. L. (1969). Socialization. In G. Lindzey & E. Aronson (Eds.), *The handbook of social psychology.* Reading, MA: Addison-Wesley.

Zigler, E., & Muenchow, S. (1992). *Head Start: The inside story of America's most successful educational experiment.* New York: Basic Books.

Zigler, E., & Valentine, J. (Eds.). (1979). *Project Head Start: A legacy of the war on poverty.* New York: Free Press.

Zingg, M. (1942). The genuine and spurious values in Tarahumara culture. *American Anthropologist, 44.*

Zinn, H. (1985). What is radical history? In S. Vaughn (Ed.), *The vital past: Writings on the uses of history* (pp. 158–171). Athens, GA: The University of Georgia Press.

Contributors

Chelsea Bailey is an Assistant Professor of Teaching and Learning at New York University. She uses postmodern, feminist, and queer theory to consider the impact of rationalist epistemologies on the research, theory, and curriculum of early childhood education.

Mark D. Bailey is an Assistant Professor of Education at Pacific University, where he is the early childhood specialist. He received his Ph.D. in Educational Psychology from the University of Wisconsin. Mark has researched and written about the role of self-concept in teachers' and students' constructions of understanding and is currently examining the role of technology in early childhood education.

Marianne "Mimi" N. Bloch is a Professor in the Department of Curriculum and Instruction at the University of Wisconsin-Madison. She is editor of the *Cultural-Ecological Context of Children's Play* (with A. Pelligrini) and *Women and Education in Sub-Saharan Africa*. Her research has multiple overlapping trajectories, including a history of early education and childcare, postmodern feminist theory and early education, and welfare state change and the impact on families and children. She has been very active in the U.S. Reconceptualizing Early Education Conference.

Marie Brennan is a Professor in the School of Teacher Education, University of Canberra, Australia. She worked for twenty years for the Ministry of Education in Victoria, Australia, before moving to Deakin University, and later Central Queensland University. Her main research interests are in areas of educational disadvantage, feminist and democratic approaches to research, new forms of technology, and community and school reform. She recently co-edited with Tom Popkewitz *Foucault's Challenge: Discourse, Knowledge and Power in Education* (Teachers College Press).

Gaile S. Cannella is an associate professor of early childhood and multicultural education at Texas A&M University. In addition to her work on social justice and teacher education, she is the author of *Deconstructing Early Childhood Education: Social Justice and Revolution*. In this critique of the field, the universalizatiion of "child" is examined through genealogical methods that challenge adult/child dichotomies, child development as a normalizing truth, and the dominant discourses of early experience, child-centered instruction, and teacher professionalism.

Deborah Ceglowski is an Assistant Professor of Early Childhood Education in the Department of Curriculum and Instruction, and Outreach Coordinator for the Center for Early Education and Development at the University of Minnesota. Her research interests include qualitative studies of the impact of policies on teachers, parents, and children and employing alternative writing strategies, such as short stories, in writing about the impact of policies. In addition to this work, she is the author of "Inside a Head Start Center: Developing Policies from Practice."

Mary Jane Fox joined the Peace Corps as a teacher trainer for the University of Guam on Woleai Atoll, Micronesia, after teaching elementary, secondary, and college level students on Long Island, New York. After completing her Peace Corps tenure she entered the doctoral program at the University of Hawaii-Manoa and returned to Yap State as Curriculum Coordinator where she pursued research on local decision making and educational change. Her recent publications include a paper on the "Discourse of Silences" and "Culturally Relevant Curriculum Development: Yap State, Micronesia." Her research interests include multicultural curriculum development, local language literacy development, and the role of local decision making in educational change.

Maria Gaiyabu is the Director of Extension Programs at the University of the South Pacific's Nauru campus. Her recent master's thesis critically engaged colonial studies as they relate to her experiences as a child raised in Australia's colonial education system in Nauru.

Lisa Goldstein is an Assistant Professor in the Department of Curriculum and Instruction at the University of Texas at Austin, where she teaches in the Early Childhood Education and Curriculum Studies programs. In her scholarly work Lisa situates the ethic of care in the contexts of classroom life and teacher education, examining the ways that caring manifests itself in the lived experiences of teachers and students. In her book *Teaching with Love: A Feminist Approach to Early Childhood Education* (Peter Lang) Lisa develops and illustrates these ideas by presenting narrative accounts of ethic of care-centered practices in a primary grade classroom.

Contributors

Susan Grieshaber (PhD) teaches in the School of Early Childhood, Queensland University of Technology, Brisbane, Australia. She works with undergraduate and postgraduate students and is very involved in professional development activities with teachers throughout the state. Susan is engaged in research with early childhood teachers about curriculum issues, and also researches with families about the construction of gender in the family context.

Kerri-Ann Hewett is currently teaching in the Elementary Cohort Program in the College of Education at the University of Hawai'i at Manoa. She is co-coordinator of two separate cohorts of preservice teachers at several schools located on the island of O'ahu. Her research interests include Native Hawaiians in teacher education and education for Native Hawaiians.

Katharina Heyning is an Assistant Professor in the Department of Curriculum and Instruction at the University of Wisconsin-Whitewater. Her research and teaching interests include teacher certification reform and change, social studies education, social foundations of education, and postmodern approaches to examining the social constructions of learning and schooling.

Janice A. Jipson is Professor of Education at National Louis University, where she teaches in the doctoral program in Curriculum and Social Inquiry and in the Interdisciplinary Studies Masters program. Recent publications include *Repositioning Feminism and Education: Perspectives on Education for Social Change* (1995) with Petra Munro, Susan Victor, Karen Froude Jones, and Gretchen Freed Rowland; *Questions of You and the Struggle of Collaborative Life* (1999) and *Daredevil Research: Re-creating Analytic Practice* (1997), both with Nicholas Paley; and *Intersections: Feminisms/Early Childhoods* (1998) with Mary Hauser. A former Head Start director, her work focuses on curriculum theory, early childhood education, and research issues of identity, intersubjectivity, and representation.

Richard T. Johnson, a former preschool teacher, is now on faculty in the Department of Teacher Education and Curriculum Studies, University of Hawai'i at Manoa. His most recent research focuses on the implications of "no touch" policies on the care of young children, work published by Peter Lang, appearing as *Hands Off!: The Disappearance of Touch in the Care of Children*.

Julie Lokelani Kaomea is a Native Hawaiian Assistant Professor in the Department of Teacher Education and Curriculum Studies at the University of Hawai'i at Manoa. Her current research focuses on curricular representations of Native Hawaiians and the potential dangers of contemporary movements toward increasing the curricular visibility of racial and ethnic minorities and other similarly underrepresented groups.

Glenda Mac Naughton is a Senior Lecturer in the Department of Early Childhood Studies at the University of Melbourne, Australia. She has a strong interest in social justice and equity issues in early childhood and in using feminist poststructuralist perspectives to inform debate on theory and practice around these issues.

Nancy Meltzoff is an Assistant Professor and a Coordinator of Graduate Programs at the Lane County Campus of Pacific University. She has worked with graduate students in teacher education for ten years, focusing on educational foundations and multicultural education. Her main research interest is in the area of community building, including the development of community in the classroom, and issues of inclusion and marginalization.

Nicholas Paley is Professor in the Graduate School of Education and Human Development at George Washington University, where he teaches courses in curriculum and educational foundations. His recent books include *Finding Art's Place: Experiments in Contemporary Education and Culture*, and (with Janice Jipson) *Daredevil Research: Re-Creating Analytic Practice* and *Questions of You and the Struggle of Collaborative Life*. He is also the author of other writings, installations, and projects that explore relationships between artistic practice and the production of educational knowledge.

Larry Prochner is an Associate Professor of early childhood education and child study at Concordia University, Montreal. He conducts research on historical and cross-national issues in early education. He is completing two books, *Early Childhood Care and Education in Canada: Past, Present, and Future* (with Nina Howe), and *The Story of the West End Creche: A Case Study in the History of Day Care*.

Christine Woodrow is Course Director of Early Childhood Studies at Central Queensland University, Australia. In addition to her leadership role in course development in early childhood teacher education at Central Queensland University and the Northern Territory University, Christine has undertaken a number of key advisory and management roles in early childhood services. These have included chair of a national council established to provide advice on policy and strategic direction in childcare to the federal government. Her main research interests include professional ethics in early childhood, images of childhood that underpin teachers curriculum and innovative models of professional development in regional and remote areas.

RETHINKING CHILDHOOD

JOE L. KINCHELOE & JANICE A. JIPSON, *General Editors*

A revolution is occurring regarding the study of childhood. Traditional notions of child development are under attack, as are the methods by which children are studied. At the same time, the nature of childhood itself is changing as children gain access to information once reserved for adults only. Technological innovations, media, and electronic information have narrowed the distinction between adults and children, forcing educators to rethink the world of schooling in this new context.

This series of textbooks and monographs encourages scholarship in all of these areas, eliciting critical investigations in developmental psychology, early childhood education, multicultural education, and cultural studies of childhood.

Proposals and manuscripts may be sent to the general editors:

>Joe L. Kincheloe
>637 W. Foster Avenue
>State College, PA 16801
>
>*or*
>
>Janice A. Jipson
>219 Pease Court
>Janesville, WI 53545

To order other books in this series, please contact our Customer Service Department at:

>(800) 770-LANG (within the U.S.)
>(212) 647-7706 (outside the U.S.)
>(212) 647-7707 FAX

Or browse online by series at:
>www.peterlang.com